Idealism
Past and Present

ROYAL INSTITUTE OF PHILOSOPHY LECTURE SERIES: 13
SUPPLEMENT TO *PHILOSOPHY* 1982

EDITED BY:

Godfrey Vesey

CAMBRIDGE UNIVERSITY PRESS

CAMBRIDGE
LONDON   NEW YORK   NEW ROCHELLE
MELBOURNE   SYDNEY

Published by the Press Syndicate of the University of Cambridge
The Pitt Building, Trumpington Street, Cambridge CB2 1RP
32 East 57th Street, New York, NY 10022, USA

ISBN 0 521 28905 X

Printed in Great Britain by Adlard & Son Ltd, Bartholomew Press, Dorking

Contents

Foreword: A History of 'Ideas'

GODFREY VESEY

Idealism in its philosophical sense is idea-lism. The root word is 'idea'. The word 'idea' has been used by philosophers in very different ways over the centuries. Properly to understand philosophical idealism one has to have followed the fortunes of the word. The changes in its use go along with fundamental changes in views about the objects of perception and knowledge, and how they are related; about mathematics; about space; about God and man; about thought, language and reality; in fact, about most of the central topics in philosophy. Much of the history of Western philosophy could be rewritten as a history of philosophers' use of the word 'idea'. To help the reader to place and assess the individual contributions to this volume of Royal Institute of Philosophy lectures I shall outline the relevant parts of the history of the word 'idea'.

The contributors are: M. F. Burnyeat, Fellow of Robinson College, Cambridge; Dr M. R. Ayers, Fellow of Wadham College, Oxford; Graham Bird, Professor of Philosophy at the University of Manchester; W. H. Walsh, FBA, formerly Professor of Logic and Metaphysics at Edinburgh University; Patrick Gardiner, Fellow of Magdalen College, Oxford; D. W. Hamlyn, Professor of Philosophy at Birkbeck College, University of London; Michael Inwood, Fellow of Trinity College, Oxford; Dr Richard Norman, Lecturer in Philosophy at the University of Kent at Canterbury; A. R. Manser, Professor of Philosophy at the University of Southampton; A. Palmer, Lecturer in Philosophy at the University of Southampton; Dr Ross Harrison, Fellow of King's College, Cambridge; Dr Crispin Wright, Professor of Philosophy at the University of Leeds; Dr Norman Malcolm, formerly Susan Linn Sage Professor of Philosophy at Cornell University; and Dr Derek Bolton, Lecturer in Clinical Psychology at the Institute of Psychiatry, University of London. Some of the papers themselves contain contributions to the history of the word 'idea'. Where this is so I shall avoid covering the same ground.

The first philosopher to advance a theory of ideas was Plato. But Plato's 'ideas' are so unlike the sort of ideas we think of as having their home in people's minds that it is better to use a semi-technical term and talk of his theory as a theory of 'Forms'.

Plato's Theory of Forms has traditionally been seen as a theory of universals. Certain passages of the dialogue *Parmenides* (e.g. 131e–132a) lend themselves to this interpretation. It was evidently favoured by Aristotle, who opposed a theory of his own about universals (*universalia in rebus*) to the one he attributed to Plato (*universalia ante rem*). But the

Parmenides passages are far from typical. There is no reference in them to any of the six central features of Plato's theory as expounded elsewhere.

The first of these six central features is the distinction between the visible world and the intelligible world. Plato introduces the distinction with what he says about 'opposites'. Opposites are things like thick and thin, tall and short, great and small, beautiful and ugly, just and unjust, holy and unholy, wise and stupid, one and many, equal and unequal. One cannot read key dialogues, like the *Phaedo* and the *Republic*, without constantly coming across talk of these opposites. In one dialogue (*Greater Hippias*, 289a–d) Plato quotes Heraclitus. Man is both wise, by comparison with an ape, and stupid, by comparison with a god. He is both wise and stupid. Wisdom and stupidity are together, confounded, in man. Plato's exposition of the significance of opposites being confounded in the visible world is in terms, not of wisdom and stupidity, but of largeness and smallness. In the *Republic* (VII, 523b–524d) he contrasts seeing that something is a finger with seeing how big it is. Vision seems adequate for the judgment that the object is a finger, but not for how big it is. The finger next to the thumb is large by comparison with the outside, or 'little' finger, but small by comparison with the middle finger. 'The great and the small are confounded' in the finger. So it cannot be by vision that one is conscious of largeness or smallness. It must be by intelligence. 'Intelligence is compelled to contemplate the great and the small, not thus confounded but as distinct entities, in the opposite way from sensation. And it is in some such experience as this that the question first occurs to us "What in the world, then, is the great and the small?" And this is the origin of the designation *intelligible* for the one and *visible* for the other' (VII, 524c). In other words, although you cannot *see* the great without its being confounded with the small, you can *think* the great by itself, pure and unadulterated, a distinct entity, separate from the small.

But what does Plato mean by calling one of any pair of opposites, by itself, 'intelligible'? What is it to think the great, or the beautiful, or the equal, by itself? This brings us to the second of the six central features of Plato's theory. To think the great is to think what greatness is, that is, how it is defined. But not just any sort of definition will do. If what is under investigation is virtue then it is no good simply listing the various virtues. It is no good saying that courage is a virtue, and temperance, and wisdom, and dignity, and many other things (*Meno*, 74a). Plato rejects what may be called 'definition by listing examples'. The definition he is after is of the 'one essential form' (*Euthyphro*, 5d) of anything. The definition of virtue must cover all the instances of virtue by specifying what is essential to anything being a virtue. It is what might be called 'definition by essence'.

But how do we come by definitions by essence of things like greatness? How do we arrive at its 'one essential form'? Do we simply get together and agree on what we are to mean by the word 'great', how we are to use it?

This brings us to the third feature. I am fairly sure that a view ascribed to Cratylus, that names 'are natural and not conventional—not a portion of the human voice which men agree to use—but that there is a truth and correctness in them which is the same for Hellenes as for barbarians' (*Cratylus*, 383ab) is Plato's own view, and is meant to apply as much to words like 'great' and 'beautiful' and 'holy' as to proper names. Plato had inherited Socrates' distaste for the conventionalism and relativism of the Sophists. This comes out in the way he formulates his questions. If it is about holiness, for instance, his question is not 'What does the word "holy" mean?' There is no mention of words in his formulation of the question. His question is 'What is the essential form of holiness which makes all holy actions holy?' (*Euthyphro*, 6d). It is a question about the thing, holiness, not about the word 'holy'.

But if 'How do we come by the definition?' means, not 'How do we *agree on* the definition?', but 'How do we *know* the definition?', what sort of knowledge is it? Is it empirical knowledge, or what? This brings us to the fourth feature. If the definition were the object of empirical knowledge (like the definition of colour as 'an effluence perceptible by sight' in *Meno*, 76d), then it would be vulnerable to new discoveries in natural science; it would be 'unsafe' (Cf. *Phaedo*, 100d). According to Plato it would not be an object of knowledge at all, merely an object of opinion. Knowledge and opinion are different faculties, naturally related to different categories of objects (*Republic*, V, 478a–b). The object of knowledge is eternal and unchanging.

Incidentally, the introduction of the doctrine about knowledge being of the eternal and unchanging calls for a revision of what was said, or implied, earlier. Vision, it was said, seems adequate for the judgment that something is a finger. But a finger is not eternally a finger. It come to be a finger from what is not a finger and, after death, changes so as no longer to be a finger. But if there can be knowledge only of what continues always to abide and exist (*Cratylus*, 440) then vision is not adequate for knowledge of a finger. Or for knowledge of anything else in the visible world, for that matter. Everything in the visible world comes to be and passes away (*Republic*, VI, 508d; *Phaedrus*, 247c–e). The original distinction between opposites, like large and small, and non-opposites, like finger, is lost when one looks at things from the standpoint of eternity. From the standpoint of eternity, finger and non-finger are confounded in whatever undergoes the change in just the same way as, at a particular instant in time, the great and the small are confounded in a finger. The ground is prepared for asking not only 'What is the essential form of largeness which makes all large objects large?' but also 'What is the essential form of finger (man, etc.) which makes all fingers fingers (men men, etc.)?'

The fourth feature of Plato's theory, the doctrine that the object of knowledge is eternal and unchanging, gives rise to a problem. As beings who exist in the changing sensible world our awareness is sensory and is of what is changing. How can we be aware of what is eternal and unchanging? Plato's answer, the fifth feature of his theory, can be approached via what he says about geometry. Geometry, he says, 'is the knowledge of the eternally existent' (*Republic*, VII, 526e–527c). And in the *Meno* (81a–86c) he propounds a theory about what it is to learn a geometrical truth. The theory draws on belief in the existence of a disembodied soul before birth. What we call 'learning' geometrical truths is really *recalling* what one had learnt, otherwise than by the use of the senses, when one's soul inhabited the intelligible world before birth. In the *Phaedo* (74a–75d) the recollection doctrine is put to use to answer such questions as 'How do we know what the real nature of equality is?' We see things in which equality is confounded with its opposite, inequality, and they remind us of what we must have known before we ever started seeing such things, that is, of what we could have known only before we became embodied, namely, what equality, by itself, is.

There is one remaining central feature of Plato's theory. Forms are somehow more real than sensible things. Plato says two things. First, he employs causal terms to describe how the intelligible is related to the sensible. Beauty, for example, is the cause of things being beautiful (*Phaedo*, 100c). Not in the sense in which a carpenter is the cause of a table, but in *some* sense. Secondly, he persistently employs words like 'imitate' and 'copy' when he is talking about how sensible things are related to the Forms. They can hardly be meant literally, but they indicate fairly clearly that Plato thought of the things in which opposites are confounded as being secondary, in some sense, to opposites by themselves, Forms. There is a hierarchy of some sort, in which Forms come above sensible things. In the *Republic*, Books VI and VII, Plato crowns the hierarchy. He posits a supreme Form, the Form of the Good. He gives it a role in the apprehension of the other Forms comparable to that of the sun in the apprehension of visible things. It 'gives their truth to the objects of knowledge and the power of knowing to the knower' and so is 'the cause of knowledge, and of truth in so far as known' (VI, 508c). The ultimate aim of the philosopher, he says, is to attain the apprehension of this supreme reality, 'the limit of the intelligible' (VII, 532b).

In *Parmenides*, 131e–135c, there is no mention of these central features of Plato's Theory of Forms. Most importantly, the original reflection about vision not being adequate for judgments about something being large or small, because large and small are opposites, and opposites are always confounded in the visible world, and about our therefore being compelled 'to contemplate the great and the small, not thus confounded but as distinct entities, in the opposite way from sensation', is replaced with a quite different reflection, namely that 'when it seems to you that a number of things are large there seems to be a certain single character which is the same when you look at them all' (132a). This is the reflection which, if taken as the justification for a Theory of Forms, makes it a theory of universals.

The third central feature of Plato's theory is that the definitions are not the product of agreement and convention; they are there to be *known*. The nearest one comes, in the *Parmenides* passages, to one of the six central features of Plato's theory is to this one. But it is no more than a similarity in a certain respect. One could argue that the distinction between a definition being an object of knowledge and its being a product of agreement and convention is a distinction between its being, somehow, objective or real, and its being, somehow, subjective or less than real. And if one thinks of thoughts as being subjective, and 'what thoughts are of' as being objective, then there is something in the *Parmenides* passages that corresponds, in respect of Forms being held to be objective in some sense, to the third of the central features of Plato's theory. For Socrates asks: 'May it not be that each of these forms is a thought, which cannot properly exist anywhere but in a mind?', to which he gets the answer that a thought must be *of* something, 'in fact, of some *one* thing that thought observes to cover all the cases, as being a certain single character', this '*one* thing' being a Form.

The sixth central feature of Plato's theory is that Forms are more real than visible things. The Form of beauty, for instance, is said to be the *cause* of things being beautiful (*Phaedo*, 100c). Plato introduces the notion of explanation by reference to Forms in the context of a discussion of scientific explanation that begins with Socrates undertaking to describe his own experience in this connection (96a). When young, he says, he puzzled primarily over such questions as 'Is it when heat and cold produce fermentation that living creatures are bred?' (96b). But then he heard someone reading from a book by Anaxagoras, and was pleased by the explanation that 'it is mind that produces order and is the cause of everything', an explanation which seemed to him to imply that 'if anyone wished to discover the reason why any given thing came or ceased or continued to be, he must find out how it was best for that thing to be, or to act or be acted upon in any other way' (97c–d). In short, he thought that Anaxagoras must be leading up to giving a teleological explanation of the ordering of things, with the *telos*, or end, being the best possible state of affairs. But when he procured the books for himself he was dismayed to find that 'the fellow made no use of mind and assigned to it no causality for the order of the world, but adduced causes like air, and aether and water and many other absurdities' (98b–c). It was as if someone had asked why he, Socrates, was where he was and had received, not the answer that it was because he thought it more right and honourable to submit to whatever penalty his country ordered, but an answer in terms of his bones and sinews. Had he not bones and sinews he could not have come to be where he was, but 'Fancy being unable to distinguish between the cause of a thing and the condition without which it could not be a cause!' (99b). The ideal explanation would be one in terms of 'a power which keeps things disposed at any given moment in the best possible way' (99b–c). But, Socrates says, he has been denied knowledge of any such power, and so has worked out his own 'makeshift approach to the problem of causation' (99c).[1]

Plato, of course, is being ironical when he describes his own approach as 'makeshift'. It is the approach on which he sets such store, his Theory of Forms. 'The one thing that makes the object beautiful is the presence in it or association with it, in whatever way the relation comes about, of absolute beauty' (100d). Absolute beauty, the Form of beauty, is the cause of things being beautiful. But this is not to say that it is the cause of beautiful things existing. There is not the problem of understanding how an intelligible thing, a Form, could bring a visible thing into existence. There is, however, a connected problem. For someone who approaches Plato via Aristotle it can be put like this. In Aristotle's conceptual scheme, 'matter' is 'in-formed' by 'forms'. What, in Plato's theory, corresponds to 'matter' in Aristotle's theory? Plato's solution to this problem is in the *Timaeus*. By the time he came to write the *Timaeus* he had left behind his original fascination with opposites. By now there were said to be Forms of fire, water and earth. These Forms are, in Plato's terminology, 'copied' in the sensible world. But the 'copies' of them are not sensible fire, water and earth conceived of as *things*. They are, rather, the fieriness, the wateriness, and the earthiness of some other 'thing'. Plato's question is: What is this other 'thing'? He needs a third form of reality, something into which the Form is copied, or, as he puts it, a 'receptacle' for the copy (*Timaeus*, 49a). It must itself be devoid of character, lest the characters it is to receive get distorted. We shall not be far wrong, Plato says, in thinking of it as 'an invisible and formless being which receives all things and in some mysterious way partakes of the intelligible, and is most incomprehensible' (51a–b). He finally concludes that the third form of reality is *space*.

> There is a third nature, which is space and is eternal, and admits not of destruction and provides a home for all created things, and is apprehended, when all sense is absent, by a kind of spurious reason, and is hardly real—which we, beholding as in a dream, say of all existence that it must of necessity be in some place and occupy a space, but that what is neither in heaven nor in earth has no existence. Of these and other things of the same kind, relating to the true and waking reality of nature, we have only this dreamlike sense, and we are unable to cast off sleep and determine the truth about them (52b–c).

[1] It would be a mistake to regard this as an irrevocable rejection of teleological explanation. It is arguable that by relating all Forms to the Form of the Good Plato reinstates teleology at the fountain head of his theory. See C. C. W. Taylor, 'Forms as Causes in the *Phaedo*', *Mind* 78 (1969), 52–54.

To Plato's brightest pupil, Aristotle, this self-confused state of unclarity about how to talk of sensible things and their essential characteristics must have seemed like an open invitation to review the whole theory.

Before turning to Aristotle, however, there is one other aspect of Plato's theory which is significant for our history of 'ideas'. In the *Phaedo* the Form of beauty is said to be the cause of sensible things being beautiful. But the Form of beauty is not a cause in the sense in which a craftsman who, with his (intellectual) eyes on the idea or Form of couch or table, is the cause of the couches and tables we use (*Republic*, 596b). Besides the Forms, the 'copies' of them, and the 'receptacle', space, Plato needs a fourth 'form of reality', a craftsman-like cause of coming-to-be and change in the sensible world. He needs what Aristotle was to call 'efficient causes'. The question then arises as to whether the efficient causes of change are all to be found *within* the natural order, conceived of as 'always in existence and without beginning', or whether there is what might be called a 'divine craftsman', outside the natural order, who created it. In the latter case, did the divine craftsman pattern it on unchangeable Forms or on something changeable? Plato considers these questions in the *Timaeus* (28a–29d). To the second question he gives the answer that, since 'the world is the fairest of creations and he [the divine craftsman] is the best of causes', he must have patterned it on the Forms. It is 'framed in the likeness of that which is apprehended by reason and mind'. In giving this answer to the second question Plato seems to have thought he had disposed of the alternative answer to the first question, viz. that the efficient causes are all causes within an everlasting natural order.

There is no suggestion, in what Plato says, that the Forms exist merely as ideas in the mind of the divine craftsman. But this is what they became in Plotinus (*Ennead*, III, 9.i), and in the Christian Neo-Platonism of St Augustine (*De Diversis Quaestionibus*, LXXXIII, Question 46) Plato's Forms became archetypal ideas in the mind of God. And the ground was laid for philosophical acceptance of the conception of ideas as *non*-archetypal things in the minds of *men*. But only the ground. Another major change was needed before the 'Way of Ideas' of Descartes and Locke could grow in that ground. Whereas Plato's 'Forms' are 'apprehended by reason and mind' Locke's 'ideas' come from sensation, or from something said by Locke to be very like it, reflection (introspection). And to understand how that change came about we need to consider both Aristotle's reactions to Plato, and Descartes's reactions to Aristotle.

Whereas for Plato sensible things are copies, in a receptacle, of the primary things, intelligible Forms, for Aristotle sensible things (individual men or horses, for instance) are substances 'in the truest and primary and most definite sense of the word', and the species within which these primary substances are included (on account of being, essentially, men or horses), along with the genera to which the species belong (in this case the genus animal), are secondary substances (*Categories*, 2a11–18). With sensible things being things in their own right and not merely copies of Forms in a receptacle, space, it is possible to treat space not as something absolute, albeit incomprehensible, but as relational, at least in the sense that to treat the concept of space in terms of place is to treat it as relational. The notion of a receptacle for a copy of a Form is replaced with that of 'matter' which, given a certain 'form' (with a small 'f', to distinguish it from Plato's 'Form'), is an individual thing. The notion of space being incomprehensible is replaced with that of prime matter (matter without any form) being only an intellectual abstraction, not something that could actually exist. Rejection of the Platonic conception of characteristics as copies of Forms in a receptacle is expressed as the logical requirement that where there is a characteristic there must be an individual thing that is characterized. The 'separate' Platonic Form is read into the individual thing; it becomes what the thing essentially is. Plato's theory of intelligible Forms becomes a theory of sensible things with intelligible essences. The Platonic heaven is brought down to an Aristotelian earth.

I said that in the *Phaedo* the Platonic Socrates describes his own experiences in connection with scientific explanation. At one time he had considered explanations of how living creatures are bred such as those in terms of heat and cold producing fermentation. Then he had been led by what Anaxagoras said about mind producing order to think favourably of the possibility of teleological explanation. But Anaxagoras had proved disappointing on that score. And Socrates, having been denied knowledge of a teleological power, settled for explanation by reference to Forms. Perhaps teleology comes back into the picture with the Form at the top of the hierarchy, the Form of the Good, or with the divine craftsman who is 'the best of causes'.

Possibly with this passage in the *Phaedo* in mind, Aristotle in his *Physics* (Bk II, Ch. 8) describes Anaxagoras as only touching on some other sort of cause than that according to which if certain things are of such and such a kind then other things *necessarily* are and come to be. He is strongly opposed to the notion that nature as a whole works 'not for the sake of something, nor because it is better so, but just as the sky rains, not in order to make the corn grow, but of necessity' (198b17). It is impossible, he argues, that this should be the true view. The true view is as follows (*On the Parts of Animals*, 639b13–16): 'The causes concerned in the generation of the works of nature are, as we see, more than one. There is the final cause and there is the motor cause. Now we must decide which of these two causes comes first, which second. Plainly, however, that cause is the first which we call the final one. For this is the Reason, and the Reason forms the starting-point, alike in the works of art and in works of nature.'

In this outline of the history of the word 'idea' I move on, now, to the seventeenth century and René Descartes. It is not difficult to relate

Descartes to Aristotle. In his *Principles of Philosophy* (I, 28) Descartes makes it clear that his programme is to replace final by efficient causes, teleology by mechanism. In his conversation with Burman he admits that when he said, in the *Meditations*, that the customary search for final causes is totally useless, he had Aristotle in mind.[2] And in a revealing letter to Mersenne (28 January 1641) he implies that the *Meditations* were written to provide a philosophical basis for his physics, and asks Mersenne not to say so lest those who favour Aristotle would have more difficulty in approving his principles. Descartes had learnt a lesson from the Church's condemnation of Galileo for his *Dialogue on the Two Systems of the World*. It was a case of 'softly, softly, catchee monkee', the monkey being acceptance of the new science.

We can restructure Descartes's thought, supposing there not to have been the awful example of Galileo. Such a restructuring will begin with something in common to Descartes and Aristotle, admission of mathematics as the paradigm of what is necessarily true. Roughly, the Greeks sought some sort of connection between relations of numbers and relations in other realms of being (or becoming) to lend authority to any claims they might want to make to knowledge in these other realms. Descartes, also, sought this. But he had the advantage of being a brilliant mathematician. He invented analytical geometry, which shows how every geometrical object or relation can be given numerical expression. It follows that if the 'extension' of spatial (i.e. physical) objects is the 'extension' of geometrical objects (something both Descartes and Kant assumed), and if 'matter' is defined, not as the correlative of 'form', but in terms of this extension, then matter is thereby brought into the domain of what is necessarily true. From being an incomprehensible 'receptacle' for number-like Forms, space is elevated to the position of being, itself, through and through numerical. Numbers, the relations between which are necessary, are shown to be constitutive of physical reality. Mathematics can be used in physics not simply for the pragmatic reason that physical objects and the changes in them lend themselves to mathematical measurement, but for the metaphysical reason that the essence of matter is extension, the same extension as is the subject-matter of analytical geometry. A new essentialism, based on a revolutionized conception of 'matter', made possible by analytical geometry, takes over from the essentialism of Plato and Aristotle.

There are a number of difficulties with this new essentialism.

The main one is that for there to be a science which explains change by one thing acting on another (e.g. one billiard ball causing a change in the position of another by striking it) there must be more to matter than mere extension. There must be something to account for one material thing's

[2] *Descartes' Conversation with Burman*, trans. John Cottingham (Oxford University Press, 1976), 19.

resistance to another's occupying the same place. In plain words, there must be some *stuff* which *has* the extension. Otherwise there is only a characteristic, being extended, and not a thing characterized, an extended thing. Descartes knew that people would have this difficulty with his theory that the essence of matter is extension, but disputed the need for any other characteristic (*HR*, I, 255–260).[3]

Another difficulty is that it does not follow from the truths of arithmetic and geometry being objectively necessary that we cannot be mistaken about them. Objective *necessity* is not the same as justified subjective *certainty*. This was a difficulty about which Descartes was prepared to do something. He recognized the need for a 'criterion', and argued as follows. The intuition 'I think, therefore I am' is true without any possibility of doubt. What assures me of its truth is my clear and distinct perception of it. Therefore clear and distinct perception of anything should be a sufficient condition of its being true. But perhaps there is some all-powerful malicious demon who makes things appear to be true which are not. There could not be both an all-powerful malicious demon and an all-powerful perfect God. I have a clear and distinct idea of the latter. It is evident by the light of nature that this idea must be caused by something with at least as much reality as that attributed in the idea. So there must be an all-powerful God. This guarantees the truthfulness of what is clear and distinct to me, such as the propositions of arithmetic and geometry, since a perfect God would not allow me to be deceived with respect to what I clearly and distinctly perceive.

This solution of the problem of the gap between objective necessity and subjective certainty raises more questions and difficulties than it is intended to resolve. I shall consider only one of them. It parallels the difficulty about extension being the essence of matter.

It might be said that all that cannot be doubted by someone, when he thinks 'I think, therefore I am', is that there is this thought. The question of who is thinking it does not arise for him. He does not observe his self. And yet Descartes writes as though the thinker is sure not only of the characteristic, thinking, but also of a thing characterized, a thinking thing. He thinks the thinker is sure of this because he (Descartes) accepts the Aristotelian requirement that you cannot have a characteristic without a thing characterized (*HR*, I, 240). He then goes on to ask himself if there is more, essentially, to this thinking thing than that it is thinking. He decides that there is not, since if I *do not know* with certainty that some-

---

[3] *HR* = *The Philosophical Works of Descartes*, trans. Elizabeth S. Haldane and G. R. T. Ross (Cambridge University Press, 1931). The reference is to Volume I, 255–260.

thing *is* the case (viz. that I am a bodily as well as a conscious being) then I *do know* with certainty that it *is not* the case.[4]

Here the parallel ends. Whereas Descartes had realized that people would feel the need for there to be more to matter than extension, so that we can understand talk of material things, in the plural, acting on one another, he seems not to have realized that people would feel the need for there to be more to people than thinking, so that we can understand talk of there being people, in the plural (and so to talk of there being a person, in the singular).

Descartes's matter/mind dualism has implications for our understanding of perception. Seeing something will now have to be construed as a case of the substance, mind, being causally affected by the substance matter.[5] An effect is produced in a mental thing by a material thing. But what are these effects, required by the theory, to be called? In his *Rules for the Direction of the Mind* (*HR*, I, 38) Descartes lists various suppositions about perception. The third is that there is a soft part of the brain which, like a piece of wax, receives shapes or forms from the external senses. Descartes calls the soft part of the brain 'the fancy or imagination' (elsewhere he refers to it as 'the corporeal imagination' to make it clear that he is not talking about something mental), and the shapes or forms impressed on it he calls

---

[4] This is the summary of the argument given by A. M. Maciver ('Is there mind–body interaction?', *Proc. Arist. Soc.* XXXVI (1935–36), 101), and described by him as a simple fallacy. Descartes's actual argument involves the additional notion that if I am able to apprehend two things as distinct they must really be distinct, 'since they may be made to exist in separation at least by the omnipotence of God' (*HR*, I, 190).

[5] Not all the seventeenth-century philosophers who succeeded Descartes agreed with him about people perceiving things by virtue of their minds being causally affected by them. One of the more interesting exceptions was Antoine Arnauld. Part of his *Treatise on True and False Ideas* (1683) is a detailed refutation of Nicolas Malebranche's Cartesian theory of perception. Arnauld argued against Malebranche that 'objective presence' to a mind does not require 'local presence'; and that for something to be objectively present to a mind is not the same thing as for it to be causally active on it. Intermediary entities called 'ideas' are needed neither as local presences nor as effects. The only 'ideas' are acts of perception, and these in no sense come between the perceiver and the object perceived. Arnauld felt all the more strongly about this because the view he was attacking was one he had himself held earlier. The first sentence of Part I of *The Art of Thinking* (1662), which he wrote with Pierre Nicole, the book sometimes referred to as the Port Royal *Logic*, was 'We have no knowledge of what is *outside* us except by the mediation of the ideas *within* us'. Arnauld's *Treatise* views were carried forward by Thomas Reid in his *Essays on the Intellectual Powers of Man* (1785). Reid says that he believes ideas, in the sense of images of external objects in the mind, to be 'a mere fiction of philosophers' (Essay I, Ch. I).

'ideas', in keeping with an old use of the word 'idea' to mean something like a shape. Descartes then proceeds to use the same word, 'idea', for the effect in the mind. Thomas Reid was later to suggest that he did this because of 'analogical reasoning from a supposed similitude of mind to body', but it seems more likely that it was because he held a very strange theory to the effect that imagining something involves the mind applying itself to a physical image in the brain (*HR*, I, 39, 185). Finally, Descartes recognizes how confusing it is to have both a shape or form impressed on the brain, and something in the mind, called by the same name, 'idea', and decides to refuse the title of 'ideas' to impressions on the brain (*HR*, II, 52).

Descartes sometimes calls the 'ideas' which are effects in the mind 'images' to distinguish them from a different category of 'ideas'. In the *Meditations* (*HR*, I, 159) he says that 'of my thoughts some are, so to speak, images of the things, and to these alone is the title "idea" properly applied'.[6] In his *Conversation with Burman* (p. 13) he calls this the 'strict and narrow sense' of the word 'idea'. There is also 'a rather extended use of the word'. Ideas in the extended sense are 'ideas of common notions'. Common notions are, for example, the notion that 'that which can effect what is greater or more difficult, can also accomplish what is less' (*HR*, II, 56).

The upshot is that Descartes's philosophy comprises *two* dualisms. There is the dualism of two sorts of substance, matter and mind. And there is also the dualism of two sorts of ideas. There are what may be called 'image-ideas' and there are what may be called 'proposition-ideas'. Furthermore, as if it were not enough that he should have reversed the Aristotelian position on the philosophy of science by elevating efficient over final causes, Descartes reverses the Platonic position on the relation of the intelligible to the sensible by making image-ideas ideas in the proper or strict sense, and proposition-ideas ideas in an extended sense. Sensible colour would be an idea in the strict sense for Descartes, but the notion that 'shape is that in which a solid terminates' (*Meno*, 76a), or that a circle is 'the thing which has everywhere equal distances between its extremities and its centre' (*Ep.*, VII, 342c), would be an idea only in the extended sense. It is not surprising that Kant should protest that anyone familiar with Plato, as he was, 'must find it intolerable to hear the representation of the colour, red, called an idea' (*Critique of Pure Reason*, A320/B377).

Given the two dualisms, a whole new range of problems, and possible solutions to them, is opened up for philosophers. Descartes is indeed the

---

[6] *Improperly* applied, according to Spinoza (*Ethics*, II, Prop. XLIX Note): 'Those who think that ideas consist of images which are formed in us by the concourse of bodies ... regard ideas as lifeless pictures on a board, and preoccupied thus with this misconception they do not see that an idea, in so far as it is an idea, involves affirmation or negation'.

Father of Modern Philosophy. I shall say something about four problems,
all of them relevant to the history of 'ideas'. They are (1) the problem of the
difference between shapes or forms impressed on the brain and ideas in the
mind, (2) the problem of the relation of proposition-ideas to image-ideas,
(3) the problem of how we know the 'external' world exists, (4) the problem
of 'ideas' which are neither image-ideas nor proposition-ideas.

  (1) The question is: Are image-ideas (i) presented to us by the senses, or
(ii) innate, the impression on the brain being merely the occasion for us to
form them by means of an innate faculty? Descartes's answer is that
'nothing reaches our mind from external objects through the organs of
sense beyond certain corporeal movements, . . . but even these movements,
and the figures which arise from them, are not conceived by us in the shape
they assume in the organs of sense', from which 'it follows that the ideas of
the movements and figures are themselves innate in us' (*HR*, I, 443). He
continues: 'So much the more must the ideas of pain, colour, sound and the
like be innate . . . for they have no likeness to the corporeal movements'.
He then switches abruptly from image-ideas to proposition-ideas, and
writes:

> Could anything be imagined more preposterous than that all common
> notions which are inherent in our mind should arise from these move-
> ments, and should be incapable of existing without them? I should like
> our friend [Regius] to instruct me as to what corporeal movement it is
> which can form in our mind any common notion, e.g. the notion that
> 'things which are equal to the same thing are equal to one another', or
> any other he pleases; for all these movements are particular, but notions
> are universal having no affinity with movements and no relation to
> them.

I think this is worth mentioning for purposes of comparison with what
Plato says about the Form of equality (*Phaedo*, 74d ff.). Descartes's doctrine
of innateness may be compared with Plato's doctrine of recollection. It is as
if, in this connection, Descartes wants to treat image-ideas as on a par with
proposition-ideas.

  (2) There is a possible solution to the problem of the relation of proposition-ideas to image-ideas in the theory that thinking is mental vision of
image-ideas (or of 'abstract ideas' obtained from image-ideas by 'abstraction') in some sort of relation. Descartes's advocacy of the mental vision
doctrine is nowhere more evident than in his *Rules for the Direction of the
Mind*. The second paragraph of Rule 9 begins: 'Truly we shall learn how
to employ our mental intuition from comparing it with the way in which we
employ our eyes' (*HR*, I, 28). In Rule 12 he says that the only mental
effort needed to know the difference between two 'simple natures' is that of
'isolating them from each other and scrutinizing them with steadfast mental
gaze': 'We must be content to isolate them from each other, and to give

13

them, each of us, our individual attention, studying them with that degree of mental illumination which each of us possesses' (*HR*, I, 46). The *Rules* were not published until after Descartes's death, but there was a manuscript copy at Port Royal. The Port Royal *Logic* took over Descartes's mental vision doctrine, and added a doctrine of abstraction. This, in turn was taken over by Locke, almost without change.

(3) It is one thing to define matter in terms of the extension which is shown by analytical geometry to be subject to the necessary laws of arithmetic. It is quite another to know that our image-ideas are caused by (or, more strictly, are formed by us on the occasion of) material things affecting our sense-organs and brain. Descartes dealt with the problem by invoking God. We know by the light of nature that our ideas of material things must be caused by something with at least as much reality as is attributed in the ideas. We have a natural impulse to believe the causes to resemble the ideas, that is, to be material things. One possibility is that God should have given us the ideas directly, without there actually being any material things. But, God not being deceitful, we can rely on the natural impulse he has given us to believe the causes to be material things. Berkeley thought otherwise. Far from our having a natural impulse to believe our ideas to be caused by material things, the notion of a material thing is incoherent. Berkeley found comfort in the thought that his idealism could not be shown to be inconsistent with language. The proper use of words being 'the marking of our conceptions, or things only as they are known and perceived by us' it follows that idealism 'is nothing inconsistent with the right use and significancy of language' (*Principles*, LXXXIII). In other words, *if* one accepts the theory that thinking is mental vision of image-ideas in some sort of order, and that language is translating such thoughts into words, *then* one must also accept that idealism is consistent with the right use of language. Berkeley is right. The question becomes one of whether Descartes was right about what thinking is. And that becomes one of whether he was right about his two dualisms, the first dualism, of matter and mind, and the second dualism, consequential upon the first, of image-ideas and proposition-ideas.

(4) There is a problem for Descartes and the philosophers who succeeded him in that some things we might be inclined to call 'ideas', such as the 'idea' of the self, and the 'ideas' of 'cause' and of 'substance', do not fit into the dichotomy of image-ideas and proposition-ideas. What makes it particularly embarrassing is that they are key ideas in philosophizing. One cannot simply write them off as fictions. And yet they cannot be shown to be 'real' as can ideas of simple natures. Simple ideas, Locke says, must all be real, because they are the effects in us 'of powers in things without us, ordained by our Maker to produce in us such sensations'. Their reality lies 'in that steady correspondence they have with the distinct constitutions of real beings. But whether they answer to those constitutions as to causes

or patterns, it matters not; it suffices that they are constantly produced by them' (*Essay*, II, xxx, 1–2).

Locke's distinction between 'real' and 'fantastical or chimerical' ideas is not altogether unlike Plato's distinction between what something, such as holiness, *is*, in itself, and what it is *said to be*, in accord with the conventions of a linguistic community. The difference between Plato and Locke is that whereas for Plato the extra-linguistic reality to which language is expected to conform is that of the intelligible Forms, for Locke it is that of the physical world. The similarity is that in neither case is the extra-linguistic reality that of the sensible world. Plato 'separated' the Forms from the sensible world. Descartes and Locke split the Aristotelian (and common-sense) notion of a sensible quality in two: it became a sensible 'idea' in the mind, and an unsensed 'power' in matter. Implicit in both Plato and Locke there is the notion that language should be shown to conform to reality, but in both Plato and Locke the status 'real' is assigned in such a way that language and reality cannot be straightforwardly compared. We have the notion of language/reality conformity, but no way of putting the notion to use.

The above are some of the problems Kant inherited from Descartes and the British empiricists. He wanted to provide an alternative answer to scepticism to those of Descartes and Berkeley. And he wanted to prove our right to use the concepts (of cause, substance, etc.) with which the empiricists had had such problems. Like Descartes, he started out from a view about mathematics and space. Space is not 'out there' at all; it is not a thing in itself. It is only a 'form' of our intuition of things. This explains the possibility of *a priori* knowledge of geometry, and it guarantees the spatiality of the things we experience. But, of course, there is a price to pay for this answer to scepticism. The spatial objects whose existence is guaranteed are merely phenomenal. We are saddled with a distinction between a subjectively conditioned spatial world and an objective non-spatial world, and with the problem of how they are related.

Kant accepted what Locke had said about why simple ideas, like those of colour, must be real—except, of course, that being a good Platonist he refused to honour them with the title 'ideas'. He called them 'empirical concepts' and said that 'experience is always available for the proof of their objective reality' (*Critique of Pure Reason*, A84/B116). But the concepts which had proved such an embarrassment to the empiricists came in for very different treatment. Kant called such concepts as those of cause and substance '*a priori* concepts', and sought to show that the very possibility of there being a world as an object of knowledge for someone, as distinct from his being affected with a meaningless buzz of sensations, is conditional on his actively 'synthesizing' his sensations according to principles corresponding to these *a priori* concepts. He called 'knowledge which has to do not so much with objects as with how we know objects, in so far as this may be possible *a priori*', 'transcendental knowledge' (B25) and he called a proof of our right to employ some concept, a 'deduction' (A84/B116). The concepts embarrassing to the empiricists are accordingly said to have a 'transcendental deduction' (A85/B117), as opposed to the 'empirical deduction' of the empirical concepts.

Kant is like Berkeley in not admitting knowledge of something lying wholly outside our sensations, but unlike him in operating with a distinction between sensations as they occur in us, and an empirical world we actively construct out of them and set up as an object for our knowledge. The point of dissimilarity between Berkeley and Kant may be described by saying that Berkeley is an empirical idealist whereas Kant is an empirical realist. To go on to describe the point of similarity by saying, without qualification, that both are idealists could be confusing. In the light of his definition of 'transcendental knowledge', and of the objects so known not being things-in-themselves, Kant's brand of idealism can be characterized as 'transcendental idealism'.

I said at the beginning of this foreword that I would avoid covering the same ground as that covered by contributors to the volume. I can see that I am in danger of doing so. Kant and the post-Kantian idealists, Fichte, Schopenhauer, Hegel and Bradley, all receive their fair share of attention from the contributors. I think my best remaining service to the reader may be to try to relate the question that is taken up at the end of the volume, the question whether Wittgenstein was an idealist, to what I have been saying about 'ideas' in Plato and Descartes, and 'concepts' in Kant.

I shall confine myself to three questions. First, does the later Wittgenstein hold the Cartesian theory that thinking is mental vision of image-ideas in some sort of relation, the theory that is conducive to Berkeley's empirical idealism? Second, does he hold the theory that was held in one form or another by Plato and Locke, and that may be described as a kind of realism, the theory that language, if it is to be correctly used and not to be merely 'a portion of the human voice which men agree to use' (*Crat.*, 383a), must conform to some extra-linguistic reality? Third, does he hold the reverse of this, the theory that instead of language conforming to reality, reality conforms to language, a theory that might be described as a linguistic version of Kant's transcendental idealism?

Without a shadow of doubt the answer to the first question is 'No'. Wittgenstein may not have read Bradley (*Principles of Logic*, Bk I, Ch. I), but he had certainly read Frege, and Frege, like Bradley, put the notion of an image-idea in its psychological place. For Wittgenstein it was what Frege called the sense (*Sinn*) of a sign which mattered for an understanding of how language works, not an associated idea.[7] To get at the sense one

---

[7] *Translations from the Philosophical Writings of Gottlob Frege*, P. Geach and M. Black (eds) (Oxford: Blackwell, 1952), 58–59. On Bradley, see the papers in this volume by Professor Manser and Mr Palmer.

has to consider the *use* of the sign, the use being something which is essentially public. The old notion, of Hobbes and Locke, that to understand thinking one has to attend to something essentially private, 'mental discourse', had been replaced by a new notion, that to understand thinking one has to attend to something essentially public, saying. Thinking is conceptually parasitic on saying; not saying, on thinking (Wittgenstein, *Philosophical Investigations*, I, 327–341). To understand different kinds of thoughts (imagining, remembering, hoping, fearing, doubting, believing, etc.) one needs to consider the grammar, in an extended sense of 'grammar', of the corresponding expression. 'One ought to ask, not what images are or what happens when one imagines anything, but how the word "imagination" is used . . . *Essence* is expressed by grammar' (*PI*, I, 370–371). To understand what remembering is we might suppose that we should introspect and catch ourselves in the act, whereas what we should attend to is the grammar of the expression 'I remember': such facts of language as that someone who claims to remember having been at a certain place at a certain time is corrected if he was known not to be there at that time. This is what gives 'remember' its sense, not 'a peculiar act of thinking, independent of the act of expressing our thoughts, and stowed away in some peculiar medium' (*Blue and Brown Books*, 43; cf. *PI*, I, 316ff.; II, xiii).

The answer to the second question, likewise, is 'No'. There is, of course, that conformity which consists in what we say being true (*PI*, I, 429). But any other supposed conformity is a metaphysical myth (see *Zettel*, 331, and *Remarks on the Foundations of Mathematics*, I, 4). Instead of saying that understanding a sentence points to a reality outside the sentence we should say 'Understanding a sentence means getting hold of its content; and the content of the sentence is *in* the sentence' (*BB*, 167). Take the sentence 'This flower is white'. According to Locke the word 'white' stands for a real idea, and according to Kant we have a right to use it, because of what Kant calls 'an empirical deduction': reality has impressed the idea or concept on us. But Wittgenstein says 'Do not believe that you have the concept of colour within you because you look at a coloured object—however you look. (Any more than you possess the concept of a negative number by having debts)' (*Z*, 332). Having a concept is not a matter of having an experience. This is as true of words for bodily sensations as it is of words for sensible qualities of things. Having the concept of pain means knowing the grammar of 'pain' (*PI*, I, 384; *Z*, 548). The word 'pain' is a word for a bodily sensation because of its grammar, but 'if someone says "If our language had not this grammar, it could not express these facts"—it should be asked what "*could*" means here' (*PI*, I, 497). 'The *aim* of the grammar is nothing but that of the language' (ibid.). Hence it makes no sense to talk of being wrong, or unjustified, in using a language-game, such as the language-game in which we talk of the existence of hands. 'A doubt about existence only works *in* a language-game' (*On Certainty*, 24, my italics; cf. 105, 370).

'The use of language is in a certain sense autonomous . . . if you follow rules other than those of chess you are *playing another game*; and if you follow grammatical rules other than such-and-such ones, that does not mean you say something wrong, no, you are speaking of something else' (*Z*, 320). In short, 'the harmony between thought and reality is to be found in the grammar of the language' (*Z*, 55), and not in some sort of causal relationship. Both Plato's 'Forms' (the causes of the characteristics of sensible things) and Locke's 'ideas' (the effects in us of powers in physical things) belong with the myth that there is some other conformity of language and reality than that which consists in what we say being true.

Finally, does Wittgenstein hold the theory that instead of language conforming to reality, reality conforms to language, a theory that might be described as a linguistic version of Kant's transcendental idealism? In an earlier volume of Royal Institute of Philosophy lectures Bernard Williams concluded a paper on 'Wittgenstein and Idealism'[8] by quoting *Zettel*, 357, and remarking that Wittgenstein's new theory of meaning 'points in the direction of a transcendental idealism'. That it does so is hotly disputed by some contributors to the present volume. I shall exercise a self-denying ordinance and leave it to the reader to decide for himself whether or not Williams is right.

This is the eleventh, and last, volume of Royal Institute of Philosophy Lectures I shall edit. I have held the office of Director of the Institute for fourteen years, and I think that is long enough. The Council of the Institute has elected me a Fellow of the Royal Institute of Philosophy, a unique honour of which I am proud. My best wishes go to my successor, Professor A. Phillips Griffiths, Professor of Philosophy at the University of Warwick, and my sincere thanks to my colleagues at the Institute, who have made the last fourteen years such happy ones.

The Open University

---

[8] In Godfrey Vesey (ed.), *Understanding Wittgenstein*, Royal Institute of Philosophy Lectures Volume 7, 1972/73 (London: Macmillan, 1974; New York: Cornell University Press, 1976), 76–95.

Idealism and Greek Philosophy: What Descartes Saw and Berkeley Missed*

M. F. BURNYEAT

It is a standing temptation for philosophers to find anticipations of their own views in the great thinkers of the past, but few have been so bold in the search for precursors, and so utterly mistaken, as Berkeley when he claimed Plato and Aristotle as allies to his immaterialist idealism. In *Siris: A Chain of Philosophical Reflexions and Inquiries Concerning the Virtues of Tar-Water*, which Berkeley published in his old age in 1744, he reviews the leading philosophies of antiquity and finds them on the whole a good deal more sympathetic to his own ideas than the 'modern atheism', as he calls it, of Hobbes and Spinoza (§354) or the objectionable principles of 'the mechanic and geometrical philosophers' such as Newton (§§250, 271). But his strongest and, I think, his most interesting claim is that neither Plato nor Aristotle admitted 'an absolute actual existence of sensible or corporeal things' (§311).

This claim is interesting not because there is any truth in it, but precisely because it is so far off the mark that the question arises what made it possible for Berkeley to read Plato and Aristotle through the distorting lens of his own philosophy. That Berkeley misread certain texts is plain enough. But in explaining this I shall be aiming at larger questions about the whole climate of thought which encouraged or allowed the anachronistic misreading. For it was not due to lack of scholarship or knowledge. Berkeley was extremely well versed in Greek philosophy, and *Siris* displays an enviable command of a wide range of the original texts. I shall argue, however, that none of those texts displays the leanings towards idealism which Berkeley thought he saw in them. Idealism, whether we mean by that Berkeley's own doctrine that *esse est percipi* or a more vaguely conceived thesis to the effect that everything is in some substantial sense mental or spiritual, is one of the very few major philosophical positions which did *not* receive it first formulation in antiquity.[1] This historical fact itself is interesting, if I can establish it, and one may suspect that the

---

* This lecture is also published in the *Philosophical Review* **91** (1982).

[1] I owe this observation, and several points pertinent to it, to Bernard Williams' brilliant survey, 'The Legacy of Greek Philosophy', in *The Legacy of Greece: A New Appraisal*, M. I. Finley (ed.) (Oxford: Oxford University Press, 1981).

history of the non-existence of idealism in antiquity will be connected with the history of what happened later to help Berkeley get it so wrong. There is thus a double tale to tell: it should teach us something about idealism and, more generally, about the relations between ancient and modern philosophy.

I

I begin, then, with the text that Berkeley had most especially in mind when making his claim that neither Plato nor Aristotle admitted 'an absolute actual existence of sensible or corporeal things':

> In the *Theaetetus* we are told that if anyone saith a thing is, or is made, he must withal say, for what, or of what, or in respect of what, it is, or is made; for, that anything should exist in itself or absolutely is absurd. Agreeably to which doctrine it is also farther affirmed by Plato that it is impossible a thing should be sweet and sweet to nobody [*Siris* §311].

There follow some qualms and qualifications about attributing the same view to Aristotle, but when all is said and done Aristotle emerges with much the same position as Berkeley ascribes to Plato on the strength of the *Theaetetus*. So let us pause to see what that position is supposed to be.

'It is impossible a thing should be sweet and sweet to nobody': that proposition is certainly to be found in the *Theaetetus* (160b, quoted below), along with much else that would be congenial to Berkeley's taste. In the first part of the dialogue a theory is elaborated according to which nothing exists outside the particular perceptual encounter in which it appears to sense. If something is sweet, not only must it be sweet for someone to whom it appears sweet, but it cannot be or appear sweet to any other percipient or to the same percipient at another time (159e–160a). The instantiation of the sensible quality of sweetness is private (*idion*, 154a; cf. 161d, 166c) to a single perceiving subject on a single occasion, and it is of such fleetingly perceived, private occurrences that the whole sensible realm consists. No wonder Berkeley seized on this theory as an anticipation of his own account of the sensible world as a succession of ideas or momentary private appearances, each of which exhibits just those sensible qualities, and only those sensible qualities, which it appears to the perceiver to have. Indeed there is evidence in *Siris* that Berkeley simply identified the *Theaetetus* theory as just sketched with his own (cf. §§311, 347–349). But in this he made two mistakes, one as to the status of the theory in Plato's dialogue, and one about its content. He was wrong in thinking that the theory gives the Platonic view of perception and the sensible world, and he was wrong in thinking that the theory is a version of his own immaterialist idealism. Of these two errors the important one for our purposes is the second, but it will be best to lead into it by a consideration of the first.

The propositions I cited from the *Theaetetus* occur in the course of a superbly elaborate argument designed to unravel the implications and commitments of Theaetetus' definition (151e) of knowledge as perception. The theory which emerges is described as an attempt to make that definition hold good (183a; cf.160e1). The attempt comprises an epistemological component taken from Protagoras and an ontological component taken from Heraclitus, the two together being worked up into an account of the world and of our relation to it in perception on the strength of which it can be claimed that all perception is knowledge and all knowledge is perception. The finished theory states a complete set of sufficient conditions for Theaetetus' definition to hold good. But since it is further suggested that this is the only set of sufficient conditions that could reasonably be devised, the sufficient conditions are also necessary conditions for the definition, inescapable commitments for anyone who purposes to equate knowledge with perception. It is then shown (160e ff.) that, when fully elaborated the Protagorean-Heraclitean theory leads to multiple absurdities, culminating in a proof (179c–183c) that if the theory were correct it would make language impossible.

Thus the structure of the argument is that of a *reductio ad absurdum*. The theorizing which attracted Berkeley represents not Plato's belief, but his spelling out of the meaning and presuppositions of the initial thesis that knowledge is perception.[2] The theory cannot give Plato's own view of perception and the sensible world if he thinks he has a good argument to

---

[2] One reason Berkeley missed this is that he translated Theaetetus' definition as 'Sense is science', taking the thesis of Theaetetus and Protagoras to be that sense alone suffices for knowing (understanding) the *connections* between things. Consequently he thought he could agree with Plato's refutation of Theaetetus and Protagoras without ceasing to approve what he supposed to be Plato's theory of perception and the flux of sensible things (§§253, 304–305). I discuss this aspect of Berkeley's reading of the *Theaetetus* in 'Aristotle on Understanding Knowledge', in *Aristotle on Science: The 'Posterior Analytics'*, E. Berti (ed.) (Padua: Antenore, 1981).

Failure to grasp that the argument is an extended *reductio ad absurdum* and that the theory of perception is not presented as Platonic doctrine is equally characteristic of modern commentators on the *Theaetetus*—although they have not Berkeley's excuse of mistranslation to disassociate the definition from the theory which supports it. This is not the place for elaborate exegesis or scholarly controversy, but the case for the reading I present can be summarily set out in three stages, as follows.

(A) We first go through the text picking out the main stage-directions, as it were, by which Plato indicates how, in his view, the three theses under discussion

show that it makes language impossible. Indeed, the dialogue makes a point of emphasizing (182e) that the theory is itself a bit of language, so that if it were correct it could not even be coherently stated.

But if Plato did not himself assent to the doctrine which Berkeley (not unfairly) formulates as a denial of 'an absolute actual existence of sensible or corporeal things', it is reasonably certain that no one else did either. The elements of the theory come from Protagoras and Heraclitus, but

---

(Theaetetus, Protagoras, Heraclitus) are related. This is best done *in abstracto*, without delving into the content of the theses themselves.

Most important, because centrally and emphatically placed at a turning point in the discussion, is 160de: the three theses 'come to the same thing' [Th↔Prot↔Her], and more particularly (e1), if Protagoras and Heraclitus are correct, perception is knowledge, as Theaetetus says [(Prot & Her)→Th]. Compare 183a, already cited: Heraclitus was brought in to make Theaetetus' definition hold good [Her→Th]. Now go back to the beginning of the discussion at 151e–152a: Theaetetus and Protagoras say the same thing in different ways [Th↔Prot]—and then follows argument (152a–152c) to show that Protagoras makes Theaetetus' definition come out right [Prot→Th]. Compare 164d: counter-examples to Theaetetus tell equally against Protagoras [Prot→Th]. Next, 152cd: Heraclitus gives the 'real truth' behind Protagoras' riddling statements [Prot↔Her]—and soon follows extended argument (153d ff.) to show that Protagoras requires a Heraclitean ontology [Prot→Her]. Compare 166b: Protagoras relies on Heraclitus to defend himself against an objection to Theaetetus' definition [(Prot→Th) & (Prot→Her)]. Finally 183b: the refutation of Heraclitus demolishes Protagoras [Prot→Her] and disposes of Theaetetus' definition [Th→Her]—unless Theaetetus can find some other method than Heraclitus' to work out his equation of knowledge and perception. This terminal qualification to the mass of evidence just listed shows that there is a difference of status between the two halves of the equivalence we began from.

It is thought to be reasonably clear that

(1) Her→Prot→Th.

The work goes into showing

(2) Th→Prot→Her,

and then that both Protagoras and Heraclitus engender absurdity. (2) is hammered out step by step through the construction of the Protagorean–Heraclitean theory down to 160de. At each step the claim is that Theaetetus has no reasonable alternative if his definition is to be vindicated (for more detail on this characteristic feature of the dialectical method, see my papers 'Examples in Epistemology: Socrates, Theaetetus and G. E. Moore', *Philosophy* **52** (1977), 381–398, and 'Socratic Midwifery, Platonic Inspiration', *Bulletin of the Institute of Classical Studies* **24** (1977), 7–16). Consequently it remains an abstract possibility at the end that Theaetetus might find some alternative to (2) to avoid the *reductio—*

there is every reason to doubt that either of these thinkers pushed the consequences of their views as far as Plato did. So, if there is a version of idealism to be discerned in the *Theaetetus*—and certainly, no other ancient text comes as near to Berkeley's position—it is not an idealism that any Greek thinker ever propounded as his own. It is a dialectical construction, which anticipates idealism only to show that it would entail the impossibility of language and other absurdities.

But is the *Theaetetus* theory a version of idealism? Do its resemblances with Berkeley, which are undeniable, include a resemblance in respect of the features which rank Berkeley as our first and foremost idealist? I take it that if the label 'idealism' is of any historical use at all, it indicates a form of monism: monism not about the number of things in existence but about the number of kinds of things. Just as materialism is the monism which asserts that ultimately nothing exists or is real but matter and material things, so idealism is the monism which claims that ultimately all there is is mind and the contents of mind. But it is just this monistic tendency which is absent from the *Theaetetus*. To explain this I need to divulge some more details of Plato's dialectical construction.

---

a possibility which is, however, foreclosed by the direct refutation of the definition which follows at 184b–187a. In sum, the Protagorean–Heraclitean theory states a complete set of sufficient conditions for Theaetetus' definition to hold good, which conditions, it is argued, are (i) necessary conditions for it, (ii) harbingers of absurdity and hence, in the end, its downfall.

(B) If commentators have almost to a man been unwilling to take at face value these manifold indications by Plato as to the intended structure of his argument (and there are many lesser confirmatory signs which I have not mentioned), that is because they have not seen the underlying philosophical connections which make (2) intelligible and plausible. So the next task is to outline the connections in a manner which will enable us to take Plato at his word: see text below (it turns out that on this aspect Berkeley's philosophical acumen scores better).

(C) Even so, even supposing that the account I shall sketch is found satisfactory, one major stumbling block will remain. To carry through the *reductio* it is necessary to remove the impression many readers have formed (most recently, John McDowell, *Plato–Theaetetus* (Oxford: Clarendon Press, 1973), 179–184, Robert Bolton, 'Plato's Distinction Between Being and Becoming', *Review of Metaphysics* **29** (1975), 66–95) that what finally gets refuted at 179c–184b is a different and more extreme Heraclitean theory than that elaborated in the earlier section to 160e. The answer here is that Plato furnishes an argument (181de) to show that there is no escaping the further developments which are to be the theory's undoing. And here too an appreciation of the underlying connections between the three theses is indispensable. For, unlike most commentators, I believe that this argument is to be taken seriously. But that is a large project which I must leave to another occasion. Our present need is to understand the theory, not destroy it.

The central contribution of Protagoras to the theory elaborated in the *Theaetetus* is the rule that whatever sensible appearances a person has, they are true for him—things really are, for him, as they appear to him to be—together with the converse rule that the only things that are real for him are those that appear to him. This is the content Plato gives to Protagoras' famous proclamation, 'Man is the measure of all things, of those that are, that they are, and of those that are not, that they are not'. The rule demands a state of affairs for every appearance, rendering that appearance true, and the converse rule demands for every state of affairs an appearance in which that state of affairs is perceived or known. Thus a thing appears white to me if and only if there obtains the state of affairs, its being white for me.[3] If the rule and its converse are correct, Theaetetus' definition is so far vindicated. Once perception is construed in Protagorean terms as the having of sensible appearances (152b9–c2), every perception will be the unerring apprehension of a particular state of affairs, and there will be no state of affairs which is not unerringly apprehended in perception. Thus all perception is knowledge, and all knowledge is perception.[4]

[3] For a defence of the claim that Plato is serious about taking Protagoras' Measure doctrine as a theory of truth and derives from it the above rule and its converse, see my 'Protagoras and Self-Refutation in Plato's *Theaetetus*', *Philosophical Review* **85** (1976), 172–195.

[4] That all perception is knowledge is explicitly and validly argued at 152ac from the rule that every appearance is true for the person who has it and the premise that perception is the same as having an appearance. That all knowledge is perception is not explicitly argued there, but it can be derived by application of the converse rule and it needs to be derived if Socrates is to prove that the whole equation of knowledge and perception follows from Protagoras' philosophy. The reason for Plato's silence here about the latter half of the package is, I think, the following: it is only where sensible qualities are concerned that one would venture to equate the having of appearances with perception—Socrates says as much at 152c1–2—and Plato wants later (161b ff.) to discuss Protagorean relativism in its most general form, as the view that things are for each person as they appear to him, whether the 'appearing' is appearing to sense or to thought. The completely general relativism will preserve the thesis that all perception is knowledge, while allowing for knowledge (veridical appearance) that is not perception. There is more to be said on this aspect (for some of it, see paper cited in the preceding note), but for present purposes it will be enough to amend our previous overall description of the argument: it is a *reductio ad absurdum* with asides, namely, those asides which treat of Protagorean relativism in a more general form than is required for sustaining Theaetetus' definition. That said, we can from now on confine attention to sensible appearances and to one half of Theaetetus and Protagoras: the thesis that all perception is knowledge and the rule that, whatever sensible appearances a person has, they are true for him.

But of course this will work only if the states of affairs are understood relativistically: what I know and perceive is what is the case *for me now*, at the time of perceiving it. The states of affairs which make the appearances true are such items as a thing's being white to my eye now, and these states of affairs must be characterizable independently of what is the case for any other perceiver, including myself at another time, and indeed independently of what is the case for (what appears to) my other senses at the present time. The reason why this must be so is that, notoriously, appearances vary and conflict, and if they are all to be true for the person who has them, as the Protagorean rule prescribes, the states of affairs which make them true must vary to match. Similar considerations apply in Berkeley's theory, for his notion of immediate perception embodies a version of the Protagorean rule: immediate perception for Berkeley is knowledge (*Three Dialogues* 206, 238);[5] what is perceived must really be as it appears to be (*Dial.* 238); hence what is perceived must alter with every variation in the sensible appearances. The argument which yields this result is simple and compelling.

The same wind cannot be simultaneously both cold and not cold, to use Plato's example, or in Berkeley's version of the identical argument, the same water cannot be simultaneously both cold and warm (*Dial.* 178–179, 189). Hence, if every appearance is to be vindicated as true, as genuine knowledge, there will be a contradiction when appearances conflict, unless what is the case for the person or the hand that feels warm and what is the case for the one that feels cold constitute distinct and independent states of affairs. In Berkeleyan terms two distinct ideas are perceived, two momentary appearances which really do exhibit the qualities they seem to have; in Protagorean terms each perception confronts its own private instantiation of a sensible quality; and neither theory can allow that the same water enters into both occurrences. And if this holds when the conflicting appearances are contemporaneous, it holds also when they come successively in the experience of one individual. Here too we need distinct states of affairs to match the appearances (for Berkeley, distinct ideas), and we must deny that the wind or the water maintains its identity through time to occur in both.[6]

---

[5] References to Berkeley's *Three Dialogues* are by page numbers of Jessop's edition: *The Works of George Berkeley*, II, A. A. Luce and T. E. Jessop (eds) (London: T. Nelson, 1949).

[6] The above summarizes a two-stage argument in the *Theaetetus*. Socrates first establishes the relativity of sensible qualities (153d–154b) and then develops its implications for the identity of objects (156a ff.). Already at stage one there are complications into which we should not enter here, but interestingly they are complications paralleled in Berkeley's *Three Dialogues*, as I try to show in 'Conflicting Appearances', *Proc. Br. Acad.* **65** (1979), 69–111.

But again, all this will only work if the world is very different from what we ordinarily take it to be. It must be a Heraclitean flux in which, for the reasons given, no two people perceive numerically the same item, and the items they do perceive cannot maintain a continuing identity from one moment to the next. Nothing is left but a succession of pairings between perceptual appearances on the one hand and the momentary states of affairs which they represent on the other.[7] Just as Protagoras supplies the epistemology which is required if Theaetetus' definition is to have a chance of survival (for the only perception which can invariably be relied upon to yield secure knowledge is what Berkeley was to call immediate perception), so Heraclitus gives the metaphysics of a world in which Protagoras' epistemology holds good. With this too Berkeley will agree (*Siris* §§344, 348–349).

Such, in outline, are the underlying philosophical connections between the three theses on which the *Theaetetus* theory is built. It all sounds remarkably like Berkeley, not only in content but also in the argument which motivates and controls the construction. The difference is that in the *Theaetetus* it is as true to say that the perceiving subject is dependent on there being something for it to perceive as it is to say that the thing perceived is dependent on a subject perceiving it. The ontological dependence goes both ways. The clearest evidence of this is the very passage that Berkeley relies on in *Siris* when he claims, in the section I quoted, that Plato does not admit 'an absolute actual existence of sensible or corporeal things'. Socrates is summing up the Protagorean–Heraclitean construction he has elaborated in support of Theaetetus' definition:

> Whenever I come to be perceiving, I necessarily come to be perceiving something; because it's impossible to come to be perceiving, but not perceiving anything. And whenever it [sc. the object perceived] comes to be sweet, bitter, or anything of that kind, it necessarily comes to be so for someone, because it's impossible to come to be sweet, but not sweet for anyone . . .

> Then what we're left with, I think, is that it's for each other that we [sc. subject and object] are, if we are, or come to be, if we come to be, since necessity ties our being together, but doesn't tie it to anything else, or indeed to ourselves. So what we're left with is that we're tied to each other. It follows that, whether one uses 'be' or 'come to be'[8] of something, one should speak of it as being, or coming to be, for someone or of something or in relation to something. As for speaking of a thing as being or coming to be anything just by itself, one shouldn't do that

[7] If 'represent' here has to be construed differently for Berkeley and for Protagoras, that is part of the ontological divergence we are coming to.

[8] This is the correct translation of *gignesthai*, which Berkeley (above, p. 20) rendered 'is made'.

oneself, and one shouldn't accept it from anyone else either. That's what's indicated by the argument we've been setting out [160ac, tr. McDowell].

In this symmetrical balance between subject and object of perception, between the appearances and the states of affairs which make them true, we have, I submit, a decisive contrast with Berkeley. In Berkeley, the object of perception is dependent on the perceiving subject, not vice versa: or if there is a dependence the other way as well, it does not carry the same weight of significance. To be sure, Berkeley insists that minds and ideas are radically different sorts of things (*Principles of Human Knowledge* §§2–3; *Dial.* 231). The being of an idea is its being perceived, the being of a mind is not. But while he says repeatedly that ideas are in the mind and cannot be conceived as existing apart from a mind which perceives them, because they cannot be conceived except as actually being perceived, he does not (in the published works)[9] suggest the converse, as the *Theaetetus* does, that minds have an essential relation to ideas and cannot be conceived as existing apart from the ideas they perceive.[10] The primacy goes to mind, not only because minds do more than perceive ideas—they are also thinking, active things (*Princ.* §27; *Dial.* 233, cf. 241)—but, more importantly, because in terms of the traditional metaphysical metaphor of support, it is minds which support ideas, not vice versa (*Princ.* §91). Ideas have to inhere in a mind; minds do not have to inhere in anything.

This is connected, of course, with Berkeley's belief that ideas, sensible things, are wholly inert; only minds have causal efficacy (*Princ.* §§25–26; *Dial.* 231). No idea would exist unless a mind brought it into existence and sustained it there. And Berkeley argues from this causal dependence to ontological dependence when he reasons that since in perception we are passively affected with ideas, these must be caused by another mind, namely God, and exist in that mind. 'The mind [sc. the divine mind] contains all and acts all' is the way he phrases this double dependency in *Siris* (§295).

Perception is passive in the *Theaetetus* also, but the causally active element is the thing perceived (159c). In truth, this is hardly a serious causal

[9] The caveat is necessary on account of a surprising group of entries in Berkeley's unpublished *Philosophical Commentaries* headed by No. 577 (obelized for rejection): 'The very existence of ideas constitutes the soul'. This belongs with the early stages of Berkeley's philosophizing studied by A. A. Luce, *The Dialectic of Immaterialism* (London: Hodder and Stoughton, 1963). It is explicitly denied at *Dial.* 233.

[10] No doubt the mind must have ideas to operate upon (cf. *Phil. Comm.* 478; *Princ.* §§27, 139; *Dial.* 231–234), but that is not enough for ontological dependence. Cf. *Phil. Comm.* 878: 'Extension tho it exist only in the Mind, yet is no Property of the Mind, The Mind can exist without it tho it cannot without the Mind'.

claim. The active item being just a momentary occurrence, it can be said to be active only in relation to the subject which perceives it here and now (157a, 160a). It has the power to stimulate a sense-organ or subject just once: it is active in relation to the equally momentary sense-organ or subject by which alone it is perceived and which perceives it alone (159e–160b). This activity is nothing but a last etiolated remnant of our ordinary assumptions about the causal role of physical objects in perception, left over when these have been whittled down to a series of distinct momentary occurrences. Plato's dialectical construction is not seriously concerned with the causal aspect of perception. Nor does he trouble to explain, what for Berkeley is a major theme, how it comes about that there is always a state of affairs to match any given appearance. He has no equivalent to Berkeley's divine agency. And his indifference to the issue of causality itself illustrates his lack of concern to award ontological primacy to one side or the other. For his dialectical purpose he can continue to work with the ordinary dualism of perceiving minds and physical objects perceived. The whittled down physical objects have indeed no 'absolute actual existence'—they exist only for the subjects which perceive them—but they are not mental things: they are not made to exist by a mind and consequently do not exist in a mind in the sense which makes Berkeley's a monistic philosophy.[11] Conversely, minds in the *Theaetetus* have no absolute actual existence either, something Berkeley could certainly not allow. There is no continuing subject of perception, any more than a continuing object of perception, but only a series of distinct subjects existing momentarily as, for example, the subject or the sense-organ which sees that white thing now.[12]

One might sum up the difference this way: where Berkeley insists that for sensible things *esse* is strictly identical with *percipi*, Plato says simply that a sensible item *est* if and only if *percipitur*, and he leaves it at that.

[11] Thus the 'mental containment' view of sense-qualities which J. N. Findlay, *Plato: The Written and Unwritten Doctrines* (London and New York: Routledge and Kegan Paul, 1974), 362, attributes to Plato in the *Theaetetus* is neither Plato nor in the *Theaetetus*.

[12] On this point the comparison is with Russell's position in *The Problems of Philosophy* (Oxford: Oxford University Press, 1912), 19, rather than with Berkeley's mature philosophy. See further my 'Plato on the Grammar of Perceiving', *Classical Quarterly* 26 (1976), 29–51. Of course, having got thus far it is only a short step, as Russell found, to abolishing the subject–object distinction altogether. But the point is that the step is not taken in the *Theaetetus*. In any case, if one detects an idealist slant in the ostensibly neutral monism of modern philosophers who have pushed further, that has a lot to do with one's knowledge that, historically, the monism is reached by way of Berkeley and presupposes Berkeley's elimination of matter. It is Berkeley's previous elimination of matter which ensured that, when Hume cut out Berkeley's substantial mind, all he could be left with was perceptions.

The etiolated remnants of the two realms of mind and matter are tied together by necessity, but they remain two, not one.

II

We have now explored in some detail Berkeley's best evidence for an ancient Greek idealism, and we have found it wanting. There is little need to dwell on Berkeley's attempt to claim a similar position for Aristotle. Berkeley quotes Aristotle as saying, 'Sensible things, although they receive no change in themselves, do nevertheless in sick persons produce different sensations and not the same' (*Met.* 1063a37–b4) and he admits that such passages 'would seem to imply a distinct and absolute existence of the objects of sense' (§311). So they do, but Berkeley counters that the existence of sensible things when not perceived is for Aristotle merely potential, not actual (§312). Here he has simply misunderstood Aristotle's doctrine that sensible qualities become actualized in perception. It is not the thesis that an apple is not actually or really red except when it is seen, but that it does not look red. The apple becomes actually red when it ripens; what is actualized in perception is not the redness but the capacity of that redness to act on or manifest itself to sight.[13] Further, even if the sensible qualities of the apple were merely potential, the apple itself in the Aristotelian scheme of things is not to be identified with the sum of its sensible qualities. It is a substantial entity in its own right,[14] which is to say that it enjoys exactly that absolute actual existence which Berkeley is so anxious to deny.

But if both Plato and Aristotle refuse to enlist in the idealist cause,

[13] See *De Anima* II, 5 and III, 2. Berkeley overlooks Aristotle's central claim (418a3–6) that the sensible object must already be in actuallity what, prior to the act of perception, the sentient subject is potentially. If the red apple's redness is a potentiality as well as an actuality, this is a *second* potentiality, on a par with the potential knowledge of a man who has actually learned something but is not currently using his knowledge, not with the potentiality which precedes the learning. Berkeley also draws on Aristotle's doctrine that actual knowledge and the thing known are one: 'Whence it follows that the things are where the knowledge is, that is to say, in the mind' (*Siris* §310). Aristotle's own conclusion is, of course, not that at all: 'It is not the stone which is in the soul but its form' (*De An.* 431b29). At *Met.* 1010b30–35 (which Berkeley should have seized on) the *aisthēta* that are conceded to depend for their existence on being perceived must be actualized sensible qualites (so Christopher Kirwan, *Aristotle's Metaphysics* Γ, Δ, E (Oxford: Clarendon Press, 1971), ad loc.), or else Aristotle will be slipping into the Megarian account of possibility which he disputes on this very issue in *Met.* H 3.

[14] In stricter moods Aristotle would not allow that an apple, as opposed to an apple tree, is a proper substance. But this hardly affects the issue, and I choose the example as being Berkeley's own (*Princ.* §1).

who remains? Various names might be suggested. Parmenides? But the fragment (frag. 3) which was once believed, by Berkeley among others (*Siris* §309), to say that to think and to be are one and the same is rather to be construed as saying, on the contrary, that it is one and the same thing which is there for us to think *of* and is there to be: thought requires an object, distinct from itself, and that object, Parmenides argues, must actually exist. Gorgias? Gorgias argued that nothing exists, that if anything did exist we could have no knowledge of it, and that even if we did have knowledge of it we could not communicate that knowledge to anyone else. But to argue that nothing exists at all is presumably not to take an idealist stance, and in any case what Gorgias was serious about was not his outrageous conclusions but the demonstration that he could impose them on you by argumentative persuasions which you will be helpless to resist. Metrodorus of Chios? Metrodorus was a sceptically inclined follower of Democritus who is credited with the obscure pronouncement, 'Everything exists that one might think of' (frag. 2). But an atomist, whatever else he may be, is at least some sort of materialist, not an idealist, and the obscure remark may rather be a version of the atomist doctrine that all possibilities are sooner or later realized somewhere in the universe. This would tie in with an argument that Metrodorus is reported to have used to establish the existence of an infinite number of worlds: it is as absurd that just one world should come to be in the infinite as that just one ear of corn should grow on a large plain.[15]

Perhaps, then, the Neoplatonists? They have been classified as idealists because they hold that the world proceeds from Intellect (Nous) and Soul. The problem is that whether this is in any interesting sense an idealist view depends on how the cosmic creation is conceived, and about that, as about so much else, Plotinus and his successors are notoriously obscure. Berkeley was content to cite evidence that 'the Platonists' believe that all nature is alive, and is made and governed by an eternal mind.[16] But that is hardly enough. Even if it can be said that in Neoplatonism the real, in so far as it is real, is in some sense spiritual,[17] it remains that matter is not. What is most revealing about Neoplatonism is that the cosmic creation (a permanent, not a temporal process) is still conceived in the old Greek way as the operation of a formal principle on matter.

Matter for Plotinus is indeed not corporeal (*Enneads* II, 4.12.34–38), for it is without any determination at all: it is the sheer negativity of not being, potentiality without a trace of actuality, darkness or privation, evil (II, 4;

[15] Diels-Kranz, *Die Fragmente der Vorsokratiker*, 6th edn (Berlin: Weidmannsche Buchhandlung, 1951), 70 A 6. Cf. 67 A 8, 68 A 38. More on Metrodorus in n. 42 below.

[16] *Siris* §§262, 266–269, 274–279, 290–291, 328, 352–353, 362–364.

[17] Cf. A. H. Armstrong, *The Architecture of the Intelligible Universe in the Philosophy of Plotinus* (Cambridge: Cambridge University Press, 1940), 87, 113.

II, 5; I, 8). But Plotinus is emphatic that this does not mean it is an empty name (II, 4.12.23–24). One arrives at the notion of matter by stripping away all determinations, including extension, and what is left at the limit of analysis is the concept of that which is other than all actual determinate being (II, 4.13.27–32). The Neoplatonic doctrine of emanation has it that through a series of stages this 'other' is endowed with reality and form in the manner in which darkness is illuminated by light. If it can be said that matter, too, is initially made by Soul, this is in consequence of, and not identical with, the imposition of form. It is actual determinate being which is the product of emanation; the making of matter is rather to be compared to the way a beam of light marks out the darkness below as what is other than itself, as that which it illuminates and informs (I, 8.7.17–24; II, 4.5). The old doctrine that everything in the world is a combination of matter and form still holds, though it has been complicated and reinterpreted in novel ways (II, 4.6; II, 4.10.23–25). It seems, therefore, that the grand cosmic metaphor of emanation is evidence less of incipient idealism in a modern sense than of the ancients' final inability to relinquish the traditional dualities of mind and object, subject and attribute. In fact, while it is not surprising that Berkeley should approve the denial that matter is corporeal (*Siris* §§306, 317–318), he is only able to embrace the full Neoplatonic doctrine that matter *is* not being,[18] the darkness illumined by form (*Siris* §§318–320), by a striking relaxation of his own earlier contention that there is no non-mental 'other' to mind because the notion of matter is just a confused fiction concocted by philosophers.[19]

A full treatment of Neoplatonic 'idealism' would have to grapple with the further difficulty that Intellect and Soul themselves proceed from an ineffable first principle, the One. It is possible that the One does in some obscure and unfamiliar sense have knowledge of itself.[20] The interpretation is not uncontroversial, but supposing it to be well founded, the motivation would probably be that it is only in an absolutely unitary and hence unitarily self-knowing first principle that the traditional duality of subject and object can be finally and completely overcome. But this means, first, that some form of duality remains at every other level; and second, that since both Intellect and its eternal intelligible objects (the Forms, which are different, yet not separate, from Intellect: III, 9.1) disappear

---

[18] *ontōs ouk on* (II, 5.5.25), to be contrasted with that which is not at all (*to pantē/panteles mē on*, VI, 9.11.36–38).

[19] This inconsistency between *Siris* and the earlier Berkeley is well noted by Naguib Baladi, 'Plotin et l'Immatérialisme de Berkeley. Témoignage de la *Siris*', in *Atti del Convegno Internazionale sul tema: Plotino e il Neoplatonismo in Oriente e in Occidente* (Rome: Accademia dei Lincei, Quaderno No 198, 1974), 597–602.

[20] For a recent discussion and advocacy of the view, see J. M. Rist, *Plotinus: The Road to Reality* (Cambridge: Cambridge University Press, 1967), chap. 4.

together into the One, it would be misleading and partial to describe the ultimate monism as a monism of mind. Even less is it a monism of mind if the controversially anthropomorphic interpretation of the One is set aside. So our quarry is not to be found in Plotinus.[21] As for the 800-odd years of Greek philosophy before Neoplatonism took over—and it is to this more congenial period that my generalizations will now be addressed— throughout that time thought and theory are dominated by an unquestioned, unquestioning assumption of realism.

Greek philosophy is perfectly prepared to think that reality may be entirely different from what we ordinarily take it to be. It may be distorted by our anthropocentric point of view and misrepresented by the conventional categories of our language, as Heraclitus held. Such fundamental features of our experience as plurality and change, time and motion, may be contradictory illusion, as the Eleatics contend. It may be that each of us lives in his own private reality, as Protagoras, had he seen as far as Plato, should have said. Or it may be, as Democritus suggests, that the only common objective reality is a colourless world of atoms and void, a world without any of the secondary qualities familiar to subjective experience. It may be, finally, that we simply know nothing of what reality is like, as various sceptics urge. But all these philosophers, however radical their scrutiny of ordinary belief, leave untouched—indeed they rely upon— the notion that we are deceived or ignorant about *something*. There is a reality of some sort confronting us; we are in touch with something, even if this something, reality, is not at all what we think it to be.[22] Greek philo-

---

[21] Authorities who are firmly against a Plotinian idealism include W. R. Inge, *The Philosophy of Plotinus* II, 3rd edn (London, New York, Toronto: Longmans Green & Co., 1929), 37ff., and Armstrong, op. cit., chap. 8. According to R. T. Wallis, *Neoplatonism* (London: Duckworth, 1972), 124, later Neoplatonists make sure that any ambiguities in Plotinus' position are resolved in the direction of realism.

[22] Objection: But Parmenides himself famously declares that the words mortals use, words like 'come into being', 'changing place', etc., are mere names (frag. 8, 38), i.e. empty names to which nothing corresponds. Answer: It is his editors who have made him say this. The authentic text, with much the best authority in the manuscripts, is not *toi pant' onom' estai* ('Wherefore all these are [sc. mere] names which mortals have laid down believing them to be true'), but *toi pant' onomastai*. The latter was vigorously defended by Leonard Woodbury, 'Parmenides on Names', *Harvard Studies in Classical Philology* **63** (1958), 145–160, with the translation 'With reference to it [sc. that-which-is] are all the names given that mortal men have instituted, in the belief that they were true'. But his defence has remained open to a technical grammatical objection (see G. E. L. Owen in *Studies in Presocratic Philosophy*, II, R. E. Allen and D. J. Furley (eds) (London: Routledge and Kegan Paul, 1975), 69). A simple solution will circumvent the difficulty: keep *toi* as 'wherefore' and take the subject

sophy does not know the problem of proving in a general way the existence of an external world. That problem is a modern invention, and the process by which it was invented will be highly germane to our enquiry later on. The problem which typifies ancient philosophical enquiry in a way that the external world problem has come to typify philosophical enquiry in modern times is quite the opposite. It is the problem of understanding how thought can be of nothing or what is not, how our minds can be exercised on false-hoods, fictions, and illusions. The characteristic worry, from Parmenides onwards, is not how the mind can be in touch with anything at all, but how it can fail to be. And I think that in this contrast there is much to be learned about the differences between ancient and modern philosophy.

For one thing, it means that the monism which comes most naturally to a Greek philosopher is materialism, as in the Stoics or, very differently and provided that an infinite void does not count as an extra item in one's ontology, Democritean and Epicurean atomism. These philosophies reduce mind to matter with a robust paucity of argument which ought to strike the historian as revealingly naive. Whereas, I suggest, a monism leaning in the other direction, from reality to mind, would be repellent to Greek thought, for it would seem to deprive the mind of the objects it must necessarily have. This inbuilt assumption of realism is well illustrated by a curious passage in Plato's *Parmenides* (132bc).

In reply to the famous Third Man Argument against the Platonic Theory of Forms, Socrates makes the suggestion that the Forms are thoughts. This would mean, he says, that a Form could not subsist anywhere but in souls, and in that way each Form would be one and would not suffer the damaging reduplication which the Third Man Argument brought about. To understand this suggestion we need to remember that Plato's forms, at least in the context of the arguments in the *Parmenides*, are entities which explain how it is that a number of things are, for example, large. Socates' answer so far has been that large things all participate in the Form, the Large Itself, which is an independent entity grasped by reasoning rather than by perception (cf. 129a–130a). But this answer has led to various absurdities, the last and most serious of which—the Third Man objection— was that the very reasoning which favours the postulation of a single Form, the Large Itself, further gives rise to an infinite number of Forms for the things that are large; and this wrecks the hypothesis, on which the explana-

---

of the verb from *to eon* in the previous line (construction as in frag. 9, 1): 'Wherefore it (the one being) is named all the names which mortals have laid down in the (mistaken) belief that they are true (of it)'. On this construal mortals continue to talk about something, viz. the only thing there is to talk about, but what they say about it is wrong and contradictory.

tory force of the theory depends, that there is just one Form for each set of things falling under the common term in question. Socrates' escape from the difficulty, as I understand it, involves the suggestion that in a certain sense there is no independently existing entity, the Form, at all, and hence nothing that could turn out to be many instead of one. Large things are large, not because they all have a relationship to a further entity, the Form, but because they are all related, in some way as yet unspecified, to a certain thought. That thought, therefore, is the Form which explains how it is that all of them are large.

Now, given that the purpose of the Theory of Forms is to explain how it is that things in the world have the characters they do, it might seem that the proposal to construe Forms as thoughts, subsisting only in souls or minds, was a move toward a form of idealism different from the Berkeleyan kind we have chiefly considered so far. The idealism which has been most influential in modern times is the idealism which asserts, in one version or another, that the world is essentially structured by the categories of our thought. And it might well seem that some such dependence of the characters of things on thought was the solution Socrates proposed to escape the difficulties he encountered with his earlier, heavily realist mode of explanation.

But consider how the argument develops. Parmenides asks, 'Is each of the thoughts one and yet a thought of nothing?' 'Impossible', replies Socrates. 'So it is a thought of something?' 'Yes.' 'Of something that is or of something that is not?' 'Of something that is.' 'Of some one thing which, being over all the cases, that thought thinks, i.e. some single character?' 'Yes.' 'Then won't this thing, which is thought to be one [or: this one object of thought] and which is always the same over all the cases, be a Form?' 'That again seems to follow.' Thus Socrates is driven back to his original realism. Thought must have an object, a really existing object independent of itself, and that object will be the Form.

What is remarkable about this argument is its swiftness and the brutality of its realism. Plato is certainly capable of more sophisticated treatment of the relation of thought to its objects. Here he is indulging an Eleatic theme which he knows very well needs careful scrutiny lest it trap one in intolerable paradox. But the very fact that he allows his Eleatic spokesman to get away with it reveals, I think, that it simply did not occur to him that there might be a serious philosophical thesis to be developed out of Socrates' suggestion that Forms are thoughts. We are confronted with the spectacle of the most audacious and creative philosophical imagination of antiquity (witness, to take just one example, the anticipatory refutation of Berkeley in the *Theaetetus*) unable to entertain seriously the idea that one might seek to explain the nature of the world by reference to the categories of our thought. He is unable to do so because, whatever his scruples about the Eleatic principle that there is no thinking of what is not, he cannot see past the idea that thought must be of something independent of itself.[23] Thought is relative, essentially of something else, and therefore it is incapable of furnishing the ultimate explanation of anything.

It is no objection to my taking this passage of the *Parmenides* as indicative of the deep hold of realism on Greek philosophy that in Hellenistic times the standard explanation of general terms, common to both Stoics and Epicureans, was a conceptualist one. General terms are associated with concepts (*ennoiai*) or mental dispositions, and no Hellenistic philosopher upholds a realist view of universals. This is no objection to what I have been saying, because the corollary of Hellenistic conceptualism is a naturalistic account of concept formation. It is our nature and our experience of the world that explain the concepts we have, not the other way round. The world is as it is independently of us, and shapes our thought accordingly. Whereas what Plato was gunning for in the *Parmenides* is not conceptualism about universals (though scholars often call it that), but the suggestion that it is thought which explains the way things are in the world. This is plain from the final twist in Parmenides' refutation, the most curious of all.

If Forms are thoughts, he argues, then the things which participate in them will themselves consist of thoughts, so that either they all think, or (an alternative absurdity) they are thoughts which nevertheless do not think. To find any sense at all in this nonsense we need to recognize that it makes use of a central contention of the Theory of Forms, that the characters of things are derived or borrowed from the characters of the corresponding Forms; so here the thought-character of Socrates' proposed Forms transfers to the things these Forms are to explain. Never mind whether Parmenides' argument plays fair with the pattern of explanation preferred by the Theory of Forms.[24] The important point for our purpose is that Plato is concerned with the explanatory, not just the classificatory function of Forms. And Hellenistic conceptualism would agree with him that it would be reversing the natural order of things to explain the world by the categories of our thought.

[23] Cf. Klaus Oehler, *Die Lehre vom Noetischen und Dianoetischen Denken bei Platon und Aristoteles* (Munich: C. H. Beck, 1962), 103ff., who sees the connection between the non-idealism of the *Parmenides* and some of the differences between ancient and modern scepticism discussed below. In the *Sophist* Plato defuses the Eleatic principle precisely by showing that to think or speak of what is not is not to think or speak of nothing. That the something thought is independent of thought is the point which, in its several ramifications, also falsifies Hegel's claim to find anticipations of his own brand of idealism in Plato and Aristotle: *Lectures on the History of Philosophy* II, trans. E. S. Haldane and Frances H. Simson (London and New York: Routledge and Kegan Paul, 1955), 1, 43, 188, 196.

[24] For an assessment which answers that it does play fair, see David Keyt, 'The Mad Craftsman of the *Timaeus*', *Philosophical Review* **80** (1971), 230–235.

III

In these last remarks I have strayed into talking about developments in Hellenistic philosophy, and it is now time to move on to the later period and pick up the question I touched on earlier, why the Greeks never posed the problem of the existence of an external world in the general form we have known it since Descartes. This is the period in which to look for an answer to that question, because it was then that the arguments from conflicting appearances which we discussed in connection with Berkeley and the *Theaetetus* were worked up into a systematic scepticism. The legacy of Protagoras and Heraclitus was a battery of arguments tending to show that we have no knowledge of anything whatsoever, indeed that we have no grounds for reasonable belief. No matter what the question, there is no reason to believe any answer rather than its denial.

This is the position of Pyrrhonian scepticism as represented by Sextus Empiricus. The strategy for inducing a total suspension of judgment may be outlined as follows.[25] We start, as sceptics so often do start, from the point that in any matter things appear differently to people in different situations or with different bodily constitutions or in different states of mind or in different cultures, and so on through an immense catalogue of varying circumstances and of the conflicting appearances to which they give rise. Faced with this conflict of appearances, the sceptic agrees with Berkeley and the *Theaetetus* that conflicting appearances cannot be equally true of a common objective world, cannot be equally representative of how things really are in themselves. Unlike Berkeley and the *Theaetetus*, however, the sceptic has no prior commitment to the thesis that perception or appearance is knowledge. So he does not accept both of a pair of conflicting appearances and then adjust his picture of the world to match. Rather, he holds on to the ordinary conception of a common objective world and looks for a criterion of truth to determine which of the conflicting appearances he should accept. Unfortunately, there turns out to be no intellectually satisfactory criterion he can trust and use. We have no adequate way of telling when things really are as they appear to be. The sceptic now finds himself in the following position: he cannot accept all the appearances, because they conflict, and he cannot decide between them, for lack of a criterion or any reasoned basis for preferring one to another. Hence he cannot accept any. He is forced to suspend judgment. Just try to believe something is true which you are fully aware that you have absolutely no

---

[25] For documentation and defence of the interpretation to be given of Pyrrhonian scepticism, see my 'Can the Sceptic Live His Scepticism', in *Doubt and Dogmatism: Studies in Hellenistic Epistemology*, Malcolm Schofield, Myles Burnyeat, and Jonathan Barnes (eds) (Oxford: Clarendon Press, 1980). The main text is the first book of Sextus' *Outlines of Pyrrhonism* (*PH*).

reason to prefer to its denial; for instance, to take the favourite example, that the number of the stars is even. Pyrrrhonian scepticism leaves you that way as regards every question whatsoever.

You may think this an uncomfortable position to end up in. But the sceptic does not find it so. The great recommendation of Pyrrhonism is that suspension of judgment on all questions as to what is true and what is false results in tranquillity. Anxiety is due either to certainty or to uncertainty. Either one holds firm beliefs—value beliefs about what is important and worthwhile and factual beliefs about states of affairs in the world which bear on one's pursuit or preservation of these goods—and then one is afflicted with hopes and fears for one's present and future happiness; or, alternatively, one is made anxious by being uncertain whether one has the right beliefs about these things. The sceptic, we are told (*PH* I, 12, 26–29), sets out on his enquiries in the hope of freeing himself from the anxieties of uncertainty. And he does get free of them—but in a manner different from that which he aimed for. He resolves his uncertainty, not by finding answers to his questions (which would only be to swap one source of anxiety for another), but by finding that they seem to be unanswerable. It is when he throws in the sponge that, unexpectedly, tranquillity ensues; just as, to use Sextus' own comparison, the famous painter Apelles only achieved the effect of showing the foam at a horse's mouth when he gave up trying and flung his sponge at the painting.

We may find this an unattractive solution to the problems of life. But we must recognize that Pyrrhonian scepticism had this in common with the rival Hellenistic philosophies, Stoicism and Epicureanism, that it offered in all seriousness a recipe for happiness. And it will become clear, I hope, that this practical orientation is of the first importance for the problem of the existence of the external world.[26] It goes without saying that a recipe for happiness is addressed to people who can live in the world and enjoy their happiness. I must now show that it did go without saying.

Sextus claims to suspend judgment about everything, but on examination we find that the scope of this 'everything' does not extend to everything that we—that is, post-Cartesian we—would expect it to cover. The limitations are of several distinguishable types, and, significantly, not all of them are explicit in the sceptical literature. First, and this is something Sextus is entirely explicit about, the sceptic's doubting and suspending judgment extend only to statements which make claims about how things are in themselves. Variants on this formulation include: how things are in their own nature, how things are in reality, what the external things are like, and (most simply) what is true. All these are what the sceptic suspends judgment about. He refrains from statements which make a truth claim

---

[26] The connection was pointed out to me by David Owen.

about what is the case in a common objective world, external to ourselves and comprising things with a nature of their own. 'Truth' in these contexts means truth as to real existence, something's being true of an independent reality. It is in this sense that the sceptic will not assent to anything as true. But he will assent, indeed according to Sextus he cannot help assenting, to such appearances as he is affected with. He acknowledges feeling hot or thirsty; he does not dispute that certain things customarily appear good or bad to him; he notes that certain arguments appear to lead to a sceptical conclusion; and so it goes for any subject you like to bring up. The sceptic finds himself assenting to a host of propositions of the form 'Such and such appears to me now thus and so', but he never finds reason to advance to the truth claim 'It is as it appears'. There is thus a large class of statements which, as Sextus puts it (*PH* I, 22), are immune from enquiry (*azētētos*). They are immune from enquiry, not open to dispute, because they make no claim as to objective fact. They simply record the sceptic's own present experience, the way he is affected (in Greek, his *pathos*), leaving it open whether external things really are as they appear to him to be.

That is the first limitation on the scope of Pyrrhonian scepticism, expressed in Sextus' own terms. The modern, post-Cartesian reader may feel that Sextus is somewhat disingenuous in offering this elucidation of what it is to suspend judgment about *everything*. But that would, I think, be a mistake. It would be a mistake for the same reason that it would be a mistake, though again a mistake that comes naturally to a post-Cartesian philosopher, to object that the sceptic has left himself some truth after all, namely, all those truths about his experience which he records in statements of the form 'It appears to me thus and so'. Surely, one wants to say, a statement of this form is true if and only if things do appear as the statement says they appear.[27] But as I have already noted, in the sceptic's book to say that an appearance, or the statement expressing it, is true is to say that external things really are as they (are said to) appear to be. 'True' in these discussions always means 'true of a real objective world', and that is how the word 'true' had been used since Protagoras and before. Protagoras' book was called *Truth* precisely because it offered an account of the conditions under which things really are as they appear to be. The Greek use of the predicates 'true' and 'false' embodies the assumption of realism on which I have been insisting all along. The correct response to this historical fact is not to object, but to ask for enlightenment: how did it come about that philosophy accepted the idea that truth can be obtained without going outside subjective experience?

That question posed, let us turn to some of the limitations on which Sextus is less explicit. Never, for example, does he claim that the sceptic

[27] Cf. Charlotte Stough, *Greek Skepticism* (Berkeley & Los Angeles: University of California Press, 1969), 142ff.

can be *certain* of 'appearing'-statements or that he *knows* his own experiences.[28] He does not, like some modern philosophers of a sceptical turn, say, 'At least I know how things appear to me, but do I know any more than that?' And there is evidence in Galen that if the question was raised—and it is not clear that it was often raised—then at least the more radical Pyrrhonists (rustic Pyrrhonists, Galen calls them) would actually deny that they had certain knowledge of appearances.[29]

It would be appropriate at this point to move a second request for enlightenment: when and why did philosophers first lay claim to knowledge of their own subjective states? But there is a complication. An earlier group of sceptics, the Cyrenaic school, did hold that we know our own experience (*pathos*) and nothing else. They put it in these terms: I know how I am being affected, but not what causes me to be thus affected. I can say, for example, 'I am being burned' or 'I am being cut', but not that it is fire that is burning or iron that is cutting me.[30] If these examples are mystifying to a modern ear, it is not just for lack of the information that cutting and cauterizing were two main operations of ancient surgery.[31] What one wants to ask is whether they mean the physical event of cauterizing or the way it feels. But to that question no answer is forthcoming.

Consider also the special vocabulary which the Cyrenaics devised to express their perceptual experiences.[32] Instead of talking, as a latter-day sceptic would do, of seeming to see something yellow and taste something sweet, or of something's appearing yellow, sweet, etc., the Cyrenaic prefers to say, 'I am yellowed, sweetened, etc.' The argument then is that if I am 'yellowed', this does not guarantee that my yellowish state is due to something yellow outside me. I may have jaundice, which makes the eyes go yellow so that everything looks yellow.[33] But now which of these, the yellowing of the eyes or the looking yellow, is the primary reference of

[28] *PH* I, 215, is an apparent exception where Sextus is in fact reporting, and resisting, someone else's attempt to assimilate Pyrrhonism to Cyrenaic scepticism, for which see below.

[29] Galen, *De pulsuum differentiis* VIII, 711, 1–3 Kühn, available also in Karl Deichgräber, *Die Griechische Empirikerschule* (Berlin: Weidmann, 1930), frag. 75, p. 135, 28–30.

[30] Aristocles *apud* Eusebius, *Praeparatio Evangelica* XIV, 19, 1 = frag. 212 in Erich Mannebach, *Aristippi et Cyrenaicorum Fragmenta* (Leiden and Cologne: E. J. Brill, 1961); cf. frag. 214. The Cyrenaic theory of knowledge was developed by Aristippus the Younger in the second half of the fourth century B.C.

[31] I am nevertheless grateful to Keith McCullough for drawing my attention to the relevance of the fact.

[32] Sextus, *adv. Math.* VII, 190ff., Plutarch, *Against Colotes* 1120b ff. = Mannebach frags 217–218.

[33] This seems to be the earliest attested citing of the familiar philosophical myth about jaundice: see further my 'Conflicting Appearances', op. cit.

the perceptual report 'I am yellowed'? Once again, there is no clear answer. Moreover, there would be reason not to expect an answer if, as seems very possible, the Cyrenaic vocabulary derives from a sceptical reading of Aristotle's theory that to perceive yellow is to acquire the form which the object already has.[34] For the ambiguity of this theory is precisely that it is unclear, and is still a matter of exegetical dispute, how literally (physically) Aristotle means to say that some part of me becomes yellow when I perceive yellow.[35] But with or without this Aristotelian connection, it looks to be anachronistic to think we must be able to 'split' the Cyrenaic notion of experience into separate mental (subjective) and physical (objective) components.

So far as I can discover, the first philosopher who picks out as something we know what are unambiguously subjective states, and picks them out as giving certain knowledge *because* they are subjective states, is Augustine (*Contra Academicos* III, 26), in this as in other things a precursor of Descartes. It is clear that Augustine means to speak of subjective states, first because he uses verbs of appearance ('This appears white', 'This tastes sweet', etc.), and second (in case anyone thinks to worry about a subjective reference for the demonstrative 'this') because he has just invented the idea that we might designate as 'the world' the totality of appearances, including the 'as if' earth (*quasi terra*) and the 'as if' sky which contains them (III, 24).[36] And Augustine thought of the claim to know items in this 'world of appearance' not as a basis for scepticism, but as a novel way to *refute* the sceptical thesis that we have no knowledge of anything.

It is not very likely that the unclarity or ambiguity just noted in Cyrenaic scepticism is merely due to the poverty of our sources. For we find a parallel unclarity or ambiguity in Sextus' talk of external things. If we ask what these external things whose nature is in doubt are external to, it appears that no sharp line is drawn such as is presupposed in the modern formulation of the problem of the existence of the external world. In the modern formulation 'external' means external to the mind, but in Sextus it means simply external to oneself, the cognitive subject, i.e. a man (cf. *adv. Math.* VII, 167)—and the question is, What does that come to? Sextus can contrast the external thing with the bodily humours which affect one's

[34] Cf. n. 13 above. The suggested derivation is due to Keith McCullough.

[35] E.g. *De An.* 425b22–24: 'That which sees has in a certain way become coloured; for in each case the sense organ is capable of receiving the sensible object without its matter'.

[36] The significance of this innovation of Augustine's as a step towards a Cartesian conception of the mind is well brought out by Gareth B. Matthews in a paper offering much that is relevant to our investigation: 'Consciousness and Life', *Philosophy* **52** (1977), 13–26.

perception of it (*PH* I, 102) or with the medium through which it is perceived (ibid. 124–127), so it seems plain that the line is not drawn in Cartesian fashion between the mind and everything else outside it, including the sceptic's own body.

By the same token 'external' in Sextus' use of it imports no Cartesian (Augustinian) break between things outside and an inner (subjective) world of things apparent. Ask Sextus what he means when he claims to suspend judgment about everything, and he will typically reply, 'Well, take honey; it appears sweet to me but bitter to people with jaundice, and there is no criterion for deciding which it really is. Likewise the tower appears round from a distance and square from close by. And so on. That's how it is with everything.' It is one and the same external thing, honey or the tower, which appears thus and so and which has a real nature that the sceptic is unable to determine. To express his scepticism Sextus continues to use the ordinary linguistic framework of reference to common objects; the familiar common objects stay on as the logical subjects of his 'appearing'-statements. Recalling Parmenides, one might put it this way: the sceptic's thinking and speaking, no less than that of his dogmatic opponents, is of something, and something that is. Of course, the sceptic is not Parmenides, and when pressed he will suspend judgment about whether these things exist to to be referred to—but he is not anxious to push that point to its logical conclusion, still less to generalize it as far as doubting whether anything exists to speak and think of at all. And I do not know a single text in Sextus which treats the sceptic's own body as something external in the now familiar epistemological sense.

About the *inside* of human bodies, to be sure, Sextus is decidedly sceptical. Historically, Pyrrhonian scepticism had connections with certain sceptical movements in medicine.[37] The Pyrrhonist arguments were used to oppose dogmatic trends in medicine which liked to theorize about the inner workings of the human body. But scepticism about one's insides hardly settles the status of one's body in the world at large. What does settle it is that Sextus is much exercised to combat an old objection to scepticism, an objection which goes back to the very beginnings of Greek scepticism and was to be important for Hume later: the objection, namely, that suspending judgment about everything must entail total inactivity and make life impossible.[38] Not at all, replies Sextus. The sceptic will carry on acting like the rest of you, responding to the way things appear to him as nature and upbringing have conditioned him to respond. Now, whatever we may think of this rebuttal, it is not the language of a man afflicted with radical Cartesian doubt as to whether he has a body to act with and a world to act in at all. One's own body has not yet become for

[37] Texts and historical discussion in Deichgräber, op. cit.
[38] On Hume's objection and Sextus' reply, see paper cited n. 25 above.

M. F. Burnyeat

philosophy a part of the external world.[39] So another question for the historian to ask is: when and why did that happen?

Meanwhile, I suggest that the reason it does not occur to the Pyrrhonian sceptic to push his doubt that far is that he is still, like any other Hellenistic philosopher, a man in search of happiness. He has a practical concern. His scepticism is a solution to uncertainty about how to act in the world; or better, a dissolution of that uncertainty. Such being his prime concern, he cannot doubt in a completely general way his ability to act in the world. It is not that he affirms the world or the role of his body in it: these Cartesian questions lie apart from the route travelled by the sceptic's inquiry, just because he is so serious, in a practical sense, about his scepticism. In that sense Descartes was very clear that his sceptical doubt was not serious (see below). It was a strictly methodological affair—in Bernard Williams' phrase, 'The Project of Pure Enquiry'.[40] And that was what enabled him to take the doubt far enough to raise in absolutely general terms the problem of the existence of the external world.

I take it to be significant in this connection that the only ancient text I have been able to find which approaches within reach of a really general doubt is not from Sextus but from an opponent of Pyrrhonism, pursuing a line of argument which is designed to be deeply embarrassing to the sceptic. It is an argument used by Galen to defend scientific medicine against his Pyrrhonist rivals.[41] Galen formulates the Pyrrhonists' position as follows: about each of the things that appear they agree that it appears but they doubt, first, whether it really is as it appears, and second, whether it exists at all. By way of illustration we have a list of examples which is, I think, very much an opponent's list, designed to embarrass, not the sort of example which is typical in Sextus. Thus, Galen says, according to the Pyrrhonists we do not know whether there is a sun or a moon, or earth or sea, or whether we are awake or even whether we are thinking or living, indeed, there is nothing in the sum total of things the nature of which we know—and here, given the context, it is further implied that there is nothing in the sum total of things the existence of which we know. Is this the generalized doubt we have been looking for? And at the same time, is the doubt about thinking and living, a hint of the materials for the Cartesian

---

[39] Caution: Platonic soul–body dualism is not to the point here, since it puts no *epistemological* barrier between soul and body. The body is part of the material or sensible world, which is not at all the same as being part of 'the external world' in the modern sense. That is one reason why Plato can vacillate over which 'mental' functions belong properly to the soul and which to the body.

[40] The reference is to Bernard Williams, *Descartes: The Project of Pure Enquiry* (Harmondsworth: Penguin Books, 1978), esp. chap. 2.

[41] *De dignoscendis pulsibus* VIII, 781, 16–783, 5 Kühn = Deichgräber, op. cit., frag. 74, p. 133, 19–p. 134, 6.

refutation of that doubt? Not quite, for see what Galen does with it. I'll grant all this, he says, just to please them, but I have one little question to ask. When the sun appears plainly in the morning sky, do they expect us to stay in bed wondering whether it is really day and time to get on with things or still night? It is just the old objection about the sceptic being unable to act if he suspends judgment about everything. Not unlike Plato in the *Parmenides*, Galen remains blind to the potential implications of the hypothetical position he is formulating. For it is a hypothetical formulation more explicitly extreme than you will find in the sceptic's own literature.[42] Like Plato's hint at idealism, it is put up for a polemical purpose and then dropped after what, with hindsight, we are likely to consider totally inadequate exploration.

IV

It must be obvious by now that it is Descartes who holds the answer to the three questions thrown up by our survey of limitations, both expressed and unexpressed, in ancient Greek scepticism. To recapitulate, the questions were:

(1) How did it come about that philosophy accepted the idea that *truth* can be obtained without going outside subjective experience?

(2) When and why did philosophers first lay claim to *knowledge* of their own subjective state?

---

[42] A couple of further texts should be mentioned here, if only that they may be discounted. (1) Xeniades of Corinth, a little-known figure of the fifth century B.C. said that everthing, i.e. every appearance and opinion, is false (Sext. *adv. Math.* VII, 53–54). Possibly what he meant by this was that nothing meets the Eleatic conditions for true being, since he also remarked that everything that comes to be comes to be from not being and everything that perishes perishes into not being. If so, the effective content of Xeniades' claim would be that none of the things that come to be are really and truly what they appear to be (cf. Melissus frag. 8). But we have no knowledge of the wider context of these assertions. (2) Metrodorus of Chios was famous for having capped the sceptical denial that we know anything by further denying that we know whether we know anything or not (frag. 1), and then on top of that he says (in one source only: Cic. *Acad.* II, 73) that we do not know whether anything exists or nothing. This, however, was the exordium to a work *On Nature* containing *inter alia* an atomist meteorology. It would seem, therefore, that for Metrodorus what we do not know we may none the less theorize about, and perhaps we may explain in terms of the atomic theory why we do not know it. I think we may be confident that if Xeniades, Metrodorus, or anyone else had come at all close to a genuinely Cartesian doubt, the sceptic doxography would have picked it up and told us loud and clear.

(3) When and why did one's own *body* become for philosophy a part of the external world?

I mentioned Augustine in connection with (2), but, as with the Cogito, the Augustinian precedent does not amount to as much as one might expect.[43] Augustine claims knowledge of his own subjective states, because they are subjective states, but he does not give that knowledge a privileged status. The claim sits side by side with the claim that he knows simple logical and mathematical truths (*Contr. Acad.* III, 21, 23, 25, 29), to which his ancient sceptical opponents had a ready reply (e.g. Cicero, *Academica* II, 91–98), and with the claim that the sceptic himself must surely know whether he is a man or an ant (*Contr. Acad.* III, 22), from Descartes' point of view an equally unpromising line of attack (cf. HR I, 150, 316–317).[44] Whatever hints Augustine may have furnished, it was Descartes who put subjective knowledge at the centre of epistemology—and thereby made idealism a possible position for a modern philosopher to take. I mean by this that it is not until someone brings the question 'Is there anything other than mind?' into the centre of philosophical attention that the replies to it—the affirmative reply of realism, and *a fortiori* the negative reply of idealism—will commend themselves as worthy of, and requiring, explicit defence. (What I have ascribed to antiquity is an unquestioned, unquestioning *assumption* of realism: something importantly different from an explicit philosophical thesis.) It remains to show that Descartes knew what he was doing, that he had a lively appreciation of the ways in which his thought transcended the limitations of the ancient tradition. With reference to the First *Meditation*, Descartes wrote:

> Nothing conduces more to the obtaining of a secure knowledge of reality than a previous accustoming of ourselves to entertain doubts especially about corporeal things; and although I had long ago seen several books written by the Academics and Sceptics about this subject and felt some disgust in warming over again that old cabbage, I could not for the above reasons refuse to allot to this subject one whole meditation [II *Rep.*, HR II, 31].

The book(s) of the Academics must be Cicero's *Academica*, the main vehicle of information about the scepticism of the Academy under Arcesilaus and Carneades. The books of the Sceptics will then refer to people who call themselves sceptics, i.e., Pyrrhonists. The works of Sextus Empiri-

---

[43] On Augustine and the Cogito, see Etienne Gilson, *Études sur le rôle de la pensée médiévale dans la formation du système cartésien* (Paris: J. Vrin, 1930), 191–201.

[44] References to Descartes are by volume and page number in E. S. Haldane and G. R. T. Ross, *The Philosophical Works of Descartes*, corrected edn (Cambridge: Cambridge University Press, 1934).

cus had become available to the modern world not quite a hundred years earlier and had been the focus of intense controversy ever since; whether or not Descartes had read Sextus, he would be acquainted with the writings of modern Pyrrhonists like Montaigne.[45] So what the passage tells us is that the First *Meditation* is a rehash of ancient scepticism.

In what sense is this so? There are three levels of doubt in the dialectical to-and-fro of the First *Meditation*, each with its precedent in antiquity. At level one (HR I, 145) Descartes argues that sense perception, since it is sometimes deceptive, cannot serve as a principle (in ancient terms, a criterion) for forming true beliefs. It is not, as sometimes supposed,[46] the invalid argument that if some perceptions are actually false, all might possibly be false, but the altogether more defensible claim that a criterion of truth which plays you false is no criterion at all (like an algorithm which sometimes gives the wrong solution). In this form the argument goes back to Carneades (Cic. *Acad.* II, 79–80; Sext. *adv. Math.* VII, 159). Carneades' Stoic opponents made a point of insisting that the wise man (if you wish, the ideally reasonable man) suspends judgment, as Descartes is now doing, on anything dubitable or uncertain (Cic. *Acad.* I, 41–42; Sext. *adv. Math.* VII, 155–157). The dispute between Academic and Stoic was then whether either sense or reason can supply a criterion for recognizing truth with unassailable certainty, in which case it is a perfectly proper first move to point out that sense perception as such will not serve since the senses sometimes deceive.[47]

This first move is met by an equally ancient distinction between favourable and unfavourable conditions of perception (e.g. Cic. *Acad.* II, 19, 53). It is one thing to be doubtful about one's view of minute or distant objects—in such unfavourable conditions it is indeed true that the senses sometimes deceive—another to query Descartes' certainty about himself sitting by the fire in his winter cloak with paper in his hands. What is new here, what shows the more radical use Descartes is going to make of his sceptical reflections, is the example. Descartes' own hands and body take

---

[45] For historical information on the transmission to modern times of the two main streams of ancient scepticism, see (for Cicero) Charles Schmitt, *Cicero Scepticus: A Study of the Influence of the 'Academica' in the Renaissance* (Hague: Martinus Nijhoff, 1972) and (for Sextus) Richard H. Popkin, *The History of Scepticism, from Erasmus to Spinoza* (Berkeley, Los Angeles and London: University of California Press, 1979).

[46] E.g. Nicholas Rescher, 'The Legitimacy of Doubt', *Review of Metaphysics* **13** (1959/60), 226–234.

[47] Further comparisons with Carneades in Pierre Couissin, 'Carnéade et Descartes', in *Travaux du IXe Congrès International de Philosophie: Congrès Descartes* (1937), IIIme Partie, 9–16; and with his Stoic opponents in V. Brochard, 'Descartes Stoïcien', in his *Études de philosophie ancienne et philosophie moderne* (Paris: F. Alcan, 1954), 320–326.

over the centre of the stage, first as an example of certainty and then, when that is challenged, as an example of something dubitable. For the next sceptical move brings up the idea that if madmen imagine that they have an earthenware head or are nothing but pumpkins or are made of glass, perhaps Descartes has no right to be certain that he does have the hands and body he takes himself to have. The appeal to the impressions had by madmen is common enough at the parallel point in ancient controversy (e.g. Cic. *Acad.* II, 88–90; Sext. *adv. Math.* VII, 61–63, 404–405), but so far as I know the examples never concern the insane person's impression of his own body. Correspondingly, when Descartes objects that he would be no less insane himself were he to accept this line of reasoning, the objection is the more telling where his own body is involved than it was in the less personally focused context of ancient debate (Cic. *Acad.* II, 54).

It is Descartes' own hands and body which again occupy his attention when he moves on to level two, the Dream doubt (HR I, 145–146). This goes back to Plato's *Theaetetus* (157e ff.), as Descartes was called upon to acknowledge (III *Rep.*, HR II, 60), but again Descartes makes a new and more radical use of it. In the *Theaetetus* the discussion remains at level one. The absence of a criterion for determining whether one is awake or dreaming supports only the conclusion that there is no rational basis for setting aside as false the impressions one has when dreaming, diseased, or insane. Every impression or appearance is true for the person who has it. Likewise in Sextus, dreams help to show that the way things appear cannot be taken as the criterion for how they really are (e.g. *PH* I, 104). The idea is that the credentials of dreams are no worse than those of waking experience. Descartes' conclusion from the same data is different and more general. It is that there is no rational basis for not setting aside as possibly false (suspending judgment about) any perceptual impression we ever have, including impressions of our own body. In other words, the credentials of (what we take to be) waking experience are no better than those of dreams. Possibly we have neither hands nor body such as we suppose we have. Any experience might be the illusion of a dream.

This is already a strikingly modern radicalization of doubt, but we have still to reach level three and the possibility of an all-powerful, deceiving deity (HR I, 147ff.) which Descartes himself characterized as a doubt additional to 'the customary difficulties of the Sceptics'.[48] Cicero's

---

[48] *Descartes' Conversation with Burman*, trans. John Cottingham (Oxford: Clarendon Press, 1976), 4. It has been said that 'it is not true . . . that Cartesian doubt is more radical than ancient scepticism' (Hiram Caton, *The Origin of Subjectivity: An Essay on Descartes* (New Haven and London: Yale University Press, 1973), 29)—this on the basis of a survey of some of our Protagorean and Pyrrhonian material. The Burman text shows that Descartes himself had a better understanding of his relation to the sceptical tradition.

Academica reports a number of the arguments which Academic sceptics used against the Stoics' theory that ordinary perceptual experience does supply a perfectly good criterion of truth, namely what they call the cataleptic impression, an impression which, being clear and distinct, gives a certain grasp of its object. Among these arguments is the following (*Acad.* II, 47). Some impressions, it is agreed, are sent by the deity, through dreams, oracles, omens, and the like, and some of these god-sent impressions are convincing but false. If, then, the deity has the power to make false impressions convincing to us, he must have the power, equally, to make convincing to us impressions which are not only false but such that they can hardly be distinguished from those which are true; and if these, then also impressions such that the true and the false are wholly indistinguishable from one another. The argument is that the deity could so arrange things that even in the best possible perceptual situation and applying the greatest care and attention, we could not distinguish the true from the false. Hence it is possible, contrary to Stoic theory, that even the most luminously clear and distinct perceptions are in fact false. But there the argument stops. The generalization which for us lies so readily to hand is not made. At no point is it suggested, as Descartes does suggest, that the malignant deity might have made every perception false (the whole totality), and every deliverance of our reasoning faculties false as well, so that we are deceived in everything.[49] This is the 'hyperbolical' doubt which alone poses in an absolutely general way the problem of the existence of the external world, where that, Descartes emphasizes once again (HR I, 148), includes the existence of one's own body. If this is the result of Descartes' rehash of ancient scepticism, the implied claim is that the traditional material supports a doubt more radical than the traditional sceptic had dared suppose. So far as I can see, that claim is correct.

It is in any case important for Descartes that the claim should be correct. One of his subsidiary purposes depends on it. His primary purpose is, of course, to find truth for its own sake, but he also held, as a matter of history, that he was the first philosopher to refute the sceptics (VII *Rep.*, HR II, 336). And this historical claim depends on the strategy whereby the traditional sceptic's own speciality, excessive doubt, is pushed to the point where

---

[49] This vital difference is overlooked by Léon Robin, *Pyrrhon et le scepticisme grec* (Paris: Presses Universitaires de France, 1944), 89–90, who claims that Carneades got as far as Descartes' evil demon doubt. Whether the evil demon was prompted, directly or indirectly, by the *Academica* is a separate issue about which I make no hypothesis. E. M. Curley, *Descartes Against the Skeptics* (Oxford: Blackwell, 1978), is well informed about the relations between Descartes and ancient scepticism, and he prefers to postulate a source in Montaigne (pp. 38–40, 68–69).

it brings us up against the truth of the Cogito. It is because the traditional sceptical materials support a doubt more radical that the traditional sceptic himself had dared suppose that they can be seen to lead, in the end, to a certainty which refutes the scepticism we began with.[50] It is because the first truths Descartes establishes in the Second *Meditation* are truths reached by the very method of doubt which is designed to call all truths in question, that they are immune to attack by the traditional sceptical devices and constitute a refutation, the first satisfactory and non-question-begging refutation, of the books of the Academics and Pyrrhonian Sceptics (cf. HR I, 101, 314–315; II, 60–61). If the Academics and Pyrrhonists could object that their arguments do not admit the further and more radical developments on which Descartes insists, Descartes would lose his entitlement to claim that he had overturned that whole tradition.

We saw earlier that ancient scepticism doubted, and gave reasons which Descartes accepts for doubting, anything that purports to be a truth about a real objective world. So it is not surprising, if Descartes thinks he has found examples of knowledge and truth which lie beyond the reach of the traditional sceptical arguments, that these examples should turn out to be truths which an ancient sceptic would hardly have recognized as *truths* at all.[51] Whereas in the First *Meditation* the discussion focuses in a largely traditional manner on what is true or false of the real world, the outcome of the doubt being, for example, that 'body, figure, extension, movement and place are but the fictions of my mind' (HR I, 149),[52] in the Second *Meditation* Descartes starts to speak of things being true or false without meaning true or false of a real objective world outside the mind. The reason is that what he now discovers is the truth of statements describing the subjective states involved in the process of doubt itself. No less true than that I exist, he says, is that I am that being who now doubts nearly everything, who nevertheless understands certain things, who affirms that one only is true, who denies all the others, who desires to know more, who is averse from being deceived, who imagines many things (all of which subjective states have been involved in the doubt)—and then comes just the type of statement which I said earlier sceptics did not call true or false: that I am a being who perceives many things, as if by the intervention of the bodily organs. It cannot be false that I *seem* to see light, to hear noise, to be warmed (HR I, 153). Subjective truth has arrived to stay,

---

[50] See Descartes' letter to Reneri for Pollot, April 1638, in *Descartes: Philosophical Letters*, translated and edited by Anthony Kenny (Oxford: Clarendon Press, 1970), 53: 'Although the Pyrrhonians reached no certain conclusion from their doubts, it does not follow that no one can'.

[51] Interestingly, this contrast was well appreciated by Hegel, op. cit., 347.

[52] Cf. *Conversation with Burman*, 3: 'Here we are dealing primarily with the question of whether anything has real existence'.

constituting one's own experience as an object for description like any other.[53]

All this adds up to Descartes seeing that he is a thinking thing, and seeing, too, that this is a truth immune from attack by the traditional sceptical devices. The beauty of the procedure is that it is a truth he has reached without applying a criterion, and so without having first to settle the ancient dispute about the criterion of truth. The Pyrrhonists argued that you cannot determine what is true and what is false without first settling on a criterion of truth. And they made sure that no proposed criterion would hold good under examination. But Descartes can go the other way round. He has got a truth without applying a criterion, and he can use this unassailable truth to fix the criterion of truth.[54] The criterion is the clear and distinct perception which is what has assured him that he is a thing that thinks (HR I, 102, 158). Once again the move is proof against all the resources of the ancient tradition.

To sum up, it is no accident that in Descartes' philosophy the following elements are found in the closest association: hyperbolical doubt and the problem of the existence of the external world, subjective knowledge and truth, the dualism which makes one's own body part of the external world—and the refutation of the ancient sceptical tradition. All these are substantially new with Descartes, and derive from the very seriousness (in one sense) with which he took the traditional sceptical materials. It is essential here that this seriousness is entirely methodological. Descartes several times associates his insistence on pushing doubt as far as it will go for the purposes of the Project of Pure Enquiry with a firm rejection of the idea of trying to carry scepticism into the practical affairs of life.[55] And what above all distinguishes the ancient sceptics in his eyes from their modern followers is that the ancient sceptics did try to live their scepticism (HR I, 206; II, 206, 335). Descartes believed the traditional story that Pyrrho's friends had to follow him around to save him from walking over cliffs and

[53] Distinguish this account from the story recently told by Richard Rorty, *Philosophy and the Mirror of Nature* (Princeton: Princeton University Press, 1979), esp. chaps. I–II, the moral of which is that indubitability or incorrigibility—the idea that we have incorrigible knowledge of our subjective states—was the innovation by which Descartes created the modern philosophical notion of the mind. Incorrigibility was there before in Hellenistic philosophy, in the shape of Sextus' description of appearance-statements as *azētētos*, immune to question or inquiry (p. 38 above). The addition of truth is what opens up a new realm for substantial knowledge, and it is knowledge not just because it is incorrigible truth but because of what Descartes will build upon it.

[54] Cf. Popkin, op. cit., chap. IX.

[55] HR I, 143, 148, 219–220: II, 44, 206, Letter to Hyperaspistes, August 1641, Kenny, op. cit., 110.

other hazards.[56] But of course what the story illustrates is that ancient scepticism even at its most extreme did not seriously question that one can walk around in the world. It did not question this, I have argued, because it was in fact entirely serious about carrying scepticism into the practical affairs of life.[57] I hope that I have made it plausible that Descartes had a very clear appreciation of the theoretical limitations of ancient scepticism and at least the beginnings of an appreciation of the practical reasons behind them.

Above all, Descartes' hyperbolical doubt, going beyond all ancient precedent in its use of the idea of a powerful malignant deity, brought into the open and questioned for the first time the realist assumption, as I have called it, which Greek thought even at its most radical never quite managed to throw off. That was what Berkeley missed. He failed to see that Descartes had achieved a decisive shift of perspective without which no one, not even Berkeley, could have entertained the thought that *esse est percipi*.[58]

[56] Diogenes Laertius IX, 62.

[57] I have illustrated this by reference to Pyrrhonian happiness, but it is manifest also in the Academic defence of the possibility of sceptical action.

[58] I am grateful for discussion at the Royal Institute of Philosophy and at the Moral Science Club in Cambridge, and for suggestions from Andreas Berriger, Henry Blumenthal, Ted Honderich, Keith McCullough, David Owen, Hans Sluga, and Richard Sorabji. From Bernard Williams have come both discussion and suggestions, and a great deal more: my starting point in the present essay was an observation of his (n. 1 above), the account in section I of Plato's argumentative strategy in Part I of the *Theaetetus* is basically his, and I am conscious of more important debts accumulated over the years which cannot be measured in terms of this idea or that. For such gifts the only proper return is the endeavour to make worthy use of what one has learned.

Berkeley's Immaterialism and Kant's Transcendental Idealism

M. R. AYERS

Introduction

Ever since its first publication critics of Kant's *Critique of Pure Reason* have been struck by certain strong formal resemblances between transcendental idealism and Berkeley's immaterialism. Both philosophers hold that the sensible world is mind-dependent, and that from this very mind-dependence we can draw a refutation of scepticism of the senses.

According to Berkeley, the scepticism which makes philosophy ridiculous 'vanishes if we annex a meaning to our words, and do not amuse ourselves with the terms *absolute, external, exist* and such like . . . I can as well doubt of my own being, as of the being of those things which I actually perceive by sense'.[1] Ideas of sense constitute 'real things': i.e. ideas caused in us by God in conformity with the principles or rules which we call the laws of nature. It is their evident external causal origin, their givenness, together with their regular association with other ideas in the order of nature, which constitute the criteria by which 'real' or 'external' things are to be distinguished from 'chimeras and illusions on the fancy'.[2]

According to Kant's Fourth Paralogism, which appeared only in the First Edition of the *Critique*, since space as the form of outer sense is 'in us', what is given in space by the senses is in us too, but it nevertheless constitutes physical reality. It can be distinguished from mere illusion because a condition of determinate location in space and time is conformity with law, so that we can employ as our criterion of reality the rule, 'Whatever is connected with a perception according to empirical laws is actual'.[3]

Both Berkeley and Kant distinguish two senses of 'external'. For Berkeley, the word may mean 'absolutely independent of mind', in which sense there are no external physical objects; or it may simply mean 'externally caused' or causally independent of us, like ideas of sense.[4] He attributes the error in the ordinary man's view of physical reality to the assumption that what is external in the second sense is external in the first.[5]

[1] *Principles of Human Knowledge*, I, 87–91.

[2] *Principles*, I, 30–34.

[3] *Critique of Pure Reason*, trans. N. Kemp Smith (New York: St Martin's Press, 1965), A376.

[4] *Principles*, I, 90.

[5] *Principles*, I, 56.

Similarly for Kant, 'external' may denote, first, 'that which as thing in itself exists apart from us', in which transcendental sense 'external' objects are entirely unknown; or it may denote 'things which are to be found in space', in which empirical sense 'external' objects are indubitably experienced. The 'transcendental realist' opens the door to scepticism by assuming that what is external in the second sense is also external in the first: i.e. that objects in space are thereby independent of mind.[6] Scepticism of the senses Kant calls 'empirical idealism', to which the antidote is a combination of 'transcendental idealism' (i.e. recognition of mind-dependence) with 'empirical realism' (i.e. employment of determinate existence in space under law as the criterion of reality). Despite differences in their arguments, these and other parallels make it natural to suppose that Berkeley had a not insignificant influence on Kant's thought.

Kant's own later efforts to distinguish his theory from Berkeley's, however, have convinced many readers that there was not in fact any such influence. Paradoxically, that is not because of his success in clarifying the difference between them, but because of his supposed abysmal failure. The Second Edition of the *Critique* and the *Prolegomena to Any Future Metaphysics* contain such seemingly inept characterizations of immaterialism that generations of commentators have held that their author could not have read Berkeley's main works, a conclusion which has been supported by the claim that neither the *Principles* nor the *Three Dialogues Between Hylas and Philonous* was available in German translation until after the First Edition of the *Critique*.

This traditional view of the relationship between the two philosophers has been challenged by contributors to a discussion initiated some years ago by Colin Turbayne.[7] Turbayne points out that (as well as *Siris*) *De Motu* and Eschenbach's translation of the *Three Dialogues* were readily available while Kant formulated his own theory. He further argues that Kant's criticisms can all be read as intelligible attempts to bring out genuine differences from Berkeley, provided that we take them to be founded, not so much on explicit doctrines, as on what Kant sees as the inevitable consequences of explicit doctrines. For Kant, Berkeley *in effect* believes these things. But in Turbayne's view Kant's main argument against scepticism of the senses, the argument which explains the term 'transcendental idealism', is not importantly different from Berkeley's. He believes that from all Kant's criticisms only minor or else irrelevant differences emerge, the significance of which Kant disingenuously exaggerates in a disreputable perversion of Berkeley's doctrines. Other commen-

---

[6] *Critique*, A373.

[7] C. M. Turbayne, 'Kant's Refutation of Dogmatic Idealism', *Philosophical Quarterly* (1955); republished as 'Kant's Relation to Berkeley' in *Kant Studies Today*, L. W. Beck (ed.) (La Salle: Open Court, 1969).

tators, however (in particular Gale Justin and Henry Allison[8]), have since argued persuasively that Kant does locate a fundamental line of distinction between himself and Berkeley. At the same time it seems in general to be agreed that Kant's criticisms do distort their object. In this paper I want to support and extend Allison's general position, but I also want to look again at the question of distortion. Since in the first part of my paper points which others have made and the additional points and modifications which I should like to make myself are sometimes rather entwined, I shall not spend time surveying previous arguments in detail. In the second part of the paper I shall be more on my own.

Absolute Space and Reality

Let us start with two notorious passages in the Second Edition of the *Critique*. First, in the Transcendental Aesthetic,[9] Kant claims that, if we ascribe objective reality to the forms of outer and inner sense, then the world of experience is 'transformed into mere illusion'.

> For if we regard space and time as properties which, if they are to be possible at all, are to be found in things in themselves, and if we reflect on the absurdities in which we are then involved, in that two infinite things, which are not substances, nor anything actually inhering in substances, must yet have existence, nay, must be the necessary condition of the existence of all things, and moreover must continue to exist, even although all existing things be removed—we cannot blame the good Berkeley for degrading bodies to mere illusion.

Secondly, in the preamble to the Refutation of Idealism,[10] Kant distinguishes two forms of 'material' (i.e. empirical) idealism. The material idealist

> declares the existence of objects in space outside us either to be merely doubtful and indemonstrable or to be false and impossible. The former is the *problematic* idealism of Descartes, which holds that there is only one empirical assertion that is indubitably certain, namely, that 'I am'.

[8] G. D. Justin, 'On Kant's Analysis of Berkeley', *Kant Studien* (1974); H. E. Allison, 'Kant's Critique of Berkeley', *Journal of the History of Philosophy* (1973). Margaret Wilson, in 'Kant and the Dogmatic Idealism of Berkeley', *Journal of the History of Philosophy* (1971), had argued that Kant's criticisms do correspond to important differences from Berkeley but also indicate that Kant did not know Berkeley's theory well.

[9] *Critique*, B70f.

[10] *Critique*, B274f.

The latter is the *dogmatic* idealism of Berkeley. He maintains that space, with all the things of which it is the inseparable condition, is something which is in itself impossible; and he therefore regards the things in space as merely imaginary entities. Dogmatic idealism is unavoidable, if space be interpreted as a property that must belong to things in themselves. For in that case space, and everything to which it serves as condition, is a non-entity.

All this may seem clear enough evidence of distortion on Kant's part, whether deliberate or unwitting. Both passages suggest that Berkeley treats all objects of the senses as illusions, ignoring his distinction between illusion and reality. Together they imply that one of Berkeley's arguments is of the form: 'Absolute space is a condition of the existence of bodies. Absolute space is an absurdity. Therefore bodies do not exist.' It is true that Berkeley does attack absolute space, in the form in which it is maintained by Newton, in the *Principles*, in *De Motu*, in *Siris* and, briefly and directly, in the *First Dialogue*. But no modern reader of all these works would naturally suppose that this attack constitutes the chief ground of his rejection of independently existing bodies.

How then might Kant's account of Berkeley be justified or excused or even understood in other terms than ignorance or dishonesty? The chief lines of the argument which emerges from recent discussion are as follows. First, Kant may have known of Berkeley's reality/illusion distinction but refused to be put off by it. It is for him a mere sop provided by someone who does not grasp that the only explanation which can do justice to the empirical reality of bodies is in terms of their determinate existence in space and time. Thus Kant regarded critics who assimilated him to Berkeley as having utterly failed to grasp the logic of his own account of the concept of empirical reality. Secondly, it is said that Kant's one-sided reading of Berkeley, supposing that he approached him through *De Motu* and *Siris*, would have made the attack on space seem more important to the critique of matter than it is.

In support of this second point it might be mentioned that in one passage in *Siris* Berkeley hints at just the kind of argument which Kant ascribes to him: 'From the notion of absolute space springs that of absolute motion; and in these are ultimately founded the notions of external existence, independence, necessity and fate'.[11] Berkeley has just cited Plotinus with approval as 'affirming that the soul is not in the world, but the world in the soul'. He thus seems to be suggesting that the belief in mind-independent bodies arises because people think of space rather than mind as the receptacle or container of bodies. In his earlier works, however, he ascribes belief in the mind-independence of ideas of sense to their involuntariness. The rival to the soul as that in which sensible objects exist is there not

11 *Siris*, 271.

space but material substance, which is postulated by those who see that sensible qualities need a support but who do not grasp that what 'supports and contains' the entire sensible world is perceiving spirit.[12] So although the diagnosis of our mistake which is proposed in *Siris* is in one way typical of Berkeley, in another way it does not seem to fit in with his earlier arguments at all well. To attribute the *general* belief in mind-independence to the *philosophical* doctrine of absolute space is, moreover, a bit odd. One might speculate that in *Siris* Berkeley was less interested in explaining that ordinary belief than in expressing his increasing conviction that Newtonian metaphysics represented the chief philosophical impediment to the acceptance of immaterialism.

It seems very possible that, after the criticism of the first edition of the *Critique*, Kant searched through translations of Berkeley for evidence of his misapprehension of the connection between the concepts of space and of empirical reality, hitting upon this passage from *Siris* as peculiarly revealing. One reason for thinking so lies in the apparent origin of another notorious characterization of Berkeley, that well-known 'British Empiricist', as driven by the principle that 'all knowledge through the senses and through experience is nothing but illusion, and only in the ideas of pure understanding and reason is truth'.[13] For this passage seems to be nothing but a mildly tendentious paraphrase of *Siris*, 264 (cf. 253 and 303f.). Berkeley's editor, T. E. Jessop, seems quite right to argue that all such denigration of the senses in *Siris* is entirely compatible with the arguments of the earlier works.[14] In all the works, after all, the objects of the senses are characterized as 'inert, fleeting, dependent beings'. In *Siris* he makes the point that the senses are incapable of carrying us beyond such low-grade objects to the principles of science, which call for a rational 'discursive faculty', or to the independent, permanent, substantial realities, spirit in general and God, which are grasped by pure intellect.[15] It is just this Platonic conception of pure intellect penetrating beyond the sensible to the immaterial and ultimately real which Kant rightly opposes to his own principles. But the present point is that Kant takes his characterizations of Berkeley from

[12] Cf. *Principles*, I, 7, 73f., etc.

[13] *Prolegomena to Any Future Metaphysics*, trans. P. G. Lucas (Manchester: Manchester University Press, 1962), 374. Numerical reference follows the pagination of the Berlin Academy edition of the Collected Works.

[14] *The Works of George Berkeley, Bishop of Cloyne*, A. Luce and T. Jessop (eds) (London: Nelson, 1953), V, 14ff.

[15] For explicit mention of 'pure intellect' in earlier works cf. *Three Dialogues between Hylas and Philonous*, I (*Works*, II, 153) and *De Motu*, 53. But the well-known theory of 'notions' is also endorsement of a quasi-Cartesian pure intellect (without innate ideas). Cf. *Principles*, I, 27f., 89, 140 and 142; *Three Dialogues*, III, 232f.

Berkeley's mature reflections upon his own theory. It is difficult to see how they could prove ignorance of that theory.

That having been said, both Kant's diagnostic characterization of dogmatic idealism in the Second Edition of the *Critique* and its possible original in *Siris* have a rather puzzling feature. For they seem to imply that transcendental realists, as such, believe in absolute space, in some strong sense of 'absolute', as an independent entity. Yet, as both Kant and Berkeley would very well know, some transcendental realists, such as Aristotle and Descartes himself, approached space in a reductionist spirit, explaining it as no more than an attribute of bodies in some way abstractly considered. For Descartes, 'the same extension which constitutes the nature of body likewise constitutes the nature of space'.[16] Body and the space it occupies are logically distinguishable as species from genus, but are not ontologically distinct. Consequently the notion of a vacuum is a contradiction. Movement, i.e. change of place, is defined relatively to surrounding bodies. The rival doctrine of absolute space as an entity achieved respectability as a consequence of powerful anti-Cartesian arguments. Hobbes did not go all the way in this respect. He poured scorn on the 'childish' *a priori* arguments against a vacuum, and argued that there is no difficulty in a conception of space empty of all bodies. Such a conception is an abstraction from our experiential conception of body: it is 'the phantasm of a thing existing without the mind simply'[17] equivalent to the idea of the *possibility* of external body. But it is distinct from the idea of body, and is required in order that body 'may be understood by reason, as well as perceived by sense'.[18] It enters into the definition of motion, for example, which is not merely relative. Yet Hobbes carefully emphasizes that space is not a thing, but is simply nothing. There is an empty space between two bodies precisely when there is nothing between two bodies which do not meet. Others, however, like Gassendi and Henry More, went much further in their rejection of the reductionist view. What can be computed cannot be nothing. Gassendi produces the principle that space and time are neither substance nor accident: consequently 'all being is substance or accident or place in which all substances and all accidents exist, or time, in which all substances and all accidents endure'.[19] He simply swallows the traditional objection that to treat space as real is to allow something other than God which is uncreated and infinite. The Cambridge Platonist, Henry More, avoids that problem by identifying space with the immensity of God, quoting what was to become Berkeley's

[16] *Principles of Philosophy*, II, trans. E. Haldane and G. Ross (New York: Dover, 1955), 10f.

[17] *Elements of Philosophy*, II, vii, 2.

[18] *Elements*, II, viii, 1.

[19] *Syntagma*, Second Part, I, ii, 1, as translated by C. Brush, *Selected Works of Pierre Gassendi* (New York: Johnson Reprint Corp., 1972).

favourite text, 'in whom we live, move and have our being'. He calls space a logical rather than physical entity, a necessary condition of existence of every particular thing whatsoever, body or spirit. Its necessity is an aspect of the necessity of God to the existence of finite beings.[20] Newton was writing in this tradition when he distinguished between sensible or relative space on the one hand, and real or absolute space on the other,[21] a distinction present in a slightly different form in Locke's *Essay Concerning Human Understanding*[22] and explicitly attacked by Berkeley.[23] Newton also supplied some famous physical arguments for accepting absolute motion (i.e. that absolute space has effects) as well as the suggestion in the *Optics* that space is, as it were, the sensorium of God.[24]

The difficulty, then, is this. Descartes certainly held that space and time, if they exist at all, are properties of things in themselves. But he did not accept the 'absurdities' in which, according to Kant, such a belief is involved. For these absurdities are simply explicit elements of *anti*-Cartesian doctrines. The only coherent interpretation of Kant's argument seems to be this: 'Transcendental realism implies the doctrine of absolute space as an independent entity, even if this not understood by all transcendental realists. It makes dogmatic idealism unavoidable for them logically, even if not psychologically.' The relation between Descartes and Berkeley would accordingly appear like this: 'Berkeley recognizes certain features of our conception of space which make it inappropriate to things in themselves, but Descartes fails to recognize these particular features. Consequently Descartes sees nothing objectionable in our conception of space—he simply does not analyse it accurately. *Qua* problematic idealist, however, he raises the question whether anything external corresponds to our conception. But Berkeley rejects our very conception of space, and with it our conception of empirical reality: i.e. he reduces all sensory representation to illusion.'

The Criteria of Reality in Berkeley and Kant

If this interpretation is right, then it must presumably have seemed irrelevant to Kant that Berkeley cobbled up his own accounts of space on the one hand and of reality on the other, arguing that they do justice to what matters in our ordinary conceptions. But the question remains why Kant should have taken such a dismissive line, rather than more sympathetically treating Berkeley as a transcendental idealist who has been driven into a

20 Cf. *Divine Dialogues*, I.
21 *Principia Mathematica*, Def. VIII Schol.
22 Op. cit., II, xiii, 10.
23 *Principles*, I, 110–116, etc.
24 *Optics*, qu. 28.

wrong analysis of our ordinary, mind-dependent conception of space by a failure to see that mind-dependence explains and makes innocuous the otherwise 'absurd' attributes of absolute space. It can only be this question, if anything, which keeps alive accusations of dishonesty and lack of generosity on Kant's part.

Perhaps what makes the difference for Kant is that, unlike Descartes, Berkeley explicitly attacks the right, logically inescapable conception of space *at all points*, as the conception of an impossible object. For, as others have remarked, the properties mentioned in his direct criticisms of Berkeley are not the only properties of space which for Kant are inescapable but which Berkeley refuses to swallow. There are also its being the common object of the senses, its being infinitely divisible, and its being *a priori*, a property manifested in the possibility of the *a priori* science of geometry. All these properties are, of course, recognized, and swallowed, by Descartes. For Berkeley, on the other hand,

> experience can have no criteria of truth because its phenomena (according to him) have nothing *a priori* at their foundation, whence it follows that experience is nothing but sheer illusion; whereas with us, space and time (in conjunction with the pure concepts of the understanding) prescribe their law to all possible experience *a priori* and, at the same time, afford the certain criterion for distinguishing truth from illusion therein.[25]

Kant's claim that he is sharply distinguished from Berkeley by his ability to derive the criteria of reality *a priori* (first from the conditions of objective existence in space and time and ultimately from the necessary unity of apperception) has been well discussed by others, and I do not have much to add. I should, however, like to give further emphasis to the point that Kant's explanation of the paradoxical properties of space, like his explanation of reality, essentially involves transcendental otherness. Space is the way things in themselves impinge on us. Empirical externality is the mode of representation of transcendental externality. To take just one example, the paradox of the purely relational difference between isomorphic incongruent figures is explained as follows: 'There is no intrinsic difference between such figures, only a relational one. The understanding assures us that there cannot be things which differ only relationally, but this "can well be the case with mere appearances".'[26] Kant does not mean that there can be entities comparable to Berkeley's ideas which differ only relationally: he means that an absolute difference may *appear* as a merely relative difference. That is the proof that spatiality, which allows such merely relational differences, is a form of appearance. Kant's appearances are

[25] *Prolegomena*, 374f., quoted by Allison, 60.
[26] *Prolegomena*, 286.

therefore, as he continually says, necessarily appearances *of* something, whereas Berkeley's ideas have no such intrinsic intentionality.

This point may seem at odds with the most 'Berkeleyan' passages, such as the Fourth Paralogism, in which Kant seems to make a sharp separation between transcendental object and empirical object, as if we could concern ourselves with the existence of the latter without any reference at all to the former. But Kant is struggling with a notably difficult area in the topic of intentionality, as we may remind ourselves if we make the comparison ('altogether insufficient' as he says it is) with secondary qualities such as colours. If what typically causes the sensation of blue is (say) a certain micro-texture of the surface of objects, is it or is it not the case that we can perceive that surface micro-texture? In a way we can, since we see it as blue. Yet in a way we cannot see it at all, and it does not appear to the closest inspection. In a way blue is the appearance on the one hand, distinct from surface micro-texture, the reality, on the other. Yet in a way the blueness of an object just *is* a certain surface structure as it appears to sight. Locke had this trouble with secondary qualities, and Kant accordingly has it with bodies. Just as Locke is led to suggest that 'blue' has two meanings, for appearance and for reality, so Kant is led to talk as if he were giving 'body' two meanings in the same breath:

> I do indeed admit that there are bodies outside us, i.e. things which, although wholly unknown to us as to what they may be in themselves, we know through the representations which their influence on our sensibility provides for us, and to which we give the name of bodies. This word therefore means the appearance of that for us unknown but none the less real object.[27]

Thus despite the famous dictum about sensations without concepts,[28] Kant's sensory ideas or representations essentially contain something which points beyond themselves: they are not wholly 'blind' effects. Their spatiality is what makes them intrinsically *capable* of truth and falsity. The concepts of the understanding come into play at the stage of distinguishing *between* truth and falsity. Testing for illusion is testing empirically, which of course means causally, that a part of space is for a time filled in such and such a way.

This admirable, profound connection of the intentionality of our sensations with their being sensations of things in space was not without antecedents. Hobbes, as we have seen, held that to form the idea of pure space just is to focus on the perceived externality or otherness of things. Very possibly it was Hobbes' view which stimulated Berkeley's concern to

---

[27] *Prologomena*, 289.
[28] *Critique*, A51 (B75). In Kemp Smith's translation, 'intuitions without concepts are blind'.

deny that distance from the perceiver, or 'outness', is immediately perceived. The perception of distance is explained by Berkeley as a hypothetical judgment about future sensations based on a regular association between ideas of the same or different senses in the past.[29] There is no other sort of 'outness' than that. Spatial externality thus does have a certain, rather accidental connection with his criteria of reality, but only because of the role of constant conjunction between ideas in his account of both. The sole theoretical basis for the connection is the notion of a divine language through which God forewarns us of the future course of experience.

It may help us to understand why space and reality should be so disconnected in Berkeley's system if we remember the influence on him in particular of Locke's theory of perception. Locke holds that we have immediate sensory knowledge of the *existence* of external objects, but strictly limited sensory knowledge of their *nature*. In what he calls 'actual sensation' we are immediately aware that 'exterior causes' are acting on us through the senses, but in this 'sensitive knowledge' we conceive of such causes or powers purely through their effects.[30] Locke does of course believe that the external powers to cause sensory ideas belong to bodies in space. He holds that ideas of space 'resemble' their causes, and distinguishes primary from secondary qualities in this respect. Yet he treats such beliefs as subsequent hypotheses or reasonable physical speculations not included in immediate perceptual knowledge itself. His general theory of representation is purely causal: simple ideas represent in thought their regular causes.[31] Such a theory treats sensations as blank data rather than as intrinsically intentional states. More accurately, it treats sensations as if the sole respect in which they are intrinsically intentional is causal. External objects are presented in sensation solely as the possessors of powers to cause sensory effects. Hence Berkeley can claim that those powers might as well belong to a spirit, indeed that that is the only intelligible hypothesis.[32] But Locke's theory of perception is inadequate. For all sensation is, as such, sensation of things in space, whether of things distant from the body, in contact with the body or, as in the case of pain and other bodily sensations, within the body itself. Unless 'external objects' were presented in

---

[29] *Essay towards a New Theory of Vision*, 45 *et passim*.

[30] Cf. *Essay*, IV, xi, 2, etc. I do not mean to imply that it is not also helpful towards understanding Berkeley to consider Descartes' rather different account of perceptual beliefs, and in fact *Principles of Philosophy*, II, 1, seems to set the scene rather neatly for the Berkeleyan theory. But Berkeley does allude specifically to the features of Locke's account described here.

[31] Cf. *Essay*, II, xxx, 2; II, xxxi, 2; etc.

[32] Cf. *Three Dialogues*, III, 239; *Theory of Vision Vindicated*, 11ff.; *Philosophical Commentaries*, 80, 112.

sensation not only as causes of sensations but as objects in space, no particular object could possibly be identified as the single possessor of a number of experienced qualities, or the cause of a number of sensations. The philosophical issue is obviously too large for the present context, but the necessary connection between the spatiality and the intentionality of sensation is one of the things which Kant offers to explain by the doctrine that space is the form of outer sense, but which goes unrecognized by Berkeley.

Infinite Divisibility in Berkeley and Kant

Kant, then, represents Berkeley as primarily a critic of objective space who thereby deprives himself of the material for a conception of objective reality. Obsessed with space in his destructive arguments, Kant's Berkeley unduly neglects it in his botched-up account of 'real things'. Is the first part of such a characterization as inept as it might, *prima facie*, seem? I shall argue that it in fact places Berkeley, not at all inappositely, within a tradition to which arguments about space were indeed of central importance, the tradition which, as Kant says, stretches from the Eleatic School.[33] Other members of that tradition, contemporary with Berkeley, were Pierre Bayle and Arthur Collier, both of whom attack our notion of objective space as vigorously as Zeno can seem to do himself. Bayle, who certainly influenced Berkeley, remarks with respect to pure space that 'an unmovable, indivisible and penetrable extension' is 'a nature of which we have no idea, and is besides repugnant to the clearest ideas of our mind'.[34] Collier's *Clavis Universalis* was, in its German translation, bound in with Berkeley's *Three Dialogues*[35] and significantly favours antinomies. One is to the effect that 'an external world, whose existence is absolute' would have to be 'both finite and infinite' in extent.[36] Both Collier and Bayle devote considerably more space to an argument even more characteristic of the tradition to which they belong. Objective extension would have to be infinitely divisible, which is absurd, and objective motion is by all our lights impossible.[37]

The topic of infinite divisibility was central to the topic of the objective determination or measurement of space and time. On the evidence of the *Principles* and *Three Dialogues*, however, one might think that it was a topic, like that of pure space, with no more than a minor role in Berkeley's argument. That appearance is misleading. Both in early and late works a

---

[33] *Prolegomena*, 374.
[34] Cf. *Historical and Critical Dictionary*, article 'Leucippus'.
[35] See Turbayne, 226.
[36] *Clavis Universalis*, II, iii.
[37] Bayle, *Dictionary*, article 'Zeno'; Collier, *Clavis*, II, iv.

concern with infinite divisibility constitutes a major preoccupation at the heart of his objections to Newtonianism.[38] But it also permeates one of his most famous arguments of all.

In the *First Dialogue* Berkeley finds contradictions arising from the conjunction of three propositions. First, the presupposition accepted by Hylas at this stage of the argument (while he represents the naive realist) that the real size of an object is the size it is perceived to be. Secondly, the ordinary assumption that when two observers of different sizes, such as a mite and a man, perceive the same object, then they both perceive its size. (The same goes for the two eyes of one observer, 'looking with one eye bare, the other through a microscope'.) And thirdly, the principle that an object's real size is at any one time single and determinate. Philonous concludes that all determinations of extension are sense-relative, and that independent material objects could not possess determinate size and shape. A similar point is made about motion, and a further argument demolishes the suggestion that an absolute extension and an absolute motion are abstractible in thought from their sense-relative determinations, great and small, swift and slow. Hylas is thus left to defend belief in a material substance to which not even extension and motion can be attributed.[39]

The structure of the *First Dialogue* can make it seem that Berkeley simply extends to primary qualities the mechanists' arguments about secondary qualities. 'Was it not admitted as a good argument', Philonous asks in direct, if unfair allusion to Locke, 'that neither heat nor cold was in the water, because it seemed warm to one hand and cold to another?'[40] Yet Philonous can only make this appeal because poor Hylas currently represents Berkeley's common man, who assumes, prior to argument, that whatever particular colour or size is immediately perceived is independently real. The corresponding argument in the *Principles* is less misleading in more than one respect. First, an extension of the mechanists' arguments against secondary qualities is there taken to prove only the sceptical conclusion that 'we do not know by sense which is the true extension or colour of the object'. Secondly, the analogy with secondary qualities is drawn only *after* an independent argument that determinates of extension and motion are sense-relative. This latter claim rather surprisingly receives as its sole credential the statement that it is 'allowed' by modern philosophers.[41] Now we might reasonably wonder how 'modern philosophers' could possibly both allow that size and speed are relative to perception and at the

---

[38] On the one hand, in the early notebooks known as *Philosophical Commentaries*; on the other, in *The Analyst* and *A Defence of Free-Thinking in Mathematics*.

[39] *Three Dialogues*, I, 188ff.

[40] *Three Dialogues*, I, 189. Cf. Locke, *Essay*, II, viii, 21.

[41] *Principles*, I, 11.

same time distinguish sense-independent primary qualities such as size and motion from sense-relative secondary ones. In fact what Berkeley is doing is placing two different arguments to be found in mechanist philosophers face to face in confrontation. The first has to do with the limitations of the senses and infinite divisibility. Even by itself, in Berkeley's view, it leads to absurd consequences.

The authors of the Port Royal *Logic*, while on the fashionable topic of the limitations of our faculties, invite us to boggle at the implications of matter's being infinitely divisible. A grain of wheat contains a whole universe, which may itself contain proportionately smaller grains of wheat, and so *ad infinitum*. We cannot even in thought identify 'any part, no matter how small, that does not have as many proportional parts as does the whole world'. Immediately before this sally against atomism we have been told that the senses cannot inform us of the 'true and natural' or 'absolute' size of a body, as the existence of lenses is evidence:

> Our very eyes are spectacles, and how do we know whether they diminish or magnify the objects we see or whether the artificial lenses believed to diminish or magnify objects may not on the contrary give their true size? Nor do we know whether others perceive an object to be the same size as we do. Two people agree that a given body measures only five feet, but each may have a different idea of a foot.[42]

These two lines of thought came to be combined by Malebranche in a single sceptical argument. Because of the infinite divisibility of matter, 'nothing but infinities are to be found everywhere'. Yet our ideas of objects are 'proportionate to the idea we have of the size of our body, although there are in these objects an infinite number of parts that they do not disclose to us'. We cannot, that is to say, indefinitely divide the immediate object of vision: 'As far as vision is concerned, a mite is only a mathematical point. It cannot be divided without being annihilated.' Microscopes, together with the thought that 'our own eyes are in effect only natural spectacles' and that there could be microscopically small perceivers, should convince us that 'we must not rely on the testimony of our eyes to make judgments about size'. Indeed, 'nothing is either large or small in itself'.[43]

Like Malebranche, Bayle combines the topics of size and infinite divisibility, including a long and elaborate exposition of geometrical paradoxes of infinity taken by themselves to prove the impossibility of extension. He returns to the 'spectacles' passage from the Port Royal *Logic*,

[42] Arnauld and Nicole, *Logic, or the Art of Thinking*, IV, i, as translated by J. Dickoff and P. James (Indianapolis 1964).
[43] *Search After Truth* I, vi, as translated by T. Lennon and P. Olscamp (Columbus: Ohio State University Press 1980).

making the very tendentious comment that it concedes outright that determinate size is relative to the senses in just the way in which, according to 'modern philosophers', colours, heat, cold and so forth are sense-relative.[44]

All these discussions make it easy to understand Berkeley's claim, as tendentious as Bayle's, that 'modern philosophers' allow that determinate size is relative, although the *Logic* and even Malebranche are in fact arguing something rather different. But very like Malebranche, if to different effect, Berkeley ties the relativity of sensible size together with the infinite divisibility of extension by imagining an infinitely variable sense by means of which the realist's infinity of worlds within worlds, parts within parts of matter, might be observed. From the doctrine of infinite divisibility,

> it follows, that there is an infinite number of parts in each particle of matter, which are not perceived by sense. The reason therefore, that any particular body seems to be of a finite magnitude, or exhibits only a finite number of parts to sense, is . . . because the sense is not acute enough to discern them. In proportion therefore as the sense is rendered more acute, it perceives a greater number of parts in the object, that is, the object appears greater, and its figure varies, those parts in its extremities which were before unperceivable, appearing now to bound it in very different lines and angles from those perceived by an obtuser sense. And at length, . . . when the sense becomes infinitely acute, the body shall seem infinite. During all which there is no alteration in the body, but only in the sense. Each body therefore considered in itself, is infinitely extended, and consequently void of all shape or figure.[45]

This argument is explicitly an elucidation of the earlier discussion of sense-relativity and primary and secondary qualities in §11. Consequently it irresistibly suggests that infinite divisibility is also in Berkeley's mind in the *First Dialogue*. Unlike Bayle, of course, Berkeley does not conclude baldly that extension does not exist. The absurdities and contradictions are supposed to attach only to *external* and *independent* extension, to the belief that each physical thing has a single determinate extent variously perceptible by various observers under a variety of conditions. Once it is recognized that what really has extension is each separate idea which goes to constitute the 'thing', the problems vanish. For the contrast between contradictory, independent extension and untroublesome, sense-dependent extension, the contrast which runs through all Berkeley's arguments against the former, involves in his mind a positive doctrine about the latter. That is the doctrine of *minima sensibilia*, which we may reasonably suppose

[44] *Dictionary*, article 'Zeno'.
[45] *Principles*, I, 47.

was inspired both by Malebranche and by Locke's suggestion that 'sensible points' are the ultimately 'simple' ideas of extension.[46] Berkeley concluded that the extension of an idea, or sensible extent, is not infinitely divisible, since it is composed of a finite number of *minima*. *Minima* are parts without parts—otherwise they would not be *minima*. Consequently the *minima* of mites and men are equal, and microscopes do not enable us to see more of them. Mites and men simply see different extensions, while the microscope 'presents us with a new scene of visible objects'.[47]

For Kant, on the other hand, as for orthodox Cartesians, infinite divisibility is mathematically proved and hence undeniable: 'the proofs are based upon insight into the constitution of space, in so far as space is . . . the formal condition of the possibility of all matter'.[48] Yet at the same time, it is necessary to conceive of the composition of substances as a composition of indivisible simples. The evident clash of these supposedly evident principles constitutes the Second Antinomy, the explanation of which, according to Kant, lies in the fact that external substances are necessarily experienced in a successive synthesis of spatial appearances. If matter is infinitely divisible then the conception of the *complete* appearance of a thing is impossible, since it is impossible to complete the task of conceiving the possible appearances of its separable parts: on the other hand, to deny infinite divisibility is to claim what is manifestly untrue, that that task could be so completed that every discernible part had actually been discerned in experience. Kant's solution seems to be that the interminable synthesis of possible appearances which is a necessary feature of experience of things in space does not correspond to a feature of things in themselves. To experience an infinitely divisible object in space is not to experience an object with an infinite number of parts—but it is not to experience an object with a finite number of parts either. The answer to the question whether an object in space has a finite or an infinite number of spatial parts is necessarily indeterminate, like a similar question about the size of the universe. The question is therefore meaningless.[49]

The difference between the two solutions is characteristic of both philosophers. Kant embraces the paradoxical property of objective extension which Berkeley, retreating to the supposedly unproblematic subjective impression, rejects outright. Yet Kant's discussion is obviously a kind of commentary on the sceptical tradition within which Berkeley wrote. One might conclude that Kant was better educated than most of us to understand the *First Dialogue*.

---

[46] *Essay*, II, xv, 9.
[47] *New Theory of Vision*, 85; cf. *Three Dialogues*, III, 245.
[48] *Critique*, A439 (B467).
[49] *Critique*, A487f. (B515f.) and A505 (B533).

The Determination of Space and Time and the Refutation of Idealism

All these issues relate to a general problem about the measurement and objective determination of space and time, and so can bring us round to the topics of the Refutation of Idealism. One discussion which seems likely to have influenced Kant considerably here was Leibniz's commentary on Locke's *Essay*.

Locke, in his account of ideas of determinate size, employs a model very like that of the Port Royal *Logic*, although without the sceptical consequences. Thus 'Men for the use and by the custom of measuring, settle in their Minds the Ideas of certain stated lengths, such as an Inch, Foot, Yard', etc. Using these as elements, we can construct an idea of any distance whatsoever, even of a quasi-infinite or indefinite distance.[50] Leibniz protests, rather profoundly, that there cannot be a distinct idea corresponding to each precise 'stated length'. 'For no one can say or grasp in his mind what an inch or a foot is. The signification of these terms can be retained only by means of real standards of measure which are assumed to be unchanging, through which they can always be re-established.'[51]

Leibniz's further discussion might suggest that this assumption of immutability depends on the assumption of immutable laws. For example, he considers the suggestion that a universal relationship, such as the length of a pendulum whose swing would take exactly one second at a specified latitude, should be used as a dependable unit of length. And it is clear that any doubt whether a particular physical standard, such as the standard metre, has changed length would have to be resolved (and would in principle always be resolvable) by means of scientific theory. So to have the notion of a foot is roughly speaking (ignoring complications having to do with the 'division of linguistic labour'[52] and so forth) to know how to determine a certain unit of physical measurement. And the possibility of physical measurement presupposes that the world is law-governed; and that might imply, and would certainly in Leibniz's time have been taken to imply, that it is composed of a law-governed substance or substances. Since the existence of determinate extension seems to presuppose the possibility of physical measurement, and it seems that extension is necessarily determinate, it also seems that we have here a proof that an extended world is necessarily law-governed, consisting of law-governed substance.

This argument is not advanced by Kant, still less by Leibniz. But a roughly parallel argument relating to time does appear in the *Critique*, in

[50] *Essay*, II, xiii, 4.

[51] *New Essays on Human Understanding*, II, xiii, 4, trans. P. Remnant and J. Bennett (Cambridge: Cambridge University Press, 1981).

[52] Cf. H. Putnam, 'Meaning and Reference' in *Mind, Language and Reality* (Cambridge: Cambridge University Press, 1975).

the Analogies. The seeds of something like this argument already exist in the *Essay* because Locke sees it as a special problem about the measurement of time that 'we cannot keep by us any standing unvarying measure of Duration', as we can of extension. A convenient measure of time must be 'what has divided the whole length of its Duration into apparently equal Portions, by constantly repeated Periods'. He first argues, however, that the succession of ideas itself gives us the idea of determinate duration, and supplies us with our first sense of 'constantly repeated periods'. For unless that were so, it would never have occurred to us, for example, that one diurnal or annual revolution of the sun was equal to the next. 'The constant and regular Succession of Ideas in a waking Man is, as it were, the Measure and Standard of all other Successions.' The primitive unit of time, the period from one idea to the next, Locke calls an 'instant'. Yet he does recognize that subjective judgments of time can be checked against objective phenomena, and he also sees that, whatever regular motion we choose as our measure, the judgment that it does measure the 'one constant, equal, uniform Course' of 'Duration itself' relies upon the judgment that 'the Cause of that Motion which is unknown to us, shall always operate equally'. In other words, he recognizes that measurement of time ultimately presupposes immutable substances and laws of nature.[53]

Leibniz, as we should expect, protests against the notion of the primitive subjective clock: 'Changes in our perceptions prompt us to think of time, and we measure it by means of uniform changes'. He seems to mean that our primitive sense of time is not a determinate measure of time. We need for that something much closer, and more evidently closer, to the operation of basic laws. He also makes the point that yardsticks are only relatively unchanging, so that they do not after all represent a fundamental distinction between time and space.

These arguments supply some of the ingredients of the Analogies and the Refutation of Idealism. (Another ingredient, which I shall ignore, is the traditional Aristotelian derivation of the measurement of time from a primitive division of time into *before* and *after* by the point *now*.) In the First Analogy Kant argues that the objective determination of time requires something permanent: succession must be conceived as the permanent undergoing change in accordance with law. The Refutation adds roughly the following argument: If I am to think of myself as more than a bare logical subject, I must have experience of myself as a thing with determinate duration in time. In that case, as well as the succession of my ideas or states of consciousness, something permanent must be the object of my senses. Inner sense, however, perceives only states of consciousness— no permanent self is perceived. I can only locate my states in determinate time by relating them to those permanent material objects, changing or

---

[53] *Essay*, II, xiv.

moving relatively to one another as the sun moves in relation to the earth, which are perceived by outer sense. Only in this way can I think of the self or subject of my states as having determinate duration, with successive states objectively ordered in time. Hence to accept one's own existence in time as indubitably given but to doubt that of external motions and clocks is incoherent, for to do the latter is to doubt the very perceptions which make experience of a permanent self possible. The concept of an enduring substance cannot be empirically employed in relation to the self unless it is first employed in relation to physical objects.

We can easily see why this argument is directed against Descartes, for whom the concept of absolute duration is quite unproblematic. The duration of a substance, whether matter or spirit, is for him not distinct from its being. The concept of duration is, moreover, prior to the concept of measurable time, which is a creation of the mind.[54] But consideration of Leibniz on Locke may also help to illuminate Kant's intentions. For Locke holds that something merely subjective, the succession of ideas, can give us a measurement of duration. A sceptic of the senses who thinks of the self as a substance in time must adopt Descartes' and Locke's presuppositions. Kant in effect turns an endorsement of Leibniz's objection to Locke into an anti-sceptical argument: i.e. we must turn to matter and the laws of physics for the possibility of that measurement of duration without which the concepts of duration and of time, of substance and of change in a substance, are empty and inapplicable. The argument presupposes that there is no identifiable empirical nature of the soul as there is of matter. Nothing in psychology corresponds to Newtonian physics. In this reasonable view there are once again echoes of such earlier writers as Gassendi, Malebranche and Locke.[55]

Kant presents the Refutation of Idealism as a proof of the existence of external objects in response to the 'problematic idealism' of Descartes. Berkeley is first set on one side with the claim that his position has already been refuted in the Transcendental Aesthetic. But there are two reasons why the Refutation might in any case be supposed an inappropriate argument against Berkeley. For any argument will work only against those who accept what it presupposes as undisputed, and the Refutation makes two such presuppositions which Berkeley rejects. First, it assumes the *concept* of a material permanent undergoing change, a concept which is not impugned by Descartes' scepticism but which Berkeley finds unintelligible and self-contradictory. Secondly, it assumes that the sceptic, like Descartes, sees the self as a substance with objectively determined duration, its states being objectively determined in time. Yet, although for Berkeley the

[54] *Principles of Philosophy*, I, 55ff.
[55] Cf. Gassendi, *Objections to Descartes' Meditations*, II, 6, 9; Malebranche, *Search after Truth*, III, ii, 7; Locke, *Essay*, IV, iii, 16f.; IV, iii, 29; IV, vi, 14.

self is a substance, on his official view he does not allow it objective duration or see its states as objectively determined in time—any more than he sees sensible bodies as objectively determined in space.

It may not always seem that Berkeley does reject objective or absolute time. For example, in an argument against absolute motion or velocity he claims that it is 'possible ideas should succeed one another twice as fast in your mind as they do in mine'.[56] Yet this argument is dialectical and *ad hominem*. It appeals, for example, to the Lockean principle that time is measured by the succession of ideas, understood to mean merely that we measure or estimate time that way. Berkeley himself actually holds to this principle in a much stronger, ontological sense: each spirit has its own time, determined or constituted by the succession of its own ideas. There is a temporal *minimum*, the instant from one idea to the next, which is without duration: 'the duration of any finite spirit must be estimated by the number of ideas or actions succeeding each other in that same spirit or mind'.[57] It would follow that the speed of the succession of ideas cannot vary from one person to another, and the only relevant intersubjective comparison possible would be between the length of time (i.e. number of ideas) between two given ideas in one person with the time between two other ideas in another person. Consequently no question of intersubjective simultaneity would be meaningful. Berkeley cannot allow, for example, that when two observers perceive, as we say, the same physical event or object, they have the ideas in question at the same time (or, for that matter, at different times). If a Berkeleyan does allow that such questions could arise, then, as the briefest reflection reveals, he will be plunged into contradictions. Berkeley's intersubjective 'reality' is so disintegrated that even time does not bind together the ideas which are supposed to constitute a real thing.

Whether Kant knew of Berkeley's extreme and wildly implausible retreat into subjectivity in the case of the determinations of time (as I have suggested he very probably did recognize the parallel move in the case of determinations of extension) is perhaps doubtful enough. Nevertheless it is one of the features of Berkeley's system which would seem fully to justify, not only Berkeley's exclusion from the scope of the Refutation of Idealism, but the charge that, with whatever sophistication, he 'degrades bodies to mere illusion'.

[56] *Three Dialogues*, I, 190.
[57] *Principles*, I, 98.

Kant's Transcendental Idealism

GRAHAM BIRD

There is a standard, traditional, picture of Kant's transcendental Idealism which runs along the following lines:

Part I

The whole of our human experience is determined by certain material conditions which cannot themselves be a part of that experience. In particular there exist objects, inaccessible to our senses, which nevertheless interact with ourselves to produce that experience. But the selves which are so affected by these objects outside our experience, and the internal mechanisms which somehow construct that experience, are also just such material conditions of, and not parts of, that experience. We might describe this appeal to material conditions of experience in Kant's technical terms as the 'intelligible' or even 'transcendental' background to our empirical experience. In its attempt to provide some explanation, in terms of things in themselves, of empirical objects (whether physical things or persons) it forms a central part of what Adickes called Kant's 'double affection' theory.[1]

Part II

However, from within our own human experience there can be detected only hints or traces of that 'intelligible' background. Such hints are given to us in a certain kind of necessity which belongs to identifiable general principles governing our empirical experience. These principles relate both to our senses and to our understanding, that is, both to the presentation of particulars and to their characterization. Such principles can be shown to be related to the systems of mathematics and natural science which form a paradigm of our human knowledge, and whose necessity provides us with those hints of a reality beyond our experience. They can be shown, moreover, to be themselves subordinate to a still more general principle of personal unity which both offers a further hint of that intelligible reality, and yet at the same time restricts our knowledge, even our knowledge of that personal unity, to our experience itself.

[1] Erich Adickes, *Kant's Lehre von der doppelten Affektion unseres Ich* (Tübingen: Mohr, 1929).

Part III

Parts I and II serve not only to explain the intelligible background to our experience, and so the latter's internal structure, but also to solve certain long-standing philosophical problems. First the account enables us to resolve certain problems about the limits of our knowledge exemplified in the traditional impasses over the spatio-temporal bounds or boundlessness of the universe. Such a resolution will make use of the suggestion that these endless debates are, somehow, about the universe construed as an intelligible object, and of the general principle (sometimes called the Principle of Significance[2]) that claims about such an intelligible reality can have no meaning for us. Second the account enables us to solve the opposite problem of scepticism with regard to our empirical beliefs. For the account shows not only that we can attach no sense to what transcends experience, but also that within experience we can have such knowledge in so far as we construct it. We process the bare contents of our sensory input so as to produce knowledge within the framework of our experience. In so doing we construct our own criteria for reality, or truth, in that framework, and no other reality is accessible or meaningful to us. So our knowledge consists of nothing but ideas, and in such a way that it is meaningless to raise questions about the reality which those ideas represent to us, that is, the material intelligible reality of Part I.

Alongside this traditional picture are the traditional complaints. Is it not inconsistent to claim in Part I that there are intelligible objects and in Part II that we can have no knowledge of them? Worse, what serious explanatory power can be attached to Part I when it is conceded in Part III that such explanations are meaningless? These problems arise immediately from the account and were raised in the earliest reviews of Kant's *Critique*. But other difficulties, less immediate perhaps but still with a long history, also arise. Kant rejects, for example, a complex doctrine of perception labelled 'empirical idealism and transcendental realism'. It is, however, entirely natural to understand this officially rejected doctrine as a conjunction of the claims (a) that our empirical experience consists of nothing but ideas, and (b) that there exist in some transcendental reality intelligible objects which bring about these ideas in us. But (a) and (b) appear to be present in the traditional story, respectively in Parts III and I. So the traditional story embodies a doctrine, as an essential part, which Kant nevertheless explicitly rejects. This difficulty might well seem so perplexing as to suggest that instead of wearily listing yet another contradiction in Kant's thought, we might instead begin to question the accuracy of that traditional picture. And the same is true, I believe, of Kant's frequent

---

[2] P. F. Strawson, *The Bounds of Sense* (London: Methuen, 1966), 16–17 and 192.

and vehement denials that he is just a standard Idealist.[3] Those who accept the traditional picture tend to overlook these denials, or else to suppose that Kant's version of Idealism is transcendental just because it admits the existence of real transcendental objects, as in Part I. But, as I have shown, that view is in gross conflict with his rejection of such a theory.

The traditional story at least has the merit of locating key elements in Kant's transcendental Idealism. It would not be possible here to offer an adequate account of Kant's theory, if it is taken to embrace the whole Critical philosophy. Even, as I shall suggest, within the limits of his epistemology, transcendental Idealism has a wider and a narrower scope. That point aside, however, the traditional picture indicates clearly what are the cruces of transcendental Idealism. They involve primarily the issue about the status of objects of perception and knowledge, the issue about the limits of our knowledge, and the issue about Kant's so-called principle of significance. I shall deal with each of these issues separately before returning to see how well the traditional picture stands up.

(1) Kant's Critical Principle

I have re-named the principle which Strawson calls the 'Principle of Significance' because I believe that name to be seriously misleading. Although Strawson's title has the merit of reproducing some of Kant's unclarity about the notion of meaning, it is nevertheless bound to suggest that Kant embodies in his principle some specific theory of meaning, or criterion of meaninglessness. In earlier times this assumption connected Kant with verificationist accounts of meaning, while nowadays it will at least raise the issue whether Kant should be associated with a non-realist semantics. Since I shall claim that Kant's principle is not connected with any specific theory of meaning I do not believe it worthwhile to pursue these further issues.

My position can be introduced by considering Bennett's account of the Critical principle. In his *Kant's Analytic* Bennett considers the principle in connection with the distinction between phenomena and noumena. He says (p. 24)

> . . . but apart from those (assertions) licensed by its definition every sentence containing 'noumenon' is unintelligible. This is because Kant ties meaning so closely to evidence; to know what a sentence means I must know something of what it would be like to have evidence of its truth. The notion of having evidence for Kant is essentially the notion of encountering a datum, running up against a brute fact, or as Kant would

[3] Kant, *Prolegomena*, section 13, Anm.II: Kann man dieses wohl Idealismus nennen; es ist ja gerade das Gegenteil davon. See also B519 and note 24 below.

say 'being given' something. But whatever is given to us is given through our senses and so cannot be relevant to any question about noumena. It follows that no synthetic sentence about noumena can be meaningful to us.[4]

Bennett then cites a passage from B506 to support this interpretation, which goes:

> A question as to the constitution of that something which cannot be thought through any determinate predicate—inasmuch as it is completely outside the sphere of those objects which can be given to us—is entirely null and void.

Bennett also (*KA*, 22) adds a brief argument to endorse the view ascribed to Kant but I shall not here consider whether that argument has any force.[5] For my purpose all that is important is whether Kant really held such a view. And here it is surely significant that in the one passage which Bennett cites Kant makes no overt reference to meaning or meaninglessness at all. What he says is that the problematic questions referred to at B506 are 'null and void', which is Kemp Smith's translation of 'nichtig und leer'. Now there is no doubt that Kant regards these questions as infelicitous in some way, but his words do not indicate that the defect is that of being meaningless. A better translation of Kant's phrase would be 'futile and empty', both because in other passages of a similar kind Kemp Smith actually translates 'Nichtigkeit' as 'futility',[6] and because 'leer', Kant's most common description of the defect, is elsewhere translated as 'empty'. On the basis of the text which Bennett cites to support his view Kant is saying not that the problematic questions are meaningless but that they are futile and empty, that is, that there is no way in which we could bring any evidence to bear on their resolution.

If Bennett's text were all that could be found to support his interpretation there could be little doubt that his account is quite unjustified. But it may be said that his mistake is to have selected the wrong text rather than to have misunderstood Kant's intentions. For certainly there are other texts where Kant appeals to the notions of sense ('Sinn') and reference

[4] Apart from the central doubt over Bennett's supposition that Kant made so strong a connection between meaning and evidence, the account of evidence ascribed to Kant in the passage is also over-simple. For Kant shows in many passages that he is aware of the fact that one thing's being evidence for another may depend on the meditation of accepted natural laws and not just on the perceptual presentation of some object. See note 10 below.

[5] The suggestion implicit in Bennett's further argument is that if Kant did not avail himself of this view, then he would lose a demonstrable benefit. But it is highly doubtful if Bennett's argument is any more successful in establishing the view than others which are generally thought to have failed.

[6] E.g. B451.

('Bedeutung') in describing similar defects. Perhaps the best known of these is at B148–149 where Kant explicitly formulates the limits to be placed on the employment of the pure categories, in which he says:

> Our sensible empirical intuition can alone provide for them (pure categories) sense ('Sinn') and reference ('Bedeutung').[7]

It would no doubt be anachronistic to ascribe to Kant any detailed Fregean account of the distinction between sense and reference. But such a distinction at least draws to our attention two different claims that Kant might be making here. In one of these he would be denying to pure categories any literal meaning (sense) at all, and in the other he would be denying to them any reference to an object beyond those given to our sensible intuition. With one proviso the preceding text indicates quite strongly that Kant's view is the latter and not the former. For he there explains:

(a) That pure categories, unlike pure intuitions, range over objects of sensible intuition in general, whether that intuition is like ours or not, and

(b) That this wider extension is, however, of no value to us, since in this context the categories are empty concepts of objects; that is, they are forms of thought without objective reality, since, *ex hypothesi*, we have no suitable intuition to which to apply them.

These claims indicate that the literal meaning of pure categories is not restricted to the range of intuitable objects to which we can apply them, but that for us such concepts, of course, have no application beyond that range of intuitable objects. And such a claim seems more accurately put by saying not that in such a context these concepts become meaningless, but that they then lack a reference for us.

The proviso that might be entered here is that when Kant speaks of 'empty concepts of an object' he is tacitly claiming that such a concept has no content, and is consequently meaningless.[8] This does not square with his other claim that such concepts are 'forms of thought' and as such play an important part in the construction of our knowledge, even though by itself such a phrase is perhaps not quite decisive. But if we look at two other passages where Kant further elaborates this claim the proviso can be seen to have no force.

---

[7] Kemp Smith translates this passage badly as: ... provide for them body and meaning. It is possible, though, that his translation was an attempt to capture the pun on the German word 'Sinn' which may perhaps account for Kant's rather untypical use of the term. Kant uses 'Bedeutung' in the *Critique* much more often than 'Sinn'.

[8] Strawson, op. cit., 190–192, assumes without argument that this is the only way to understand Kant's notion of emptiness.

In the Schematism (B186–187) Kant again tries to explain his view of pure (unschematized) categories. He makes the same points about the extension of the range of pure categories beyond our sensible intuition, and about the uselessness of such an extension to us. But he then goes on to claim that such concepts have a 'logische Bedeutung' which is not by itself enough to provide a reference to an object. Thus the pure concept of substance is that of something that can be thought only as a subject and not as a predicate. These logical forms, or functions, are, then, not totally meaningless for Kant, though their use is precisely limited for us to that range of objects accessible to our sensible intuition.

In the Amphiboly (B346–349) Kant further provides a more general doctrine of emptiness. This account, not much noticed by commentators, is important precisely because it is this term which provides Kant's most favoured description of the defect we are considering. In it he distinguishes between the emptiness of a contradictory concept, and the emptiness of a concept, like that of a 'noumenon' or a 'fundamental force', which has no application for us. It is made clear that the phrase 'leere Begriff' in the latter context does not mean 'empty of content' or 'meaningless', but does mean 'lacking reference to an object', or 'having no application in our sensible intuition'.[9]

These considerations should certainly prevent us from ascribing verificationism to Kant as a theory or criterion of meaning. Bennett's view is not only unjustified in terms of the text he cites, it is also unjustified in terms of other texts which may initially seem to support his view. Nor is it in general at all surprising that this should be so. For such verificationist claims are naturally associated with the empiricist belief that not only our knowledge but also our grasp of meaning must derive solely from our senses. Kant's anti-empiricism comes out in the passages examined in his view that although we can attach meaning to *a priori* (non-sensory) concepts, these concepts can have application for us only within the range of our sensible intuition. Such a view is, of course, an integral part of Kant's further explanation of certain metaphysical errors, namely that in them we allow the meanings of some concepts to outrun our capacity to exemplify them in experience. This lack of identity between the meaning of such expressions and their range of application for us suggests perhaps a realist rather than a non-realist semantics. But, though I believe that Kant has said enough to indicate certain requirements which would have to be satisfied in a Kantian theory of meaning, I do not believe that he has said enough to indicate more precisely what that theory is.

[9] B347: thus the object of a concept to which no assignable intuition whatsoever corresponds = nothing. That is, it is a concept without an object . . .

(2) Transcendental Idealism in the Antinomy

Transcendental Idealism has a broad significance in its solution to Kant's dialectical problems. In these passages Kant attempts to show how philosophers may fail to recognize the limits of the use of reason and so make claims which there is no way of assessing and indulge in disputes which there can be no way of settling. But the doctrine has also a narrower signficance in its specific treatment of problems of perception. Although the two issues can be separated only artificially I shall deal with the broader aspect here and reserve the narrower for the final section.[10]

As in the case of the Critical principle I introduce an account of Kant's Idealism in the Antinomy by means of a dominating line of thought in a recent interpretation. After reviewing the strict validity of the arguments in the thesis and antithesis in the Antimony, Strawson in his *The Bounds of Sense* (pp. 184–185) raises the question of the general nature of Kant's problem. He says:

> Even if we do not regard the arguments as valid we are still, on Kant's view, faced with a philosophical problem. We are still faced with the cosmological questions themselves, with an apparent choice between two mutually contradictory answers to each of them. We cannot, Kant points out, claim inevitable ignorance regarding the answers to these questions on the ground that they refer to supersensible objects (B506–507). They refer, if they refer to anything, to things in space and time. On the other hand he insists—and the point is central to the whole of the ensuing discussion—that 'the solution to these problems can never be found in experience' (B512). The philosopher cannot simply pass the problem on to the natural scientist. He must solve it himself.

I shall accept the initial point here that on Kant's view even if the

---

[10] Thus, despite Strawson's insistence (op. cit., 194–196) that transcendental Idealism in the Antimony is essentially a phenomenalistic theory, it is worth noting that Kant often expresses his view in the passage without any such explicit commitment, e.g. at B521:

> The objects of experience, then, are never given *in themselves*, but only in experience, and have no existence outside it. That there may be inhabitants in the moon, although no one has ever perceived them, must certainly be admitted. This, however, means only that in the possible advance of experience we may encounter them. For everything is real which stands in connection with a perception in accordance with the laws of empirical advance.

It is surely not enough to express a phenomenalistic theory that one should require that claims about empirical reality be testable against perceptual experience in conjunction with natural laws. The passage also indicates a more complex account of evidence in relation to perceptual experience than that summarily offered by Bennett. See note 4 above.

opposed arguments are not valid we still face a problem about the opposed cosmological claims themselves.[11] But once that initial point is accepted two further aspects of Strawson's treatment of the Antinomy become puzzling. First it is puzzling that almost all of his subsequent discussion turns on the idea, in Kant's resolution of the problem, that the opposed arguments are valid and on the formal corollaries of this. Now it would plainly be wrong to disregard this formal side of Kant's account in attempting to give a comprehensive treatment of his text. But if it is also true that the problem arises independently of that formal treatment, then it would seem to be equally wrong to neglect alternative accounts of the problem and its solution. Since I wish to offer such an alternative account, once it is conceded that it exists, it is not therefore necessary for me to comment on these formal issues. Even if Kant were generally mistaken in his assessment of the opposed arguments, and even if his formal apparatus of presupposition and of analytical and dialectical opposites were unacceptable, this need not impair such an alternative account.

It is, second, also puzzling that in his characterization of that alternative account Strawson should stress what seem to be inconsistent elements in it. Thus on one side we cannot resolve the problem by pleading our unavoidable ignorance of supersensible objects, for the problem is framed in terms of spatio-temporal objects which are within the scope of our senses. And yet, on the other side, the solution to the problem cannot be found in experience, for the concepts in terms of which the problem is framed are not such as we 'could ever have empirical grounds for applying'. It seems impossible to avoid the conclusion here that any alternative account cannot be coherently stated, since it seems to require that the problem concerns both empirical and non-empirical objects. Strawson does not make it clear in this passage whether he believes there is a coherent alternative or not, but the fact that he entitles this section 'A Problem in Any Case?' suggests that he intends his readers to think that there is no such alternative account. In what follows I shall try to explain how such an account might be given despite Strawson's initially unpromising way of presenting it.

It is essential to recall here Kant's opening remarks in the first edition Preface (Ai–ii). There Kant refers first to the fate of human reason to be faced with questions which are both unavoidable and yet unanswerable. In more detail he explains that we may start with principles relating uncompromisingly to ordinary experience but may be forced, or tempted, into the position of seeking some final or complete account of some area of enquiry. In doing, so, he claims, we may appeal to principles which go beyond any possible application to experience. No imagination is needed to associate such a view with the subsequent discussion in the Antinomy.

[11] This point is also made in Al-Azm, *The Origins of Kant's Arguments in the Antinomies* (Oxford: Oxford University Press, 1972). See 'The First Antinomy', and especially p. 21.

We might see that section primarily as an attempt to fulfil the tacit promise expressed in the Preface to show how this transition from ordinary or scientific questions to metaphysical bewilderment takes place. Not much imagination is needed to expect that the fulfilment of this promise will involve the ideas both of completeness and of a transition from questions which can be answered in experience to those which cannot.

It would be natural, too, to expect that, once this pattern of explanation is demonstrated, Kant will say that disputes over rival answers to these metaphysical questions violate the Critical principle and are simply futile. Yet, as Strawson points out, Kant apparently denies at B506–507 that we can claim inevitable ignorance of these answers on the ground that they refer to supersensible objects. There may seem to be a serious conflict here, but an examination of the passage at B506–507 resolves it. For what Kant is claiming in that passage is not that the pattern of transition from empirical to metaphysical questions has no relevance to the resolution of the Antinomy. What he is claiming is that the reference in the questions to the world, or the universe, is to the set of objects in space and time of which we have some experience. But the questions themselves ask of the universe whether it has a beginning in time, or a limit in space, and it is this reference to an absolute totality to the completion of the series of temporal world states for example, which effects the transition from science to metaphysics.[12] So the apparent incoherence which Strawson's presentation suggested is not real. In its place we have instead, as a central part of Kant's analysis, the idea that these cosmological questions have both an empirical, or scientific, aspect, and a transcendental, or metaphysical, aspect. And this idea brings another with it, namely, that it is importantly our failure to notice the transition from one to the other, a confusion between what Kant calls the empirical and the transcendental import of such terms as 'world', 'whole', and 'totality'[13], which leads to these futile debates.

[12] B507: the cosmological ideas alone have this peculiarity that they can pre-suppose their object, and the empirical synthesis required for its concept, as being given. The question which arises out of these ideas refers only to the advance in this synthesis, that is, whether it should be carried so far as to contain absolute totality—such totality, since it cannot be given in any experience, being no longer empirical.

[13] B447: The ideas with which we are now dealing I have above entitled cosmological ideas, partly because by the term 'world' we mean the sum of all appearances, and it is exclusively to the unconditioned in the appearances that our ideas are directed, partly also because the term 'world' in the transcendental sense, signifies the absolute totality of all existing things. B511: in its empirical meaning the term 'whole' is always only comparative. The absolute whole of quantity (the universe) . . . (has) nothing to do with any possible experience . . . Yet it is just the explanation of this very whole that is demanded in the transcendental problems of reason.

If this is right, then we should expect that, just as in the case of dialectical illusions in psychology, there will be room both for a spurious rational cosomology and for a genuine empirical cosmology. Although Kant draws some distinction between the psychological and the cosmological cases in the passage at B506–507, it is not a distinction which excludes that parallel. If there were such a parallel, then we should have to note another gap in Strawson's quoted account. For if Kant's view is compatible with the existence of a genuine scientific cosmology, then while it would be true that the philosopher could not pass the metaphysical question on to the natural scientist it would also be true that he should pass the scientific question on to him.

Such an account goes scarcely any way towards exemplifying these distinctions, and I therefore offer a sketch of one such way. Let us suppose, in relation to the question about the temporal origin of the universe, that we have scientific evidence for the recession of large-scale objects (galaxies) at speeds proportional to their distance from us. Let us further suppose that in accordance with accepted physical laws and from some given distribution of such objects and their velocities it is possible to retrodict their location or distribution systematically over a range of past times. With these assumptions we might be led to believe that at some point in the past these objects were not distributed discretely through space, but converged on some point. We might be led to speak of such convergence as showing the origin of the universe, and to treat it as a working scientific hypothesis rather than as a matter for metaphysical debate. It is clear that already within such an account there is room for ordinary scientific disagreement of an empirical or theoretical kind. In this respect the hypothesis, though spectacular, is no different from other scientific hypotheses, and questions about what it calls the origin of the universe are part of a genuine scientific cosomlogy.

But although it seems reasonable for such an hypothesis to be described in these terms a philosopher might argue that it has not provided an adequate account of what he understood by the phrase 'origin of the universe'. All that the hypothesis has provided, it might be said, is a relation between an earlier distribution of matter in the universe and a later distribution. If some account of the *origin* of such matter had been provided, then we should have had to know the origin of that earlier distribution, and about this the hypothesis said nothing. Two points emerge from such an exchange. First, the philosopher's demand may continue to be made whatever hypothesis is put forward, and if this is so, then what he calls the 'origin of the universe' is no longer expressible in any such scientific hypothesis. Second, the philosopher may nevertheless present a semblance of scientific respectability, since at any particular point for which he raises his further demand it is in principle possible for some other scientific hypothesis to satisfy that demand. So his demand is satisfiable at any particular point, but not totally satisfiable. The total or final demand would require for its satisfaction a completed scientific cosmology that could no longer be revised or amended. We might hesitate to say that such a demand, and such terms as 'universe' and 'totality' in it, are meaningless, but it is apparently unsatisfiable.

Like Strawson's four models for understanding Kant's argument this model does not meet every textual requirement. It has, however, many advantages from a textual point of view and is preferable to Strawson's 'weak' model, which it most closely resembles. Unlike that interpretation, however, it does not merely stress the difference of category between talking meaningfully of the start of a series of events in the universe and meaninglessly of the start of the universe itself.[14] Unlike the weak model, too, it finds room for Kant's important distinction between empirical and transcendental questions about cosmology, and so offers a fulfilment of that passage from the Preface. It does not, like so many other accounts which over-emphasize the mathematical aspects of the formal arguments in the thesis and antithesis, need to get involved in these aspects of what is primarily a physical issue. And it shows how, once the transition has been made from scientific to metaphysical questions, it is inevitably but uselessly to such mathematical models that the debate will turn. But in one crucial respect the model may seem to be seriously at fault. For Strawson's view of his 'weak' interpretation is that it is too weak to be Kant's own view. If this is true of that interpretation, then it will be true of mine as well. The objection here is that it reduces transcendental Idealism to evanescence, where that doctrine is itself interpreted as in Part I of the traditional picture, or as in some more standard Idealism with regard to the objects of perception. Both of these features are present in Strawson's later section on the metaphysics of transcendental Idealism.[15] It is, therefore, to that latter aspect of the doctrine that I finally turn.

(3) Transcendental and Empirical Realism: Transcendental and Empirical Idealism

Most recent commentators on Kant's epistemology have paid close attention to the four-fold division between transcendental and empirical Realism on one side, and transcendental and empirical Idealism on the

[14] Bennett, *Kant's Dialectic* (Cambridge: Cambridge University Press, 1975), 287, and Al-Azm, op. cit., both take this view, which was put forward in my 'The Beginning of the World', *Proceedings of the Aristotelian Society*, Supplementary Volume (1961).

[15] Cf. Strawson, op. cit., 235–277, where essentially the traditional doctrine outlined in Parts I, II and III is identified as the metaphysics of transcendental Idealism.

other. Kant employs these contrasts essentially to separate his own theory of transcendental Idealism plus empirical Realism from that of transcendental Realism with empirical Idealism as opposed theories about the objects of perception and knowledge. But such commentators have disagreed about the significance of the four-fold division, and I introduce an account of it by contrasting the views of two such commentators.

In *Kant's Criticism of Metaphysics* (pp. 28–33) Walsh explains Kant's preferred theory in the following way. First he stresses Kant's official rejection of any claim to know things as they are in themselves, that is, out of all relation to our senses. Second he notes that to call the objects of perception (or intuition) 'appearances' is not to use the term in its customary way, and specifically not to suggest that such objects are in any way illusory. The sense in which these objects are, transcendentally, ideas or appearances is for Kant compatible with their being, sometimes, empirical, spatial, physical objects. In order to achieve this reconciliation, according to Walsh, Kant allows that

> ... we can speak of the reality of things at two quite different levels. First, we can speak at what may be called the level of common sense ... and of scientific thought. Second, we can think and talk at the level of critical philosophy, which takes account of factors that common sense and science alike find irrelevant (p. 29).

Earlier Walsh had usefully explained the meaning of Kant's term 'transcendental' by summarizing Kant's own account from B80–81. He says (pp. 15–16):

> ... a transcendental enquiry into the possibility of knowledge directed particularly to the question of *a priori* knowledge.

Such a view fits naturally into Walsh's account. For it emphasizes the difference of level involved in philosophical considerations as against those of common sense or science. Such a difference, moreover, might naturally be exemplified in the earlier distinction between a scientific cosmology and a philosophical treatment of problems arising out of such a discipline.

Walsh goes on to point out two corollaries of his view. First he shows that the contrast between appearances and reality can be drawn at *both* levels. At a common sense or scientific level we could contrast in this way the primary and the secondary qualities, for example, so that to restrict our experience to appearances would be to restrict it to such items as a sweet taste. But at the philosophical level the contrast between appearance and reality is quite different. At that level the aim is to contrast items given to our senses as appearances, including for example both primary and secondary qualities, with other purported items which exist independently of, and out of all relation to, our senses. Second, therefore, Walsh wishes to separate on Kant's behalf two senses of the terms 'idea' and 'appearance', in one of which these are contrasted (empirically) with public spatial objects, and in the other of which they are (transcendentally) contrasted instead with supersensible things.[16] He says:

> In order to make this general theory work Kant has to provide at the transcendental or philosophical level for two sorts of appearances: for those which belong to the experience of particular individuals, and for those which belong to the experience of men as such.

Later (section 17) Walsh also offers some clarification of this contrast in terms of the distinction between the objective character of judgments and the private character of particular experiences.

Bennett, however, in *Kant's Analytic* offers a quite different account of the four-fold division. He begins (pp. 22–25) by defining the term 'appearance' in Kant's theory as 'all those objective things, processes and events which we can know about by means of our senses, but not . . . our sensory states themselves'. He then explains the four-fold division by ascribing to Kant the doctrine that statements about phenomena are equivalent to statements about actual and possible sensory states. He says:

> Kant calls this account of statements about phenomena 'transcendental Idealism'—'transcendental' because it is a thesis about meanings, and Idealism because of the primacy it gives to sensory states. It must be sharply distinguished from empirical Idealism, which, without reducing statements about non-mental items to ones about mental items, says that there are in fact only mental items. Whereas transcendental Idealism offers an analysis of statements about chairs and tables, empirical Idealism denies that there are any chairs and tables . . . Transcendental Realism which denies that non-mental statements reduce to mental ones is 'Realism' because it gives to the concept of a non-mental item an irreducible place in our conceptual scheme; while empirical Realism says tritely that there are non-mental items in the world (p. 23).

It is clear from this passage that Bennett simply treats transcendental Idealism as some form of phenomenalism, and he later offers (p. 126) a passage from A104–105 to support his view.

> The object is viewed as that which prevents our modes of knowledge from being haphazard or arbitrary, and which determines them . . . in some definite fashion. For in so far as they relate to an object they must necessarily agree with one another, that is, must possess that unity which constitutes the concept of an object.

---

[16] These views are similar to those outlined in my *Kant's Theory of Knowledge* (London: Routledge and Kegan Paul, 1962), Chs. 1–3.

Which of these two accounts should be preferred? I think there can really be no question but that whereas Walsh's account is tied firmly to the text at almost every point, Bennett's can scarcely be tied to it at any point. Walsh's account of the term 'transcendental' echoes indisputably what Kant himself says, as does the distinction between the two levels and the dual function of the contrast between 'appearance' and 'reality'.

By contrast Bennett's account of the term 'transcendental', his appeal to the text to support Kant's phenomenalism, and his grasp of the four-fold division are all seriously at fault. I list some of the problems in his account quite summarily.

(i) It is clear that Bennett's account of the term 'appearance' is mistaken, for Kant importantly uses the term to cover items belonging both to outer and to inner sense, that is, both to spatial objects and to sensory states.[17]

(ii) Kant nowhere says that the term 'transcendental' applies to any thesis about meanings. Bennett no doubt believes that Kant may be understood in this way because of his verificationist version of Kant's Critical principle, but, as I have argued, there is little justification for that either.

(iii) Kant in fact characterizes empirical Idealism as a doctrine which may either doubt or deny the existence of outer objects, and not merely as a doctrine which simply denies such existence.

(iv) There is evident obscurity over the relation between phenomenalism, empirical Idealism, and Berkeley. Bennett's account strongly suggests that Berkeley is not, as Kant believed, an empirical Idealist. Indeed Berkeley seems likely to emerge as a precursor of transcendental Idealism. Such a view, or a weaker claim to the effect that Kant is closer to Berkeley than he believed, has often been canvassed, but it seems unsatisfactory to achieve the result by definition.[18]

(v) Transcendental Realism, in Bennett's account, as a mere denial, or rejection, of phenomenalism is compatible with a naive Realism which

---

[17] E.g. B50–51, B69, B155–156, and A386. But apart from these explicit commitments it is surely undeniable that Kant requires parity between our knowledge of outer objects and our knowledge of our empirical selves, in so far as both are classified as appearances.

[18] There is, of course, here a serious problem of interpretation, which cannot be satisfactorily tackled merely by claiming, as some commentators have, that Kant was closer to Berkeley than he (Kant) believed (see Strawson, op. cit., 22, 35, 192, 197). For just as Kant's views are not entirely determinate, independent of their interpretation, so the same is notoriously true of Berkeley as well. But to suggest that within the range of views ascribable to Berkeley some are close to views within the range ascribable to Kant is to say virtually nothing. It is essential in such matters to 'fix' one or other view, and then compare it with some interpretation, or range of interpretations, of the other. In this case I believe that it is vital to consider where Berkeley and Kant stand with respect to the denial or rejection of common sense beliefs.

simply does not match Kant's claims in rejecting it. Moreover transcendental Realism may even *entail* empirical Realism in Bennett's account, and this would have the unwelcome consequence that the conjunction of transcendental Realism with empirical Idealism is actually inconsistent. Kant certainly wishes to reject that complex theory, but he does not suggest that it is simply inconsistent.

(vi) The passage at A104-105 certainly carries no clear commitment to phenomenalism at all, but may be taken to express a general consistency requirement for any concept of an object.

Walsh's account is, therefore, to be preferred, but not just negatively because of Bennett's inadequacies. The primary reason for preferring Walsh is that his account takes seriously the difference of level implied in Kant's distinction between empirical and transcendental enquiries, while Bennett is prevented by his misinterpretation of the term 'transcendental' from capturing this crucial point. But even if Walsh's account is preferable it raises two further problems. First it leaves Kant's four-fold division still imperfectly explained. Second it raises, as Walsh admits, the difficulty of elucidating the contrast between empirically private ideas and ideas belonging to men as such. It may be objected to that contrast not only that it is obscure, but also that it begs the traditional questions about objectivity which Kant was trying to answer. We need, then, some further explanation of these points, and I offer two models to deal with them.

First, and most obviously, we need a model with which to understand Kant's four-fold division. We know that empirical Idealism is a doctrine which doubts or denies that outer objects exist, and, we may presume, does so on the basis of a traditionally Idealist view about the immediate objects of perception. To call these ideas is to raise at once the traditional issues over the justification for our beliefs about outer objects. We know also that empirical Realism is the opposed doctrine that outer, spatial, objects do exist. But there is, perhaps, a problem about how we should understand the conjunction of empirical Idealism and transcendental Realism. Kant, of course, is not claiming that all empirical Idealists are transcendental Realists. In the central passage where he explains these terms (A367-495), he indicates only that someone who succumbs to transcendental Realism will tend to adopt also empirical Idealism.

Such a tendency is well illustrated in the cases of both Locke and Leibniz. In both there is what Bennett agreeably calls a 'veil of perception' doctrine,[19] which admits ideas as the immediate objects of perception and prevents us from gaining direct access to the real objects so represented to us. Both philosophers require some general principle of inference to enable

[19] See J. Bennett, *Locke, Berkeley, Hume* (Oxford: Oxford University Press, 1971), 68–70. In relation to Leibniz I gratefully acknowledge the help of Guy Stock in pursuing the detail of Leibniz's views.

us to recover a justified belief in such real objects; and in both there is a reference to the power of science to penetrate the veil of perception. It may well be that neither Locke nor Leibniz should in the end be understood in this way, but, for example, Locke's principle of inference from ideas to primary qualities, and Leibniz' account of 'confused' perception clearly make them vulnerable to such an interpretation. A transcendental Realist, on this model, is one who wishes to justify our belief about real objects but, no doubt unwittingly, places them beyond the veil of perception, or, as Kant says, out of all relation to our senses.

It is evident that such a transcendental Realism may naturally be associated with empirical Idealism. One who, for example, begins with a Platonic conception of a non-sensory reality unveiled by science will tend to regard our common sensory experience as concerned only with private, and possibly confused, ideas. In a similar way, more closely associated with Locke than Leibniz, one who begins with a conception of the senses as directed immediately to our ideas will tend to construe the common belief in outer objects as a belief in a supersensible reality. It might be claimed, then, that Kant's preferred composite theory can be grasped simply as the denial of this complex doctrine. An empirical Realist will be one who neither doubts nor denies the existence of outer objects; and a transcendental Idealist will be one who denies the belief in a world of objects beyond the reach of our senses, at least as any serious way of resolving the doubts of empirical Idealism.

This way of understanding Kant's four-fold division is not, I believe, basically wrong. It is one which arises quite directly from Kant's text in the Fourth Paralogism. But it also faces difficulties which need to be resolved. For one thing it may seem too weak a doctrine for Kant to have held. However, given that the traditional picture of Kant expressed earlier is under review, it would merely be circular to appeal to that. But a claim about the weakness of this transcendental Idealism might also be based on the view that as a mere denial of a fairy story about a supersensible reality it denies nothing worth denying and so has no explanatory value. Two things can be said to answer this. First, even if these, transcendental Realist, doctrines appear as preposterous fictions, still there can scarcely be any doubt that philosophers have sometimes succumbed to them. Moreover, such views are not, generally, presented just as fictions, but arise confusedly from reflection upon our common, or scientific, experience. They are, indeed, generally offered as accounts which philosophical reflection compels us to give of that experience itself. Given this confused and uneasy background a clear account of what such doctrines imply, and a clear denial of their truth or value, have some merit on their own, and this must certainly have seemed so to Kant.

Second, however, Kant was not concerned only to present such a bare denial. He wished also, as the account of the Antinomy has shown, to offer some explanation of the way such doctrines make the transition from common experience to transcendent metaphysics. So a part of Kant's objection to transcendental Realism coupled with empirical Idealism is that it fails to acknowledge just that transition. His preferred theory has, then, some explanatory value in so far as it clarifies the confusion which brings that transition about. It is designed to show how the doctrine to be rejected, although intended to acknowledge certain beliefs from our common experience, nevertheless deviates radically from it. In such a demonstration the contrast between empirical and transcendental enquiries and the Critical principle can be expected to play a vital part.

But it may still be urged that even if there is room for some such explanation it is not clear how Kant's apparatus provides it. For this purpose we need another model, namely that of a 'framework' as outlined by, for example, Carnap and Körner.[20] It is not necessary for me to elaborate the formal structure of such frameworks, though partly for reasons which Körner's outline makes clear I do not think it helpful to characterize them as 'conceptual' frameworks. From Carnap, then, we may take the idea of a set of discriminations governed by certain principles which at least make clear the standard procedures for testing the application of such discriminations. In the case of a mathematical framework, for example, we are provided with formal accounts of the elementary concepts and with procedures for determining whether some number has or lacks a particular property such as that of being prime. In his sketch of a framework for ordinary spatio-temporal objects there are similarly procedures for determining whether some object exists at a specific spatio-temporal location and whether it has some specific property.

Carnap used this apparatus primarily to separate what he called 'external' and 'internal' questions. His distinction is complex and not without its difficulties, but for my purposes it can be taken as a distinction between questions whose answers are, at least in principle, provided for in the framework and questions for which this is not true. It is not hard to see that Carnap's distinction might also have been labelled in terms of the contrast between 'empirical' and 'transcendental' questions. For with this apparatus it is possible again to illustrate Kant's account of the different levels of these enquiries and to elaborate further the four-fold division.

We could say, for example, that the empirical Idealist does not accept our spatio-temporal framework of objects of perception. For he raises a question about the rationale for applying the framework's tests to resolve its internal questions. In questioning the framework itself he is raising not an internal empirical but an external transcendental question. Yet his position is less clear, more confused, than this. For he raises this external

[20] F. Carnap, 'Empiricism, Semantics, and Ontology', *Revue Internationale de Philosophie* (1950); S. Körner, *Categorial Frameworks* (Oxford: Blackwell, 1970).

question on the basis of an acceptance of part of the framework itself, namely that part in which we describe the way in which objects are represented, or appear, to us. It is characteristic of such an Idealist that he should take this internal use of 'appearance' or 'idea', in which it is contrasted with physical objects, and transform it into an external use, in which it includes physical objects, and so makes an unacknowledged transition from Kant's empirical to his transcendental level of enquiry. Such an Idealist may also intend actually to justify the other part of the framework in which we refer to and describe spatio-temporal objects themselves. But the consequence, in transcendental Realism, is only to re-write the framework. It is not merely to fail to justify our ordinary beliefs, but also to put them apparently beyond justification. So the transcendental Realist–empirical Idealist persistently confuses the contrast between internal and external questions; he persistently makes the transition from empirical internal enquiries to their external transcendental counterparts without realizing the significance of this move. What makes his problem seem urgent is his reliance on part of the framework, but what prevents his solution from succeeding is his compulsion to transcend that framework.

There is a further important corollary of this model. Kant indicates in his discussion of the four-fold division (A371–372) that psychologists are liable to fall into these mistakes, and it is easy to see why. Even nowadays when psychologists are apt to speak of representations or models of reality rather than simply of ideas, their terminology makes them vulnerable to the temptations of transcendental Realism and empirical Idealism understood in this way. Any account in which it is supposed that we construct representations of reality from our basic sensory input is liable to raise the philosophical questions about the justification for a belief in the reality so represented. But modern pyschologists, unlike those to whom Kant referred, evade these philosophical issues by treating their questions only as internal and empirical. They regard the independent reality as simply given by the framework, and so raise issues only about the correlation between representations and reality and its development from birth to maturity. Such issues have no concern with the attempt to justify a belief in reality and consequently avoid the dangers of the transition from empirical to transcendental questions. They arise within the framework and do not question it. Such an empirical task is one which Kant believed Locke to have undertaken, and which he distinguishes from his own task of justification in the Transcendental Deduction. It is clear that Kant regarded that part of Locke's enquiry as both genuine and important, and many of his own comments on the psychological origins of our knowledge, for example in the preliminaries to the first edition Deduction, also belong to such an enquiry. It is primarily for that reason, I believe, that Kant so often appears as a phenomenalist. The term 'phenomenalism' of course stands for no single clear philosophical doctrine, but in so far as it claims that our knowledge or experience is somehow constructed from our sensory input then Kant would certainly have accepted it.[21] But only, if the above account is right, as an internal empirical programme in psychology and not as an attempt philosophically to justify our beliefs about outer objects.

That view is confirmed by another consideration. It may be objected here that Kant's appeal to our framework for spatio-temporal objects is simply an appeal to ordinary language. But not only are such appeals nowadays rightly regarded as inadequate, it is also true that Kant himself, in the *Prolegomena*,[22] makes it clear that this is not his intention. Such an objection can be answered in two ways. First Carnap's appeal to frameworks is not itself an appeal to ordinary language. Exactly the same apparatus can be applied to any framework however technical it may be. Moreover it is not part of Carnap's thesis that frameworks cannot be revised or even abandoned. What is important in the argument is the apparatus for separating the distinct questions that may arise in relation to frameworks so that the confusion about such questions can be avoided. Second, however, on Kant's side nothing is plainer than that he is not simply appealing to our framework for spatio-temporal objects in order to justify it. Certainly the apparatus of empirical and transcendental enquiries has a part to play in clarifying the issues, but the key element in his own attempt to justify that framework is a general argument in the Transcendental Deduction and the Refutation of Idealism to show that such a framework is a necessary condition of any possible experience. That line of thought has, in recent years, been extensively surveyed and there may be controversy about its success. But there can surely be no controversy about its presence in the *Critique*. That line of argument, however, seems to have little to do with standard philosophical phenomenalism. If Kant had wished to offer a standard phenomenalistic solution to these problems one would expect to find it strongly emphasized in the Refutation of Idealism, but there is no trace of it in that passage.

Two other features of transcendental Idealism, viewed in this way, indicate typical aspects of a more common Idealism. First, in line with Kant's Copernican revolution, Kant stresses that he is not approaching the traditional problems in the traditional way. The difference of level between empirical and transcendental enquiries, which Walsh and I have empha-

---

[21] I indicated above (note 10) that such a claim is not sufficient for phenomenalism, but it is at least necessary. Philosophers have not, generally, stressed the different variety of phenomenalistic theories, for example, the substantial differences between a theory such as Ayer's in *The Foundations of Empirical Knowledge*, and one such as Goodman's in *The Structure of Appearance*.

[22] Kant, *Prolegomena*, Introduction.

sized, is a revolutionary way of approaching those problems. It involves, for one thing, an awareness of the differences between scientific and philosophical problems and of the associated differences between internal and external questions. Beyond this, too, Kant's Copernican hypothesis attaches a new priority to the frameworks in which our knowledge of objects is constructed rather than to the objects themselves which we claim to know. In this way Kant explicitly associates himself with the typically Idealist thesis that we somehow impose an order on reality or even construct that reality itself. The thesis remains, of course, ambiguous and unclear. Kant has not analysed it with the completeness, or in the way, we would now prefer; but it is clearly present in the account I have offered.

Kant's theory, so understood, offers also some explanation of Walsh's appeal to the ideas of men as such. The priority accorded to our frameworks indicates a way in which our beliefs are unavoidably restricted to the frameworks we accept.[23] It indicates a kind of subjectivity which is, however, not that of an individual's private sensory experience but is rather that of a certain relativism associated with a system of belief. Transcendental Idealism offers in its transcendental distinction between appearances and intelligible objects a contrast not between a private, eventually solipistic, experience and a public experience of outer objects, for that contrast is already an empirical internal part of our framework. Instead it offers a contrast between the revisable beliefs which we accept as that framework and some ultimate form of knowledge in which no revision or change is possible. Kant has, of course, two qualifications to make to this contrast. First he argues that such an absolute system of knowledge is beyond our reach, and perhaps has a function only in its heuristic guidance towards improving our system of beliefs. Second he is also often thought to hold that certain aspects of our framework, for example those associated with Aristotelian logic and Euclidean geometry, are strictly unrevisable. If he indeed does hold this latter view, then we have no need to follow him there. But the basic notion of a relativism which is for us unavoidable is a fruitful idea with strong echoes in post-Kantian Idealism and in very recent philosophy.

(4) The Traditional Picture

I hope that it will be already reasonably clear which parts of the traditional picture survive in the account I have given, and which parts can be put aside. I summarize the main points and add one quite general comment on its failings.

[23] It also begins to explain Kant's references to the collective 'we' throughout the *Critique*, which have evidently puzzled commentators. Cf. Strawson op. cit., 197, 257.

(1) In my account the Critical principle is not a principle of significance and does not derive from a specific theory or criterion of meaning. This at least avoids the conflict between holding that Part I has explanatory value but is strictly meaningless.

(2) Nevertheless it may be said that there remains a conflict. For Part I at least asserts the existence of intelligible objects while the Critical principle tells us that we have no evidence for such a claim. Now Kant certainly commits himself to the existence of such objects, although he also makes many qualifications about the claim and many of his expressions of such a commitment are implicit rather than explicit. But in my account the strongest commitment he makes here is to a belief in a real limitation of our own cognitive, especially sensory, faculties, which would not entitle us to claim that the objects *we* are presented with in the frameworks *we* accept are the only possible ones. To assert the existence of such objects beyond our capacities is to underline the modesty with which we should view our own frameworks of belief. This view has some explanatory value; as I indicated earlier it is connected importantly to Kant's belief that we make certain metaphysical mistakes because we can construct meanings which are beyond our capacity to exemplify. But this is not to ascribe to Kant the purported material explanation which gives Part I its central flavour.

(3) My account of the Critical principle plainly affects its use in the Dialectic. In particular in my account the principle is used primarily to show the manifold temptations to overstep the bounds of experience. It is used also to explain such errors as arising from a confused transition between the different levels of what Kant calls empirical and transcendental enquiry.

(4) The same important difference between empirical and transcendental considerations must also affect Kant's treatment of the problems of perception and the four-fold division. In my account the remaining commitment from Part I to intelligible objects has no real bearing on these problems. In particular Kant is not himself a transcendental Realist, and the conflict between Part I and his rejection of the transcendental Realist-empirical Idealist theory vanishes. More importantly Kant's own preferred theory does not involve a commitment to phenomenalism, except in so far as it can be construed as a non-philosophical, internal, empirical theory in psychology. Instead the favoured theory, with its associated contrast between empirical and transcendental questions, indicates a kind of subjectivity that has to do with the notions of a framework and of framework-relativity.

One final comment is worth making about the attractions of Part I and its apparent conflicts with much of Parts II and III. One general way of understanding Part I is as a material correlate of the formal conditions of experience already present in the other parts. If we consider, for example, a neutral Kantian claim to the effect that there are conditions of experience which are not themselves part of that experience, we may interpret this either in material or in a formal way. In the material construction in Part I the claim then indicates a realm of purported objects which materially, causally, condition our experience. In the formal construction, however, the claim merely indicates those dominant, and perhaps unrevisable, principles which formally define our framework of belief. The temptation to believe Part I might, then, be seen as a failure to distinguish the material from the formal aspect of the general claim. Now Kant himself frequently employs precisely this kind of explanation.[24] Our notion of an object in general may be taken either as a purported reference to real intelligible objects, or instead only as a formal requirement of objectivity to be satisfied in any comprehensible framework. The notion of the self, similarly, has such a misleading material construction, when, properly understood, it has only a formal significance. It could not be said that Kant has fully worked out or explicitly presented all the consequences of such a view, but the ingredients for such a view are present in the *Critique*. To attribute the traditional picture to Kant all that is required is that we should believe that he totally failed to appreciate their significance.

[24] E.g. for objects, B50–52, B306–307, B337, B345–346, B522–523. For selves, A397–398, B404, B409, B426–427, B429. And on Idealism itself see B519 note, which reads:

I have elsewhere called it (transcendental Idealism) *formal* Idealism in order to distinguish it from material Idealism, i.e. the usual sort which either doubts or denies the existence of outer things. It seems sometimes prudent to use this terminology rather than that used above in order to prevent any misunderstanding.

Kemp Smith's translation omits the final sentence from this passage.

Plato twice, Aristotle and Descartes once each; Hume doesn't get a mention). There is plenty of evidence to show that Hegel repeatedly read Kant in particular. Leaving aside the early writings, which might be said to constitute a continuing *Auseinandersetzung* with Kant on topics bearing on morals and religion, there are at least three places in his works as we have them now where Hegel undertakes a full review and criticism of the Kantian philosophy: in the essay *Glauben und Wissen* of 1802, in the introductory section which formally leads into the part on Logic in the *Encyclopaedia of the Philosophical Sciences* and which mostly dates from the second edition of 1827, finally in the posthumously published *Lectures on the History of Philosophy*. There are also repeated references to and discussions of particular Kantian doctrines in Hegel's most elaborate and most important work on theoretical philosophy, the *Science of Logic* (1812–16). What makes these passages remarkable when we compare them with their counterparts in Kant himself or in Hume is the detailed knowledge they reveal on Hegel's part of the doctrines under discussion. In *Glauben und Wissen* Hegel not only quotes Kant's actual words (or at any rate something quite like them) in examining particular doctrines; he also refers to individual arguments of his author in a way which shows that he had grasped not just the main thesis being put forward, but also how Kant tried to work it out. There is, for example, in this essay considerable emphasis on Kant's doctrine of the productive imagination and the 'figurative' as opposed to the 'intellectual' synthesis spoken of in §24 of the second edition Deduction. There is also a full and accurate account of what Kant had to say in the *Critique of Judgment* about intellectual intuition, with a correct indication of the grounds on which Kant concluded that intuition of this sort is not available to human beings. The treatment of Kant in the *Encylopaedia* passage is more general if also more trenchant, but not so general that Hegel loses sight of the particular points Kant wanted to establish. In both works, and again in the more lengthy (though also of course less authentic) discussions in the History of Philosophy lectures, Hegel pays particular attention to what might be called the unity of the Kantian philosophy: the fact that its author produced three Critiques and not one only, and intended the conclusions established in the *Critique of Pure Reason* to be complemented or supplemented by those argued for in the two later works. Hegel was particularly sensitive to the importance of the *Critique of Judgment*, and saw, as some modern critics (including myself) have not, that it was not intended to be simply a series of appendices to the other two Critiques, but to advance Kant's argument by showing that the gulf between Nature and Freedom may well be less absolute than at first sight appeared. He was also alive, in this again differing from many later students of the Critical philosophy, to the crucial part played in Kant's thinking by the doctrine of the Postulates of Pure Practical Reason, which he presented as being central to Kant's ethics, rather than an eccentric appendix to it. That the main ambition of the *Critique of Pure Reason* was to abolish knowledge in order to make room for faith was a dictum not lost on this author.

But it is one thing to grasp a philosophical system correctly, another to agree with it, and the fact of the matter is, of course, that Hegel disagreed with Kant in all sorts of important ways. Not only did he reject Kant's denial of the possibility of metaphysical knowledge, with its corollary that we never know reality as it is in itself, but only as it appears to us; he rejected the whole idea of a critical examination of the powers of pure reason, supposed to be conducted in advance of any first-order enquiries. It was certainly a proper demand (cf. *Encylopaedia*,[2] §41, Zusatz) to require that the forms of thought be subjected to examination, but

> what we want is to combine in our process of inquiry the action of the forms of thought with a criticism of them.

The examination, in other words, has to be internal, not external; reason must criticize itself in the course of its operations, which are essentially concerned with the attaining of truth, i.e. knowledge of reality.[3] The project to suspend metaphysicians from their office until they have satisfactorily answered the question, 'How are synthetic cognitions *a priori* possible?' is accordingly absurd. To say that we know only appearances is to say that we know nothing. And to add that it does not matter because as regards what really concerns us, namely God, Freedom and Immortality, we can always fall back on pure rational faith is not only to comfort ourselves with a theory that will not bear serious examination, but more important to re-erect the barrier to free thought set up in the darkness of the Middle Ages. The Kantian philosophy ends in a denial of the rights of reason, and as such can never be accepted by modern man.

'People in the present day', wrote Hegel on the page following the last quotation,

> have got over Kant and his philosophy: everybody wants to get further. But there are two ways of going further—a backward and a forward. The light of criticism soon shows that many of our modern essays in philosophy are mere repetitions of the old metaphysical method, an endless and uncritical thinking in a groove determined by the natural bent of each man's mind.

[2] Quoted here and elsewhere in the translation by William Wallace, *The Logic of Hegel*, 2nd edn (London: Oxford University Press, 1892).

[3] I do not discuss these objections here but have done so in a subsequent paper: 'The Idea of a Critique of Pure Reason: Kant and Hegel', forthcoming in *Akten des 5. internationalen Kant-Kongresses*, Mainz, 1981.

It appears from this that for all its shortcomings Kant's philosophy per-
formed an essential service, and indeed Hegel never denied that it did.
Hegel's picture of pre-Kantian metaphysics, discussed under the heading
'First Attitude to Objectivity' in the *Encyclopaedia*, is not exactly like
Kant's, since Hegel presents its exponents as having made a naive attempt
to grasp reality with inadequate and unexamined resources rather than as
aiming at the impossible goal of knowledge of what transcends experience.
But Hegel follows Kant in describing these thinkers as 'dogmatists', and
takes that term to mean that they were insufficiently sceptical about their
own intellectual equipment. They embarked on their enquiries into the
Soul, the World and God without asking themselves just what these subjects were and whether they could be properly spoken of in the sharply
defined terms—finite, infinite, etc.—which naturally occurred. Kant's
philosophy had in this respect the useful, if unintended, consequence of
showing that this form of metaphysics was essentially a metaphysics of the
understanding, and hence of clearing the way for speculative truth, which
holds opposing formulae 'in union as a totality, whereas Dogmatism
invests them in their isolation with a title to fixity and truth' (*Enc.*, §32,
Zusatz).

What Hegel is insisting on here is the element of scepticism which he
regards as indispensable to successful philosophical thought, the feature
which provokes the ruthless and continuing self-examination and self-
criticism which give rise to and constitute dialectical thinking. Puzzled
Kantians may well wonder why their hero should be credited with the
invention, or the fostering, of dialectic, seeing that one of Kant's explicit
aims was to combat scepticism and in view of the fact that much of his
philosophy rests on the acceptance of forms of thinking as being in order
as they are, in mathematics, in natural science and in dealing with the
moral life. Hegel's answer is to point to features of Kant's text which
foreshadow his own larger conceptions: the passing remark added in the
second edition of the first Critique that 'the number of the categories is
always the same, namely three', the third category arising 'from the combination of the second category with the first' (B110), the discovery, partial
and incomplete as it was, of the Antinomies and thus of the antinomial
nature of thought. Hegel would certainly not have denied that there is
much in Kant which is dogmatic or, as he put it in his early works,
'unphilosophical'; he sees Kant's official attitude to science, mathematics
and common moral conceptions as complacent and uncritical. Philosophy
cannot properly take for granted that any branch of enquiry or area of
human activity is in order as it is, without need of unfettered
examination. But he also believes that Kant's practice is sometimes
better than his professions might lead one to expect (an interesting
example is the 'construction of matter from powers and activities' in the
Metaphysical Foundations of Natural Science, praised by Hegel in his

Lectures[4] (E.T., III 456) as having been 'of great service' to the incipient philosophy of nature despite the restrictions within which Kant worked). And he claims that though Kant remained at heart a philosopher of the Understanding and in consequence had a quite inadequate grasp of Reason and its Ideas, he was not entirely unaware of the other ways of thinking about the cognitive situation, nor wholly unwilling to grant them authenticity. This comes out particularly in the *Critique of Judgment* where, as the point was put in *Glauben und Wissen*[5] (E.T., 91),

> Kant himself recognized in the beautiful an intuition other than the sensuous. He characterized the substratum of nature as intelligible, recognized it to be rational and identical with all Reason, and knew that the cognition in which concept and intuition are separated was subjective, finite cognition, a phenomenal cognition.

Hegel grants that for Kant there was no going beyond such finite cognition: the most human beings could do was form the Idea of an intuitive understanding, not use it as a standard in judging claims to knowledge. He thinks even so that the presence of such thoughts shows that Kant's philosophy has a 'truly speculative aspect', and that this constitutes its central interest.

I shall return to this topic. But first I must consider a feature of Hegel's system which connects with Kant more obviously and less controversially, his idealism. The most striking aspect of Kant's analysis of experience when we compare it with that of his predecessors is the emphasis he puts on the subject of knowledge. Any item in experience which lays claim to objectivity must be connectible according to universal rules with other such items in a consciousness recognised or recognisable as one; whatever is real must relate to the same unitary point, the continuing unity of apperception. Experience is all experience for a subject, the world exists only so far as it is constituted in judgment. Through judgment the mind imposes necessary and universal form on the material of the senses and thus in a way 'makes' nature, though only from the formal point of view. Kant's idealism, which carries the corollary that we know only phenomena, consists in his theses that what there is exists for a subject, and that that subject imposes form on whatever comes into consciousness. Now Hegel had many reservations about this whole line of argument. He denied absolutely the Kantian conclusion that we know only appearances, he complained that Kant had given no account worth serious consideration of how the categories proceed from the unity of apperception, how the latter as it were expresses itself in them, he laid special stress on the heterogenity Kant saw

[4] *Lectures on the History of Philosophy*, 3 vols, translated by E. S. Haldane and F. H. Simson (London: Kegan Paul, Trench, Trübner & Co., 1892–95).

[5] Translated as *Faith and Knowledge* by Walter Cerf and H. S. Harris (Albany: State University of New York Press, 1977).

between understanding, the source of form, and sensation, the provider of matter, and asked how in this scheme of things knowledge was possible at all. Was it not a standing miracle that I turn out to be able to unite the whole manifold of sense in a single consciousness? And is not the result Kant argues for, that the world exists only so far as I constitute it, with universality and necessity belonging only to the knowing mind, no part of things as they are in themselves, paradoxical in the extreme? An idealism of this kind must be described as 'subjective', for all Kant's preoccupation with objectivity. Hegel even stoops sometimes to the accusation that the mind which makes nature in Kant should be understood as that of some particular person, thus rendering the whole structure arbitrary and absurd, though elsewhere he acknowledges that 'it is not the mere act of our personal self-consciousness, which introduces an absolute unity into the variety of sense' (*Enc.*, §42, Zusatz). As I have argued elsewhere, it is the impersonal subject of judgment, something which is or should be the same in all of us, that Kant has in mind.

These criticisms notwithstanding

> It is one of the profoundest and truest insights to be found in the *Critique of Pure Reason* that the unity which constitutes the nature of the Notion is recognized as the original synthetic unity of apperception, as unity of the I think, or of selfconsciousness (*Science of Logic*,[6] E.T., 584).

The unity which constitutes the nature of the Notion is for Hegel a unity which belongs to things as much as to thoughts, since the Notion (the peculiar Hegelian *Begriff*) has what might be called an inbuilt tendency to express itself in particulars rather than to stand over against them in isolation as do the concepts of the understanding. We see here how, for all his complaints against Kant, the Kantian unity of apperception is the germ of Hegel's doctrine of Spirit. The unity of apperception might be said at a pinch to subdue or appropriate the manifold of sense by forcing the latter to enter into relations with itself; Hegelian Spirit similarly appropriates and subdues whatever presents itself as its opposite, ending up not so much with a world it has made as with one in which it is writ large. The differences are first that while Kant is posing his question at a fairly modest level, asking how we can make judgments which state what is the case as opposed to what merely seems to be so, Hegel is concerned with the larger problem of the intelligibility of the universe as such, which he thinks can be solved only by seeing it as the self-expression of Spirit; second and perhaps more immediately important, that Kant sets up his structure on the supposition that the manifold of sense is initially alien to the intelligence which informs it, whereas Hegel says (*Glauben und Wissen*, E.T., 70) that the 'original,

[6] *Hegel's Science of Logic*, translated by A. V. Miller (London: Allen and Unwin, 1969).

synthetic unity must be conceived ... as a truly necessary, absolute, original identity of opposites'. I take these cryptic words to mean that the dualism of sense and thought found within ordinary experience is not to be taken as absolute, but must be seen as itself the product of mind or Spirit. As Fichte had first argued, the original 'I' posits itself as something not itself which it subsequently works on and exhibits as its own.

In a celebrated 'open letter' published in 1799 Kant dismissed the *Wissenschaftslehre* (without of course having read it) as 'a totally indefensible system' (Zweig, *Kant's Philosophical Correspondence*, 253–254); there is no reason to believe that his declared attitude to Hegel would have been any different. Hegel's obsession with the production and reconciliation of opposites, which underlies his whole conception of dialectical thinking and manifests itself in every part of his philosophy, would without doubt have struck him as far-fetched. Yet we know that Kant himself took steps to reduce the sharpness of some of the oppositions in his own thought, for example by making transcendental schemata function as intermediaries between pure concepts of the understanding and the empirically given, and it is a fact that in his last years he was himself preoccupied with the problem of the gap between pure and empirical physics, and toyed with the idea of 'positing' as a way of filling it. If he never quite reached the full Fichte/ Hegel standpoint he came quite close to it (see Vleeschauwer, *L'Evolution de la Pensée Kantienne*, 197–217). And even if we neglect the fragments of the *Opus Postumum* as products of Kant's dotage we are still left with his insistence in the *Critique* itself on the original, i.e. ultimate character of pure apperception, on its synthesizing function and on its spontaneity. The development from Kant to Hegel on this point would certainly not have been to the liking of the Kant of 1781, but could not all the same be described as wholly unnatural. It is arguable that the restricted idealism Kant presented in the *Critique* had within itself the seeds of something more ambitious. Hegel and others (Fichte and J. S. Beck among those personally known to Kant) cultivated these seeds and so were in a position to claim to have taken Kant's thought to its logical conclusion.[7]

Before proceeding let me attempt to summarize how Hegel saw Kant's idealism. He described it as 'subjective' in contrast to his own 'absolute' idealism, and meant by 'subjective' that it restricted itself to the imposition of form on the matter of experience, eschewing the very idea of grasping reality as it is in itself. Kant offered as the sole object of knowledge an artificial world constituted or contaminated by human thought; that this should be taken as objective, for all Kant's elaborate story about synthesis, was to Hegel quite incredible. A true idealism must not stop half way but,

---

[7] For a discussion of this issue see my paper 'Subjective and Objective Idealism', to be published in the proceedings of the Hegel Congress at Stuttgart, 1981.

as it were, go over into things; Hegel's absolute idealism, in which Spirit took over from the mere unity of apperception, professed to show how this could be done. Further, Hegel maintained that Kant's idealism was unsatisfactory because of the empirical elements it contained. It proffered a doctrine of categories and explained their general function, but made little attempt to discover which concepts answered the description or how they were interconnected. 'Kant, it is well known, did not put himself to much trouble in discovering the categories' (*Enc.*, §42): he simply relied on the supposedly complete table of judgment forms in formal logic in drawing his own list up. Hegel's complaint is formally incorrect, for we know now from Kant's papers that he hunted hard and long for a satisfactory 'clue' to the categories and rejected other candidates before finally settling for the table of forms of judgment (see Vleeschauwer, op. cit., 85ff.). Yet it has to be agreed that Kant knew or suspected that some concepts were categories before he even tried to draw up a full list; he 'picked them up as they came his way', to use the phrase he himself used of Aristotle (B107/A81). And he certainly had no thought of speculating in the Hegelian manner on the relations of one category to another; the whole idea of categories cancelling or superseding one another was foreign to his thought. It is, however, arguable that his treatment in the Analogies suggests that the three categories of Relation are not as separate as his theory required, and that the antinomy of mechanism and teleology in the *Critique of Judgment* conceals a conflict between rival sets of categories, though that is not of course how Kant presents it. If Kant did not think about this problem, perhaps he should have done.

Had he done so, might he have come somewhere near Hegel's conception of absolute idealism? He could not have done that without radically changing two central doctrines in his philosophy, that we know only appearances and that there is an absolute gulf between concepts and intuitions, in human experience at least. Hegel has interesting, though not necessarily convincing, things to say about both of these. As regards Kant's confining knowledge to appearances he appears to say that this conflicts with his all-important doctrine of the synthetic *a priori*. Kant, we read in *Glauben und Wissen* (E.T., 69), reproached Hume for not envisaging the problem of the synthetic *a priori* in its full universality, but himself 'stopped at the subjective and external meaning of this question'.

Hegel goes on:

How are synthetic judgments *a priori* possible? This problem expresses nothing else but the Idea that subject and predicate of the synthetic judgment are identical in the *a priori* way. That is to say, these heterogeneous elements, the subject which is the particular and in the form of being, and the predicate which is the universal and in the form of thought, are at the same time absolutely identical. It is Reason alone that is the possibility of this positing, for Reason is nothing else but the identity of heterogeneous elements of this kind.

I am not sure what this means, nor can I get much out of a parallel passage in the *Lectures* (E.T., III, 430) in which Hegel said that

> Synthetic judgments *a priori* are nothing else than a connection of opposites through themselves, or the absolute Notion, i.e. the relations of different determinations such as those of cause and effect, given not through experience but through thought.

But one point he may be making in the first passage at any rate is the general one that judgment in its fundamental form ascribes a predicate to a particular which is experienced as real, and to that extent can be seen as claiming to state truth about the world, not about some unreal appearance. As Bradley argued, judgment is the ascription of an ideal content to a reality experienced though not articulated in feeling, and owes what grip it has on fact to that. If Hegel is making this point he is saying something important which may well be relevant to the question whether true knowledge is possible, even if it has little to do with the special problem of the synthetic *a priori*. But we should notice that to grant him this point would not in Hegel's view dispose of the problem of appearances. For to arrive at truth we need to have not just a point of contact with reality, but also an intellectual apparatus which is adequate for its proper characterization. One of Hegel's most insistent criticisms both of Kant and of his predecessors is that they employ concepts without sufficient reflection: they fail to ask themselves whether the terms in which they frame their questions are appropriate to the subject-matter. This explains why when the terms turn out not to be appropriate, for example in the area of rational psychology, the tendency is to put the blame on the things, instead of devising fresh ways of thinking better fitted to capture their real nature. 'Criticism of the forms of the understanding', wrote Hegel in the introduction to his *Science of Logic* (E.T., 46), 'has had the result that these forms do not apply to things-in-themselves. This can have no other meaning than that these forms are in themselves something untrue.' To proceed from appearance to reality we do not need, as Kant apparently thought, to exchange our human discursive consciousness for another form of apprehension; we need to improve our categories. Kant had already seen that the world is nothing apart from thought. But it does not follow that reality can be specified in terms of the first thoughts which occur to us. The chances are rather that our first thoughts on the subject will be inappropriate, incoherent or both. We can arrive at truth about reality only when we learn to reject all one-sided views, and in fact to characterize the world in terms of the Hegelian Idea.

But suppose we do proceed to the Idea: are we not still faced with the possibility that our thoughts may not be true of reality? I said just now that for Kant the world is nothing apart from thought, referring here of course to what Kant called the phenomenal world. Kant himself would have insisted that this was at best an exaggeration: there would be no (phenomenal) world apart from thought, but equally there would be none apart from intuition. 'Thoughts without content', i.e. without application, 'are empty'; they must be brought to bear on intuitions if they are to have full significance. But (and this is the crucial point) in the case of human beings concepts and intuitions originate in sources which are apparently quite distinct, concepts in the understanding, intuitions in the sensibility. No intuition is available to us but sense-intuition, and though we can form the idea of an understanding which produced intuitions of itself, an intuitive understanding as Kant calls it, it is evident that such an understanding must be entirely different from our own. We can see this by reflecting that, were there to be such an intelligence, it would diverge from ours not only in the nature of its intuitions, but also in its concepts: as Kant put the point in the *Critique of Judgment*, they would be synthetic, not analytic, universals, concepts possession of which would at once give access to their instances. Such concepts would in fact be self-specifying, as ours most evidently are not. Indeed, the whole contrast between actuality and possibility which is so distinctive a feature of human experience would not be found in the experience of an intuitive understanding: in thinking something as possible it would automatically know it as real.

It is not surprising that Hegel was continuously preoccupied with issues arising out of the Kantian dichotomy between concepts and intuitions. At the beginning of his philosophical career he wrote a passage in *Glauben und Wissen* (E.T., 68) which makes clear what he thought Kant got right and what he got wrong:

> The Kantian philosophy has the merit of being idealism because it does show that neither the concept in isolation nor intuition in isolation is anything at all; that intuition by itself is blind and that the concept by itself is empty; and that what is called experience, i.e. the finite identity of the two in consciousness is not a rational cognition either. But the Kantian philosophy declares this finite cognition to be all that is possible. It turns this negative, abstractly idealistic side into that which is in itself, into the positive. It turns just this empty concept into absolute Reason, both theoretical and practical. In so doing, it falls back into absolute finitude and subjectivity, and the whole task and content of this philosophy is, not the cognition of the Absolute, but the cognition of this subjectivity.

Kant is just a latter-day Locke, a miserable epistemologist when he should have been a serious metaphysician. But what should Kant have done to avoid this fate? Hegel's answer is that he should have rethought his fundamental distinction along Hegelian lines. He should have recognized that the abstract concepts of the understanding are not the only concepts; there is also what translators call 'the Notion', the *Begriff par excellence*. The third book of the *Science of Logic* is devoted, in Hegel's own words (E.T., 591), to 'the exposition of how the Notion builds up in and from itself the reality that has vanished from it.' It may be useful to quote his further remarks at some length.

> It has therefore been freely admitted that the cognition that stops short at the Notion purely as such, is still incomplete and has only as yet arrived at abstract truth. But its incompleteness does not lie in its lack of that presumptive reality given in feeling and intuition but rather in the fact that the Notion has not yet given itself a reality of its own, a reality produced from its own resources. The demonstrated absoluteness of the Notion relatively to the material of experience and, more exactly, to the categories and concepts of reflection, consists in this, that this material as it appears apart from and prior to the Notion has no truth; this it has solely in its ideality or its identity with the Notion. The derivation of the real from it, if we want to call it derivation, consists in the first place essentially in this, that the Notion in its formal abstraction reveals itself as incomplete and through its own immanent dialectic passes over into reality; but it does not fall back again on to a ready-made reality confronting it and take refuge in something which has shown itself to be the unessential element of Appearance because, having looked around for something better, it has failed to find it; on the contrary, it produces the reality from its own resources.

The Notion is thus at any rate similar to the self-specifying concept Kant dismissed as unreal for human beings. What is more, its functioning was virtually recognized by Kant himself. In *Glauben und Wissen* (E.T., 69–70) Hegel adduces the productive imagination and the figurative synthesis in support of this claim, saying that this

> shows that the Kantian forms of intuition and the forms of thought can-cannot be kept apart at all as the particular, isolated faculties they are usually represented as. One and the same synthetic unity . . . is the principle of intuition and the intellect.

In the *Lectures* (E.T., III, 441) schematism is portrayed as a means whereby 'pure sensuousness and pure understanding, which were formerly expressed as absolute opposites, are now united'. Hegel adds that this process involves an intuitive understanding or an intellectual intuition, though Kant regrettably failed to see the point. But it is in his references to the *Critique of Judgment* that Hegel is most insistent on Kant's being his forerunner. 'The Reflective Power of Judgment', he declares without qualification in the *Encyclopaedia* (§55), is invested by Kant with the function of an Intuitive Understanding. That is to say, whereas the particulars had hitherto appeared, so far as the universal or abstract identity was concerned, adventitious and incapable of being deduced from it, the intuitive understanding apprehends the particulars as moulded and formed by the universal itself. Experience presents such universalised particulars in the products of art and of organic nature.

This is why, in a passage already quoted from *Glauben und Wissen* (E.T., 91), Hegel could say that 'Kant himself recognized in the beautiful an intuition other than the sensuous'. Of course he did nothing of the kind, and Hegel knew that he did not. Kant said we have to judge beautiful natural objects and living things according to special principles which are not objectively valid in the way the principles of the understanding are objectively valid; we have to look at them as if they were designed when we have no reason to think that they are. When something is designed it is produced according to a concept in a sense; the concept determines what shall come into existence and what relations its different parts shall have one to another. In so far as we make reference to design in judging beauties of nature or living things it might be said that we apprehend particulars 'as moulded and formed' by some universal. But it is not true, of course, that the design itself conjures the particulars into existence—it might remain unexecuted—and in any case Kant insists that it is only a question of thinking *as if* design were involved; we have no right to say that it is.

Kant's caution about design in the third Critique was certainly not to Hegel's taste; as Hegel saw it Kant had grasped the truth in this area, only to turn away from it in an almost arbitrary way. And the same thing was broadly true of the discussion of the idea of an intuitive understanding to be found in §§76–77 of the *Critique of Judgment*. 'It will always stand out as a marvel', wrote Hegel in the *Science of Logic* (E.T., 592),

> how the Kantian philosophy recognized the relation of thought to sensuous reality, beyond which it did not advance, as only a relative relation of mere Appearance, and perfectly well recognized and enunciated a higher unity of both in the Idea in general and, for example, in the Idea of an intuitive understanding, and yet stopped short at this relative relation and the assertion that the Notion is and remains utterly separate from reality—thus asserting as truth what is declared to be finite cognition, and denouncing as an unjustified extravagance and a figment of thought what is recognized as truth and of which it established the specific notion.

According to *Glauben und Wissen* (E.T., 89) Kant admitted that we are 'necessarily driven' to the Idea of 'an archetypal intuitive intellect', but nevertheless refused it reality. He preferred to rely on 'experience and empirical psychology' for his conclusion that 'the human cognitive faculty essentially consists in the way it appears, namely in this process from the universal to the particular or back again from the particular to the universal'. As if, Hegel adds, he had no counter-experience in his own grasp of the idea of an intuitive understanding. 'He himself shows that his cognitive faculty is aware not only of the appearance and of the separation of the possible and actual in it, but also of Reason and the In-itself.' Both thoughts were present to his mind, that of an intuitive and that of a discursive understanding, but 'his nature depised the necessity of thinking the Rational . . . and decided without reservation for appearance'.

This argument as it stands is so embarrassingly bad that it demands further consideration. It begins, presumably, from Kant's frequent description of the human intelligence as 'discursive', meaning in the first place that it operates on material supplied to it from without. If we are to understand the notion of a discursive intellect we must have some idea of what it would be for an intellect not to be discursive, and that perhaps is all that is involved in the necessity of the idea of an intuitive understanding. Kant sometimes says (e.g. B139) that we cannot 'form the least conception' of an understanding of that sort; he may mean by this that we cannot characterize its knowing in any positive way, but only in negative terms, by contrast with our own. It seems to be such a conception that is put forward in §§76–77 of the *Critique of Judgment*. Now Hegel says nothing about the antithesis suggested here between a negative and a positive idea of an intuitive understanding, just as Descartes in the third Meditation made no distinction between a positive and a negative conception of the idea of God which he said he found within himself. Descartes argued that the 'objective reality' of this idea was such that it could have been caused by nothing else than an actually existent God; his argument is weakened, if not destroyed, if we have to define the content of the idea in negative terms ('intelligent, but not subject to the limitations of human intelligence; active, but free of the obstacles which obstruct human activity', etc.). Hegel of course produced no such crude inference from effect to cause. But it looks as if Kant's choice of discursive consciousness as setting the standard by which philosophical theories are to be judged, a choice so much derided by Hegel, may well have had something to do with his belief that the alternative remained shadowy and indeterminate, like its counterpart the noumenon in the positive sense of the term (B307). Hegel would have disagreed with this characterization, but it is not clear that the view he presents is couched in a truly positive way.

Had, however, Kant been questioned about his choice he would certainly have said that he made it primarily because experience shows that ours is a discursive consciousness: we do make a distinction between possibility and actuality, and we do think that no amount of reflection on concepts will show in what particular situations they apply. Concepts and intuitions are different in kind, even it if is only when they co-operate that we have the chance of attaining knowledge. Hegel does not deny that Kant is right as far as the appearances are concerned. But he maintains, in effect, that a philosophical theory such as Kant is putting forward cannot be authenticated by a simple appeal to fact in this way. Philosophy, as opposed to the special sciences, is not subject to judgment by appeal to fact, since facts reflect theories and hidden presuppositions, and can stand only if these can survive critical examination. To authenticate a philosophy you have to compare it with rival theories, subject it and them to careful internal criticism, and see if your view survives unscathed. Hegel would not have allowed that the theories which lie behind our ordinary consciousness of the world and our everyday experience of ourselves can survive such critical scrutiny, and the elaborate story he tells in the *Phenomenology* and elsewhere is intended to show both why we naturally adopt such views and why and how they must be superseded.

What this comes to, perhaps, is that it is unfair to judge Hegel on the assumptions of his opponents, seeing that he explicitly dissents from these assumptions. We cannot properly reproach him with confusing the concept of what he called (*Science of Logic*, E.T., 789) 'the self-producing Notion' with the actuality of something answering that description, since he did not accept the implied distinction between concepts as mere possibilities and intuitions as actualities. We can, however, ask him to clarify his own account of the relationships between thoughts and things on the one hand, and thought and sensation on the other. The quotations given above already show that this is not an easy subject. They present the picture, particularly apparent in the long quotation from the *Science of Logic* on p. 103, of a thinking which is not complete in itself but positively demands embodiment in the concrete; they also suggest that it is a mistake to think of such thought as exercising itself on a material which has an independent nature of its own. The antithesis between subject and object is one formed within an original unity, not something we have to accept as valid as it stands. This view disposes of subjective idealism, since it shows that the mind which makes nature cannot be the finite mind of everyday experience. But does it explain why reality takes the particular form it does? To answer that we must consider what Hegel made of sensation and in what way he supposed that it contributed to knowledge. Let us be clear from the start that he never claimed that sensation was an eliminable factor in human knowledge, however refined that knowledge became. Leibniz presented sensation as confused thinking; for him the content of every sense judgment could ideally be re-expressed in terms which were purely intellectual. Hegel by contrast associated sensation with the immediate element in knowledge, and argued that there could be no knowledge at all unless and until it was there. Sensation had to do with the sensibility, and the sensibility connected with the senses, the sense-organs and in general the body.

The knowledge in which Hegel was interested was knowledge obtained by a mind which was essentially embodied, and sensation could not be dismissed without forgetting the embodiment. Those who think of Hegel as an arch-rationalist should read the section on 'the Soul' in the third part of Hegel's *Encyclopaedia* and notice what Hegel has to say not only about the physical basis of feelings but also about the corporeal expressions of inner states.

But though sensation can thus no more be left out of account in the Hegelian scheme of things than can the body, that still says nothing of its actual part in knowledge. Plainly Hegel cannot think of it as a source of fully formed data in itself, as some modern philosophers have done. To do that would be to make it wholly independent of thought, and in so doing revive the possibility that thought cannot get at reality. But if it is neither reducible to thought nor independent of it, what is it? The Hegelian answer must be that it is what thought naturally makes articulate, something which thought presupposes and develops but which cannot be described at its own level. Sensation or feeling is an indispensable element in sense-perception, and indeed in knowledge generally; without it concrete grasp of what is individually real would not be possible. But it is not experienced in isolation: we become aware of it only as we make its content explicit in judgment. Sense-perception is, as Kant said, a process in which concepts are brought to bear on intuitions. But it is not true, as he seemed to suggest, that concepts and intuitions, though significant only in combination, nevertheless *exist* in isolation, each with a nature of its own.

This view that the relationship of sense and thought is not one of outright opposition but rather of complementary development seems to me to deserve independent attention. It has the advantage of allowing us to say that not just concepts but percepts too have no real existence apart from judgments; it goes along with the view that the world is everything that is the case, the totality of facts not of things. But of course those who subscribe to these doctrines rarely have much to say about 'the self-producing Notion' and tend to regard talk about intuitive elements in the human understanding with deep suspicion. Is this simply prejudice on their part?

It must be confessed that Hegel's own position on this subject appears to involve an important ambiguity. On the one hand he argues, as we have just seen, for the indispensability of sensation, which he sees as the immediate component in knowledge. But at the same time he opposes the Kantian view that the human intellect is purely discursive, suggests that this is true, if at all, only of the abstract thinking of the understanding and holds out the prospect of a superior form of thinking, revealed by and exemplified in philosophical thought, which will 'pass over into' or 'produce' reality from 'its own resources'. That Hegel took Kant's idea of an intuitive understanding as embodying an ideal for human thought and not just a sketch of what might be involved in the workings of a divine mind is apparent from his numerous critical comments. Yet intuitive understanding as described by Kant was a form of experience in which mediacy and immediacy, to use Hegel's language, were inextricably intertwined, so much so that in it no distinction could be drawn between merely possible thoughts and actual situations answering to them. Whatever such an understanding thought would *ipso facto* be actual, just as whatever Midas touched turned to gold. It is hard to see how on these terms Hegel could say that thought finds sensation indispensable. It perhaps needs it to get started on the road to knowledge, but once it is in its stride simply swallows it up.

Hegel is consistently scornful of the Kantian idea that the ideal of pure reason, to cast the results of our first-order enquiries into fully systematic form, has a purely regulative force; to speak in this manner is, he thinks, to be content with a mere 'ought to be' and leads on naturally to faith in the transcendent (the ideal is not realized in the world we know, but in another world which lies beyond this one and is not accessible to reason). Yet in practice he comes near accepting something like the Kantian notion himself, in so far as he takes the results of the sciences and tries not to replace them but to find sense in them. He hopes to rethink these results and represent them in the light of the resources of philosophy, but has no thought of producing new facts from the depths of his own consciousness. The Notion as he operates with it certainly strives to 'understand the world, to appropriate it and subdue it' to itself, to use phrases quoted earlier from the *Encyclopaedia*; it does its very best to 'idealize' phenomena, to employ another Hegelian term. But how much it can achieve depends upon something more than mere ingenuity or depth of thinking; it depends also on the nature of the material on which the philosopher brings his thought to bear. Hegel is quite clear that he cannot as philosopher take any liberties he pleases with material of this sort. And it is interesting to observe that, for all his criticisms of empiricist philosophies, he expressed in one of his early essays a strong respect for what he called 'pure' empiricism, which insisted against philosophers of the understanding on attention to concrete facts. Empiricism is here the standpoint of common sense, and it is important to make clear that Hegel thought of himself as in a way its champion, certainly not as an opponent pledged to its destruction (see *The Scientific Ways of Treating Law*,[8] E.T., 69–70).

Yet if we allow Hegel to appear on the scene in this moderate guise it is difficult to see any difference of principle between his philosophy and Kant's. There are of course many differences of detail, some of them of very considerable importance. Kant thought that the categories were fixed for all time; so far as he was concerned there was no question of deepening

[8] Translated by T. M. Knox (Philadelphia: University of Pennsylvania Press, 1975).

our understanding of the experienced world, except by acquiring more facts or establishing more empirical connections. Hegel by contrast argued that categorial thinking was of its nature endlessly self-critical; history had shown that there were many sets of terms in which to take the world, and philosophy could do something to put them in an order of adequacy. The categorial apparatus proffered by Hegel is altogether richer than Kant's, who after all put forward only five principles of the understanding (six if we count the general principle of the Analogies), together with a small group of regulative principles of reason and reflective judgment. Although, as Hegel saw, Kant laid the foundations for philosophy of nature (and philosophy of history as well) he did so almost with reluctance, laying constant emphasis on how little way philosophy could go in these matters. Hegel had no such reservations: he was confident in his pure philosophy and extraordinarily bold in its application. He also had, as it happened, a wealth of empirical knowledge, especially of the social world, considerably greater than Kant's. He sometimes, no doubt, talked nonsense, as Kant rarely did, but he also produced applied philosophy of a brilliance which exceeds anything in Kant. We do not find in the latter's writings anything to match the perceptive analysis of the *Philosophy of Right*, or even the discussions of the *Philosophy of World History*. Yet it must be insisted that there is nothing in these works which could not in principle have been produced by Kant, had his interests been different and his imagination wider. The pretence Hegel makes in his logical writings to have laid bare a way of thinking which Kant glimpsed dimly but then turned away from altogether is not made good when we turn to other parts of his work. Hegel had an endless love/hate relationship with Kant. He admired him and at the same time he despised him. Perhaps he should have asked himself whether the shortcomings he saw in Kant were not necessarily features of his own thought as well.

Fichte and German Idealism

PATRICK GARDINER

Fichte's reputation at the present time is in some respects a curious one. On the one hand, he is by common consent acknowledged to have exercised a dominant influence upon the development of German thought during the opening decades of the nineteenth century. Thus from a specifically philosophical point of view he is regarded as an innovator who (for good or ill) played a decisive role in transforming Kant's transcendental idealism into the absolute idealism of his immediate successors, while at a more general level he is customarily seen as having put into currency certain persuasive conceptions which contributed—less directly but no less surely—to the emergence and spread of romanticism in some of its varied and ramifying forms. On the other hand, however, it is noticeable that detailed consideration of his work has not figured prominently in the recent revival of concern with post-Kantian thought as a whole which has been manifested by philosophers of the English-speaking world. Although his name is frequently mentioned in that connection, one suspects that his books may not be so often read. In part this may be due to his particular mode of expounding his views, which at times attains a level of opacity that can make even Hegel's obscurest passages seem comparatively tractable. It is also true that Fichte's principal theoretical works—if not his semi-popular writings—are largely devoid of the allusions to scientific, historical, psychological or cultural matters with which his German contemporaries were prone to illustrate their philosophical doctrines and enliven their more abstract discussions: there is a daunting aridity about much of what he wrote which can raise nagging doubts in the modern reader's mind about the actual issues that are in question. Yet the fact remains that by the close of the eighteenth century his ideas had already made a profound impact, capturing the imagination of a host of German thinkers and intellectuals. The problem therefore arises as to what preoccupations, current at the time, they owed their indubitable appeal and to what puzzles they were welcomed as proffering a solution. If these can be identified, it may become at least partially intelligible that Fichte should have been widely regarded as having provided a framework within which certain hitherto intractable difficulties could be satisfactorily reformulated and resolved. Let me accordingly begin by saying something about them.

Fichte once described his own philosophy as amounting from beginning to end to no more than an 'analysis of the idea of freedom'. However that may be, it is undoubtedly true that from an early stage in his philosophical career the question of whether, and if so in what sense, human freedom could be vindicated assumed an overwhelming importance in his eyes and that it continued in one form or another to haunt him for the rest of his life. Nor was he alone in this. Thus he came to intellectual maturity in the seventeen-eighties, during a period when the belief that the operations of the human mind were as susceptible to mechanistic explanation in terms of invariant regularities or laws as those of physical nature had in many quarters achieved an almost axiomatic status. Upholders of such a view, which was associated in the first instance with representatives of the Enlightenment in France but which also found eloquent adherents elsewhere, may have differed amongst themselves as to the precise nature and foundations of the laws in question. None the less, that were united in the conviction that in the final analysis all that men thought and did could be explained as the necessary consequences of antecedent factors—whether physiological, psychological or environmental—which determined them as rigorously as those that governed occurrences in the inanimate sphere investigated by the natural sciences; only irrationality or a misplaced vanity could lead people to imagine that they were somehow exempt from the causal uniformities that manifested themselves throughout the universe and whose ubiquity had been triumphantly demonstrated by the successes of Newtonian physics. If followed that there was no acceptable alternative to treating the human world, in all its aspects, as a mechanically ordered system wherein traditional doctrines of 'free will' had no place: the latter must either be ruthlessly re-interpreted in the interests of intellectual hygiene or else simply discarded, along with other outdated theological and metaphysical dogmas, as the contemptible remants of pre-scientific superstition. If these consequences were repugnant to orthodox religious opinion this was hardly a matter for surprise, still less for regret.

Yet while there were some, in Fichte's time as in our own, who were prepared happily, even eagerly, to embrace such a conclusion, there were others (especially in Germany) for whom it was a source of intense disquiet; moreover, their discontent, though partly influenced by religious concerns, by no means wholly derived from these. Two further considerations, both of which later found expression in Fichte's own writings and struck a responsive chord in his readers, may be picked out as being of particular significance in the present context.

The first involved a deep distaste, not easy to define with any precision but nevertheless profoundly felt, with an overall picture of the universe in which human existence was seemingly conceived as a mere appendage of nature and where nature itself was presented in a way that reduced it ultimately to no more than an abstract system of interacting material particles—'the same old atoms shuffling about in accordance with the same old laws', as one modern commentator has succinctly put it.[1]

[1] A. O. Lovejoy, *The Reason, the Understanding, and Time* (Baltimore: Johns Hopkins Press, 1961), 150.

Apart from anything else, a picture of this kind was considered to rob human life of the spontaneity and variety which were its distinctive features and to obscure something to which all history, including that of the sciences themselves, bore witness at every point—the palpable creativity of the intellect and its capacity for transforming both itself and the world in novel and unpredictable ways. The second consideration, though not unconnected with the first, was more specific and pertained to the asseverations of immediate practical experience. Thus it was all very well to speak as if doctrines affirming the freedom of the will belonged to the prehistory of human knowledge and could be treated as so much metaphysical lumber which we should be far better off without. It was not clear, however, that those who adopted this confident tone had understood the full implications of what they were proposing. For the ideas they dismissed in so cavalier a fashion could not properly be portrayed as if they were no more than the ghosts of antiquated theory, with about as much relevance to everyday thought and behaviour as the abstractions and rarefied essences of the schoolmen. On the contrary, they remained alive and active, being intrinsic to our awareness of what it was to participate as purposive agents in the world and representing an essential component of the structure within which our practical consciousness as a whole, and in particular our moral consciousness, was set. When such points were recognised and taken into account, the suggestion that to accept a thorough-going determinism need entail no radical dislocation of our ordinary beliefs acquired—to put it mildly—a paradoxical air. How far was it really possible to do so without undermining the entire conception of ourselves as autonomous sources of deliberation and choice, capable of determining our behaviour in accordance with reasons which we had freely decided upon or endorsed? Was not such a supposition, even if it were granted that it could be coherently entertained, destructive of the very notion of human action as this was customarily used and understood?

It was, of course, precisely contentions of the latter kind that were accorded primacy of place in the moral philosophy of Kant. Unlike some of his compatriots, however, Kant did not think that it was justifiable, or indeed possible, blankly to reject the determinist thesis out of hand; rather he believed that an account of man's status as a rational and practical being could be provided which fully accommodated the considerations just mentioned without in any way impugning the legitimacy of treating human behaviour as being at the same time subject to invariant causal laws. The materials for resolving the alleged dilemma were in fact to be found in the doctrines of transcendental idealism, according to which a fundamental distinction must be drawn between the phenomenal world, or reality as it appears to a conscious subject, and the noumenal or 'intelligible' world of things as they are in themselves. Regarded as empirical entities we necessarily belong to the former realm and as such must be conceived of as conforming to the same ordering principles as those that govern the rest of nature; to that extent the scientifically minded theorists associated with the Enlightenment had been correct. But, notoriously, this was for Kant by no means the whole story. For he also maintained that another standpoint could be adopted that transcended the limits of a purely naturalistic approach and from which human beings might be viewed, not as phenomenal 'appearances' falling under the causality of nature, but rather as non-empirical centres of consciousness and will; in this sense they could be regarded as members of the noumenal sphere, capable of issuing and obeying laws which were 'independent of nature' and which had their source in reason alone. Moreover Kant claimed, somewhat obscurely, that these two distinguishable ways of looking at ourselves were entirely compatible with one another and that no clash need therefore occur between, on the one hand, the scientific conception of what went on in the human world and, on the other, those assumptions about the reality of freedom which were, he fully agreed, integral to our outlook as practical and moral beings; as he himself put it, 'that our reason has causality, or at least that we represent it to ourselves as having causality, is evident from the *imperatives* which in all matters of conduct we impose as rules upon our active powers'.[2]

In a general way, and whatever Kant might have thought it appropriate to affirm at the empirical level about human beings and their activities, his own version of idealism appeared to his contemporaries to involve a drastic transformation of the terms in which it had become customary to present the relation between the human mind and the natural order. Prevalent views typically subordinated the former to the latter and portrayed consciousness, under both its cognitive and its practical aspects, in a manner that conformed to the interpretative scheme which had been successfully applied to the investigation of the natural world; hence the various mechanistic models and hypotheses that had been introduced to explain thought and action alike. In place of these Kant had elaborated notions which stressed the creative and constructive functions of the intellect, such functions being envisaged as in some fashion set apart from the realm of nature and as contributing to its overall character. Theoretically speaking, they were seen as responsible for the pervasive structure and form, though not for the sensory content, which the world of experience as a whole displayed; while at the level of practice they were to be understood as generating rational principles which could prescribe courses of action opposed to those prompted by the sensuously conceived inclinations and passions emphasized by much Enlightenment psychology. Mind and nature had thus been pictured in a profoundly changed perspective. Kant himself might have believed that, in so presenting them, he had not really

[2] *Critique of Pure Reason*, A547, B575.

put in question the essential insights embodied in the Enlightenment position; his aim had rather been one of providing a corrective to certain limitations inherent in it, both by removing defects in its theory of know-ledge and by making room for dimensions of human thought which it tended to ignore or override. To Fichte, however, it seemed that the innovations introduced carried far-reaching implications which even their author had not adequately appreciated. Only when these had been fully explored and developed, and their misleading association with the relics of superseded doctrine finally severed, could their truly revolutionary import at last become manifest. Fichte claimed to have performed such a service in his own philosophy. To this claim we must now turn.

Fichte first encountered Kant's ideas through the *Critique of Practical Reason*, which he read in his late twenties, and it was this work above all others that made a lasting impact upon his mind. His own philosophical reputation originally derived from a contribution to critical theology so deeply influenced by Kantian conceptions that it was taken to be by the master himself; when its true authorship became known he was appointed to a professorship at Jena at the early age of thirty-two. During the same year (1794) the first version of his most famous book, the *Science of Knowledge* (*Wissenschaftslehre*), appeared, and in this case he went out of his way to stress its Kantian affiliations through two Introductions to the work which he appended three years later. In the first of these he expressed his indebtedness to Kant's revisionary achievement in phil-osophy, while in the second he argued for the view that what he had written was 'perfectly in accordance with the teaching of Kant' and that this had been 'increasingly confirmed by the continuing elaboration of his system'.[3] Yet he was at the same time quite aware that such an opinion was by no means shared by reviewers and critics of the *Wissenschaftslehre*, many of whom dissented from it and one of whom had cited Kant himself as firmly dissociating his position from Fichte's own. In reply, Fichte was mainly content to argue that, since Kant's basic theses had been generally misunderstood, it was not surprising that their true relation to his own philosophy had been correspondingly misapprehended; while if Kant, too, had demurred, it might be because that 'reverend sage' had not read Fichte's actual writings and had relied instead on inaccurate expositions of them. In any case he wished to insist that his system was in all essentials continuous with the Kantian.

Despite the vehemence of his language one wonders how far Fichte really believed this. Admittedly his attitude towards those who dis-agreed with him was seldom conspicuously temperate; but the peculiar irritation he showed in the present instance may have been due to an

---

[3] *Science of Knowledge, with the First and Second Introductions*, ed. and trans. P. Heath and J. Lachs (New York: Appleton–Century–Crofts, 1970), 43.

uneasy sense that his claims must appear to the most sympathetic reader as somewhat lacking in plausibility. It was one thing to hold that he had taken as his starting point certain leading Kantian themes; it was another to assert that the conclusions he had reached were consistent with Kant's own doctrines. The latter contention was extremely hard to square with any natural interpretation of Kant's views, if only because Fichte's thinking seemed to have issued in the construction of a speculative ontology which was sharply at variance with Kant's conception of philosophy as a pre-eminently critical enterprise directed towards establishing the scope and determinate limits of human reason. Such an outcome, however unexpected, had—as we shall see—two principal sources. Partly it arose through emphasizing and exploiting the libertarian and idealist strands in the Kantian theory, especially its insistence upon the autonomy of the self and upon the contribution made by the subject to the character of experience. And partly it derived from an attempt to eliminate what Fichte was not alone in conceiving to be a glaring inconsistency in Kantian epistemology, although he was exceptional in attributing it to Kant's interpreters rather than to Kant himself: this was the claim, already referred to, that there exist noumena or things in themselves upon which the realm of phenomenal appearance is in some way dependent. The consequence was a system that stood to its predecessor in a relation not without parallels in the genealogy of philosophical theories. Certain features characteristic of its ancestor were preserved in an accentuated form; others, by contrast, had either not survived at all or else re-emerged in so altered a shape as to be barely recognizable. In any event, the face it presented to the world seemed beyond question to be a new one. And if there were some whom it disturbed or dismayed, there were also those over whom it exerted a powerful fascination.

Fichte made his central preoccupation with the problem of freedom apparent at the outset, when he declared that the outstanding philosophical issue of his time concerned the status of what he called 'dogmatism'. For him dogmatism covered an amalgam of notions which he sometimes explicitly connected with a Spinozist conception of reality but which he also employed in a more general way to embrace all scientifically inspired attempts to provide materialistic or mechanistic accounts of human consciousness and behaviour. Such accounts, whatever form they might take, were viewed by him as constituting a *prima facie* threat to the validity of ideas like choice and responsibility which were fundamental to our experience as moral beings; thus far, at least, his concerns may be said to have paralleled those shown by Kant when confronted by similar considerations. But Fichte's reaction was altogether more extreme. In the first place, he implied—unlike Kant—that some element of spiritual weakness, of temperamental passivity or inertia, attached to the upholders of such interpretations of the human condition; the idea of being a mere appendage or product of nature, acted upon rather than acting and forever governed by factors beyond their control, possessed a certain lure for many persons who were by no means averse to regarding themselves as helpless objects rather than as self-determining subjects—'the majority of men', he wrote at one point, 'could sooner be brought to believe themselves a piece of lava in the moon than to take themselves for a *self*'.[4] Thus he often spoke as if there were something perverse and self-deceiving, and not just mistaken, in adhering to beliefs of this sort. Fichte's reaction was, however, more extreme in a further respect and one that was of greater relevance to the development of his own system. Kant had attempted to mediate between a deterministic and a libertarian outlook, holding that we could consistently treat ourselves from a theoretical standpoint as subject to the natural order and from a practical one as essentially free; for him, moreover, it was characteristically within contexts demanding the exercise of moral reasoning and choice that we found ourselves committed to a libertarian position. Fichte's philosophy, on the other hand, involved a wide-ranging and comprehensive extension of Kant's conception of the practical dimension of human consciousness, an extension which took as its point of departure the direct intimations of subjective self-awareness and which finally issued in a perspective on life and experience that was far removed from anything to be found in what Kant himself had written. It is true that Fichte did not wish to deny that it was possible, and for certain purposes quite legitimate, for us to regard ourselves under an aspect in which we appeared as what he called 'organized creations of nature'; he did not, however, believe—for reasons which he never perhaps made sufficiently clear—that this entailed a radical dualism of the kind enshrined in the Kantian attempt to show how the respective requirements of the theoretical and the practical consciousness could be rendered mutually coherent. Rather, he implied that it was necessary at the outset to acknowledge the primacy of the practical standpoint, according priority to the crucial part played by the notion of agency in any adequate account of our role in the world and of the terms in which we conceived it. And it is here, if anywhere, that one touches upon the nerve of his thought, the focal point from which his claims to originality as a philosopher who exercised a potent influence upon subsequent speculation ultimately derived. Yet the contention as it stands is a vague one, open to more than one interpretation. How should it be understood?

As an initial step towards unravelling what Fichte had in mind it is necessary to look at his account of the concept which he himself treated

---

[4] Ibid., 162. In his tendency to treat philosophical views as owing their appeal to emotional or temperamental factors, and not merely to intellectual considerations, Fichte anticipated a variety of other nineteenth-century writers, including Kierkegaard and Nietzsche.

as fundamental. This was the notion of the 'I' (*das Ich*)—the self or ego—which represented an ineliminable component of every aspect of our conscious life and which could be immediately recognized through what Fichte was prone to term 'intellectual intuition'. The latter expression, with its rationalist associations and the suggestion it carries of referring to a faculty of non-empirical cognition, might lead one to suppose that he had in view something recondite or mysterious. He hastened to inform his readers, however, that this was not so. What he was talking about was, on the contrary, wholly familiar and such that a moment's reflection would show it to occur in the most mundane everyday experience. To grasp what was meant we need only consider what was involved in doing something, however trivial; for it amounted (in Fichte's words) to 'the immediate consciousness that I act, and what I enact: it is that whereby I know something because I do it'.[5] In this sense, it could be affirmed that whenever we engaged in activity of any sort we were aware of ourselves as performing, or as intending to perform, whatever it was that was in question; such consciousness of ourselves as active, which was primitive and underived, both accompanied and at the same time was distinguishable from our knowledge of the actual content—the observable or describable features—of what we did or proposed to do. If, for example, I decide to put into effect some course of action, subsequently carrying it out, then I am certainly aware of what is aimed at and of its eventual realization. But (Fichte thinks) we shall seriously distort the situation if we portray it as being one in which all that happens, all that I am conscious of, is a sequence of discrete presentations—in this case, the idea of a certain thing's being performed followed by a perception of the actual performance. Such a picture, reminiscent of the accounts offered by empiricists like Hume, treats consciousness as an 'inert stage on which presentations succeed one another', and it is quite unacceptable. For it omits something indispensable, namely, my concurrent awareness of myself as the 'active principle' that is responsible for the formation of the intention and for its fulfilment in reality alike. It is precisely because of the continuing awareness I possess of my 'real efficacy' that I treat the intention as being more than simply an ideational content which happens to be followed by a sensory presentation involving my behaviour. Yet that would be all that it could conceivably be for me if my consciousness were reducible to a flow of impressions, passively apprehended, on the Humean pattern. Fichte believed that the latter model was in fact profoundly untrue to the pervasive conception we have of ourselves in the course of our ordinary experience: 'I cannot take a step, move hand or foot, without an intellectual intuition of my self-consciousness in these acts; only so do I know that *I* do it,

[5] Ibid., 38.

only so do I distinguish my action, and myself therein, from the object of the action before me'.[6]

In putting forward such phenomenological points—which in some ways invite comparison with those propounded by his French contemporary, Maine de Biran—Fichte was none the less insistent that he should not be taken as trying to revive the idea that self-consciousness implied awareness of the ego as some kind of immaterial or mental 'substance'; whatever his dissent from him on other counts, on this one he was in agreement with Hume. The 'intuition' referred to was of 'sheer activity', not of a 'static' thing or entity, and he thought that all attempts to reify the self, to freeze it within the categories of objective existence and to endow it with substantial properties was already to take a fatal step on the road to 'dogmatism' and the denial of the subject's essential freedom. Instead we were obliged to think of ourselves as 'self-active', 'not as determined by things but as determining them'[7]—a notion which, as he acknowledged, had strongly Kantian overtones. For all that, however, his own account embodied a significant shift in outlook and emphasis. Not only was Kant's theory of the self formulated within the framework of an obscure dualism, according to which deterministic assumptions still held good at the purely cognitive level. It was also stated in a fashion that implied further divisions: the theoretical use of reason was contrasted with its practical employment, while within the sphere of the practical itself a fundamental distinction was drawn between behaviour governed by respect for the moral law and behaviour motivated by purely sensuous inclination. Fichte, in effect, drastically simplified this picture and in doing so radically changed its outlines.

In the first place, he treated awareness of self-activity as a residual but none the less irreducible and pervasive feature of consciousness under all its varying forms; such awareness was sufficient, without transcending the bounds of experience, to preclude us from assimilating ourselves to the category of merely objective or 'natural' phenomena. Secondly, he asserted that there was no justification for insulating our moral propensities from our non-moral ones; both could in the end be traced back to the same volitional source, the behaviour that issued from them representing simply the distinguishable ways in which we were capable of expressing ourselves as unitary beings. Thirdly, and perhaps most significantly, he implied that a true recognition of our essentially active nature as revealed by self-consciousness set in a quite fresh light the general question of how we apprehend reality and attempt to understand it. Traditional distinctions between knowing and doing, which neatly separated the two into independent compartments, appeared less convincing when we

[6] Ibid., 38.
[7] Ibid. 41.

were seen to be primarily centres of activity, the initiators of projects which we sought to realize in concrete form. For, once this was granted, it was no longer plausible to assume that our habitual modes of approaching and interpreting experience could be considered in isolation from the needs and interests that informed our attitudes as purposive agents. As Fichte put it in his essay, The Vocation of Man', 'we do not act because we know, but we know because we are called upon to act—the practical reason is the root of all reason'.[8] Cognition being ultimately dependent upon practical demands and requirements, it followed that the forms taken by the first could not adequately be comprehended without reference to the second; the practical orientation of our thinking had a vital bearing upon the ways in which we grasped, ordered and conceptualized what was presented to us and upon the classifications we found it natural to impose. In this manner the world as we experienced it was not the 'neutral', self-sufficient domain it was typically portrayed as being. On the contrary, when viewed as the field of our diverse needs, aims, and—Fichte was at pains to stress— moral aspirations, it was in a crucial sense 'our world', falling within a perspective that could not fail to reflect these at every turn. At the level of day-to-day living, phenomena were characteristically apprehended 'through want, desire and enjoyment': 'not by the mental conception', Fichte wrote, 'but by hunger, thirst and their satisfaction, does anything become for me food and drink'.[9] And it was partly in the light of similar considerations that he claimed that, from an ethical standpoint, 'my world is the object and sphere of my duties, and absolutely nothing else; there is no other world for me, and no other qualities of my world than what are implied in this'.[10] Governed throughout by my moral preoccupations, it inevitably bore their imprint.

Thus far, and with these aspects of his thought before us, it is not unreasonable to see Fichte as the forerunner of a host of philosophers, ranging from the pragmatists of the last century to existentialist and analytic writers of the present one, who have—albeit in widely varying ways— emphasized the role played by agency in shaping and structuring human knowledge and who have protested that exclusively contemplative models of cognition have been responsible for pervasive errors in epistemology. Both Heidegger and Sartre, for instance, have underlined the extent to which the world of everyday life is necessarily experienced in 'instrumentalist' terms, our apprehension of what we find being filtered through the complex network of tasks and practical concerns which determines our approach to it and from which whatever we perceive derives its particular significance or 'meaning'; in Sartre's words, 'since

[8] *Fichte's Popular Works*, I, trans. W. Smith (London: Trübner & Co., 1889), 421.

[9] Ibid., 418.

[10] Ibid., 419.

the world reveals itself across our conduct, it is the intentional choice of the end which reveals the world, and the world is revealed as this or that (in this or that order) according to the end chosen'.[11] And if such points are often reminiscent of what Fichte had to say on the same theme, so too—although from a quite different angle—are the recurrent suggestions in Wittgenstein's later work that the quest after indubitable foundations in the sense typified by much traditional epistemology is misconceived, and that the process of cognitive justification comes to an end, not in certain propositions 'striking us immediately as true', but rather in our readiness to act in certain ways.[12] At one point Wittgenstein quotes from Goethe's *Faust* the dictum 'In the beginning was the deed', and this could almost serve as a motto for Fichte's own approach to problems of the kind that philosophers have frequently raised regarding the status of our fundamental beliefs. In our capacity as agents, Fichte maintained, we found ourselves unavoidably committed to an interpretation of experience which was not in the final analysis susceptible to justification in theoretical terms and which instead had its roots in the demands we made as beings with concrete purposes to fulfil and projects to realize: it was here, not elsewhere, that we should look for an answer to the sceptical doubts apt to assail us when we indulged in free-floating reflection of the sort that involved an abstraction from the practical dimensions of our life and thought. For within the context of practical endeavour and moral striving questions concerning the reality of what we encountered in consciousness, of a world or 'non-ego' set over against the active subject or self, lost all force and substance and could not even properly be said to arise; we were bound to posit such a world in the course of fulfilling our aims or duties and could not coherently envisage ourselves as agents without it. As Fichte himself expressed the point, in so far as 'we are compelled to believe that we act, and that we ought to act in a certain manner, we are compelled to assume a certain sphere for this action'; ultimately it was from 'this necessity of action' that our 'consciousness of the actual world' proceeded, and not the other way about.[13]

Yet, whatever the intrinsic interest or merits of such claims, it would none the less be wrong to suppose that they represented all, or even the major part, of what Fichte finally wished to maintain. It might be true that, when discussing the structure and conditions of ordinary experience, he offered an account in which the primacy of agency was stressed. It was, however, no part of his purpose to question the role played in such experience by the idea of an objectively conceived natural order; rather,

[11] J.-P. Sartre, *Being and Nothingness*, trans. H. E. Barnes (London: Methuen, 1957), 477.

[12] L. Wittgenstein, *On Certainty*, trans. D. Paul and G. E. M. Anscombe (Oxford Basil Blackwell, 1969), §§ 110, 148, 204, 342.

[13] *Fichte's Popular Works*, I, 421.

as has just been seen, the latter was treated by him as a necessary correlative or counterpart of the notion we have of ourselves as active subjects. But this was only part of the story. For he also believed that it was possible to provide an interpretation of existence as a whole which transcended the everyday standpoint and according to which the primordial activity of the ego as revealed in self-consciousness could be shown to have much more extensive and dramatic implications than any mentioned so far. To understand his reasons for making this claim we must go back once more to Kant, in this case to the doctrine of things in themselves.

That doctrine (it will be recalled) involved the contention that, while the overall *form* of the phenomenal realm derived from the operations of the intellect, the sensuous representations that constituted, so to speak, its 'filling' had a non-empirical source or 'ground' which was necessarily inaccessible to consciousness: to this extent, the world of nature was only in part of our own making, its sensory content having an independent origin. But was such a theory plausible, or even intelligible? In Fichte's view it was utterly unacceptable, amounting to a 'reckless' attempt to combine elements that had been drawn from two inherently opposed philosophical positions: from materialism the notion of 'things in themselves making impressions upon us', from idealism the notion of 'all existence arising solely out of the thinking of the intellect'.[14] Furthermore, it stood in palpable conflict with a cardinal thesis which Kant had repeatedly proclaimed throughout the *Critique of Pure Reason*, the thesis, namely, that categories of the understanding, like *substance* and *cause*, could not validly be employed outside the field of possible experience. Hence there could be no warrant for using them to arrive at 'the assumption of a something distinct from the self, as a ground of the empirical content of knowledge'.[15] Yet this was just what the theory in question required us to do.

In general, indeed, Fichte considered the doctrine of the *Ding an sich* to be so radically confused, so sharply at variance with the central tenets of the critical teaching, that he was reluctant to ascribe it to Kant himself, preferring instead to lay the blame on commentators who in his opinon had misconstrued those passages in the *Critique* where the notion of noumena was discussed. Such an interpretation of Kant's intentions, whereby he was to be seen as simply articulating a presumption of ordinary thought rather than as propounding an ontological claim of his own, has not found many adherents, either in his time or since; but however that may be, the objections Fichte brought against the doctrine itself retain their pertinence. And, if their force is granted, it is not too hard to understand why his own thinking took a direction which, in its eventual outcome, involved a total reversal of the priorities he attributed to the scientifically inspired theorists of his day. For he did not challenge what he conceived to be the

14 *Science of Knowledge, p.* 56.

15 Ibid., 54.

essence of the Kantian view, in which it was affirmed that the entire
spatio-temporal realm of phenomena existed purely for the subject and had
no independent reality. On the contrary, he spoke as if it were clearly
true. But if so, and if at the same time one eliminated the obverse conception of things in themselves, there appeared to be no alternative to opting
for a thorough-going and unadulterated idealism according to which the
world of experience under all its aspects derived from the operations of the
ego alone. Primacy in the fullest sense would thereby be ascribed to the
active subject; instead of the latter's being treated as if it were in some
way subordinate to nature, it would be necessary to regard the natural
world itself as being ultimately no more than the expression or manifestation at the level of the empirical consciousness of an ungrounded and
spontaneous spiritual activity. It was with such considerations in mind
that Fichte felt justified in concluding that 'to the idealist, the only positive
thing is freedom'.[16]

Fichte was, of course, aware that an uncompromising commitment to
idealism along the lines proposed might appear to pose a problem in the
light of his earlier, equally uncompromising, insistence upon the part played
in our ordinary experience by the notion of an objective world. Yet his
various attempts to deal with it, both in the *Wissenschaftslehre* and elsewhere, are not easy to follow. Part of the difficulty arises from the indeterminacy of his fundamental concept of the self or ego, an indeterminacy
which frequently leaves it unclear whether it is intended to carry implications
of the sort customarily associated with its use in everyday contexts or
whether, on the other hand, it is to be interpreted in a fashion that involves
a more or less complete severance from these. In so far as he initially
implied that his system was founded upon the direct deliverances of
self-consciousness and nothing more, it is scarcely surprising that he was
taken by some of his original readers to be propounding an extreme and
paradoxical solipsism, with everything in the Fichtean universe traced
back to Fichte himself. This was a criticism which—again perhaps unsur-
prisingly—he bitterly resented, and he went out of his way to repudiate it
as constituting a gross misrepresentation of his whole position. For it
overlooked (he maintained) the vital distinction he wished to draw between
the 'finite' or personal subject of everyday life and what he was prone to
term, by contrast, the 'infinite' or 'absolute' subject. It was the second, not
the first, that was the ultimate creative agency, expressing itself under one
aspect in the form of finite centres of self-conscious activity and under the
other in the form of phenomenal objects and events. As finite subjects,
we are necessarily aware of ourselves as being affected or impinged upon
in certain ways; in Fichte's words, we are apprised of 'something *given*
to reflection, as the material of presentation', without being conscious of

16 Ibid., 69.

'the manner in which it arrived there'.[17] The suggestion here seems to be that, through an opaque process involving what is sometimes referred to as 'the productive imagination', the absolute ego gives rise to sensory representations which are susceptible to a projective interpretation in the shape of an objectively conceived spatio-temporal world. Thus our everyday 'firm conviction of the reality of things outside us' can be accommodated within the framework of a philosophical theory which entails no departure from a fundamentally idealist standpoint.

While such an account of his position may have protected Fichte from the particular objection he was concerned to rebut, it is nevertheless hard to square with his original contention that all knowledge is necessarily confined to what lies within the sphere of consciousness. Nor, in the end, was it easily reconcilable with other claims he wished to make regarding our relations both to nature and to each other. And such difficulties were, indeed, symptomatic of a more general lack of tidy fit between the epistemological and ontological departments of his system which was to become increasingly manifest. As we have already noticed, there was from the beginning a discernible tension between his professed adherence to the cognitive principles laid down by Kant and the speculative impulse by which so much of his own thinking was actually guided and propelled. In the subsequent development of his philosophy the gap separating the two widened, with the more critical and epistemologically orientated elements in his thought tending progressively to recede into the background. What replaced them was a metaphysical interpretation of reality as a whole, an interpretation which was imbued with teleological and ethical ideas and which represented a kind of massive projection, on a cosmic scale, of of what he conceived to be the true nature and destiny of human beings in the world.

Thus the notion of an absolute subject or self, which lay at the centre of Fichte's comprehensive vision, can be said to reflect his conviction that the categories of agency and will formed the basis of any scheme in which the significance of human life and consciousness could be adequately presented. Certainly nature, regarded as a system of interconnected phenomena, would also play an indispensable role in such a scheme, but it would only do so in a manner that exhibited it as being a prerequisite for the constructive activity and self-development of free autonomous persons. As dramatized by Fichte, this was transformed into the claim that the world in general must be envisaged as a dynamic self-differentiating totality, the natural sphere now being portrayed as a direct or immediate manifestation of the absolute ego rather than as something merely posited by it through the mental processes of the finite human subject. In a sense it could still be affirmed that—as he once put it—'the world is the product of my whole

---

[17] Ibid., 208.

spirit', but only if this was understood to mean that I, as a particular individual, was constituted by the same self-active principle that expressed itself, on the one hand, through the medium of other conscious agents like myself and, on the other, in the shape of an opposed realm of nature against which I must exert my will. So conceived, the spiritual character of reality in no way implied that it should be regarded as a seamless or harmonious whole: its inner 'striving' essence entailed conflict and division, such division being, so to speak, self-generated and involving it in a continual struggle to overcome constraints and obstacles that had their source in its own primordial activity. Human beings were the vehicles of this process and, as such, could fulfil themselves only by pitting themselves against a resistant natural world whose ultimate function was to afford them the opportunity for realizing their potentialities as free self-determining beings. A close colleague of Fichte—F. K. Forberg—once described him as teaching on every possible occasion that 'action, action, action' was the proper destiny of man, and this indeed is the message that his philosophical system seems continually to proclaim. Despite, however, his emphasis upon the unitary character of the human psyche, he was also anxious to stress that man only attained his full stature when his conduct and motivation were of a certain kind. For action, as he understood it, implied the vindication at the level of self-conscious experience of the spontaneous creative principle which underlay reality in general; and for that to be adequately achieved human behaviour must exhibit a complete independence of the influence of external factors—it must (in his words) be a manifestation of 'absolute self-activity'. In practice, this meant that the agent's motivation should be governed by laws which he, as a self-conscious subject, imposed upon himself and made the ground of his conduct. But conduct so actuated was, for Fichte, nothing less than moral conduct; it was only when what was done was performed simply on the basis of 'an immediate consciousness of our determinate duty' that we fulfilled our true vocations as agents in the world. Thus the practical conclusion of Fichte's metaphysic was a form of ethical idealism, designed to confirm the reliance of the ordinary person upon the direct deliverances of his conscience. Whatever his divergences from Kant in other respects, here at least he remained true to the spirit of his master.

From a present-day standpoint, Fichte's speculative excursions inevitably appear bizarre and invite the question of why, in order to protect human freedom against the threat allegedly posed by what he stigmatized as 'dogmatism', he should have felt compelled to propound so sweeping and all-embracing a theory. Nor is it always clear what kind of freedom he principally had in mind: the notion that we are free inasmuch as our actions are not subject to natural necessitation tended, as he proceeded, to give way to more 'positive' interpretations of the concept, such as those in which it implied self-legislation and the determination of behaviour by principles

Schopenhauer on Action and the Will

D. W. HAMLYN

There are certain metaphysical theories which present a view of the world and of the position of human-beings within it which have seemed attractive or at least impressive to many irrespective of the arguments that are marshalled in their favour. That is certainly true of Schopenhauer. His identification of the inner nature of reality with the will, and the conclusions which he drew from this as regards the nature of human-beings and their place in the world, have seemed striking and perhaps even illuminating to many thinkers, not all of whom have been philosophers in the most obvious sense and not all of whom have had much concern for the under- lying argument that led Schopenhauer to his conclusions. It is in this way too, perhaps, that certain of Schopenhauer's *ideas* have become well known—his emphasis on the will to live, his pessimism and his views on suicide, and his thoughts about human nature and about sex that have been seen as something of an anticipation of Freud. In recent times attention has also been directed to his influence on Wittgenstein. In all these respects, however, it is Schopenhauer's *ideas* that have been influential, rather than the argument that underlies them. Indeed it is sometimes said that Schopenhauer was not a very systematic thinker at all. If that *seems* true it is so in the sense that Kant too has seemed to some unsystematic in the details of his argument. That does not mean that the main structure of the argument is not clear. So it is with Schopenhauer.

It is true not only that there are metaphysical theories that are impressive irrespective of the arguments marshalled in their favour. It is true also that there are certain extended arguments for metaphysical conclusions that have a grandeur and magnificence about them despite their final invalidity. That is the case, or so it seems to me, with Aristotle's argument for the existence of a Prime Mover in the last book of his *Physics*; on a quite different scale, it seems to me also the case with Kant's general argu- ment in the *Critique of Pure Reason*, although here, as I have already implied, one is called upon for a very considerable patience and tolerance over the details. So again is it with Schopenhauer. That is perhaps not very surprising, since he was a great admirer of Kant, and thought of himself as carrying forward the Kantian spirit in the face of what he considered, and expressed in no uncertain terms, as the meretricious philosophical out- pourings of Hegel and other German contemporaries. Not that he thought that Kant was entirely right; but in many ways the framework for his own theory was derived from Kant. He accepted some of Kant's premises but came through them to the very un-Kantian conclusion that Kant's unknowable 'thing-in-itself' could, despite all that Kant had said about our inability to give any positive account of it, be identified with the Will—the one, single, will which is the underlying reality but which manifests itself to one degree or another not only in human willing and animal impetus, but also in the various forces that govern inorganic matter.

What I intend to do is to try to give some general account of the outlines of his argument for this surprising conclusion and then to concentrate on one point in the argument—the step in the making of which he argues that it is the will which is the 'thing-in-itself'. I shall do this partly because I think that the argument has an interest of its own at this point despite the invalidity of the argument as a whole. He is after all trying to do something that Kant had taken himself to have shown to be absolutely impossible. I also think, however, that what Schopenhauer says about the will at this point together with the argument that turns on it have considerable interest for the philosophy of action. Indeed there is something there that we ought perhaps to learn from him. Unfortunately, however, for present purposes, Schopenhauer's overall argument is complex and what I present of it will inevitably be schematic. I have tried to give an account of one part of it on a previous occasion—in 'Schopenhauer on the Principle of Sufficient Reason' in *Reason and Reality*, Royal Institute of Philosophy Lectures, Vol. 5 (1970–1).[1]

The first premise of his argument is in effect his idealism—summed up in the idea of the world as representation (*Vorstellung*). Schopenhauer thought that one of the great Kantian discoveries was the truth of transcendental idealism—that as far as experience is concerned we can be acquainted with phenomena only, never a reality beyond perception, even if within phenomena we can distinguish between mere appearance and what we ordinarily think of as reality. For Kant this is summed up by saying that phenomena or certain aspects of them are empirically real but transcendentally ideal. Since Schopenhauer, however, saw nothing wrong in the idea that a metaphysical thesis might be given or found confirmation in empirical fact, he thought that there were supposed empirical facts that gave credence to idealism, and he saw a closer relation between Berkeley's empirical idealism and Kant's transcendental idealism than Kant himself was prepared to see. He thus laid great weight upon the causal processes involved in perception, as he saw them, and summed the matter up by saying that what both Berkeley and Kant had shown was that everything in the supposedly real world was in truth a phenomenon of the brain. (There is a marvellous passage at the very opening of the second volume of his main

[1] There is also a more elaborate discussion in my book on *Schopenhauer* (London: Routledge and Kegan Paul, 1980).

work, *The World as Will and Representation*, which states that position forcefully.)

The details of Schopenhauer's account of perception are complex and in the end not very coherent, and I shall not go into them here. The argument for the thesis that the world is a phenomenon of the brain is, however, one that is familiar from other philosophers. It argues from the fact that perception is inevitably subject to causal conditions to the conclusion that what we perceive must be merely the effects of those causal conditions —that is to say, whatever is produced by what happens in the brain and therefore something essentially subjective. He thinks, moreover, that the contrary view—that, as he puts it, 'the *objective world would exist* even if there existed no knowing being at all'—can be shown to involve a contradiction. For, he says (*WR*, II,1, p. 5),[2] 'If we try to *realize* this abstract thought, in other words, to reduce it to representations of perception, from which alone (like everything abstract) it can have content and truth; and if accordingly we attempt to *imagine an objective world without a knowing subject*, then we become aware that what we are imagining at that moment is in truth the opposite of what we intended, namely nothing but just the process in the intellect of a knowing being who perceives an objective world, that is to say, precisely that which we had sought to exclude.' By 'realize' here Schopenhauer means something like what Husserl was to express by speaking of the fulfilment of a thought—giving its cash-value, so to speak, in perceptual terms. It is perfectly true that if we are to *imagine* a world at all it must be from a point of view; the representation of it is in that sense in perceptual terms. It does not follow from that that the world which we imagine contains an imaginer. *A fortiori*, it does not follow that the attempt to imagine an objective world without a knowing subject is bound to end in frustration because the terms of reference involve a contradiction. It is a further question again whether the abstract thought of an objective world without a knowing subject *needs* to be realized in imagination, *needs* to have a fulfilment in that sense. The claim that it does need this involves, to say the least, a controversial verificationism, which links the sense of a proposition to the conditions under which the state of affairs described by it may be perceptible. It might even be said that Schopenhauer's claim that the abstract thought must be reduced to representations of perception presupposes the very idealism for which he is arguing.

However that may be, Schopenhauer thinks that it is clearly true that there can be no object without a subject. Indeed, to be an object for a subject and to be a representation are for him the same thing; and in his

---

[2] *WR = The World as Will and Representation.* I use the admirable translation by E. F. J. Payne (New York: Dover, 1969), and all page references are to that edition.

criticisms of Kant, Schopenhauer takes him to task for making an illegiti-
mate distinction between representations and their objects—objects *are*
representations (*WR*, I, 444). He also thinks that there can be no subject
without an object—without, that is, a representation of some kind; but I
shall not discuss further that claim here. The outcome of it all is the further
claim that the phenomenal world, the world as representation, is a world of
representations for a knowing subject or intellect. The phenomenal world
has, he says, two poles, two limiting cases—intellect and matter without
form or quality. These are, however, limiting cases indeed. They are presupposed in the idea of knowledge of objects, but the only actual knowable
objects are representations for a subject. This is the nature of the world for
each of us, considered simply as knowing subjects, and the idea of a
knowing consciousness is in effect Schopenhauer's point of departure for
his inquiry, as he makes very explicit in the *Fourfold Root of the Principle
of Sufficient Reason* (41).[3] His account of the principles which govern
representations for us is thus also a kind of unfolding or 'exposition'
(in the Kantian sense) of what is involved in the idea of a knowing
consciousness.

I have attempted to give some account of that 'exposition' elsewhere
(ibid.). What Schopenhauer thinks is the guiding principle is that 'all our
representations stand towards one another in a natural and regular connection that in form is determinable A PRIORI' (*Fourfold Root*, 42).
Nothing can become an object for us without there being such a connection
with other representations. Schopenhauer thinks that he can show that
such a connection can take four forms, and only four forms, and that these
four forms determine four classes of object for our 'knowing faculty'. The
four forms are constituted by four forms of the principle of sufficient
reason. Representations, that is, are governed by four principles of necessary connection such that one representation constitutes a sufficient reason
for the occurrence of another, and no representation can occur which is
not so governed. This is not meant to be a mere empirical observation
about our experiences and thoughts. Schopenhauer thinks that it is
possible to recognize *a priori* the necessity of each kind of connection; but
all such necessities are for him relative, and while the principle of sufficient
reason constitutes a transcendental truth (i.e. its truth is a necessary condition of the possibility of its being true that we, as knowing conscious-
nesses, have objective experience in the form of representations) he does
not think that there is anything like a proof to be given of it. A proof would
have to provide absolute necessity, and Schopenhauer does not think that
there is any such thing. In his view, there is no such thing as a transcendental argument, conceived as a proof. One can, however, get people to

[3] Translated by E. F. J. Payne (La Salle: Open Court, 1974). That translation
was not available when I wrote my previous paper on Schopenhauer.

recognize *a priori* that something is so, even that it is a transcendental truth that it is so.

The form of reason provided by the *ratio* or *principium fiendi* (becoming) is causality—every change presupposes a cause. That provided by the *ratio* or *principium cognoscendi* (knowing) is one or other form of truth-ground—every judgment depends for its truth on some ground. That provided by the *ratio* or *principium essendi* (being) is that provided by mathematical relations (which Schopenhauer interprets along more or less orthodox Kantian lines as involving intuitions of space and time)—every division within space and time is determined for each other by such relations in accordance with our intuitions of space and time. The fourth and last form of reason, that provided by the *ratio* or *principium agendi* (acting) is motivation—every action is conditioned by some motive, which Schopenhauer characterizes as 'causality seen from within'.

I have said nothing of the details of the argument for this theory; nor shall I do so here. The point to note, however, as I have in effect already indicated, is that every necessity that attaches to representations on this theory is a conditional necessity. If such and such representations must occur it is because they are necessary relative to whatever constitutes the reason for them. Moreover, the occurrence of representations of whatever kind is for us subject to such a conditional necessity. No representation can be conceived as known unconditionally by a knowing consciousness. We are always aware of such an object as being subject to one or other of the kinds of reason that have been delimited; hence our knowledge of such an object cannot be in a proper sense immediate or unconditional.

It may at first sight seem odd that Schopenhauer includes acting among those things that constitute objects for a knowing consciousness. Why is it, to use terms that he himself sometimes uses in this connection, that acting is included as something that has to do with Sensibility, Understanding and Reason? The answer is that Schopenhauer makes reference to action simply in so far as we are aware of ourselves as engaging in it, as acting. It is his belief—and he makes something of an issue of it in connection with his discussion of the idea of freedom of the will—that all our actions are subject to causes which we are aware of as motives for those actions. Causes in the narrowest sense apply to changes that occur within inorganic phenomena. When we come to organic life, to plants and 'the unconscious part of animal life', causes feature as stimuli. In animals that have knowledge and in human-beings causes feature as motives, and cannot function as such without the medium of knowledge. What seems to be true in all this is that motives as such can be attributed only to beings who are capable of doing things knowingly, i.e. intentionally. I have myself suggested elsewhere[4] that any feature that figures in a description of an action as in-

4 'Unconscious Intentions', *Philosophy* (January 1971), 12–22, esp. pp. 13–14.

tentional can be referred to as a motive for that action. Schopenhauer's conception of motives seems to be narrower than that; it is clear that for him the feature in question must not only explain the action but must also be seen by the actor as doing so. It is in this sense at least that motives are causes seen from within. (It should be said, however, that in the end this dictum turns out to have for him a more profound sense—what we are aware of in this way as motives is *literally* the same thing as we perceive as causes in other phenomena. There is a delightful and typical passage in *WR*, I.24, p. 126, where he comments on a remark of Spinoza's to the effect if a stone thrown through the air had consciousness it would imagine that it was flying of its own will; Schopenhauer agrees but adds that in fact the stone would be right.)

Because motives must, on Schopenhauer's view, be seen by the actor as explaining the action, they might be said to be the causes simply of the *phenomena* of action—that aspect of the action which appears in the form of representation. Because they have to do with phenomena they presuppose knowledge at least to the extent that they imply a knowing subject, since that, for Schopenhauer, is true of all manifestations of the principle of sufficient reason. Nevertheless, in so far as they are causes seen from within they in fact presuppose more than just that; they exist as motives only *qua known*, and not merely as something knowable because belonging to a knowing subject. I am inclined to think that despite what is often said about Schopenhauer's anticipations of Freud, and despite what he himself said about our ignorance of our real nature and about our tendencies to self-deception, he cannot admit the possibility of unconscious motives. If there are things that affect our bodies, and thereby what we do, without our knowledge, they function as stimuli, as is the case with, as he puts it, 'the unconscious part of animal life'. In this respect I think that Schopenhauer makes the mistake made by many other philosophers of equating knowledge too much with consciousness. However that may be, Schopenhauer's view of the phenomena of action is that the representations involved are subject to the same conditional necessity as other representations, even if the form that that conditional necessity takes is peculiar to action.

What then makes those representations those of action? It is at this point that the will enters the picture. Like Kant, Schopenhauer argues that we can have no direct knowledge of ourselves as a knowing subject. The situation is somewhat different, however, as regards knowledge of ourselves as agents. I say 'somewhat different' because we are not just agents. There is a passage from *WR*, II.18, p. 197, which brings out fairly clearly the point at issue. He says, 'For even in self-consciousness, the I is not absolutely simple, but consists of a knower (intellect) and a known (will); the former is not known and the latter is not knowing, although the two flow together into the consciousness of an I. But on this very account, this I is not *intimate* with itself through and through, does not shine through so to speak, but is opaque, and therefore remains a riddle to itself.' Later, in the next chapter (p. 209), he uses the image of the will as a strong blind man carrying the intellect as a sighted but lame man on his shoulders. But this is in some ways to anticipate, since I have not as yet properly introduced the will. It is a cardinal point of Schopenhauer's doctrine that as far as human-beings are concerned the will manifests itself only in doing, and it is this point that has been seized upon by some commentators, e.g. Patrick Gardiner,[5] as a line of connection with some contemporary philosophy of mind, particularly that inspired by Wittgenstein. It follows from this cardinal point of Schopenhauer's, as he goes on to say after the passage that I quoted just now, that while our inner knowledge of our agency as such is 'free from two forms belonging to outer knowledge', namely space and causality, it is still subject to time. In consequence, as he says, 'everyone knows his *will* only in its successive individual *acts*, not as a whole, in and by itself'. He adds that for that reason no one knows his character *a priori*, but only by way of experience.

There is at first sight a problem in all this. If willing manifests itself only in doing, and if that is a phenomenon that involves time, and *qua* phenomenon is subject to a form of the principle of sufficient reason in being conditioned by motives as causes seen from within, how can our knowledge of ourselves as agents be in any better case than our knowledge of ourselves as knowers? That knowledge must, on the premises, still be indirect at best. The problem can, I think, be solved through the making of a distinction, which it may be that Schopenhauer himself is not always clear about, perhaps because of the terms in which he discusses the issues. It is perfectly true that, if willing manifests itself in our case only in doing, we can be aware of *what* we will only in *what* we do, and in so far as we are aware of that we must, on Schopenhauer's terms be aware of something conditioned, i.e. subject to motives. But knowing *what* we do is not knowing *that* we do. Knowledge of *what* we do is in effect knowledge of a phenomenon, and is for that reason subject to the same constraints as knowledge of other phenomena. The same is not true of knowledge *that* we act—knowledge of agency simply as agency. This, Schopenhauer thinks, we know directly and unconditionally, and it is in this sense that the will is the only direct and unconditioned object of knowledge. It is for this very reason that Schopenhauer identifies the will with the thing-in-itself, as the underlying reality behind phenomena. An act of will, he says (*WR*, II.18, p. 197), 'is indeed only the nearest and clearest *phenomenon* of the thing-in-itself', but he adds that if other phenomena were known just as immediately and intimately we should have to regard them too 'precisely as that which the will is in us'. In other words what he says about an act of

[5] Patrick Gardiner, *Schopenhauer* (Harmondsworth: Penguin, 1963), e.g. pp. 169ff.

133

will is true of the *phenomenon* that we are aware of in acting—what we do—but that still leaves open the possibility of a direct knowledge of the will in the consciousness of ourselves that we have as acting. The object of that consciousness must, on Schopenhauer's terms, be something distinct from mere phenomena, simply because it is an object of direct and unconditional knowledge; it is not therefore subject to the principle of sufficient reason and must thus lie outside the range of any phenomena. So Schopenhauer concludes that it must be the thing-in-itself.

Such in very brief, and no doubt oversimplified, form is the crucial move in Schopenhauer's argument for the identification of the will with the thing-in-itself. Several questions arise from it. First, given the premises, is the argument valid? In other words, if it were accepted that anything phenomenal is knowable only in a conditional way but that there is something which is knowable in an unconditional way, would it follow from that that the something in question is something non-phenomenal, something different from anything phenomenal? For these purposes we can leave aside the question of the further nature of that non-phenomenal something and of its relation to the phenomenal, and confine our attention to the question of the simple validity or otherwise of the argument. In this bare form it is of course an argument similar to one that has been used against the mind–body identity thesis. It has been argued that sensations are (to put the matter in terms which are no doubt controversial but which are parallel to those of the argument with which we are primarily concerned) knowable directly, brain processes are not knowable directly, so sensations are not identical with brain processes. It has generally been pointed out with regard to that argument that it involves referential opacity, so that one cannot use in that way the principle of the indiscernibility of identicals or its contrapositive the non-identity of discernibles. In other words, nothing follows about identity or difference from considerations about knowability or ways of knowability unless the differences in knowability turn on other properties of the things in question; and of course if that is so, we do not need the argument based on considerations about knowability. That would apply to Schopenhauer's argument too, and if so the argument for a non-phenomenal entity must be invalid.

It might be argued that it is not necessary to put the argument in terms of identity. The Schopenhauerian argument might be put in the following way: if any *x* is phenomenal, it is not knowable unconditionally; the will is knowable unconditionally; therefore, the will is not phenomenal. The first premise of that argument involves in effect quantification into a referentially opaque context, and if that were objectionable *per se*, it would constitute an objection to the whole argument concerning phenomena; the whole argument would be misconceived since no valid conclusion *could* be reached from a premise stated in that form. It may very well be the case that Schopenhauer's argument *is* in fact misconceived, in that no *a*

priori argument of the sort which he uses could show that nothing phenomenal is knowable unconditionally, while nothing less than an *a priori*
argument would be sufficient for his general purposes. That objection,
however, is quite different from one based simply on the fact of quantification into referentially opaque contexts. It is far from clear that *that is*
objectionable in itself, apart from uses to which it might be put. I conclude
that it is at least not *clear* from that consideration that Schopenhauer's
argument is formally invalid, as long as it is enough that its conclusion
should be that the will is not phenomenal (although whether the premises
are acceptable is not something that I propose to say anything more about
here). Unfortunately I do not think that it *is* enough that the conclusion
should be that the will is not phenomenal. To say that it is not phenomenal
is to say that it is not, in Schopenhauer's terms, representation. Much more
is required to show that it is the thing-in-itself, even if there are no over-
riding objections to the premises and the earlier stages of the total
argument.

The point might be made in another way. Much turns in the argument
on the notion of the phenomenal. If that notion is an epistemological notion
purely and simply, that obviously affects the status of the conclusion of an
argument about it which turns on questions of knowability. To say that the
will is non-phenomenal would simply be to say that it is not known in the
way that representations are. That does not as yet justify a conclusion
about the will's distinctive ontological status. We are still confined to
epistemological considerations and have not yet reached a conclusion which
states that the will has a quite different ontological status from anything
else. The idea of a thing-in-itself might justifiably be thought to be of that
kind, i.e. ontological rather than simply epistemological. If that is so,
Schopenhauer is not entitled on these considerations alone to equate the
will with the thing-in-itself.

Is there, however (and this is my second question), anything to be learnt
from all this about action and the will? Is there, that is, anything to be
learnt from the considerations that Schopenhauer takes to lead to his final
conclusion, even if they do not in fact take him there? In my earlier paper
on Schopenhauer, I said that it was odd that he combines in his theory 'a
tenet which is central to contemporary philosophy of mind—the direct,
non-inferential knowledge that we have of what we do in intentional action
... with a tenet that is often rejected by those who espouse the same
philosophy of mind—that motives are causes seen from within' (ibid.,
160). Given what I have said here, it will appear that I was wrong to say
what I said then in one respect. The direct, non-inferential knowledge is
not of *what* we do in intentional action, but of the *fact that* we are acting. In
Schopenhauer's view motives determine the will so that we act in the way
that we do. If we ourselves are will, then motives determine *us*.

Schopenhauer often says quite categorically that we are indeed the will;

we are indeed the thing-in-itself. Moreover, since plurality is merely a function of space and/or time, in that it is these forms which provide the basis for division and distinction, plurality is an aspect of the phenomenal alone. Hence the will as the thing-in-itself is one, and it is this point which Schopenhauer uses in order to set out the metaphysical basis of ethics— we have an inkling on occasion that differences between us are merely phenomenal and that we are really one, this being the basis of sympathy which is for Schopenhauer that on which ethics itself rests. It is difficult, however, to take Schopenhauer as saying that the *only* reality is the will; if it were, there would be no explanation of the phenomenal. The world is will *and* representation. It would not even do to say that the phenomenal is illusion, as is implied by Schopenhauer's often quoted allusions to representations as the veil of Maya; for illusions have to be such *to* someone or something. There cannot be just will; there has to be the knowing subject also. If it be said that the will simply objectifies itself in knowing subjects among other things, it remains true that there is no explanation available as to why it should do that. It is surely not enough to say with Schopenhauer that the will is blind. That simply emphasizes the irrational element in his metaphysics. It is an important fact that Schopenhauer cannot *explain* the existence of knowing subjects, even if he seems to think that he can explain the nature of a whole range of phenomena by reference to the will. (It is perhaps worth adding that similar considerations arise in connection with Kant, and will do so for any philosopher who makes a distinction between phenomena and things-in-themselves, whether or not the latter are thought to be identifiable in any positive way.)

I said that for Schopenhauer motives determine the will. They can do so, however, only because we are knowing subjects as well as willing ones. That is at least part of the force of saying that motives are causes seen from within, and also the point of the analogy of the strong and lame men. It is thus not possible to get rid of the aspect of knowledge in explaining how the will manifests itself in action. In acting, we know directly, or can do so, the fact *that* we act, and we know in a way conditioned by the part that motives play in *what* we do. The latter knowledge is not direct in the way that the former is. That means in effect that we cannot know what we do, or cannot know this clearly or exactly, without also knowing why we do it, when and as long as that 'Why?' is to be answered by reference to motives. One might say that we know *a priori* that what we do is subject to motives, or at least that is Schopenhauer's doctrine; to know *which* motives what we do is subject to is to know more clearly what we do.

I made the qualification 'when and as long as that "why?" is to be answered by reference to motives' because if what we do is caused in, for example, the way in which a reaction can be caused and thereby elicited by a stimulus, the point about motives no longer applies. Schopenhauer thinks that where the will is determined by stimuli it is so determined without reference to knowledge, but directly; and that the will is involved at all in such cases is made clear, he thinks, by the general teleological nature of the processes involved—the fact that there is a tendency towards a goal or end. Presumably, therefore, if some stimulus were to call out a reaction in our body, then if we were prepared to allow that that might be characterized as a doing on our part, it would be a doing which we might become aware of only by observation of ourselves. The representation that we might have thereby would indeed be conditioned and would be an inevitable result of the cause in question. But, as I understand the situation, there would, in Schopenhauer's view, be no necessity that in being aware of what we did in this way we should also be aware of the reason why even if we knew that there had to be some reason or cause. The case is different where the action is subject to motives, just because motives are, so to speak, intrinsically known; that knowledge enters into the identification of the act in a way that it does not where the act is subject only to stimuli.

There seems to me much to be said for this point of view.[6] It would not do to say without any qualification that the identity of an action is given by the motive or intention with which it is performed. There are after all unintentional actions. Even in the latter case, however, it is at least arguable that there must be some description under which what is done is done intentionally. Thus if what is done brings about some effect which was not intended by the actor, then to the extent that that effect can be brought within a description of the action (as it normally can be) what was done under that description was done unintentionally. It remains the case that there is some description under which what was done was done intentionally. To say that is to say that there is some description under which what was done was done for some motive, even if the sole motive was the performance of the action itself. That is, I believe, familiar philosophical doctrine. It is, for example, the sort of thing that Donald Davidson says in his philosophy of action. Moreover, it is Davidson's view that, given that an action is intentional under some description, it takes place because of, and thus has its cause in, some combination of belief and desire. In that context, the Schopenhauerian doctrine is, in effect, that to *know what* one is doing one has to place the action in a context of beliefs and desires— that being what knowledge of one's motive, and indeed the very existence of the motive, comes to. Knowing *that* one is doing something is, however, in a different case.

Davidson's initial doctrine about the explanation of action seems to

---

[6] There might have to be qualifications put on it in the light of the possibility of unconscious motives; and the force of the principle involved may vary for acts with different descriptions. I discuss the matter further in my book, *Schopenhauer*.

have been subject to modification in more recent writings of his,[7] largely because it seems to be possible for such beliefs and desires (such motives, one might say) to be present and for these to be the apparent cause of what is done without the action being done for that reason, for that motive. It has been suggested that such anomalous cases might be dealt with by distinguishing between normal and abnormal causal routes in the way that is at least implicit in the Gricean causal theory of perception. Whatever may be the case, however, in connection with perception and causality, the relation between action and motive is, if Schopenhauer is right, too intimate to make that a satisfactory course to take. In saying that I do not mean to suggest a return to any thesis to the effect that an internal relation between the concept of an action and the concept of an intention or motive rules out the possibility that such an intention or motive may be construed as the cause of the action. There are several things that make that thesis implausible, including perhaps the imprecision of the word 'cause'. It is not at present in dispute, however, that motives can be causes. The problem is this: given that a combination of belief and desire can function causally as a motive in connection with an action when it is intentional, and that that same combination of belief and desire can function causally in some different way in connection with an action when it is unintentional, how exactly are we to understand the difference?

There are in fact two points of difference—the presence and absence of intention, and the difference in causality. The suggestion that we can simply appeal to differences in causality or causal routes presupposes in effect that there is nothing further to be said about the presence or absence of intention; indeed it is implied that *that* difference can be explained in terms of the difference in causality. But, if Schopenhauer is right, that ignores the point that motives are causes *seen from within*. That is to say that it ignores the part that knowledge plays in it all. To act from a certain motive is not simply to act as the effect of a certain combination of belief and desire; there must also be the question of how that combination of belief and desire are seen by us as knowing actors. That is in effect a question about the way in which the action is intentional. It will not do to say that for an action to be intentional under a certain description there has to be a certain kind of causation—not as an account of what makes it intentional. Some account of that intentionality is *presupposed* in an understanding of the kind of causality involved in motivation. One cannot, that is, dispense with reference to the way in which an actor is also a knower. That is the central point in what Schopenhauer has to say in this area.

It might be said, however, that what Schopenhauer is talking about in all

---

[7] Particularly perhaps in 'Freedom to Act' in *Essays on Freedom of Action*, T. Honderich (ed.) (London: Routledge and Kegan Paul, 1973), also in D. Davidson, *Actions and Events* (Oxford University Press, 1980), 63–81.

this is still what is from his point of view knowledge of representations. That is to say that the knowledge of what we are doing, conditioned as it is by motives in such a way that we cannot properly know what we are doing unless we know how it is conditioned in this way, is still a kind of observational knowledge. So it would be if an action were an event like any other event, a representation like any other representation. But Schopenhauer's crucial point, the point that takes him to the idea of the will as the thing-in-itself, is that an action is not just an event, not just a representation; it is a direct manifestation of the will and this we somehow know directly and unconditionally. (And if he is wrong about the thing-in-itself that does not make him wrong on this point.) Hence, knowledge enters into intentional action in two ways—the direct knowledge of ourselves as acting and the conditioned knowledge of what we do and why. We have the latter knowledge only because we have the former. There is a sense in which that holds good in the reverse direction also, in that unless the will manifested itself in action there would be no occasion, so to speak, for the unconditional knowledge of the will to manifest itself either. To put the matter in other, less Schopenhauerian terms, we can know *what* we do and *why* only if we know *that* we do, and we can know *that* we do only if we know *what* we do and *why*. None of this applies to ordinary events, and it may thus be inferred that actions are not to be constructed as such events.[8]

It might be said that such a conclusion is premature, since what I have had to say is about *knowledge* of action, as opposed to knowledge of events generally, and for the reasons connected with referential opacity and identity that were discussed earlier nothing follows about a difference between actions and events generally from any considerations about knowledge of them. That would be true but for one thing. That is the fact that knowledge enters into action in a way that it does not do so with events generally. In the sense of 'action' that we are concerned with only knowers can be actors. An action has to be intentional under some description, even if it is unintentional or perhaps non-intentional under others. Intention involves at the very least knowing that one is doing whatever one is doing (and this will hold good even if one admits unconscious intention); to the extent that it involves also knowing what one is doing it will also involve, as I have tried to show is implied by what Schopenhauer has to say, knowledge of the causes of one's action in the sense of the motives for it. Whether this has any kind of necessity will depend on how far causality of any kind enters into our understanding of what is said to be so caused. It is clear, however, that there is at least a good deal to be said for what Schopenhauer believes concerning this matter.

In sum, even if we scorn the idealism that Schopenhauer accepts, and even if we distrust the subsequent argument for the identification of the

---

[8] There is again a further discussion of the point in my book.

Hegel on Action

MICHAEL INWOOD

One of the things that makes Hegel hard to understand is the difficulty of identifying the problems and questions to which he was responding, at least in a form in which we can appreciate them. There are several reasons for this. Firstly, he was involved in the intellectual life of his time, and many of the themes which engaged him have now lost their urgency. Secondly, because he wanted to connect every topic into a single, coherent system, and because the transition from one topic to the next usually depends on some problem which cannot be solved unless the transition is made, some of the problems he unearths seem fairly insubstantial. Finally, his desire to philosophize without making any presuppositions[1] means that he is reluctant to state the problems which he is trying to solve in advance. Any problem involves presuppositions, both of facts and about the meaning and coherence of the words or concepts used in stating it. Problems arise within Hegel's system, therefore, and they do so in a guise appropriate to their context. To some extent, the appreciation of the problems presupposes an understanding of the system.

There is, therefore, some strain involved in focusing on a mere fragment of Hegel's system—in this case, his account of human action—and in attempting to disentangle the questions which it is designed to answer. Nevertheless a not wholly arbitrary starting-point can be found in his account of self-consciousness.[2] When a man is self-conscious, he is aware of himself as a simple entity, a centre of awareness, and he is conscious of a variegated and expansive world confronting him. The connection between self-consciousness and action is twofold. Action is both

---

[1] E.g. *Enz*, I, 1 (W. 3); *Wiss. Log.* I, 65ff. (M. 67ff.). References are to the following German editions and English translations of works by Hegel: *Enzyklopädie der philosophischen Wissenschaften*, E. Moldenhauer and K. M. Michel (eds) (Frankfurt am Main, 1970): I. *Die Wissenschaft der Logik* [*Enz*. I] (*Hegel's Logic*, trans. W. Wallace (Oxford, 1975)³ [W.]); III. Die Philosophie des Geistes [*Enz*. III] (*Hegel's Philosophy of Mind*, trans. W. Wallace and A. V. Miller (Oxford, 1971) [W.]). *Wissenschaft der Logik*, E. Moldenhauer and K. M. Michel (eds), 2 vols. (Frankfurt am Main, 1969) [*Wiss. Log.*] (*Hegel's Science of Logic*, trans. A. V. Miller (London, 1969) [M.]). *Phänomenologie des Geistes*, J. Hoffmeister (ed.) (Hamburg, 1952) [P.G.] (*Hegel's Phenomenology of Spirit*, trans. A. V. Miller (Oxford, 1977) [M.], *Grundlinien der Philosophie des Rechts* G. Lasson (ed) (Leipzig, 1921)² [P.R.] (*Philosophy of Right*, trans. T. M. Knox (Oxford, 1952) [K.]).

[2] P.G. 133ff. (M. 104ff.); A. V. Miller (Oxford, 1977) [M.]). *Grundlinien Enz*. III, 213ff. (W. 165ff.).

intimately involved in my becoming self-conscious, and it is, along with cognition, a response to the problem which self-consciousness presents.

Hegel believes that action, as opposed to knowledge or contemplation, is especially connected with self-consciousness. At the most primitive level, action arises from self-centred desires,[3] for example, the desire to eat this piece of meat. I, as an individual, figure essentially in the desired state of affairs; my desire is the desire that I should eat the meat, not simply that it should be eaten. By contrast, the expression of the cognitive attitude is non-egocentric: such-and-such is the case. Again, it is in acting that I come into conflict with other things—feel their resistance, push, pull, and devour them—and thus distinguish myself from them. In action I both require and confirm my awareness of my body as that fragment of the sensible world with which I am particularly associated, as a specially pliant and ever-available instrument for the realization of my purposes.[4] When I contemplate my foot, say, it appears as just one, albeit peculiarly persistent, item in my visual field. But when I manipulate or kick objects, knowledge of my own spatial position in the world and of the boundaries of my own body becomes central. I also come into conflict with other people and develop the notion of myself as one person among others. It is when I act that others recognize me as a person and thus confirm my self-awareness.[5] Finally, I do not need to say which person I am, or which foot is my foot in giving a factual account of the world. I might, of course, say how the world ought to be, and contrast this with how it is, without bringing egocentric knowledge into play. But more usually and more reasonably I focus on what is to be done by me, and this obviously involves my self-awareness.

Secondly, Hegel sees a problem in the co-existence of my simple self and an expansive diversified world.[6] It is a problem to which our practical and cognitive assaults on the world are the response. It is not entirely clear what the problem is. There is a cluster of problems which arise out of the contrast between myself and the world, for example that of the mind–body relationship, of how an extended materal world can make a sensory and intellectual impact on the self, and that of freedom. But the appreciation of these problems already presupposes considerable knowledge of the world. At this stage the problem seems to be, rather, how there can be any intelligible relationship between two such disparate items as the self and the world of which it is conscious.

One response to this problem, according to Hegel, is subjective idealism,[7] the view that the world is my ideas or sensations. This establishes some

[3] P.G. 139f. (M. 109f.); *Enz.* III, 215f. (W. 167f.).
[4] *Enz.* III, 189ff. (W. 145f.).
[5] P.G. 140ff. (M. 110ff.); *Enz.* III, 219ff. (W. 170ff.).
[6] P.G. 133ff. (M. 104f.); *Enz.* III, 213ff. (W. 165ff.).
[7] P.G. 175ff. (M. 139ff.).

sort of relationship between myself and the world. Moreover the more specific problems associated with this dichotomy—those of mind and body, freedom, and the origin of my ideas—do not, on this view, arise, at least in the same form. Fichte, for example, believed that freedom could be secured only by the truth of some version of subjective idealism.[8] Hegel, too, hoped to solve these problems by some type of idealism, but his idealism is not that of Berkeley, Kant, or Fichte. The contrast is pointed by the fact that whereas Dr Johnson thought that kicking a stone refuted idealism, Hegel held that, if anything, it confirmed it. Realism, according to Hegel, maintains that physical objects are independent of oneself. Practical involvement with them—eating them or possessing and using them—both establishes that they are not independent and persistent, and expresses one's belief that they are not.[9] The familiar, subjective idealism is, he implies, uninteresting. The claim that the world is my idea or ideas does not in itself establish an intelligible relationship between my simple self and the diverse objective-seeming ideas which it has. It is no more clear how the self can be the source of such ideas or why it has just the ideas it does have than it is how the self is related to the external world. The disparity and incommensurability remains in either case.[10]

The proper response to the problem is rather, for Hegel, to get to know and to act on the world of which I am conscious.[11] This does not only show that some state of affairs, some relation, for example, between myself and the world, obtained all along, whether by the sheer fact that I am able to know and act on the world at all or by some specific discovery which my practical and cognitive endeavours unearth. Rather, these endeavours produce some state of affairs, establish a relation between myself and the world which did not obtain before, much, perhaps, as familiarizing myself with a strange town establishes a relationship between myself and the town, rather than revealing something that held good all along. Thus rather than saying that idealism is true whatever men do or think about it, Hegel is inclined to say that men make idealism true: 'mind negates the externality of Nature, assimilates Nature to itself and thereby idealizes it'.[12] Part of the point of this is that, on Hegel's view, one should in giving an account of the world, include men's beliefs about it, their philosophical beliefs as well as their non-philosophical ones, as part of the world which is to be accounted for, but it suggests too, that men's beliefs and actions radically change nature, and do not merely constitute a new factor, alongside nature, of which the philosopher has to take account.

[8] *Fichtes Werke*, II, I. H. Fichte (ed.) (Berlin, 1845/1846), 169ff. (*The Vocation of Man*, by J. G. Fichte, R. M. Chisholm (ed.) (New York, 1956), 5ff.).

[9] P.G. 87f. (M. 65); P.R. 54 (K. 41f.); P.R. 298 (K. 236).

[10] P.G. 180ff. (M. 144f.); *Enz.* I, 119 (W. 70f.).

[11] P.G. 183ff. (M. 145ff.). Cf. n. 9.

[12] *Enz.* III, 23 (W. 13).

So far it is not clear whether Hegel is saying that men's cognition and action do in fact solve the self-world problem or whether he is attempting to explain men's cognitive and practical activities by reference to this problem. These are not equivalent. For what a problem, even if we recognize it as such, leads us to do need not solve the problem, and if we do do what solves the problem, it need not be the recognition of the problem which explains our doing it. In many cases it could not do so on its own, for there are alternative solutions or alternative routes to a single solution, as well as promising-looking cul-de-sacs. However, Hegel seems to want to explain our activities in terms of the problem, as well as to present them as the solution to it. The contrast between myself and the world produces the sort of cognitive discomfort which impels at least some men to attempt to solve it, and the response it evokes from them is the one that will solve it. Moreover, there is only one route to the solution, but this is, in part, because Hegel sees false starts, blind-alleys and even attempts to evade the problem as essential parts of a single journey.

This suggests, however, that Hegel takes an excessively intellectualist view of our actions. He might be interpreted, for example, as claiming that our desire to eat is in some way rooted in an urge to eliminate or nullify the world.[13] But clearly most actions are not motivated by intellectual unease about the co-existence of my simple self and the complex world. He can be allowed two concessions. Firstly, almost any type of action could be motivated by a desire to reduce the external to order and familiarity, and some types of action, for example, artistic creation, empire-building and spring-cleaning, are especially open to such an interpretation. Again, many of the trappings of our everyday actions, for example, what kind of things we eat and when we eat them, might be explained in this way. Secondly, some men reflect upon their actions as a whole and form a general conception of the course of their life. I may not merely give money to charities and so on, but see my life as a sort of crusade against suffering and injustice. Even if all or most of my particular actions have a successful outcome, I might decide that my general plan of action is somehow absurd or unsatisfying. I might reflect, for example, that, since my plan of action requires the presence of what it purports to remove, I really desire the presence of injustice and suffering, as well as desiring to remove them, so that my conflict with them is not in earnest.[14] Such a general conception of my actions might be found wanting because it fails to solve the problem which Hegel finds in the contrast between myself and the world. But even if such considerations lead me to abandon or modify my actions, it does not follow that they are primarily motivated by a desire to solve this problem.

[13] P.G. 139 (M. 109); *Enz.* III, 215 (W. 167).
[14] Cf. P.G. 438f. (M. 378); *Enz.* I, 386f. (W. 291).

The response to this problem, according to Hegel, was our getting to know the world, as well as our acting on and in it. He is concerned to stress the interdependence of knowing and doing. I cannot, for example, have a purpose unless I can form a conception of what I want to bring about,[15] and to realize a purpose I must exploit, and therefore understand, mechanical and chemical processes.[16] Conversely, experiment plays a part in my acquisition of such knowledge.[17] He also emphasizes the resemblances between cognition and action. It is not the case, for example, that the one is wholly passive, and the other wholly active; both are, in a sense, productive.[18] This, together with other features of his thought, makes it hard for him to distinguish between them. Sometimes he does so by reference to their products: the product of cognition is the word, while that of practical activity is enjoyment, or, again, the deed.[19] But Hegel is aware that words play a part in non-cognitive activities, in, for example, flattery.[20] Sometimes, again, he suggests that knowledge aims at the true, while action aims at the good.[21] But not all action aims at the good, at least in the moral sense, and Hegel's own concept of truth is not confined to cognition, but ranges over practical activities as well.[22] Another distinguishing feature might be that while knowledge is concerned with (discovering) what is the case, action is concerned with (producing) what ought to be the case. Hegel, however, does not regard action proper, or action properly conceived, as designed to bring about what ought to be the case but rather as a contribution to a satisfying, on-going system.[23] It is not clear whether what he is objecting to in this regard is a certain type of action or a certain conception of action, but in neither case would he want to distinguish action from cognition in terms of the notion of 'ought' (*Sollen*).

Hegel's official account of the distinction turns on the contrast between objectivity and subjectivity, although in other passages he shows an exemplary awareness of the ambiguity of these terms.[24] As theoretical, the mind makes the objective material given to it subjective. This is 'the activity by which the seemingly *alien* object receives, instead of the shape of something given, isolated and contingent, the form of something inwardized, sub-

---

[15] P.R. 287 (K. 227).

[16] *Wiss. Log.* II, 451ff. (M. 745ff.).

[17] P.G. 191f. (M. 152f.).

[18] *Enz.* III, 238f. (W. 186f.).

[19] Ibid.

[20] P.G. 370f. (M. 315f.).

[21] *Wiss. Log.* II, 498ff. (M. 783ff.); *Enz.* I, 378ff. (W. 283ff.).

[22] Cf. 'Truth and Self-satisfaction', by Robert C. Solomon, in *The Review of Metaphysics* **XXVIII**, No. 4 (June 1975), 698ff.

[23] E.g. *Enz.* III, 317ff. (W. 253ff.).

[24] P.R. 293f. (K. 232f.); *Enz.* I, 115f. (W. 67f.).

jective, universal, and rational'.[25] This activity does not consist primarily in acquiring more information about the world, but in ordering, categorizing and conceptualizing what is given: 'What I find and feel, I transform into mental representations, at the same time making it into an external object. But I recognize this content, when I bring my understanding and reason to bear on it, as being at the same time not merely isolated and contingent but an element of a great interrelated whole, as infinitely *mediated* with other contents, and by this mediation, becoming a *necessary* content'.[26] Practical mind, by contrast, makes what is subjective, objective: 'it does not start from the seemingly alien object, but from its own aims and interests, that is, from subjective determinations, and *then* proceeds to make these into an objectivity'.[27] Cognition and action are both ways of overcoming the self-world contrast. At the cost of some awkwardness they are presented as complementary attempts to assimilate the self and the world, proceeding in contrary directions.

One of the problems that is rooted in the contrast between myself and the world is that of freedom. Hegel believed that the will is free, and this belief is one of the guiding threads of his account of human action. Freedom constitutes the will, just as heaviness constitutes, in part, a stone.[28] 'Free' differs from 'heavy', however, in that it is interestingly and multiply ambiguous. Hegel is aware of this, but he is less inclined than we perhaps are to suppose that men might be free in one sense but not at all in another, and leave it at that. What he does want to say is not wholly clear. It is not always that if a man is free in one sense, then he is necessarily free in some other sense. Sometimes it is that if men are free in one sense, then they, or at least some of them, will become free in some further sense, or, again, that if a man is free in some primary sense, then he should be free in another sense, he should not, for example, be enslaved or sign away his right to decide moral and religious questions to an external authority.[29]

If Hegel is doing history, then his procedure is not unreasonable. Men are, perhaps, initially free in one sense, and this generates aspirations and problems which require them to become free in some further sense, and so on. Different senses of 'freedom' would then be related by their related roles in this process and would not be sharply distinct. Analogously, there might be no clear, single sense of the word 'science' in which Thales and Einstein were both scientific. Thales was scientific in a way which enabled him to pose problems which could only be solved by one who was scientific in a different sense, and so on. For a man, procedure or theory

[25] *Enz.* III, 237 (W. 185).
[26] *Enz.* III, 166f. (W. 127).
[27] *Enz.* III, 237 (W. 185).
[28] P.R. 285 (K, 225f.); *Enz.* III, 199f. (W. 153f.).
[29] P.R. 68 (K. 53). Cf. P.R. 27 (K. 20).

to be scientific in a general sense would then consist in its playing a part in a continuing tradition of problem solving, and not in its possessing some single feature.[30] Something similar might be said about art and religion. In such a developing tradition, one would not expect to find all the central features present at the beginning, any more than one does in an infant or an acorn. At the same time men's changing conceptions of freedom, science or art—conceptions which may be more or less vague, ambiguous or incoherent—affect, and are affected by, their practice.

Hegel is not, however, concerned only with history, and cannot be, if he is right in supposing that there are important logical relationships between different types of freedom such that history can be seen as the development of a sort of rational plan. If this is so, it should be possible to uncover the plan, disregarding the concrete events and agents in which it is embodied. There is, of course, some looseness of fit between the plan and its historical embodiment; the connections Hegel draws between them often seem strained and arbitrary.

Hegel is untroubled by what is often taken to be a potent threat to free will, namely causal determinism. He seems to have had some such thought as that since it is I who cognize external reality, any view according to which external reality engulfs me and deprives me of my freedom is self-refuting. Freedom is a feature of the theoretical mind, as well as of the practical mind. The picture with which we started, of the simple self confronted by a diverse and expansive world, already involved a sense of the independence of the self from its world, as well as of its uncommensurability with it. The freedom of this self and its ability to rise above its environment is a constraint on its cognitive activities.

This general principle is supported by several of Hegel's more particular doctrines. First, he holds that, in causal action, the effect is a simple continuation of the cause.[31] For example, when rain makes the streets wet, the wetness of the streets is just the same liquid in a different position. Or, again, when a moving object strikes and propels another, it imparts to it some of its own motion. But more complex objects like plants, animals, and men do not receive causal impacts in this way. Rather they transform them into something different. This is a matter of degree. Infants and invalids are more susceptible to neat causal influences than healthy adults, and men are more adaptive and self-determining than vegetables.[32]

[30] Cf. H. Putnam, in *Mathematics, Matter and Method* (Cambridge, 1975), 222f.: 'Of [certain meta-scientific terms, for example, "science" itself] we might say . . . that they are not defined in advance—rather science itself tells us (with many changes of opinion) what the scope of "science" is, or of an individual science, for example, chemistry, what an "object" is, what "physical magnitudes" are'.

[31] *Wiss. Log.* II, 225f. (M. 560f.); *Enz.* I, 297f. (W. 215f.).

[32] *Wiss. Log.* II, 227ff. (M. 561ff.); *Enz.* III, 52ff. (W. 36ff.).

Secondly, mechanical explanation cannot, in any case, deal satisfactorily with wholes like living organisms. Causal explanation is piecemeal; a composite whole is explained by giving separate explanations of its several parts. But an organism, in particular a self, is not a whole consisting of distinct parts like a pile of stones.[33]

The same point figures in Hegel's discussion of phrenology. It is absurd to suppose that the bumps and hollows of the skull represent different mental faculties and tendencies. For a man's powers and tendencies are not distinct and separable like bumps and hollows; the mind is not a bundle of faculties and dispositions like balls in a bag. Again, there is nothing in the skull corresponding to the power of the ego to transcend itself, for example, my power if I discover that I have a tendency to cruelty, to overcome this tendency in the light of my self-knowledge. It does not follow from this that the mind is in no way dependent on or associated with the brain, but it does mean that we cannot assign different powers and tendencies to different compartments of the brain, and that the brain cannot be, like the skull, a determinate and fixed lump of stuff. The brain must be fluid and plastic, more mind-like than we ordinarily take matter to be.[34]

Hegel argues that, in any case, the disparity between mind and matter has become less stark. For scientists in his day recognized weightless matters, like heat, light, and vital matter, and these are not matter in the ordinary sense at all.[35] Hegel was also receptive, though not uncritically so, to reports of phenomena such as mesmerism and telepathy, and argues that they suggest that 'the soul pervades everything'.[36]

Scientists' attempts to discover laws relating man and his natural and social environment have, Hegel holds, failed to produce non-trivial, exceptionless generalizations. This is, in part, because a man can as well reject as accept the conventions and institutions of his society. Which of these two attitudes he adopts cannot be explained by reference solely to his society.[37] Hegel does, however, suggest that a man is, to a degree depending on how independent he is, governed, even constituted by, the web of social relationships to which he belongs.[38] This is true at least to the extent that a man cannot do certain things, for example, pay his rates by cheque, unless he inhabits a certain social environment, though he can, of course, still decide to withhold his rates. And it suggests a difficulty for the view that what I do or intend to do is wholly determined by states of my body, namely, that if this were so, the brain-state corresponding to the

---

[33] *Wiss. Log.* II, 82f. (M. 446f.).
[34] P.G. 239ff. (M. 196ff.).
[35] *Enz.* III, 43ff. (W. 29f.).
[36] *Enz.* III, 143 (W. 109).
[37] P.G. 223ff. (M. 182ff.).
[38] P.G. 226f. (M. 184f.).

intention to pay one's rates by cheque might conceivably occur in a palaeo-lithic cave-dweller.[39]

Hegel believes, then, that it is the autonomy of the self which is the constant factor rather than physical science. For it is we who propose scientific theories and decide whether or not to accept them. But in any case there is no rigid contrast between a simple autonomous ego and an external world governed by mechanical causal laws. Mechanistic causality is not the only way of making sense of things. Chemical action, living organisms, and above all, social institutions mediate between mind and raw matter. The urge to take mechanism as primary and to explain other levels of being in terms of it is groundless. Matter, if we probe it, becomes more mind-like than mind becomes material.

In his main accounts of freedom, however, Hegel concentrates not on such points as these, but on the will itself. The primary sense in which the will is free is its ability to abstract from everything.[40] What is meant by this is not simply that I can distinguish myself from the particular desires, inclinations and attachments which I have and conceive of their being different, but that I can refrain from acting on, suspend the operation of, any particular desire or attachment of mine, and, indeed, rid myself of it if I wish. In this respect, men differ from animals, which cannot stand aloof from their prevailing desire and cannot refrain from acting on it.

But this abstractive freedom, Hegel argues, is not enough. A plausible reason for this would be that, granted that I do not have to pursue any particular inclination or to submit to any particular state of affairs, if I am to act in some definite way I must opt for some desire, or at least for some purpose, or other. Abstractive freedom alone does not enable me to do anything in particular. Hegel does in part want to say this,[41] and thus to regard abstractive freedom as an element in all human action. But he also wants to say that certain types of action—mystical withdrawal, destruction and suicide—especially display abstractive freedom, and that in certain periods, during the French Revolution, for example, men have acted in such ways on a large scale.[42] On Hegel's view, a Jacobin or a suicide is not so much doing something definite as rejecting everything definite and display-ing his independence of it.

However, if we leave aside these historical specifications of abstractive freedom and regard it as a feature of all human action, then my next step is to survey my inclinations, pick one of them and act on it. This is the freedom to pick and choose (*Willkür*) but it is not, according to Hegel,

---

[39] Cf. N. Malcolm, in *The Mind/Brain Identity Theory*, C. V. Borst (ed.) (London, 1970), 176ff.

[40] E.g. P.R. 28f. (K. 21f.).

[41] P.R. 29f. (K.22f.).

[42] P.R. 28f. (K.29); P.R. 287f. (K. 227f.).

genuine freedom.[43] There are several ideas involved in his dissatisfaction with it. Firstly, to act on one of the desires that I happen to have is seen as a surrender of my autonomy, rather like delegating my decisions to an external authority, even if the authority is of my own choosing.[44] There is, secondly, the disparity between the will, the thinking self in its practical guise, and the particular decision which it adopts.[45] The will is universal. In respect of his will alone, for example, a man does not differ from other men. But the decision it takes is particular, contrasting with a range of other possible decisions. Even if I aim at happiness, my happiness is still particular, depending on the nature and relative strengths of the desires I happen to have. Sometimes Hegel speaks of the will as if it were a concept, attempting to find an adequate instantiation of itself.[46] Less obscurely, a man should express himself adequately in the external world, should act in ways which express his essential nature. Acting on some particular desire which I have or even in pursuit of my long-term happiness fails to meet this requirement, a requirement which coheres with Hegel's view that the point of action is to bridge the gulf between myself and the world. This view also suggests that a man's actions should be concerned with what is central in the universe, and not with what is marginal and trivial. But the pursuit of my own happiness, however reflectively and rationally conceived, assigns to my activities a peripheral role in the world as a whole, and this may have been one source of Hegel's objections to it.

Finally, Hegel felt that my actions, like my beliefs, should be governed by objective interpersonal standards, and should not, any more than my beliefs, depend on contingent, subjective states which I do not share with other men. 'When I will what is rational, then I am acting not as a particular individual but in accordance with the concepts of ethics in general. In an ethical action, what I indicate is not myself but the thing. But in doing a perverse action, it is my singularity that I bring on to the centre of the stage. The rational is the high road where everyone travels, where no one is conspicuous.'[47] This is clearly connected with the requirement that action should express the universality of the will.

Hegel does not, then, regard free choice as genuine freedom. When speaking of genuine freedom, he often uses such formulae as 'the will wills itself', 'the will wills freedom', or 'freedom wills freedom'.[48] (No important difference is intended here, since freedom constitutes the nature of the will.) This implies that the will is self-contained. It does not depend on anything else for its object nor is this object, when it is realized, anything

[43] P.R. 35f. (K. 27f.).
[44] Ibid.
[45] E.g. *Enz.* III, 299 (W. 237f.).
[46] E.g. P.R. 39 (K. 30f.).
[47] P.R. 291 (K. 230).
[48] E.g. P.R. 38f. (K 29f.).

other than the will itself. Hegel employs the image of a circle, a line which is unbounded but finite, though he sees it rather as truly infinite.[49]

However, the formula as it stands has no clear sense. Hegel does not mean that a man is free only when he seeks freedom, since the Stoic and the Jacobin sought freedom, but this does not guarantee that they were genuinely free. Nor does he mean that a man is free only if he acts morally. Following Kant, Hegel sees this as acting for goals which are derived from my own resources, namely my capacity for rational thought. This would, indeed, meet some of the objections raised against acting on a desire or in pursuit of my own happiness. For example, a man's capacity for thought is, on Hegel's view, more intimately a part of him than his desires are, so that he is more truly autonomous when he decides what to do by thinking. Again men do not differ in their capacity for thought, in the way that they differ in their tastes and desires. To the extent that they settle an issue by thinking, they should arrive at the same result. So if goals could be established by thinking, such goals would be ones that all men could share. However, Hegel believed that one cannot derive substantial practical guidance from thinking, at least from the sort of thinking that Kant had in mind. He also objected to what both he and Kant took to be an implication of morality, that the point of action is to progressively approach a goal which ought to be attained, but which cannot be attained in a finite time.[50]

These difficulties are resolved, on Hegel's view, once we realize that a man is genuinely free, his will wills itself, only in the ethical, as opposed to the moral, life, that is, only when he lives and acts in accordance with the norms of his society.[51] The content of the will is then universal. Laws are universal. They are expressed in general terms and they apply alike to all citizens.[52] Again, our desires are, in a way, universalized. They are embodied in and satisfied within public, social institutions. For example, our sexual urges are regulated and informed by, as well as gratified within, the legal institution of marriage.[53] Our desire for gain is integrated into a system in which each individual's satisfaction of his needs promotes and is promoted by every other individual's satisfaction of his needs.[54] Our aims and activities have the universality, interpersonality and objectivity which is appropriate to the will. Thought plays a part here, just as it did in morality, because universality is, on Hegel's view,

[49] E.g. P.R. 293 (K. 232).

[50] P.G. 301ff., 423ff. (M. 252ff., 364ff.); P.R. 95ff. (K. 75ff.); *Enz.* III, 312ff. (W. 249ff.).

[51] P.R. 131ff. (K. 103ff.); *Enz.* III 317ff. (W. 253ff.). Hegel distinguishes this conception, *Sittlichkeit*, from *Moralität*.

[52] E.g. *Enz.* II, 303ff. (W. 241f.).

[53] P.R. 135ff. (K. 107f.); *Enz.* III, 296f. (W. 235f.).

[54] P.R. 154ff. (K. 122ff.); *Enz.* III, 321ff. (W. 257f.).

essentially connected with thought.[55] But the thought involved in social institutions is not the thought of a particular individual on a particular occasion.

An important feature of this conception is that, on Hegel's view, our actions are contributions to the maintenance of what is the case, and are not designed to bring about what ought to be the case. This is true not only of the routine actions of ordinary citizens, but also of the deeds of great men. Thus in a passage which is intended to show how, 'mind negates the externality of Nature, assimilates nature to itself, and thereby idealizes it', Hegel distinguishes two types of action. First, there is the case where 'the activity of our willing . . . is confronted by an external material which is indifferent to the alteration which we impose upon it and suffers quite passively the idealization which falls to its lot'. Secondly, 'a different relationship obtains with the mind or spirit that makes world history. In this case, there no longer stands, on the one side, an activity external to the object, and on the other side, a merely passive object: but the spiritual activity is directed to an object which is active in itself, an object which has spontaneously worked itself up into the result to be brought about by that activity, so that in the activity and in the object, one and the same content is present. Thus, for example, the people and the time which were moulded by the activity of Alexander and Caesar as *their* object, on their own part, qualified themselves for the deeds to be performed by these individuals; it is no less true that the time created these men as that it was created by them; they were as much the instruments of the mind or spirit of their time and their people, as conversely, their people served these heroes as an instrument for the accomplishment of their deeds.'[56]

Hegel muddies his point here by concentrating on great historic deeds. It could be as well made by contrasting such actions as sweeping a floor with a broom with, for example, dancing with a co-operative partner. It is not a matter of the relative difficulty of these actions; dancing is, for some, harder than sweeping. Rather, my dancing-partner co-operates, shares my purposes, whereas the broom does not. Again, the contrast does not depend on whether or not my action involves other people. For we can distinguish between making a remark in order to break an awkward silence and contributing effortlessly to a smooth-flowing conversation. Similarly, I might push a wheel to start it moving or push it when it is already moving in order to keep it going. Hegel gives the contrast more credit than it deserves by focusing on the deeds of great men.

Hegel feels, however, that a type of action which is designed to bring about what ought to be the case is radically defective, and the fault extends

[55] *Enz.* III, 288f. (W. 228).
[56] *Enz.* III, 23f. (W. 13).

to any view which conceives action in this way. He does not mean, though he sometimes verges on saying, that our actions do or should make no difference to what happens. Rather our actions are, or should be, designed to keep things moving, and not to stop or start them, or to change their direction. There are several reasons for this. Firstly, if all action is designed to produce what ought to be the case, to remedy unsatisfactory states of affairs, then we are engaged in a labour of Sisyphus.[57] Hegel would have a special reason for objecting to this in the light of his view that the point of action is to bridge the gulf between man and the world. Secondly, freedom, on his view, involves acting in an unresisting medium, rational and universal like oneself, and this excludes the supposition that one's environment is in need of constant alteration by oneself.[58] Thirdly, large-scale alterations of the world are impossible to justify, if they go against the accepted values of one's time.[59] The criteria for assessing projects must be derived from within the world as it is. Finally, the view that I and my projects are good, while the rest of the world is bad, introduces an explanatory gulf between myself and the rest of the world. We can, on Hegel's view, explain Caesar's aims and actions in terms of the world to which he belonged, but we could not have done so if he had been wholly at odds with it.[60] Hegel's view seems to be, then, not only that we cannot justify projects for wholesale change, but also that we cannot coherently conceive them. Nor can our actions be seen only as attempts to bring about small-scale changes. It does not follow that we cannot bring about change, or, at least, that change will not occur. The point is, rather, that we do, or should, swim with the tide, and this does not entail anything about the speed or direction of the tide.

Among the many difficulties and unclarities involved in this view, I shall mention two. It is, firstly, unclear whether Hegel is assessing types of action or, rather, conceptions of action. Often he seems to be distinguishing types of action, effortful manipulations of material objects and easy intercourse with other men. But the former type of action is constantly involved in our everyday social life and in great historical deeds; even heroes and civil servants have to mow their lawns and mount their horses. Probably Hegel has both points in mind. First, he wants to contrast breaking awkward silences with easy conversation. Secondly, he advocates a switch of perspective on our apparently change-producing actions. Filling in a form, for example, should be seen not so much as bringing about a change which ought to be produced—replacing an empty by a completed form—as contributing to the maintenance of an on-going institution.

[57] *Wiss. Log.* I, 144ff. (M. 133ff.); *Enz.* I, 386f. (W. 291). Cf. n. 50.
[58] E.g. *Enz.* III, 23f. (W. 13); *Enz.* III, 303f. (W. 241f.).
[59] P.R. 6ff. (K. 4ff.).
[60] P.R. 15 (K. 11); *Enz.* III. 23f. (W. 13).

Almost any action can, of course, be seen or described as the maintenance of something or other, so that this manoeuvre tends to deprive the contrast between types of action of its point.

Secondly, it is hard to see why Hegel regarded keeping things moving as less Sisyphean and pointless than changing unsatisfactory states of affairs, unless it is because he selects examples favourable to his case. Part of his answer to this is that a man in his youth tends to espouse ideals for improving the world, but later on he becomes reconciled to it and his position in it; 'he gets to be completely at home in his profession and grows thoroughly accustomed to his lot'. Before this becomes too tedious, he dies; death rounds out the natural pattern of a man's life.[61] This is only part of the answer, since the endless repetition of human lives can seem as pointless as endless repetition within a single life. He therefore supposes that mankind as a whole has a goal, though not necessarily one of which it is aware, towards which it progresses. Effortful activity is transferred from the individual to the world-spirit. How satisfactory this is depends in part on the answer to a question too large to be discussed here: what Hegel supposed was left for us to do after Hegel.

[61] *Enz.* III, 85f. (W. 63f.).

The Primacy of Practice: 'Intelligent Idealism' in Marxist Thought[1]

RICHARD NORMAN

I

> The chief defect of all previous materialism (including that of Feuerbach) is that things, reality, the sensible world, are conceived only in the form of *objects of observation*, but not as *human sense activity*, not as *practical activity*, not subjectively. Hence, in opposition to materialism, the *active* side was developed abstractly by idealism, which of course does not know real sense activity as such (Marx, *Theses on Feuerbach* I, trans. T. B. Bottomore).

There can be no question of looking for a *correct* interpretation of these words. They were never developed by Marx into a fully articulated philosophical theory. Like other similar suggestions elsewhere in his works (for example, in the *1844 Manuscripts* and in the *Notes on Wagner*) they were left simply as cryptic remarks. The question to which I shall therefore address myself is not: What did Marx mean? but: What kind of theory *could* Marx have developed along these lines? He was, it seems, looking for a theory which would draw on the idealist recognition of the importance of *practice* for human thought and knowledge, but which would incorporate this insight into a materialist philosophy.[2] My question is: Can such a theory be found? Can one assert the primacy of practice in a way which is both epistemologically interesting and compatible with materialism?

Before moving to an examination of what I take to be a plausible version of such a theory, I shall list certain other possible interpretations of Marx's words, and offer my reasons for not dwelling on them.

(a) It would be possible to understand such remarks as asserting some more or less naive form of pragmatism. When Marx says, in the second

---

[1] 'Intelligent idealism is closer to intelligent materialism than stupid materialism' (Lenin, *Philosophical Notebooks*, Collected Works Vol. 38 (Moscow: Progress Publishers, 1972), 276).

[2] Doubts have sometimes been raised as to whether Marx should properly be called a philosophical materialist. His own view on the matter is sufficiently clear, if not from this first Thesis on Feuerbach, then from the ninth and tenth Theses, where he contrasts the 'old' ('contemplative') materialism with a 'new' materialism which must surely be his own.

Thesis on Feuerbach, that 'the dispute over the reality or non-reality of thinking that is isolated from practice is a purely *scholastic* question', one could take this to be, at its crudest, a philistine rejection of any philosophical speculation which has no practical upshot. A somewhat less crude theory which could also be read into such remarks would be the standard pragmatist claim that practical utility is the criterion for the truth of beliefs. Marxists have sometimes been found advocating a class-relativist version of pragmatism, to the effect that those beliefs the acceptance of which would promote the interests of a class are thereby constituted as true for that class.[3] I shall not expand on this idea. It may be what Marx had in mind, but I regard it as plainly false.

(b) Another possible interpretation would be along lines developed by Engels in some of his later writings: that practice is the *means* whereby we obtain verification of beliefs and theories. This idea occurs in two well-known passages, one in *Socialism Utopian and Scientific* and the other in *Ludwig Feuerbach and the End of Classical German Philosophy*.[4] In the latter passage Engels refers to the Kantian denial of the possibility of knowing things-in-themselves, and comments as follows:

> The most telling refutation of this as of all other philosophical crotchets is practice, namely, experiment and industry. If we are able to prove the correctness of our conception of a natural process by making it ourselves, bringing it into being out of its conditions and making it serve our own purposes into the bargain, then there is an end to the Kantian ungraspable 'thing-in-itself'. The chemical substances produced in the bodies of plants and animals remained such 'things-in-themselves' until organic chemistry began to produce them one after another, whereupon the 'thing-in-itself' became a thing for us, as, for instance, alizarin, the colouring matter of the madder, which we no longer trouble to grow in the madder roots in the field, but produce much more cheaply and simply from coal tar.

My objection to this idea, unlike the previous one, is not that it is false. On the contrary, I regard it as both true and important—but not *epistemologically* important. Certainly it is the case that the development of new technical processes makes possible new kinds of knowledge, and this fact in its detailed exemplifications may be of great interest for the history of ideas or the sociology of knowledge. But the fact that, for example, alizarin can be produced out of coal tar does not mean that practice constitutes the *verification* of hypotheses about the chemical constitution of alizarin. Practice here puts scientists in a position where they can make new and

---

[3] See for example Peter Binns, 'The Marxist Theory of Truth', in *Radical Philosophy* 4.

[4] Marx and Engels, *Selected Works*, II (Moscow: Foreign Languages Publishing House, 1951), 92f. and 335f. respectively.

relevant observations; but it is still the observations, not the practice, that constitute the mode of verification. (We should note also that Engels' suggestion fails to solve the problem of the thing-in-itself. His example shows only that we can correct appearances and extend our knowledge within the limits of experience; it does nothing to undermine the Kantian idea of a thing-in-itself which lies outside all possible experience.)

(c) Marx could also be interpreted as pointing to the active character of theory formation in human knowledge. Knowledge, he might be saying, is not just the passive reception of data; the data themselves have to be interpreted in the light of a theory, and this theory must be actively constructed, it cannot be simply read off from experience. This would be in keeping with Marx's insistence, in *Capital*, that capitalist society cannot be adequately understood in its own terms. A good example is Marx's discussion of wages, in which he asserts that the everyday category 'value of labour' or 'price of labour', though required by capitalistic relations of production, reveals only the phenomenal form and conceals the essential relations. It perpetuates the illusion that the worker is paid for each hour of his labour. Only by formulating the category 'value of *labour-power*' can we adequately grasp the hidden substratum beneath the surface phenomena—the fact that what the labourer sells is himself as a commodity.[5]

This line of thought I see as both true and epistemologically important, and to be set against a simple reflection theory of the kind which Lenin sometimes appears to advocate. But it also seems to me that Marx, in the *Theses on Feuerbach*, is after something more. He explicitly emphasizes not just *theoretical* activity but *practical* activity, '*human sense activity*', and the role of this in human understanding. What then are we to make of this emphasis?

In answer I turn to what I regard as the most philosophically stimulating interpretation of Marx's epistemological remarks. A particularly full and persuasive version is to be found in the essay by Leszek Kolakowski on 'Karl Marx and the Classical Definition of Truth', and I shall begin by summarizing Kolakowski's account.[6]

[5] *Capital*, I, Part VI, ch. XIX.

[6] The essay is in Leszek Kolakowski, *Marxism and Beyond* (London: Pall Mall Press, 1969), to which page references are given. The same collection of essays has also been published under the title *Towards a Marxist Humanism* (New York: Grove Press, Inc., 1969). Similar interpretations of Marx's epistemology can be found in, for example, Shlomo Avineri, *The Social and Political Thought of Karl Marx* (Cambridge: CUP, 1968), chapter 3, and Alfred Schmidt, *The Concept of Nature in Marx* (London: New Left Books, 1971), ch. 3 B-C. It will be apparent that the ideas to be considered are not confined to Marx or his interpreters. Similar ideas have, since 1845, been developed in various ways by other philosophers. One might mention, for example, Nietzsche's perspectivism, Dewey's instrumentalism, Merleau-Ponty's work in *The Phenomenology of*

II

Kolakowski accepts the claim, central to the idealism of Kant and Hegel, that there can be no pre-conceptualized experience. Particular entities can be objects of experience only in so far as they are brought under general concepts. Thus

> Every thing as an object of cognition establishes the existence of man's conceptual apparatus, thanks to which one can differentiate that thing from the rest of the world (op. cit., 65f.).

How is this conceptual apparatus created? Kolakowski attributes to Marx the following answer:

> The assimilation of the external world, which is at first biological, subsequently social and therefore human, occurs as an organization of the raw material of nature in an effort to satisfy needs. . . . All consciousness is actually born of practical needs, and the act of cognition itself is a tool designed to satisfy these needs (ibid., 64).

The human conceptual apparatus, then, picks out those features of the world which are important for human activity aimed at the satisfaction of practical needs. This conceptual apparatus comes to be enshrined in language, which is not 'a transparent glass through which one can contemplate the "objective" wealth of reality', but rather 'a set of tools we use to adapt ourselves to reality and to adapt it to our needs' (ibid., 69). Hence it can be said that the world which we experience is itself a human product:

> Human consciousness, the practical mind, although it does not produce existence, produces existence as composed of individuals divided into species and genera. From the moment man . . . begins to dominate the world of things intellectually . . . he finds that world already constructed and differentiated not according to some alleged natural classification but according to a classification imposed by the practical need for orientation in one's environment. The categories into which this world has been divided . . . are created by a spontaneous endeavour to conquer the opposition of things (ibid., 66).

My first and rather guarded comment is that there are at any rate some grounds for attributing something like this view to Marx. Apart from the *Theses on Feuerbach*, and the *1844 Manuscripts*, on which Kolakowski mainly bases his interpretation, such a theory is strongly suggested in a

---

Perception, and the work of contemporary philosophers such as Stuart Hampshire (in his *Thought and Action*). For an interesting survey of some of this material, see Richard Bernstein, *Praxis and Action* (London: Duckworth, 1972).

passage in Marx's 1880 *Notes on Adolph Wagner*.[7] My second comment is that it has an authentically idealist lineage, and could reasonably be described as having been 'developed abstractly by idealism'. Though Kolakowski underplays the Kantian affiliations,[8] we are immediately reminded of Kant's account of the categories which, imposed on the sensory manifold by the understanding, create the possibility of ordered human experience. The categories of Hegel's *Logic* are likewise held to be constitutive of the reality which we experience, though they are for Hegel the product of absolute spirit rather than of finite human minds. The distinctively Marxist innovation would be the suggestion that the categories are created not just by mental activity but by human work upon the material world. This idea too Marx owes to Hegel, and he acknowledges the fact. Above all, his debt is to Hegel's discussion of the master–slave relation in the *Phenomenology of Mind*. But his complaint is that though Hegel recognizes the importance of practical work, this is in the end swallowed up in the purely theoretical activity of absolute spirit.[9]

---

[7] 'For the doctrinaire professor, man's relation to nature is from the beginning not practical, i.e. based on action, but theoretical. . . . But men do not begin by standing "in this theoretical relation with the objects of the external world". Like all animals they begin by eating, drinking, etc., i.e. they do not "stand" in any relation but are engaged in activity, appropriate certain objects of the external world by means of their actions, and in this way satisfy their needs (i.e. they begin with production). As a result of the repetition of this process it is imprinted in their minds that objects are capable of "satisfying" the "needs" of men. Men and animals also learn to distinguish "theoretically" the external objects which serve to satisfy their needs from all other objects. At a certain level of later development, with the growth and multiplication of men's needs and the types of action required to satisfy these needs, they gave names to whole classes of these objects, already distinguished from other objects on the basis of experience. That was a necessary process, since in the process of production, i.e. the process of the appropriation of objects, men are in a continuous working relationship with each other and with individual objects, and also immediately become involved in conflict with other men over these objects. Yet this denomination is only the conceptual expression of something which repeated action has converted into experience, namely the fact that for men, who already live in certain social bonds (this assumption follows necessarily from the existence of language), certain external objects serve to satisfy their needs.' (Quoted in Alfred Schmidt, op. cit., 110f. Cf. Karl Marx, *Texts on Method*, trans. and ed. T. Carver (Oxford: Basil Blackwell, 1975), 190.)

[8] 'This vision of the world does not in the least derive from a Kantian position' (Kolakowski, op. cit., 69).

[9] Both the acknowledged debt and the complaint are in Marx's 'Critique of Hegel's Dialectic and General Philosophy', in the *Economic and Philosophical Manuscripts of 1844*.

A full acknowledgement of the theory's idealist lineage enables one to state the theory more effectively than Kolakowski himself does. He says at one point that what the human mind creates is the division into 'species and genera'. If this means 'biological species and genera', the claim does not seem to me to be convincing, nor is it much more so if the phrase 'species and genera' is taken to mean natural kinds in general. Once the empirical sciences are established, it would seem that disinterested enquiry, abstracted from any direct serving of practical needs, is capable of *discovering* new natural kinds in a quite straightforward sense—discovering rather than creating. More promising is Kolakowski's reference to the human creation of *categories*. Taking up this idea we might, as I have suggested, look at the Kantian and Hegelian categories, and especially at the Kantian triad of 'substance', 'causality' and 'reciprocity', which give us our primary ontology of a world of relatively enduring material things located in space and time and interacting causally within a single causal system. It can, I think, plausibly be argued that this ontology, this categorial framework, is fashioned by human beings from the perspective of human agency, of human work upon the world. I shall now attempt to elaborate the claim.

III

I shall begin with the category of substance, and I shall ignore what I take to be the Kantian ambiguity in the use of the term, as between 'substance' as thing' and 'substance as stuff'. What I really want to examine is the category of 'material thing'. I shall begin with some fairly superficial points and move on from there.

When philosophers want to give uncontroversial examples of the furniture of the universe, they invariably cite precisely that: furniture—chairs and tables. Now this may be simply because chairs and tables are the things which philosophers always have most readily at hand. But what it also suggests is that one of our most natural paradigms for a material thing is provided by human artefacts. Are there other paradigms which are similarly persistent? There are two, I think. First, other living things—plants and animals. Here we can note that these are picked out as important for human beings in so far as they are sources of food or raw materials, and also, in the case of animals, in so far as they are seen as other agents partially comparable with human beings—agents against whom humans may have to defend themselves, and whom they can also put to work for them. The other class of paradigmatically material things is constituted by features of the landscape. And what are the basic units of the natural terrain? How do we cut up the geographical continuum? Into things which constitute obstacles to human activity, or means to be utilized in human activity—rocks and stones, rivers and lakes and seas, hills and valleys, etc.

The suggestion so far, then, is that the paradigmatic constituents of our ontology are artefacts, other living things, and features of the natural landscape, and that these are picked out in virtue of their relevance to human activity and human work. To provide a contrast here, consider the phenomenalists' ontology of colour patches. Given the kind of categorial framework which we in fact have, we identify colour patches as the colours of the sorts of material things I have been talking about—the green of the tree, the red of the post office van, the brown of the rocks. The alternative to identifying colour patches as the colours of trees and rocks and post office vans is identifying them by direct ostension or by their spatial relation to material things, and then our vocabulary of colours and shapes is just not rich enough for us to say much. I can talk about 'this red spot' or 'that square-shaped patch of yellow six inches to the left of the clock', but if I want to talk about the pattern of browns and blacks formed by the grain of the table, I have to do precisely that: talk about the grain of the table. Now in a sense we *could* have a categorial framework in which colour patches were basic, and a very different language which embodied that alternative ontology, an ontology in which the basic units were patches of colour homogeneous within very narrow limits, and in which we talked not of things changing their colour, or looking different with changes of lighting and perspective, but of new colour patches coming into being. I say: *in a sense* such an ontology would be possible. But it could be employed only by beings utterly different from ourselves. If we had to operate with such an ontology, even our most rudimentary attempts to act on the world would require a massively complex conceptualization. The kind of ontology we in fact have is the kind of ontology appropriate to human work.

So far the thesis is a fairly modest and perhaps even a trivial one. It may be said that all I have provided is an explanation of why certain kinds of examples most naturally occur to us as examples of material things; I have not shown that these examples have any ontological primacy, or reveal what is essential to the concept of a material thing. A more fundamental consideration is the following. What is definitive of our conception of a material thing is the evidence of touch rather than the evidence of vision or the other senses. And this needs to be put more strongly, for under the influence of the empiricist tradition we may be inclined to think of the sense of touch as consisting in the passive having of tactile sensations. This, however, is a radically diminished notion of 'touch', which more properly is the capacity to grasp things, to manipulate things. And what I am now suggesting is that our primitive conception of a material thing is of that which can be grasped and manipulated—or more generally, as Kolakowski puts it, it is 'the opposition encountered by human drives', that which both puts resistances in the way of human action and can then be handled and worked on to overcome this recalcitrance. Take the classic case of Macbeth's dagger, of which he says:

> Come, let me clutch thee.
> I have thee not, and yet I see thee still.
> Art thou not, fatal vision, sensible
> To feeling as to sight? or art thou but
> A dagger of the mind, a false creation,
> Proceeding from the heat-oppressed brain?
>
> (*Macbeth* Act II Scene I)

If Macbeth had been unable to see the dagger but could nevertheless touch it, could clutch it and use it, he would have an *invisible dagger* (and all the more useful for that, no doubt). Since he can see it but not touch it or grasp it, what he sees is not an *untouchable dagger* but 'a dagger of the mind, a false creation'.[10]

I said that what we can encounter and manipulate in action provides our 'primitive' concept of a material thing. In part I intended this to have connotations of 'historically primitive' or 'psychologically primitive'. It provides our naive and unsophisticated concept of a material thing, and this concept subsequently has to be deepened and extended. But I also intended 'primitive' to mean 'logically primitive', for when the concept of a material thing comes to be given a more extended application—when it is a matter of demonstrating the corporeality of air, for example—this is done by showing that the entities in question act in ways essentially similar to the more primitive paradigms.[11] Again, we shall get into difficulties if we cling to this primitive concept of a material thing within the realms of scientific theory, and envisage sub-atomic particles or fields of force in accordance with this model. But the fact remains that what these scientific theories

---

[10] In connection with the primacy of touch over the other senses, Yukio Kachi has pointed out to me that something of this idea is to be found in Aristotle, who states that touch is the one sense which all animals possess, and explains this from the fact that 'touch is the sense for food' (*De Anima* II.3). Berkeley also maintains the primacy of touch in his *New Theory of Vision*, and this might seem to invalidate my remarks about the empiricists' diminished conception of touch. It is to be noted, however, that Berkeley subsequently regards his position in the *Principles* as the more consistent one, for if experience consists simply in the having of sensations, touch can be no more privileged than any of the other senses.

[11] Lucretius, for example, argues for the corporeality of air by pointing to the fact that, though we cannot see it (nor indeed manipulate it in any obvious sense), we are aware of the way in which it acts as a destructive force, like a stream in flood. In the same passage he defends the existence of invisible corporeal particles by referring to such phenomena as the wearing away of a ring or a plough or a pavement and asserting that this must be produced by the same process of rubbing and breaking which is more grossly experienceable in other cases. See *De Rerum Natura* I, 265–328.

provide an account of is nothing other than the world of material things defined by our engagement with them in practical activity.[12]

I turn now to the category of 'causality', about which I want to make the same suggestion: that the category gets its meaning from the human experience of working on the world, resisting it and utilizing it. The point is made by Engels in the following passage:

> Not only do we find that a particular motion is followed by another, we find also that we can evoke a particular motion by setting up the conditions in which it takes place in nature, indeed that we can produce motions which do not occur at all in nature (industry), at least not in this way, and that we can give these motions a predetermined direction and extent. *In this way*, by the *activity of human beings*, the idea of *causality* becomes established, the idea that one motion is the *cause* of another. True, the regular sequence of certain natural phenomena can by itself give rise to the idea of causality—the heat and light that come with the sun; but this affords no proof, and to that extent Hume's scepticism was correct in saying that a regular *post hoc* can never establish a *propter hoc*. But the activity of human beings *forms the test* of causality. If we bring the sun's rays to a focus by means of a lens and make them act like the rays of an ordinary fire, we thereby prove that the heat comes from the sun.[13]

This is not entirely unambiguous. Engels is partly concerned with the idea we noted earlier, of practice as a tool, a means for finding out about the world. The more interesting suggestion, however, is that what we *mean* by 'causality' can be understood only from the standpoint of human practice.

[12] The primacy of touch and manipulability can be linked with the idea that primary qualities are more centrally constitutive of a thing than are its secondary qualities. Especially interesting here is Jonathan Bennett's article 'Substance, Reality, and Primary Qualities', in which he points out that the reality and objectivity of primary qualities can be shown by innumerable manipulative tests; we can demonstrate that one cup is *bigger* than another by pouring water from the bigger into the smaller until the latter overflows, by passing a hand across the top of the smaller and bringing it up against the side of the bigger cup, and so on. There are very few comparable manipulative tests for demonstrating the existence of colours, etc.; in general, either we see them or we don't. Bennett adds, without pursuing it further, the suggestion that 'this difference between primary and secondary qualities is closely connected with the fact that the former alone involve the sense of touch'. See op. cit., 105–117, in C. B. Martin and D. M. Armstrong (eds), *Locke and Berkeley* (London: Macmillan, 1908). The article originally appeared in *American Philosophical Quarterly* **2** (1965).

[13] F. Engels, *Dialectics of Nature* (Moscow: Progress Publishers, 1974), 230. Engels' example is, as it stands, unsatisfactory, and would have been less so if he had said that by focusing the rays so as to produce heat we prove that the heat comes from the *light-rays*.

He implies that Hume's failure to see in causality anything other than constant conjunction stems from his failure to see the relationship between causality and practice. This, though it does not entirely dispose of Hume's sceptical treatment of causality, seems to me to be essentially right. Hume says:

> All ideas are derived from and represent impressions. We never have any impression that contains any power or efficacy. We never, therefore, have any idea of power.[14]

The claim that our experience contains no impression of power or efficacy could be made only by ignoring the fact of human labour. Of course if one's experience is that of the detached spectator, all that one can experience is the behaviour of one thing accompanied or followed by the behaviour of another. All that one can *see* is the water flowing and the mill-wheel turning, and to that extent one does not see the water causing the wheel to turn, or exerting any force on the wheel. But just *try to stop* the wheel turning, just 'put your shoulder to the wheel', and you will soon have an impression of power and efficacy.[15]

Here, then, we have the idea of 'force' as that which resists human agency, and hence as that which can be redirected by human agency to bring about some desired state. The force of the flowing water, acting on us when we try to resist it, can be utilized by us, through the mill wheel, so that it becomes our power, the power to grind corn, etc. I would suggest that it is in this kind of context that the concept of 'cause' also has its original application; the cause of an event is the natural force by the utilization of which we can bring about the event when we desire it. As Collingwood and others have noted, 'cause' is in origin a practical concept. Gasking puts it like this:

> When we have a general manipulative technique which results in a certain sort of event A, we speak of producing A by this technique. (Heating things by putting them on a fire.) When in certain cases application of the general technique for producing A also results in B we speak of producing B by producing A. (Making iron glow by heating it.) And in such a case we speak of A causing B, but not vice versa. Thus the notion of causation is essentially connected with our manipulative techniques for producing results. Roughly speaking: 'A rise in the temperature of iron causes it to glow' means 'By applying to iron the general technique for making things hot you will also, in this case, make it glow'.[16]

[14] Hume, *Treatise of Human Nature*, I (Everyman Edition), 159.

[15] I have said that this does not dispose of Hume. In particular, it leaves as yet untouched the problem of induction.

[16] D. Gasking, 'Causation and Recipes', *Mind* LXIV (1955), 483.

Again, as with the category of 'substance', the concept of 'cause' is one that can be extended beyond immediate practical contexts. But it can be extended in this way only on the basis of the original meaning which it is given from the standpoint of human agency. To quote Gasking again:

> ... one may say that the rise in mean sea-level at a certain geological epoch was due to the melting of the Polar ice-cap. But when one can properly say this sort of thing it is always the case that people can produce events of the first sort as a means to producing events of the second sort. For example, one can melt ice in order to raise the level of water in a certain area.[17]

I have been sketching a way in which the Kantian categories constitutive of human experience could be seen to be fashioned not just by human mental activity, but by practical work on the world. I see this as a possible way of developing the theory attributed to Marx by Kolakowski, and plausibly so attributed, in my view, though the way in which I have been setting it out goes way beyond anything that Marx actually said. I further agree with Kolakowski that 'this embryo of an epistemology . . . is not only found in Marx's thought, but is also philosophically worthy of continuation' (op. cit., 78). In continuing it, one would have to beware of overstating it. I do not, of course, want to claim that an understanding of the fundamental categories is available only to the worker. All the same, it does seem to me that Hume's class position would play its part in an explanation of his espousing an 'empiricism of the detached spectator'. More importantly, it is because work is so central to human social life that it determines the fundamental categories of human cognition (a statement which I shall qualify at the end of this paper). Again, I don't want to say that, in the individual case, the child cannot learn the meaning of these categories until it learns to work. But though the young child is hardly a worker, he or she is acquiring the manipulative skills essential to human work; she builds with toy bricks, plays with toy cars, she learns to throw, to balance, to fetch and carry. I would claim that the acquisition of these manipulative skills plays a vital role in the acquisition of the conceptual framework. (We might think here of Wittgenstein's stress on locating language within 'language-*games*', where the latter means not just doing things with words, but the practical activities within which language gets its meaning.) Throughout this section I have deliberately oscillated between the phrases 'human work' and 'human agency'. The wider term is needed to give the thesis its proper plausibility. But not just any human act counts as 'agency' in the required sense. Manipulating objects does; wriggling one's toes does not.

However, I cannot attempt here to elaborate the thesis in further detail.

[17] Ibid.

For the remainder of this paper I want to concentrate on one particular line of objection to it.

IV

The objection has to do with the question I posed at the beginning of this paper. Is the theory we have been looking at incompatible with materialism? Is it, perhaps, not only traceable to an idealist ancestry, but itself inescapably tainted with idealism? Can one make use of the relevant idealist insights, while detaching them from their idealist context?

At one level, what I have been trying to do so far is precisely to *establish* a materialist ontology, by showing how our conception of a world of causally interacting material things is grounded in human work. But it may be said that this materialism is bought only at the cost of a second-order idealism. It may be seen, in Kantian terms, as an empirical realism resting on a transcendental idealism. For it may be thought that the thesis which I have been developing from Kolakowski involves the claim that the world of substances and causes is a world *created* by human practice. And should not an authentically materialist philosophy, on the contrary, incorporate the objectivist claim that the world which we experience is as it is, *independently* of human interaction with it?

Kolakowski's thesis has in fact been criticized on these grounds by Andrew Collier, in a paper entitled 'Truth and Practice'.[18] Collier sees Kolakowski's interpretation of Marx as running directly counter to what he calls the 'essentially materialistic' stipulations

> ... that reality precedes and is independent of thought, that thought lays claim to reflect and correspond to reality, that the truth or falsity of a thought is determined by reference to the reality it claims to reflect, and that the meaning and identity of a thought are determined by the conditions which would make it true (op. cit., 10).

From this standpoint Collier formulates objections to Kolakowski's thesis which seem to boil down to the following two:

(1) 'Precisely in order to serve our needs, cognition must attain a certain independence of them' (op. cit., 12). The world is not fashioned by human thought, it is as it is, independently of our understanding of it. We could

[18] Andrew Collier, 'Truth and Practice', in *Radical Philosophy* **5** (Summer 1973). I should like to emphasize the extent to which I have been impressed by this article, and been forced by it to think out my own view on these issues. A position similar to Collier's is advocated by David-Hillel Ruben in his book *Marxism and Materialism* (Sussex: Harvester Press, 1977)—another impressive piece of Marxist philosophy. Unfortunately I did not read the book until I had written most of this paper, but I think that what I say in response to Collier is largely applicable to Ruben also.

not act effectively on the world and master it through work unless we were in a position to obtain objective knowledge of it, uninfluenced by our needs.

(2) Just because we are capable of this independent and objective knowledge of the world, we can understand *how* our view of the world is sometimes influenced by our needs. 'We can study human needs objectively, and revise our account of "external" reality in so far as it was in the first place distorted by their influence' (ibid.).

A first point that can be made in response to Collier is this. Collier fails to distinguish between the claim that *specific beliefs* are the product of human needs, and the claim that an *overall categorial framework* is the product of human needs. The distinction is vital. The second thesis, that the categorial framework is a human product, is entirely compatible with the recognition that *within this framework* specific beliefs may either correspond or fail to correspond with objective reality. My belief that, as I write, a car is being driven past my window is objectively true or false, quite independently of my needs or of any human needs. I can, quite straightforwardly and empirically, ascertain that the noise I hear is in fact produced by a car, that the car stands in a certain spatial relation to my window, that its movement is controlled by someone sitting in the driver's seat, and so on. To such beliefs the correspondence theory of truth (in some suitably wide formulation) is indeed applicable. But *any* experiences which might serve either to confirm or falsify such beliefs would themselves have to be structured in accordance with our categorial framework of enduring things causally interacting in space and time. And just because *all* our experiences are structured in this way, the framework cannot itself be assessed in the way that the specific beliefs can. We cannot stand outside this all-embracing framework and compare it with an independently existing reality, in the way that we can stand outside our specific beliefs and assess their degree of correspondence with an independent reality.

The same goes for Collier's second objection: that we can ascertain *how* our view of the world is affected by our needs, and can revise it accordingly. Consider Collier's example: 'I may believe that a woman still loves me, when she does not', and my believing it may be a result of my need to do so, because 'it would be too painful to admit the truth to myself' (op. cit., 11). Here again what we are talking about is the determination of a *specific belief* by the believer's needs. Certainly, then, we can distinguish here between what is objectively the case and what I need to believe about it. Accordingly, we can show also how the effect of my needs is to *distort* my understanding of reality. And we can show this because we can *identify independently* those features of the world which I distort because I want them to be other than they really are. But there can be no question of identifying independently the reality which we experience within our categorial framework, and thus of asking whether this framework, shaped by our needs, distorts or faithfully reflects that reality.

The point, then, is this. Collier attacks Kolakowski's theory as incompatible with objectivism. But the theory in fact leaves room for an objectivist, correspondence theory of truth as applied to all our specific beliefs or sets of beliefs; and Kolakowski himself points this out (though not as clearly as he might have done).[19] What the theory is concerned with is the status of a categorial framework.

As a reply to Collier, however, this only takes us a certain way, for it may still be said that despite these concessions to objectivism the theory remains radically idealist. It still seems to imply, at the level of categorial frameworks, that the world is as it is *because* we comprehend it that way; the world is a world of material things causally interacting in space and time because those are the categories which we apply to it and within which we experience it. Notice again how Kolakowski formulates the matter:

> Human consciousness, the practical mind, although it does not produce existence, produces existence as composed of individuals divided into species and genera (op. cit., 66).

The suggestion here is not simply that human beings create the genus-terms with which they describe the world—which, as a claim about language as a human product, is obvious enough. Rather, the suggestion is that human beings create the world in so far as it falls under that description. Again, we find Kolakowski saying:

> From the point of view of this anthropological, or anthropocentric, monism, the picture of reality sketched by everyday perception and by scientific thinking is a kind of human creation (not imitation). . . . In this sense the world's products must be considered artificial. In this world the sun and stars exist because man is able to make them *his* objects (ibid., 67f.).

Here we have a move from the claim that 'the *picture* of reality' is 'a kind of human creation' to the claim that the sun and stars are *themselves* a kind of human creation.[20]

---

[19] 'To this reality [i.e. the reality common to all human beings in virtue of the constancy of basic human needs] one can also apply the Aristotelian concept of truth'; but it 'applies to [a] world upon which man has already imposed "substantial forms" ' (Kolakowski, op. cit., 77).

[20] Kolakowski finds similar formulations in Marx's own early writings. He quotes him as saying that

> Nature, considered abstractly, in and of itself, perpetuated in its separation from man, is *nothing* to him (op. cit., 63; cf. K. Marx, *Early Writings*, trans. T. B. Bottomore (London: Watts, 1963), 217).

Despite such remarks, Kolakowski disavows the label of 'idealism'. He asserts that 'the qualities of things arise as human products, yet not in the idealist sense', since they are not 'created out of nothingness' (p. 67). What does this mean? Kolakowski is acknowledging the reality of what he calls a 'pre-existing chaos' (p. 75) independent of human consciousness. He likens man as the creator to 'the God of the Averroists, who organizes the world out of previously existing material. Once created, this world becomes the only one, and the act of creation annihilates the primal chaos' (p. 77). This would seem to mean that the world, as some kind of undifferentiated reality, does exist independently of human consciousness, but that the components of the world—things and their causal and spatio-temporal relations, in my version of the thesis—do *not* exist independently of human consciousness. But that, of course, is not enough to rebut the charge of idealism.

Kolakowski's formulations, then, make the theory an incontrovertibly idealist theory. Can it be reformulated in non-idealist terms, while still retaining its substantive import?

More indicative, perhaps, is the following sentence, in a passage where Marx envisages the eventual unification of the natural and human sciences:

> Nature, as it develops in human history, is the act of genesis of human society, is the *actual* nature of man; thus nature, as it develops through industry, though in an alienated form, is truly *anthropological* nature (*Early Writings*, 164).

Envisaging the future realization of this in a non-alienated form, he says:

> . . . it is only when objective reality everywhere becomes for man in society the reality of human faculties, human reality, and thus the reality of his own faculties, that all *objects* become for him the *objectification of himself*. The objects then confirm and realize his individuality, they are *his own* objects, i.e. man himself becomes the object (ibid., 160f.).

In the same vein, Marx seems to argue that we will cease to look for a divine creator when we come to see nature, including man himself, as a human creation:

> Since . . . for socialist man, the *whole of what is called world history* is nothing but the creation of man by human labour, and the emergence of nature for man, he therefore has the evident and irrefutable proof of his *self-creation*, of his own *origins*. Once the essence of man and of nature, man as a natural being and nature as a human reality, has become evident in practical life, in sense experience, the quest for an *alien* being, a being above man and nature (a quest which is an avowal of the unreality of man and nature) becomes impossible in practice (ibid., 156f.).

But it has to be admitted that none of these passages lends itself unequivocally to a strong epistemological interpretation. For a caution against reading too much into the *1844 Manuscripts*, see Ruben, op. cit., ch. 3.

V

An obvious step to take would be the following. We have seen that Kolakowski shifts from saying that our *picture of reality* is a human creation to saying that *reality in so far as it conforms to this picture* is a human creation. So can we not simply interrupt this slide? Can we not retain the essence of the theory by saying that the categories, but not the world to which they apply, are the product of human practical needs? Well, that is in fact what I want to say. But before resting content with that formulation, we need to see why the slide to the stronger position can seem so attractive.

If we are to resist Kolakowski's idealist formulation, we shall have to say something like this. Human beings create a categorial framework with which they describe a world of material things causally interacting in space and time. Now we do not want to say, with Kolakowski, that they thereby *create* such a *world*. So it looks as though the alternative is to say that they apply the framework to a world *which is in fact* a world of material things causally interacting in space and time (what I shall from now on call, for short, a 'Kantian world').

But now consider this. A crucial and indispensible element in the theory is the claim that the world *could have been categorized differently*. And this is not just to say that, though our categorial framework gives us a correct picture of the world, it might have happened that we got it wrong. It is to say that, as it were, the world can lend itself to alternative categorizations. For what I have stressed is that it is the nature of *human needs* and *human practice* that determines why we have the categorial framework that we do have. This implies that, if human needs had been different, we would have had a different set of categories, and these too could have been just as applicable to reality. It is the nature of the needs, not the nature of the reality, that is decisive for which framework we actually have.

So now we are landed with the following assertions. The Kantian categories are applied by us to what is in fact a Kantian world. If our needs had been different, we could quite appropriately have applied a different set of categories. Putting these two assertions together, we have to say, it seems, that if our needs had been different we could appropriately have applied non-Kantian categories to what is in fact a Kantian world. But that does not seem satisfactory; if they were non-Kantian categories, and if they were applied to a Kantian world, how could they be applied 'appropriately'? One can now see, I think, how tempting it is to say that *if* it had been appropriate for us to apply non-Kantian categories to the world, the world to which we applied them would *ipso facto* have been a non-Kantian world. Which seems to lead us inexorably to the conclusion that which set of categories we apply determines what kind of world it is.

Let us try another way of putting it. We might say something like this. 'There is no limit to the number of possible classifications of objects', and which classification we choose will depend upon 'human interests and human purposes'; but 'there is no classification of any set of objects which is not objectively based on genuine similarities and differences'. I quote these sentences from Renford Bambrough's article on 'Family Resemblances'.[21] Along these lines we might say that there are innumerable similarities and differences between features of the world, from which we pick out those which give us demarcations suited to our purposes; and that this is what makes for the possibility of *alternative* categorizations, each of which is *objectively based*. Here is Bambrough's example. Suppose we visit a South Sea island where various kinds of trees are cultivated. We find that the islanders regularly describe as 'the same' trees which seem to us to have nothing in common, and vice versa. We may at first be puzzled by their classification; but it turns out that they can teach us their principles of classification, and can point out to us genuine similarities and differences, not marked by our classification, on the strength of which they assign trees to 'the same kind' or 'different kinds'.

> It may be that the islanders classify trees as 'boat-building trees', 'house-building trees', etc., and that they are more concerned with the height, thickness and maturity of the trees than they are with the distinctions of species that interest us (op. cit., 221).

Likewise our own system of classification can be taught to the islanders, since it too is based on features which we can point out to them.

This example, and what Bambrough says about it, are adequate to Bambrough's purposes in his paper. To some extent also they can be utilized to serve our present purposes. The idea of picking out certain similarities and differences rather than others provides us with a model which is in some ways less misleading than Kolakowski's talk of 'creation'. It helps us to see how alternative categorizations can be different, yet each objectively grounded. Nevertheless, there is a vital difference between the case Bambrough is considering and the one we are concerned with. Bambrough's case is one where there is a wider shared framework, a wider vocabulary, *from within which* different groups pick out different features. The islanders and the visitors share the concept of a tree, they have shared concepts in terms of which they can talk about leaf shapes, etc., which are the basis of the visitors' classification, and features such as height, thickness and maturity which might be the basis of the islanders' classification. Here is another example of the same kind, from Whorf's *Language, Thought, and Reality*:[22]

---

[21] Renford Bambrough; 'Universals and Family Resemblances', *Proceedings of the Aristotelian Society* LXI (1960–61), 220–222. Also in G. Pitcher (ed.), *Wittgenstein—the Philosophical Investigations* (London: Macmillan, 1968), 202–204.

[22] Benjamin Lee Whorf, *Language, Thought, and Reality* (Cambridge, Mass.: MIT Press, 1956), 216.

> We have the same word for falling snow, snow on the ground, snow packed hard like ice, slushy snow, wind-driven flying snow—whatever the situation may be. To an Eskimo, this all-inclusive word would be almost unthinkable; he would say that falling snow, slushy snow, and so on, are sensuously and operationally different, different things to contend with; he uses different words for them and for other kinds of snow.

Here too the fact that we treat falling snow and slushy snow and the rest as different states of some one stuff, snow, whereas the Eskimo treats them as different stuffs, should not be allowed to conceal the obvious fact that the demarcations made by the Eskimos' conceptual system *can* be identified quite naturally within our own system of concepts, even though they are not marked by single words. The point about both these examples is that although the different conceptual systems pick out different features to emphasize, they do so from within a wider framework which is common to them both. And it is precisely the existence of this wider framework which enables us to talk about 'picking out' here. It is in the terms of this wider framework that we can say *what it is* that the different systems pick out.[23]

Now this aspect of the examples is precisely what is missing from the case we are concerned with. What we want to talk about there are alternative *total* frameworks which can each be grounded in objective features of reality. And *ex hypothesi* there is no way of standing outside these frameworks and saying what it is that the different frameworks pick out. In Bambrough's example we can describe a neutral world of trees and their sizes and shapes, and can describe the features which the islanders pick out

[23] The same goes for conflicting scientific theories, and the way in which observation statements may be relative to a specific theory. Hanson, in *Patterns of Discovery* (Cambridge: CUP, 1958), says:

> Let us consider Johannes Kepler: imagine him on a hill watching the dawn. With him is Tycho Brahe. Kepler regarded the sun as fixed: it was the earth that moved. But Tycho followed Ptolemy and Aristotle in this much at least: the earth was fixed and all other celestial bodies moved around it. *Do Kepler and Tycho see the same thing in the east at dawn?* (p. 5).

Although, as Hanson argues, in an important sense they do *not* see the same thing, the fact remains that, as with the previous examples, there does exist a wider framework, neutral as between the different scientific theories, in terms of which we can say *what it is* that the alternative theories lead one to see differently. As Hanson says, there is *some* sense in which Tycho and Kepler see the same thing. And this is because neither's conceptual framework is confined to the conceptual framework of the particular scientific theory he holds. There is a wider frame of reference. I mention this kind of case because there are affinities between Hanson's position and Marx's view of the creative character of scientific theorizing which I mentioned above (p. 2f.). We can perhaps now see how that Marxist view is both linked with, and distinct from, the stronger thesis I have been examining.

as the basis of their classification and the features which the visitors pick out as the basis of their classification. But there is no neutral description we can give of the world from which a Kantian categorial framework picks out some features and a non-Kantian categorial framework picks out others.

So then, what are we to say now? I want to avoid Kolakowski's idealist formulation. I do not want to say that human needs and human thought *create* a certain kind of world. I want to hang on to the claim that the categories which human beings employ, though they are determined by human needs, at the same time have an objective basis in a world which exists independently of human cognition. I should like to say, following Bambrough, that different systems of categorization could each be based on objective similarities and differences. But now the problem is: how can we describe this world from which different categorial systems could pick out different similarities and differences? There is no neutral framework; so how describe the world to which both Kantian categories and non-Kantian categories could be applied? Well, I want to describe it as just that—no more and no less. It is a world to which both Kantian categories and non-Kantian categories could objectively be applied.

That may seem an incredibly lame and uninformative conclusion. It doesn't tell us anything positive about the nature of such a world. Of course it doesn't. The impossibility of doing so is just the impossibility of conceptualizing a pre-conceptualized world. But it does enable us to avoid any talk of Kantian unknowable things-in-themselves. It enables us to avoid Kolakowski's idealist supposition of a world which is created by our categorization of a primal chaos. And it enables us to meet Collier's requirement, the entirely proper requirement that any theory of knowledge which is to count as a Marxist theory must recognize 'that reality precedes and is independent of thought' and that human beings are capable of obtaining objective knowledge of that independent reality.

VI

I want finally to return to Collier's second objection. This was that we are capable of giving an account of *how* our thought is influenced by our needs, and therefore of revising our thought accordingly. In the light of what I have been saying, however, there is an important sense in which we *cannot* give such an account. Of course this whole paper has been taken up with trying to give one. But we now have to notice the peculiar difficulty of stating the thesis. Consider again Collier's example: a woman no longer loves me, but I need to believe that she does. This is unproblematic, because there is no problem about how to describe my needs and the objective situation independently of my beliefs about it. But as I have been emphasizing, what we are really concerned with is the way in which a total categorial framework is determined by human needs. And since there is no way of standing outside the framework, there is no way of giving any description of the independent reality and the independently existing needs whose interaction creates the framework. We can describe them only within the terms of those categories which are already shaped by those needs.

The problem shows itself as a practical difficulty. A part of the thesis is that alternative frameworks are possible. To make the thesis convincing, we ought to be able to say what such alternatives might look like. But now it would seem that we cannot do so; for any such description would have to be given from within the framework that we actually have. As such, it would not be a description of an *alternative* framework, but a sketch of a set of concepts parasitic upon our existing ones. Kolakowski falls into this trap, as Collier is quick to note. To provide some kind of contrast, Kolakowski asks us to imagine

> . . . a world where there would be no such such objects as 'horse', 'leaf', 'star', and others allegedly devised by nature. Instead, there might be, for example, such objects as 'half a horse and a piece of river', 'my ear and the moon', and other similar products of a surrealist imagination. The surrealist world seems more 'strange' to us than the usual one only because we do not have names for its components and do not use it in technology (op. cit., 68).

But as Collier comments, the world created in surrealist art is one which trades on the ways in which human fantasies distort our objective knowledge of the world. It is not an authentically independent alternative.

Nevertheless, in our attempt to envisage contrasting frameworks, we are not altogether helpless. For a start, we can, from within our existing framework, gesture at possible alternatives. One possibility I have already mentioned is that we might contrast a substance-causality ontology with a sense-datum ontology. In some of its versions the concept of sense-data seems to me to be radically incoherent—but not in all versions. An ontology of colour patches would, I think, be a possible ontology; that is, it would be impossible only in the sense that it would be pragmatically impossible, given the kinds of beings that human beings are and the ways in which they need to act in the world. We cannot say in detail what such an ontology would be like, for within our own Kantian ontology colour patches are characteristically identified as the colours of things, the latter being regarded as ontologically primary. For us, then, a colour patch ontology has to be parasitic on a substance ontology. Nevertheless this is a case where, as I have put it, we can 'gesture towards' the possibility of an alternative ontology from within our own framework.

A similar example would be the possibility of an ontology in which things ceased to exist when they were not perceived. Generations of students have been initiated into philosophical study by being asked 'How do we know that an object continues to exist when it is not perceived?' The point is, of course, that *ex hypothesi* no perceptual experience could establish that it does continue to exist. Therefore what we might call a 'phenomenalist' ontology would be a possible way of conceptualizing the relevant experiences.[24] We could talk about a new object coming into existence with each continuous sequence of experience. Again we cannot spell out what this ontology would be like. The concept of an object in such an ontology would be very different, and the kinds of attribution we make within our existing ontology (e.g. the attribution of causal agency to unperceived objects) would have to be articulated in ways which we cannot envisage. But at any rate we can say enough to indicate that such an ontology would be theoretically possible, that it would be an alternative way of conceptualizing the relevant experiences conceptualized by our existing ontology, and that the superiority of the latter is a pragmatic superiority.

There is, in addition, another way of setting up the required contrast, viz. by contrasting the different conceptual frameworks of different human cultures. And this introduces an important modification into the theory, which I have until now kept deliberately over-simple. I have implied that the Kantian categorial framework represents the total conceptual apparatus of all human beings and all past and present cultures. Of course that is not so. As a way of comprehending the actual diversity, let me sketch an ideal-type alternative. I have said that the Kantian framework represents the way in which the world is experienced by human beings in so far as they work on the world to satisfy their needs. But in fact this is not the only way in which humans interact with their environment. They work on the world, but they also interact with other persons. Corresponding therefore to these two kinds of interaction, work and personal interaction, we can identify two sets of categories, the Kantian categories of impersonal 'substances' and 'causes', and 'personalist' categories of the kind which we ourselves normally apply to human persons. A hypothetical purely personalist ontology would make no distinction between persons and things, between the animate and the inanimate, but would include all the components of the world in the category of persons and would describe them entirely in the terms which we normally reserve for animate (and especially human) beings. There are innumerable residual traces of something approximating to a personalist ontology in our own vocabulary, in our talk of angry skies, fierce winds, gentle slopes, and so on. We may be inclined to think of these as metaphors, but we can envisage the possibility of their being

---

[24] I am making rather free use of the label 'phenomenalism', which in its orthodox form does not assert that objects cease to exist when unperceived, but simply offers an analysis (in terms of hypothetical perception-statements) of what is meant by saying that they continue to exist.

treated as natural and literal descriptions of the world. The undeniable resemblances between one's experience of an angry sky and one's experience of an angry person would not then be regarded as cross-categorial comparisons, but as sufficient to bring both experiences within a single category. They would be *the same experience*.

The idea of a 'personalist' ontology could provide us with another hypothetical contrast to a Kantian ontology. As I have indicated, however, personalist categories also function as an actual component of human categorial frameworks. How they can still nevertheless provide the required contrast, I shall try to explain in a moment. I want first to suggest that the ontology of any human culture will be some combination of personalist and impersonalist elements. Between the hypothetical extremes of pure personalism and pure impersonalism there is a continuum on which we can locate actual categorial systems. For example, perhaps the nearest historical approximation to pure personalism would be an animistic world-view. But it is important to recognize that animism is not itself a purely personalist ontology. However extensively the members of a primitive culture may populate the natural world with spirits, they still have also a technical relationship to the natural world; they make tools, they know how to manipulate their environment by means of technical skills, and, as I have been claiming, impersonal causal categories are rooted in this technical relationship. Notice also that the distinction between interpersonal and technical relationships to natural phenomena is reflected in the distinction between the natural phenomena themselves and the spirits which inhabit them. The spirit inhabiting the tree, for example, is distinguished from the tree itself, and thus we have here a degree of depersonalization as compared with our hypothetical extreme which would consist simply in characterizing the tree itself in wholly personalist terms.[25] Further degrees of depersonali-

[25] In this respect it may be that there are historical instances of world-views closer than typical animism to the personalist extreme. R. R. Marett, for example, in his criticism of Tylor's 'animism' theory, coined the term 'animatism' and explained it as follows:

> . . . when a thunderstorm is seen approaching in South Africa, a Kaffir village, led by its medicine-man, will rush to the nearest hill and yell at the hurricane to divert it from its course. Here we have awe finding vent in what on the face of it may be no more than a simple straightforward act of personification. It is animism in the loose sense of some writers, or, as I propose to call it, *animatism*: but it is *not* animism in the strict scientific sense that implies the attribution, not merely of personality and will, but of 'soul' or 'spirit', to the storm (R. R. Marett, *The Threshold of Religion* (London: Methuen, 1929), 14).

There appear to be comparable elements in Shinto:

> The woodlands, the flowers of the field, crops in their seasons, the dust of the road and the water that lays the dust and the germs of disease in the dust,

zation would be represented by e.g. Greek polytheism or Christian monotheism, in which personalist categories have a role to play in the comprehension of the natural world, but where personality is more decisively
located outside the natural phenomena themselves. And of course a
modern secular culture would represent a point even further towards the
impersonalist pole of the continuum.

However, the personalist and impersonalist elements within a categorial
framework do not always peacefully coexist. They also come into conflict
with one another. Classic instances of this conflict are, of course, provided

---

animal life and humanity, beneficial or harmful, are all divine spirit. Fire,
mountains, seas, every material as well as every living form of the universe is
Kami or divine spirit, for to Shinto there are not two entities, divine spirit and
Nature. Nature *is* divine spirit come forth from subjectivity as the objective
universe. Mountains and seas do not have spirits dwelling in them. Everything
is divine spirit . . . (J. W. T. Mason, *The Meaning of Shinto* (New York: E. P.
Dutton and Co., 1935), 62).

For guidance in connection with the empirical material relevant to these questions, I am grateful to Lewis M. Rogers and Peter Appleby. Even if I had the
space to do so, I would be incompetent to deal at all usefully with the issues in
the fields of comparative anthropology and comparative religion which are
raised by my remarks here. I would, however, like to make two suggestions:

(a) In the following paragraphs I allude favourably to an evolutionary approach
to religion, and especially to primitive religions, of the kind which held the stage
in the late nineteenth and early twentieth centuries but appears now to be out of
fashion (see E. E. Evans-Pritchard, *Theories of Primitive Religion* (Oxford:
Clarendon Press, 1965), especially chapter V). Of course it is important to
recognize the dangers of forcing a genetic interpretation on cross-cultural comparisons, and of oversimplifying a complex process. Nevertheless I would have
thought it difficult to deny that just as increasing technological mastery of nature
brings with it a change from a predominantly religious to a predominantly secular
view of nature, so also at an earlier stage it goes along with a development from
something like animism to some kind of monotheism. Here I am assuming that
the thesis of the relatively primitive character of animism can be defended
against the counter-theses of primitive monotheism (see e.g. the criticisms in
Robert H. Lowie, *Primitive Religion* (New York: Liverlight, 1948), 124–133),
and of the 'mana'-doctrine as a pre-animistic belief in an impersonal divine or
magical force (see e.g. Evans-Pritchard, op. cit., 110, and Raymond Firth, 'The
Analysis of Mana: An Empirical Approach', in *The Journal of the Polynesian
Society* **49** (1940), for criticism of excessive claims made for the 'mana'-concept).

(b) Tylor and others tended to look at animism from the standpoint of a
modern scientific outlook, as some kind of false inference (e.g. a mistaken
generalization from the experience of the 'separation' of the soul from the body
in dreams; see E. B. Tylor, *Religion in Primitive Culture* (New York: Harper
Torchbooks, 1958; a reprint of chs. XI–XIX of *Primitive Culture*, originally
published 1871), esp. 12f., 194f., 270f.). The trouble with this approach is that it

by the struggles between religious and secular views of the world. This fact of conflict constitutes a very important qualification of the overall thesis I have been considering. I have until now given the impression that since all our thinking takes place within a categorial framework, the framework itself must always be beyond question. We can now see that a questioning of the framework does take place, not however as the impossible feat of standing outside the framework and examing it, but in the form of the working out of the conflicts within it. We can best illustrate this by referring to the role of philosophy in the process. Various classical philosophical dilemmas and debates can be seen as attempts to adjudicate between the rival claims of personalist and impersonalist categories. The pre-Socratics are an excellent example. They inherit a world in which 'everything is full of gods'. They inherit personalistic and biological models with which to describe the origin of the universe and its continuing processes. We can observe their thought becoming increasingly impersonalistic and mechanistic as they search for new kinds of model derived from technological control of the world; natural processes are described in terms of combination and separation, quantitative proportions, the causal interaction of lifeless atoms. Other examples are available from modern philosophy. Descartes for one is obviously concerned to draw a clear line of demarcation between the personal and the mechanical in the light of the emergent scientific outlook. The Kantian categorial framework which I have been referring to throughout this paper is, when seen in the context of Kant's total philosophy, another attempt at the same task. And in our own time it is a matter for philosophical dispute whether personalist categories are even applicable to persons. Conflict centres around the claim that the categories of intention and purpose are eliminable even from our experience of human life, and that the causal and mechanistic categories implicit in our manipulation and control of the natural world are the appropriate categories in which to understand our own human activity.

To return now to my main theme: from the point of the Marxist thesis I have been considering, these philosophical disputes would have to be seen as attempts to articulate an ontology already implicit in the practical relation of human beings to the world. To the extent that human beings acquire practical mastery over the non-human world, they experience it less and less as the behaviour of wilful persons, now hostile, now benign, and increasingly as the behaviour of impersonal forces which can be

---

then seems implausible that such a mistaken theory should have been formulated in the first place and perpetuated thereafter. I suggest that it may be more helpful and more plausible to understand an animistic ontology not as a 'theory' at all but as a basic way of categorizing experience; and not as an aberration from a scientific outlook, but as a qualified version of the hypothetical ontology which I have called 'personalism'.

manipulated and controlled. It is in this way that, in our understanding of the natural world, the categories of intention and purpose, of motive and emotion, come to be replaced by the category of causality. The struggle between personalist and impersonalist categorizations of experience is initially fought out at this level.[26]

In short, though the philosophers have an important part to play in this process, their role is essentially that of tidying up. Like Hegel's philosophical Owl of Minerva, they come on the scene when the crucial preliminary work has already been done. The creation of an adequate categorial framework is, in the first place, a task performed by human beings in their engagement with the world, in work, in practice. And if 'the primacy of practice' means the primacy of the worker over the philosopher, that is not such a bad conclusion.[27]

[26] Such a perspective is suggested by the following passage:

Consciousness is at first, of course, merely consciousness concerning the immediate sensuous environment and consciousness of the limited connection with other persons and things outside the individual who is growing self-conscious. At the same time it is consciousness of nature, which first appears to men as a completely alien, all-powerful and unassailable force, with which men's relations are purely animal and by which they are overawed like beasts; it is thus a purely animal consciousness of nature (natural religion) just because nature is as yet hardly modified historically. (We see here immediately: this natural religion or this particular relation of men to nature is determined by the form of society and vice versa. Here as everywhere, the identity of nature and man appears in such a way that the restricted relation of men to nature determines their restricted relation to one another, and their restricted relation to one another determines men's restricted relation to nature.) ... This sheeplike or tribal consciousness receives its further development and extension through increased productivity, the increase of needs, and, what is fundamental to both of these, the increase of population (Marx and Engels, *The German Ideology* Part One, C. J. Arthur (ed.) (London: Lawrence and Wishart, 1970), 51).

[27] I should like to thank the members of the Department of Philosophy at the University of Utah, to whom I read a first draft of this paper, and from whom I received valuable help. I am also grateful for comments from Chris Cherry, Andrew Collier, David-Hillel Ruben, Sean Sayers, and Godfrey Vesey.

Bradley and Internal Relations

A. R. MANSER

Bradley is often described as an Anglo-Hegelian, and hence it is assumed that his doctrines derive from Hegel. It is true that his first two works 'The Presuppositions of Critical History' and *Ethical Studies* are heavily influenced by Hegel. *The Principles of Logic* is much less so: it certainly contains a number of both laudatory and critical references to Hegel, but the whole design of the book is completely unrelated to his treatment of logic. *Appearance and Reality* seems to me not to be Hegelian at all. The interesting logical discussions occur in the *Principles*, and it is here that we can find points of comparison between Bradley and Frege and Russell. This is in part because all three were agreed that it was impossible to account for logic by reference to psychology. Bradley's doctrine of internal relations first emerges in this context, though it is given a more metaphysical interpretation in the subsequent *Appearance and Reality*. However, most who have talked of internal relations have taken their view from the latter work, and have found the doctrine either confused or silly. This quotation from *Appearance and Reality* seems to bring out all that is objectionable in the view:

> And if you could have a perfect relational knowledge of the world, you could go on from the nature of red-hairedness to these other characters which qualify it, and you could from the nature of red-hairedness reconstruct all the red-haired men. In such perfect knowledge you could start internally from any one character in the Universe, and you could from that pass to the rest . . . For example, a red-haired man who knew himself utterly would and must, starting from within, go on to know everyone else who had red hair, and he would not know himself until he knew them. But, as things are, he does not know how or why he himself has red hair, nor how and why a different man is also the same in that point, and therefore, because he does not know the ground, the how and why, of his relation to other men, it remains for him relatively external, contingent, and fortuitous. But there is really no mere externality except in his ignorance (*AR*, 520–521).[1]

Few have even paused to wonder why the stress was on relations and not on properties, for the example of the red-haired man would seem more

[1] The books of Bradley are referred to in an abbreviated form as follows: *AR*, *Appearance and Reality*; *ETR*, *Essays on Truth and Reality*; *PL*, *Principles of Logic*.

naturally to be taken as an instance of the latter. Certainly the discussion of the topic has not distinguished between these two. Relations are not seen nowadays as particularly problematic in philosophy; properties are one-place predicates, relations two-place or many-place predicates; both are susceptible of the same treatment. The formal difficulties in handling relations, the fact that they can be transitive, intransitive or non-transitive, symmetrical or non-symmetrical, seem of little philosophic interest, of no more concern than the fact that the old syllogistic logic could only represent the obviously valid argument 'A is greater than B, B is greater than C' 'Therefore A is greater than C' as committing the fallacy of four terms. Hence it is surprising that Russell could write in 1924:

> The question of relations is one of the most important that arise in philosophy, as most other issues turn on it: monism and pluralism; the question whether anything is true except the whole of truth, or wholly real except the whole of reality; idealism and realism, in some of their forms; perhaps the whole existence of philosophy as a subject distinct from science and possessing a method of its own.[2]

However, there seems to have been relatively little written about the controversy that Russell though so important. Moore's well-known paper on the topic was published in 1917, and in 1935 Ryle and Ayer debated the question at a Joint Session, evidence that at least the committee thought it a worth-while topic. The two symposiasts, however, found the doctrine of internal relation absurd. They did not take the obvious step demanded by philosophic charity and ask whether they had misunderstood a view which seemed to them patently ridiculous. The same applies to more recent commentators on Bradley; Wollheim explains 'internal relations' thus:

> In the first place, some of a term's relations are *internal*: by this is meant that the term in question necessarily stands in these relations, or that, if it did not stand in these relations, it would not be what it is or would be other than what it is. So for instance, a husband necessarily stands in the relation of being married to someone: if he were not married to someone, he would be other than what he is. Hence the relation 'being married to someone' is internal to him. Similarly the relation of being disloyal to one's country is internal to a traitor, that of being indifferent to culture is internal to a philistine, that of being printed before 1500 is internal to an incunabulum.[3]

Pears, writing on Russell, says much the same:

[2] 'Logical Atomism' in *Logic and Knowledge*, Marsh (ed.) (London: Allen and Unwin, 1956), 333.
[3] *F. H. Bradley* (Penguin, 1959) 104–105.

A relation is internal if the proposition attributing it to an individual is true *a priori*. For instance the married state is a relation between two individuals, and the proposition that a particular husband is married, or a particular wife is married, is true *a priori*, because it it guaranteed by definition. So in these two cases we have an internal relation.[4]

Thus both these philosophers reduce 'internal relations' to simple analytic truths. Neither of them raise the question of why Bradley, if he wished to maintain all true propositions to be analytic, did not make use of the Kantian terminology, which was certainly known to him (cf. *PL*, 49 n.). Neither did they ask why, if analyticity were the issue, both Bradley and Russell talked of relations in this context, rather than of properties. In this they seem to be following the tradition of Moore, Ryle and Ayer.

Strangely enough, in spite of these dismissals of the terminology, some contemporary writers have taken to using the word 'internal' when what is at issue is a conceptual connection; for example Peter Winch employs 'internal' or its synonym 'intrinsic' frequently in *The Idea of a Social Science*. He says in a section entitled 'The Internality of Social Relations':

> An event's character as an act of obedience is *intrinsic* to it in a way which is not true of an event's character as a clap of thunder[5] . . .

There certainly is a conceptual connection between a command and its being obeyed. If someone does what he was ordered to, though unaware of the order, his act was not one of obedience. This would be generally agreed, as would the reason, namely that it was due to the meaning of the words 'command' and 'obedience', not to the particular command that was given. We are still at the level of analytic truths: there is no important difference between Winch's example and Wollheim's. That Winch thinks that internal relations involve generality is made even more clear by his taking conventions as examples of them.[6] Even though I do not want to follow Bradley's doctrines in his later works here, it is perhaps significant that the example from *Appearance and Reality* was of a particular red-haired man. Certainly in the *Principles of Logic* 'internal relations' hold between particulars, not between concepts. However, Winch does also use an example which at first sight seems different. He is talking of a scene from the film *Shane*:

> And what I want to insist on is that, just as in a conversation the point of a remark (or of a pause) depends on its internal relation to what has gone before, so in the scene from the film the interchange of glances derives

---

[4] *Bertrand Russell and the British Tradition in Philosophy* (Fontana, 1967), 162.
[5]. Op. cit. (Routledge, 1958), 125.
[6] Op. cit., 131.

its full meaning from its internal relation to the situation in which it occurs: the loneliness, the threat of danger, the sharing of a common life in difficult circumstances, the satisfaction in physical effort, and so on.[7]

Unfortunately this type of example will not give true particularity, and hence is not different from the earlier examples. If we surprised an actual glance between two men digging out a tree root, there would be room for discussion of its meaning or even for doubt as to whether it had a meaning. In the film this doubt is not liable to arise, because the significance of the glance has been indicated by the way the camera lingers on it, changes in the incidental music, etc. No doubt the director told the actors to give the glance that particular meaning as they rehearsed the scene. But I doubt that their actual expressions could convey all that Winch rightly says it means in the film. For that we need the rest of the story. If Shane had later eloped with the crofter's wife, then we would have to interpret the glance differently; it would no longer be the same.

The fact that what happens subsequently in the film alters, or can alter, our interpretation is relevant here, for it shows that the connections are both to what has happened and to what will happen. This is part of what is meant by calling the film a work of art. In such a work, the links between the different parts are more like conceptual connections than like those that exist in real life between individuals. The structure of the whole is normally designed to force a certain interpretation on us and in this it resembles a proof in logic or mathematics rather than a description of events in the world. Of course I am not denying that the author or director intended the completed whole to look like a simple description, like the chronicle of a series of real events; I am concerned with its logical status. For an actual series of events does not force an interpretation; it is generally open to several and part of the difficulty is to discover the correct one, to understand it aright. But the notion of a correct interpretation is different for a piece of history and a story. In the latter there is in principle an 'authoritative' interpretation, that of the author himself. In the former a different view is always possible. For new facts may come to light which compel us to change our interpretation. In a story the 'facts' are given us complete; it does not make sense to try to discover what the author did not tell us. Hence even if certain connections in the story are like logical ones, it does not follow that analogous connections in life are of the same sort. If the term 'internal relation' is defined as that which holds between such items as the glance and its background in the passage qoted from Winch, then it is a very different relation from the one with which I am concerned, or the one which Bradley dealt with in his *Logic*. The argument I am putting forward here is that the relations that Winch calls 'internal' hold

[7] Op. cit., 130.

between universals, those of Bradley between particulars. Shane is not a particular or 'Shane' is not a proper name—there is no such person. Nor will it do to say that he is an imaginary individual, for to be that is not to be a particular either. I am claiming that a story, as distinct from a chronicle or a piece of history, is in essence not concerned with particulars—although it is nominally about individuals. There are no individuals in a novel. Hence it is more like a philosophic argument than like a slice of history. If internal relations hold between particulars, and all Bradley's examples suggest this, then his topic is radically different from that of Winch.

It seems that a similar stress on particulars as the bearers of internal relations was in Wittgenstein's mind when he wrote:

> A property is internal if it is unthinkable that its object should not possess it.
> This shade of blue and that one stand, *eo ipso*, in the internal relation of lighter to darker. It is unthinkable that these two objects should not stand in this relation.[8]

This remark is a puzzling one, which will perhaps become clearer when Bradley's views have been explained. Here I cite it to bring out the kind of difference I am trying to indicate. If an author says that A was wearing a darker suit than B it does not make sense to challenge this, except in the trivial case where he says the opposite a few pages later. Wittgenstein is not thinking of such a case but one where two actual shades of blue are presented or pointed to.

Thus it is necessary to reject various interpretations of 'internal relation' that have recently been offered. For a more positive consideration of the topic it might be best to begin with the fact that relational propositions differ from ordinary predications. We may feel untroubled about the meanings of the words used in 'The book is red', but in 'The book is on the table' we face a problem about what 'on' stands for. This might be brought out by a question about how many 'elements' there are in the two propositions. Some would say both contained three, taking the copula in the first as an element; others would say the first contained two, the second three or even four. Wittgenstein thought the second only had two elements:

> Instead of, 'The complex sign "*aRb*" says that *a* stands to *b* in the relation *R*', we ought to put, '*That "a" stands to "b" in a certain relation says that aRb*'.[9]

I take it that Wittgenstein meant that we are forced by our language to include 'on' as an 'element'. though in a more perspicuous notation it

[8] *Tractatus Logic-Philosophicus*, 4.123.
[9] *Tractatus Logico-Philosophicus*, 3.1432.

A. R. Manser

might be possible to eliminate it by a device that 'pictured' reality better, e.g.

'The book
the table.'

Here there would be no temptation to think of 'on' as a term or element. The new method of representation could be compared with musical notation. The situation only consists of a book and a table. It would be different if the book were attached to the table with a piece of string, for the string would need to be mentioned in any proposition that described the situation. Here there exists a contrast which is not too distant from that between internal and external relations. Roughly it could be said that a relation that would have to be represented in a perspicuous language would be an external one. That the details of Wittgenstein's remarks are connected with his 'picture theory' of language does not vitiate the point I am making, for the argument can be presented without substantive reference to that theory.

Russell, in his earlier period, certainly thought of relations as 'terms', which he said meant the same as 'unit, individual and entity'.[10] Later he was still concerned with the issue:

> For my part, I think it as certain as anything can be that there are relational facts such as 'A is earlier than B'. But does it follow that there is an object of which the name is 'earlier'? It is very difficult to make out what can be meant by such a question, and still more difficult to see how an answer can be found.[11]

Thus, at least for Russell, the question of the 'reality of relations' was a question about the existence of entities, not just the logical query as to whether relational propositions could be reduced to subject–predicate ones, though that was also an element in the total problem. Here I do not wish to go into the details of the controversy between Bradley and Russell, which would involve a great deal of space to explain the shifts in the latter's views. It is clear, however, that if 'earlier' is an existent or entity, then there is a problem about its link to the other elements of the proposition. Russell would here seem vulnerable to an argument he tried to use against Bradley, but which Bradley had himself used to show that a relation could not be an entity in its own right, namely that if R could exist by itself, it would need a relation R' to attach it to a in the proposition 'aRb'. If R' also could exist by itself, it would need a further relation R" and so on (*AR*, 27–28). Much the same would apply in the case of subject–predicate propositions if the copula is regarded as the element which links the two terms together,

[10] *Principles of Mathematics* (London: Cambridge University Press, 1903), 43.
[11] *My Philosophical Development* (Unwin, 1975), 128.

186

in other words if it is taken to function as a relation. Bradley argued that:

> ... if the copula is a connection which couples a pair of ideas, it falls
> outside judgment; and, if on the other hand it is the sign of judgment,
> then it does not couple (*PL*, 21).

Part of his reason for saying this is that a question has the same content
as an assertion. That the problem about copulation can also be seen as
involving the existence of relations helps to show why Russell thought the
issue so central.

One possible way out of the difficulty is to say that relations are special
sorts of entities, which just have the property of linking other entities.
This could be put formally by saying that a relation is a two-place function,
properly written ( )R( ), just as a predicate can be represented by a one-
place function, F( ). Relations, like predicates, could then be described
in Fregean terms as 'unsaturated' to indicate that they demand completion
by a pair of terms which can stand on their own, such as proper names;
in Frege's words:

> For not all parts of a thought can be complete: at least one must be
> 'unsaturated' or predicative; otherwise they would not hold together.[12]

(This passage occurs in an explicit discussion of relations.) The notions
of 'completeness' and 'unsaturation' are, as he makes clear, only meta-
phorical. It is not because they are such that they are unsatisfactory,
but because they fail to explain what they purport to. Certainly if we
translate 'Socrates is mortal' or 'John loves Mary' into F(a) and (a)R(b)
and then omit the constants 'a' and 'b' we get forms which contain a
blank and which thus appear to demand completion in a way that the
constants themselves do not. In ordinary language 'is mortal' also appears
to demand completion, but perhaps 'loves' looks as if it can stand on its
own feet. Geach accuses Dummett of making a similar mistake:

> ... the thought that John hit Mary has three component parts: the sense of
> 'John', the sense of 'hit' the sense of 'Mary'. He does not tell us how
> these cohere into a whole, and into the right whole at that, rather than
> into the thought that Mary hit John.[13]

There are two problems here, the first about the coherence of Frege's
views, the second about the way in which a proposition forms a unity,
which Geach mentions. If we accept Frege's (and Bradley's) view that a
word only has *Bedeutung* in the context of a sentence, it is hard to see
why any distinction should be made between different sorts of words.
In the case of predicates it can be argued that their correct form should be

---

[12] *Philosophical Writings of Gottlob Frege* (Oxford: Blackwell, 1952), 54.
[13] Review of Dummet's *Frege, Mind* (1976), 444.

'is mortal', 'is red', etc., but I am not sure that this makes a great deal of difference. In any case, 'hit' or 'loves' are single words. But it is hard to see why, if all words are, as it were, incomplete until they are set into a sentential context, one group should be singled out for special attention as 'unsaturated'. The problem that this notion was introduced to solve is, of course, that of the unity of a judgment or assertion; only if there was some linkage would the parts hold together. The suggestion that one part of the sentence is unsaturated is meant to account for the unity. Dummett even talks of 'the process whereby an atomic sentence is put together out of its parts'.[14] But it is not because '—— is mortal' demands completion by some such expression as 'Socrates' that we say 'Socrates is mortal', but because Socrates *is* mortal. Similarly, 'That flash of lightning was followed by a very loud clap of thunder' is said because it was, not because 'was followed by' demands some such completion. In a sense the whole of the doctrine of 'internal relations' is contained in this remark. What Bradley was primarily concerned about, at least as far as the *Principles of Logic* dealt with the issue, was the question of what made a judgment into a unity.

One possible answer is that some kind of 'logical cement' holds the parts (or terms) together. Many traditional logicians took the copula to be this special ingredient which transformed a string of words into a piece of meaningful discourse. It was because the copula, and only the copula, performed this function that all propositions had to be reducible to subject–predicate form. To argue for the possibility of other forms, such as relational ones, was to claim that there were other things that could join words together. The Fregean talk of 'unsaturated elements' can be seen as another effort to find this 'logical cement'. Certainly as far as sentences are concerned, it is true that verbs have the function of transforming lists of words into properly formed grammatical units which can stand by themselves; in general I cannot make myself understood by uttering a string of words. But, and this seems to be the nub of Bradley's views, neither can I make sense just by uttering any sentence, even though that sentence happens to be true. It is here that Bradley's use of the term 'judgment' in preference to 'proposition' or 'sentence' becomes significant; what a philosophical logic is concerned with is not merely well formed formulae but with what can form a part of intelligible discourse, and for such intelligibility more is needed than consonance with grammatical and logical rules. Part of what is denied by the thesis of internal relations is the extensionality of logic, the view that all complex propositions are truth-functions of simple or atomic ones. This is perhaps shown by what is, to our eyes, the very curious treatment of disjunction by Bradley in *PL*. Bk. 1, Ch. IV. Without going into the details, the kind of example that he relies on is 'A is b or c', whereas the form we are familiar with in contemporary logic texts is 'p ∨ q' where

---

[14] *Frege* (London: Duckworth, 1973), 23.

'p' and 'q' are propositions. The only relation between 'p' and 'q' is that given by the truth-table for 'v', so that a well-formed disjunctive proposition could be 'Either it is raining or Stalin is not dead'. Bradley would claim that no one could possibly *judge* this, or that there are no conceivable circumstances when anyone would want to utter, in an ordinary conversation, such a form of words. Of course he is aware of the emphatic use of the disjunctive form to assert the truth of one of the disjuncts: 'Either this is the case or I'll eat my hat', but this gets its force because it is clear that the consumption of headgear is not at issue. Normally the disjunctive form is used because the user is aware of a connection between the two disjuncts, which is why the form 'A is b or c' is a better analysis of it than 'p v q'. 'The murderer is either Smith or Jones' would be a possible candidate for judgment. In other words a theory or judgment has not only got to make it impossible to judge a nonsense in the formal sense but also in what could be called a material one.

Thus the issue of the internality or externality of relations, as far as Bradley was concerned at this period of his life, is one which at other times has been represented by questions about the copula or about the 'unsaturatedness' of certain terms. Although there are some unclarities in the passage, this at least would seem to be clear in the following:

> In their ordinary acceptation the traditional subject, predicate and copula are mere superstitions. The ideal matter which is affirmed in the judgment, no doubt possesses internal relations, and in *most* cases (not all), the matter may be arranged as subject and attribute. But this content, we have seen, is the same both in the assertion and out of it . . . So that it is impossible that this internal relation can itself *be* the judgment; it can at best be no more than a condition of judging (*PL*, 21).

It is not explicitly 'relational' propositions that Bradley is talking about, but any possible proposition. This point is perhaps brought out even more clearly by a later passage in which he is explicitly arguing with Russell:

> Let us take Mr Russell's instance of 'between'. 'Between' requires a multiplicity of terms, and 'between', it is said, is a relation, and so much may seem obvious. But, I reply, to my mind it is not true that 'between' is a relation, and the opposite of this I even venture to regard as evident. 'Between' is certainly a feature which appears in a relational arrangement. But the arrangement is not itself a relation, and still less could it be the relation of 'between'. What is 'between' is one piece of the related whole, and it could never be that whole itself (*ETR*, 306).

(Bradley refers in a footnote to Russell's *Problems of Philosophy* and to Ch. XXV of the *Principles of Mathematics*.) The relations with which he is concerned are those that make a judgment into a unity; elsewhere he expresses this by saying that a judgment consists of one idea, not several.

For the purpose of analysis it may be necessary to distinguish different 'ideas' in a unity, but we must not assume that these ideas are therefore independent existences. Russell, Bradley could claim, falls into this trap by his talk of 'terms' and his statement that:

> The notion that a term can be modified arises from neglect to observe the eternal self-identity of all terms and all logical concepts, which alone form the constituents of propositions.[15]

The central core of Bradley's view is best expressed in the following passage:

> The relations between the ideas are themselves ideal. They are not the psychical relations of mental facts. They do not exist between symbols, but hold in the symbolized. They are part of the meaning and not of the existence. And the whole in which they subsist is ideal, and so one idea (*PL*, 11).

It is possible to translate Bradley's terminology into more familiar terms:

> The relations between symbols are themselves symbolic. They are not the physical relations between marks on paper. They do not exist between the symbols but hold in the symbolized. They are part of the meaning of the symbols and not features of their existence as matters of fact. And the whole in which they subsist is symbolic, and so is one symbol.

If it is accepted that a word only has meaning in the context of a proposition, then it seems to follow that the whole proposition is in some sense a single symbol, that, as Bradley argues, a judgment is a unity. There is a sense in which the doctrine of internal relations can be seen as a denial of relations, as in the passage quoted above about 'between'. There are not self-subsistent entities which need to be connected together by some device such as a copula or relation, but only parts which are artificially isolated for the purpose of understanding. In this sense the 'doctrine of internal relations' is not a special metaphysical thesis for which Bradley was offering arguments in the *Principles of Logic*, but only another formulation of the central doctrine of the book. It is for this reason that he seldom refers to it explicitly there.

The first two sentences of my 'translation' are easily dealt with; symbols are physical objects and as such have physical relations. To have grasped the essence of symbolism is to have understood that these relations are not the important thing. And the same applies to 'ideas'; the logician is not engaged in any sort of psychological investigation. Hence the connections which we are interested in are those that hold in

---

[15] *Principles of Mathematics* (London: Cambridge University Press, 1903), 444.

the real world. To take the example which Bradley uses on the next page, the perception of a wolf eating a lamb. We express this by saying 'The wolf eats the lamb', of which Bradley says:

> We have a relation here suggested or asserted between wolf and lamb, but that relation is (if I may use the word) not a *factual* connection between events in my head. What is meant is no psychical conjunction of images (*PL*, 12).

What we express by the judgment is that an actual wolf actually ate a lamb, that something occurred in the real world. The means by which we express this necessarily involves the use of some 'material', ideas or symbols, but that is not what we are talking about. Here it is possible to begin to see Bradley's meaning. He is not here suggesting that there is any necessity involved in the wolf eating the lamb, but that the proposition, if true, describes an actual event. The fact that it is asserted is the claim that it is true. The judgment or proposition reaches right out to reality. Thus ' "The wolf eats the lamb" expresses an internal relation' does not mean that it could have been deduced that this would happen (nor that the lamb is now inside the wolf). It is not about the world at all, but about the way in which we can talk about the world. One way of expressing this would be to say that internal relations are shown by the use of language, but that they cannot be expressed in language. This is not the way Bradley here puts it, but it helps to bring out the kind of claim he is making.

To use the example of the book and the table again, when I say that the one is on the other, this is because of what I have seen, but I did not see something called 'on' which connected the two objects. None the less it is true that the book is on the table, and the relation between the two is 'internal' in the sense that it is something which is the result of our methods of symbolization, not an extra object existing in addition to the two (real) objects, the book and the table. An 'external relation' would be a physical connection, like the piece of string which tied one thing to another and which would have to be mentioned in any description of the state of affairs. Wittgenstein talks of the confusion between 'internal relations and relations proper (external relations), which is very widespread among philosophers' and adds:

> It is impossible, however, to assert by means of propositions that such internal properties and relations exist: rather they make themselves manifest in the propositions that represent the relevant states of affairs and are concerned with the relevant objects.[16]

Bradley makes much the same point when he says:

> In this ideal content there are groups and joinings of qualities and

---

[16] *Tractatus Logico-Philosophicus*, 4.122.

relations, such as answer to nouns and verbs and prepositions. But these various elements, though you are right to distinguish them, have no validity outside the whole content (*PL*, 12).

Internal relations are products of our symbolism, not features of the real world. But they do not represent *de dicto* necessity; there is all the difference in the world between 'The wolf eats the lamb' and 'A bachelor is an unmarried man', for the latter is about symbols, the former about an event in the world. But it is not legitimate to argue that the former must represent *de re* necessity, for if my argument is correct Bradley is not claiming any sort of necessity for 'internal relations' at this period. Indeed, it is hard to see how he could so long as he remains at the level of logic. And it is clear that the *Principles of Logic* does not discuss metaphysical questions but leaves them for subsequent discussion.

Thus the doctrine of internal relations is the consequence of the view that judgment consists of one idea and hence that the separate 'ideas' of particular things which we normally think of as going to make up or compose the judgment are not fully independent entities but only the products of analysis. In the linguistic mode this is equivalent to saying that words only have meaning in the context of a proposition. To understand a word is to be able to make sense of sentences in which it appears. The contextual principle leads to the view that any word is dependent on others, and hence is only the word it is in relation to other words. Its existence as a word depends on its relation to other words, and so these relations are 'internal', make the word the word it is. It also follows that there is no particular item in the sentence which has the role of making it into a unity, no such thing as a copula or 'unsaturated item', for every part is equally dependent on every other. It seems clear that it is impossible to hold both to what may be called contextual principle, a word only has meaning in the context of a proposition, and to a belief in the copula or the unsaturated nature of predicates, and in so far as Frege did hold both these view he must be considered wrong. The contextual principle can be glossed as maintaining that all words are unsaturated, because they all depend on internal relations to other words to do their job.

It may legitimately be objected that my analysis of the doctrine of internal relations has rendered it plausible at the cost of removing from it all that was objected to by Russell and his followers when they upheld their doctrine of external relations. They were against a set of metaphysical views, in particular those of *Appearance and Reality*, in which a rather different doctrine of internal relations played a vital role. Consequently it is necessary to look briefly at how Bradley managed to get a set of substantive, and very odd, philosophical theses out of what I claim is merely a logical doctrine. But before turning to that question it is worth pointing out that Russell did have serious problems with the unity of the proposition.

Wittgenstein argued that a correct explanation of the form of the proposition 'A believes that p' must show that 'it is impossible for a judgment to be a piece of nonsense. (Russell's theory does not satisfy this requirement.)[17] If any word can be juxtaposed with any other word, then nonsense is liable to to result. But if words are independent entities, each existing in its own right, then there is nothing to stop this occurring. If the theory that all relations are external is construed in this manner, there is nothing to be said against nonsense judgments.

What turns the issue from one of logic to one of metaphysics is a confusion between sense and truth. 'John is bigger than Joan' and 'Joan is bigger than John' are well-formed sentences, but clearly both cannot be true at once. The normal way of deciding between them is to look at John and Joan in order to see which applies, in other words to rely on a correspondence between the judgment and the world. The error comes in carelessness over the way in which this is expressed. Russell, in his criticism of the doctrine of internal relations, put it thus:

> . . . there is the fact that, if two terms have a certain relation, they cannot but have it, and if they did not have it they would be different; which seems to show that there is something in the terms themselves which leads to their being related as they are.[18]

Here the word 'terms', as so often, serves to confuse the issue. For it is not clear if it refers to 'John' and 'Joan' or to John and Joan. If two human beings have a certain relation then it is true that they would be different if they did not have it. John's height is something which he actually has, and if he had a different height he would be different from what he is, and it might turn out that 'John is bigger than Joan' is no longer true. This seems to be something which no one would wish to challenge. In other words, if we take 'terms' as referring to the individuals in question, the 'doctrine' turns out to be a harmless truism. On the other hand, if we take 'term' to refer to 'John' we seem to be in a different position, for he was not given that name because he had a particular height. The confusion might be said to arise because there is a failure to distinguish between the fact that, if I am looking at the two standing side by side, I cannot but say that John is taller than Joan and the idea that it is necessary that John is taller than Joan. The latter is the position that Bradley gets into in the passage I quoted at the beginning of this chapter, where he suggests that starting from any one piece of knowledge it would be possible to reach all others by a chain of deduction.

It is not difficult to see how he gets to this position from a view of ʲudgement which is perfectly respectable. A judgment is a unity, and

---

17 *Tractatus Logico-Philosophicus*, 5.5422.
18 *Philosophical Essays* (London: Longman, 1910), 143–144.

to abstract a part from the judgment is to falsify that part, for it is only what it is in the context of the judgment. The fatal move is to say that it follows that the reality which is the true subject of the judgment is therefore also a unity, and to extract one part from that is to falsify it. All judgments have the form 'Reality is such that S is P' for Bradley, but this did not imply a separation between the two things; judgments 'reach right up to reality'. The 'elements' which compose the judgment are internally related. But in *Appearance and Reality* he seems to come to believe that reality itself must be 'internally related'. This view is forced upon him by his adoption of a coherence theory of truth in the latter work, a doctrine which itself is connected with his attempt to make language and reality coincide. For, he claims, any judgment we utter is partial, abstracts from the full situation it is meant to describe. We say 'The book is on the table', but it must be in a particular position on the table for which accurate co-ordinates could be given. And it is there because I put it there half an hour ago, no doubt for particular reasons. The table is where it is because . . . The account could be extended indefinitely. At the present moment there is a large number of different 'books on tables'; only if the full account were (*per impossibile*) to be given would it be clear that the judgment referred to this particular book, only then could it be really true. The only way of ensuring that general words can 'latch on' to reality is to go on specifying until absolute particularity is reached. A passage from the appendix to *Appearance and Reality* shows this:

> For a thing may remain unaltered if you identify it with a certain character, while taken otherwise the thing is suffering change. If, that is, you take a billiard-ball and a man in abstraction from place, they will of course—as far as this is maintained—be indifferent to changes of place. But on the other hand neither of them, if regarded so, is a thing which actually exists; each is a more or less valid abstraction. But take them as existing things and take them without mutilation, and you must regard them as determined by their places and qualified by the whole material system into which they enter (*AR*, 517).

'Abstraction' is here the enemy, and the only way to guarantee the reference to this actual billiard-ball is to bring in all the circumstances, even though they would be infinite. Hence only the whole truth can really be said to be true at all. This is why the red-haired man, in the passage quoted at the beginning of the paper, could only grasp his red-hairedness if he knew everything about it. Even at this stage, however, it is clear that the doctrine of internal relations is concerned with particulars, not with universals. Indeed, it seems as if it is because universals fail in the task of firmly anchoring what we say to the reality about which we are talking that a device for reaching particularity is needed. To this end in *Appearance and Reality* Bradley adapts what he has earlier said about the unity of judgments, giving it a metaphysical air which it does not have in the *Logic*. Hence he now thinks that there can only be a single unity, which is the totality of things; anything less is not really a unity at all. I think this later view is a falling away from the interesting and probably correct analysis of the nature of judgment and language which he gives in the *Principles of Logic*.

It is also clear that Russell and subsequent philosophers totally failed to understand what Bradley had been trying to do when he originally introduced the notion, partly because they took it to belong primarily to metaphysics, which they were committed to attacking, instead of to logic. I have tried to show that without a detailed look at its logical background, the notion of an internal relation does not make sense. Further because it was believed that the Fregean route was the right one for logic, there was no incentive to study Bradley's logical work in detail. Finally, I think it would be better if any contemporary use of the term should either refer to something like Bradley's meaning or be abandoned altogether. If it is necessary to talk of connections between concepts which are not simply analytic, then they could be called 'conceptual connections' *tout court*.

Parasites Cut Loose

ANTHONY PALMER

A. J. Ayer has made the point that

> Whether any property is internal to a particular object may be taken to
> depend upon the way in which the object is described. Thus it is not an
> internal property of Scott to have been the author of *Waverley*, neither
> is it an internal property of the author of *Ivanhoe*. But what of the author
> of *Waverley*? Is the proposition that the author of *Waverley* composed
> *Waverley* necessarily true? On one interpretation of it it surely is. Even
> so, one can attach a sense to saying that the person who was in fact the
> author of *Waverley* might not have been so. All that is needed for this is
> that he be capable of being otherwise identified (*Russell and Moore, the
> Analytic Heritage*, 158).

This way of handling the problem of internality and thereby dismissing
the work of those philosophers who, like Bradley, laid great stress upon
it is now, I think, fairly generally accepted. It has indeed become part of
our analytic heritage that the doctrine of internal relations held by idealist
philosophers is just false, and that the correct way to look at internal relations is to see them as relations between descriptions, or what amounts to
the same thing, to see them as relations between particulars in so far as they
are identified by means of descriptions. Many of Wittgenstein's remarks in
the *Tractatus* have been interpreted in this way. For example his view that
'a property is internal if it is unthinkable that its object should not possess
it' (*Tractatus* 4.132) has been seen as reminiscent of earlier attempts in the
history of philosophy to formulate the nature of necessary truths. It has
been ranked alongside Leibniz's 'true in all possible worlds' and Hume's
'truths the contradictories of which are unimaginable'. It also seems to be
congruent with Wittgenstein's account of logical truths as tautologies,
since that after all is what 'The author of *Waverley* composed *Waverley*'
seems to boil down to. The doctrine of internal relations has thus been
changed into some version of the distinction between analytic and synthetic truths, and there seems to be general agreement that 'the dispute about
the internality of relations is in general no longer an exciting one' (Gilbert
Ryle, *Collected Essays*, 2, 100). So far as the original doctrine itself is concerned it only remains for sensible philosophers to sort out why anyone
should ever have held such an absurd view. Needless to say such sortings
out are seldom attempted, no doubt because it is difficult to see what
possible philosophical value they could have. In this lecture I shall argue

that such an interpretation avoids, but does not resolve, the issues that the doctrine was intended to clarify. These issues seem to me to be important.

What both Bradley and Wittgenstein say about internal relations arises out of a consideration of the nature of symbols. Wittgenstein uses interchangeably the terms 'symbol' or 'expression' to signify 'any part of a proposition that characterises its sense' (*Tractatus* 3.31). What has sense is a proposition. 'Only propositions have sense' (3.3). Bradley's *Principles of Logic* begins with an examination of the notion of judgment. But it is clear that he regards judgments as the bearers of sense. A proposition for Wittgenstein is the visible aspect of sense. 'In a proposition a thought finds expression that can be perceived by the senses' (3.1). Bradley on the other hand is interested in the way in which a thought finds expression in mental contents, that is to say in ideas. Wittgenstein himself recognizes the similarity of concern. At *Tractatus* 4.1121 he writes:

> Does not my concern with sign-language correspond to the study of thought processes which philosophers used to consider so essential to the philosophy of logic? Only in most cases they got entangled in unessential psychological investigations, and with my method there is an analogous risk.

And again in a reply to one of Russell's queries about the *Tractatus* he writes:

> I don't know what the constituents of a thought are but I know that it must have such constituents which correspond to the words of Language. Again the kind of relation of the constituents of the thought and the pictured fact is irrelevant. It would be a matter of psychology to find out (*Notebooks 1914–16*, Appendix III, 129).

It is this entanglement in unessential psychological investigations that Bradley's account of judgment seeks to avoid. Just as in the *Tractatus* Wittgenstein is only interested in signs in so far as they are symbols or expressions, so for Bradley ideas from the point of view of logic are only of interest in so far as they serve to characterize the sense of a judgment. Considered from any other point of view they are no more relevant to logic than any other momentary psychical state.

> We might say that, in the end, there are no signs save ideas, but what I here wish to insist on, is that, for logic at least, all ideas are signs. Each we know exists as a psychical fact, and with particular qualities and relations. It has speciality as an event in my mind. It is a hard individual, so unique that it not only differs from all others, but even from itself at subsequent moments. And this character it must bear when confined to the two aspects of existence and content. But just so long as, and because, it keeps to this character, it is for logic no idea at all (*Principles of Logic*, Ch. 1, section 6).

What then is it for something, either a mental entity (if such there be) or a mark on paper to be a symbol or an expression? At *Tractatus* 3.318 Wittgenstein tells us that 'Like Frege and Russell [he] construe[s] a proposition as a function of the expressions it contains'. In order to obtain an expression or a symbol which a proposition contains and of which the proposition is to be construed as a function we hold one part of the proposition constant and allow the rest of it to vary. A symbol or an expression precisely is part of a proposition held constant while the rest is allowed to vary. If we begin with the proposition 'Socrates is wise' and allow 'Socrates' to vary then we are left with a part of 'Socrates is wise' which serves to characterize its sense. We are left with the expression '. . . is wise'. The symbol '. . . is wise' is a propositional variable whose values are the propositions which contain it. It can serve to characterize their sense just because it represents what is common to them all. When we consider signs from a logical point of view what we are doing is to regard them as propositional variables and that, from a logical point of view, is all that is relevant. Any other characteristic they might possess is irrelevant.

Now although Frege's *Begriffsschrift* was published three years before Bradley's *Principles of Logic* it is clear that Bradley had not read it. The Fregean notions of function and argument were not available to him. And even in his later writings when they were available to him through the work of Russell he tended to dismiss anything mathematical-looking as beyond his comprehension, giving the impression of an old dog who could not be taught new mathematical tricks. Yet in his attempts to articulate what from a logical point of view is essential about ideas he comes up with something which is strikingly similar. Moreover it is this insight which motivates much of his later work. He acknowledges this much in the appendix to *Appearance and Reality*. Incidentally this in itself shows the misleadingness of the picture which seems to have been accepted since Wollheim introduced it, of Bradley being 'like a man forced backwards, step by step, down a strange labyrinth, in self-defence, until at last finding himself in the comparative safety of some murky cave he rests among the shadows' (*F. H. Bradley*, 18). On my reading of Bradley such an account is quite wrong. Bradley begins with an insight into the nature of logic, and the seemingly extravagant views contained in his later work are largely seen by him to be consequences of it. The insight, expressed in his idiom, is into what with regard to ideas can properly be considered ideal. For him what distinguishes ideas from other mental contents is the capacity we have by means of them to form judgments. What is special about them is their connection with sense or meaning. It is only with regard to judgments that the question of the ideality of ideas arises. What he saw was that if we think of them *as* mental contents, if we consider them with the speciality they have as events in our minds, we are prevented from making precisely that connection. So considered an idea belongs entirely with the reality of which judgments can be made and not with the judgments that are made of it. So he tells us that

> for logical purposes the psychological distinction of idea and sensation may be said to be irrelevant, while the distinction of idea and fact is vital. The image, or psychological idea, is for logic nothing but a sensible reality. It is on a level with the mere sensations of the senses. For both are facts and neither is meaning (*Principles of Logic*, Ch. 1, section 8).

Bradley's contention is then that when ideas are considered in their ideal nature, that is to say as they enter into judgments, their characteristics as psychical entities are irrelevant. The big thing for logic is not to be sidetracked by such psychological irrelevancies. But more than this the steering clear of such irrelevancies in and of itself provides an insight into the ideal nature of ideas. If in their psychological nature ideas are irrelevant to logic what will be relevant, given that ideas are in some way involved, will be the way in which ideas can be construed when stripped of their nature as psychical entities. As psychological realities they are hard, individual, unique but from a logical point of view they are none of these. Their ideality will consist in their generality. Throughout *The Principles of Logic* and *Appearance and Reality* Bradley returns again and again to this point, and in order to characterize it he employs some of his most picturesque vocabulary.

> Neither [the image or psychological idea] is cut from a mutilated presentation, and fixed as a connection. Neither is indifferent to its place in the stream of psychical events, its time and relations to the present congeries. Neither is an adjective to be referred from its existence, to live on strange soils, under other skies and through changing seasons. The lives of both are so entangled with their environments, so one with their setting of sensuous particulars that their character is destroyed if but one thread is broken. Fleeting and self-destructive as is their very endurance, wholly delusive their supposed individuality, misleading and deceptive their claim to reality, yet in some sense and somehow they *are*. They have existence; they are not thought but given. But an idea, if we use idea of the meaning, is neither given nor presented, but is taken. It cannot as such exist. It cannot ever be an event, with a place in the series of time or space. It can be a fact no more inside our heads than it can outside them. And if you take this mere idea by itself, it is an adjective divorced, a parasite cut loose, a spirit without a body seeking rest in another, an abstraction from the concrete, a mere possibility which by itself is nothing (*Principles of Logic*, Ch. 1, section 8).

The positive descriptions we have here of ideas is derived directly from the negation of the characteristics that ideas possess in their aspect of psychical entities. It is because from the point of view of logic ideas cannot be considered as existing things that we are obliged to regard them as parasites cut loose, spirits without bodies, divorced adjectives, or mere possibilities which by themselves are nothing. The same theme recurs in *Appearance and Reality*.

> The predicate is mere 'what', a mere feature of content, which is used to qualify the 'that' of the subject ... Judgment adds an adjective to reality, and this adjective is an idea, because it is a quality made loose from its own existence, and is working free from its implication with 'that' ... When we turn to the subject of the judgment, we clearly find the other aspect, in other words the 'that'. Just as in 'this horse is a mammal' the predicate was *not* a fact, so most assuredly the subject is an actual existence. And the same holds good with every judgment. No one ever *means* to assert about anything but reality, or to do anything but qualify a 'that' by a 'what' ... The point is whether with every judgment we do not find an aspect of existence absent from the predicate but present in the subject, and whether in the synthesis of these aspects we have not got the essence of judgment. And for myself I see no way of avoiding this conclusion. Judgment is essentially the reunion of two sides, 'what' and 'that', provisionally estranged. But it is the alienation of these aspects in which thought's ideality consists (pp. 144–145).

Now it is my contention that Bradley's picturesque extravagances point logic in the same direction as the *Tractatus* aphorisms. 'Divorced adjectives' and 'parasites cut loose' point to the conclusion that Wittgenstein saw followed from regarding a proposition as a function of the expressions it contains. It directs our attention to the central notion in logic of the variable. The view which both of these philosophers hold is that in logic we are only interested in signs in so far as they are symbols and that symbols are variables. In the case of Wittgenstein this is easy to show since he says as much

3.311 An expression presupposes the forms of all the propositions in which it can occur. It is the common characteristic mark of a class of propositions.

3.312 It is therefore presented by means of the general form of the propositions that it characterizes.

In fact, in this form the expression will be *constant* and everything else *variable*.

3.313 Thus an expression is presented by means of a variable whose values are the propositions that contain the expression.

(In the limiting case the variable becomes a *constant*, the expression becomes a proposition.)

I call such a variable a 'propositional variable'.

3.314 An expression has meaning only in a proposition. All variables can be construed as propositional variables.

(Even variable names.)

What I am maintaining is that Bradley's 'parasites cut loose', etc., are articulations of the same point of view. His descriptions of the ideality of thought provide us with a formula for the production of a propositional variable. In judgment we have the combination of a 'this' and a 'what', but the ideality of thought, what is from the point of view of logic ideal about ideas, consists in a provisional estrangement of them.

Now it is important to notice just what is being said when it is being said that a symbol is a variable, just because if we were asked about the nature of a variable our initial response would be no doubt to say that a variable is a symbol that has certain characteristics. So, for example in 1908 Russell tells us that 'A variable is a symbol which is to have one of a certain set of values without its being decided which one' (quoted in Jean van Heijenoort, *From Frege to Godel* (1967), 10). But if we say this we deprive ourselves of the notion of a variable in any explanation of symbols since the description of it presupposes that we understand them. Frege, who is often credited with the first clear introduction of the notion of a variable into logic, when presented with this definition of Russell's was suitably mystified.

> Would it not be well to omit this expression [variable] entirely, since it is hardly possible to define it properly? Russell's definition immediately raises the question what it means to say that 'a symbol has a value'. Is the relation of a sign to its significatum meant by this? In that case however we must insist that the sign be univocal, and the meaning (value) that the sign is to have must be determinate; then the variable would be a sign. But for him who does not subscribe to a formal theory a variable would not be a sign, any more than a number is. If, now, you write 'A variable is represented by a symbol that is to represent one of a certain set of values' ... what is the case then? The symbol represents first the variable and, second, a value taken from a certain supply without its being determined which ... accordingly it seems better to leave the word 'symbol' out of the definition ... So we come to the definition 'A variable is one of a certain set of values, without its being decided which one'. But the last addition does not yield any closer determination, and to belong to a certain set of values means, properly, to fall under a certain concept (ibid.).

Now Bradley will sometimes put these points about thought's ideality in a way which has turned out to be misleading by saying that judgments always have the form 'S (R) P'; they have the form 'Reality is such that S is P'. Again he will sometimes say that reality as a whole is the subject of any judgment. But from his own point of view this is a misleading thing to say, since in moving against 'S is P' and settling for 'S (R) P' all he seems to have done is to change the subject of the judgment. What the 'S (R) P' form is meant to highlight is the connection between judgment and truth. Judgments are what can be true or false. Without these notions we cannot make sense of the notion of judgment at all. The 'S (R) P' notation obscures this point just because it makes it look as though a judgment's being about reality is one thing and its truth another. In judgment, according to Bradley, we have a naked 'this' to which a 'what' gets appended. But of course there are no naked 'thises'. And yet the ideality of thought consists in the appending of a 'what' to a naked 'this'. We have, that is, a 'what' attached to a mere something. With this it seems to me that we have come as close as non-technical language will permit to the notion of a propositional function. A correct understanding of the ideality of ideas generates the conclusion that the general form of judgment is 'This is so how'. Or, as the *Tractatus* has it, the general form of the proposition is 'This is how things are'. The general form of judgment is given once the ideal nature of ideas is understood, once, that is, we have stripped them of their psychological irrelevancies. In logic signs are only of interest in so far as they are symbols and symbols are variables. The nature of the variable gives us the general form of the proposition.

Given the ideal nature of ideas it follows straight away that we cannot think of judgments as consisting of unions of ideas. Such a view is a reversion to psychological irrelevancies. Although relational judgments in particular might make it look as though in judgments we have linkings of ideas the very notion of such a linkage prevents what gets linked from having anything to do with judgments. A relational judgment seems to consist of two terms related by a relation. But if the relation is part of the judgment then it will itself have to be considered as an idea, and whereas before it looked as though we had two ideas now we have three. More relations would now be needed to link these. But again if these relations are considered part of the judgment then the argument just repeats itself. Relations between ideas seemed to be able to weld ideas together into a judgment but no part of a judgment could serve that function, for a part of a judgment is an idea considered in its ideal nature. Bradley's point is that when we understand the way in which ideas enter into judgments it is clear that there can be no relations between ideas. The criticism that is often put forward of this argument that it misses the mark because it treats relations as terms in a proposition itself misses the mark because that is precisely what Bradley is insisting on. His argument is that if a relation were part of a judgment it can be so only in the way in which anything can be part of a judgment that is as an idea or a symbol. When we understand ideas we see that judgment cannot consist of linked ideas. Since the constituents of a proposition are the different ways in which the proposition can be regarded as a variable it is inconceivable that there should be parts of propositions which link other parts.

From the fact that a symbol is a variable or an idea is a parasite divorced, a doctrine about internal relations follows. In our attempts to understand what it is for a proposition to have sense we cannot dispense with the notion of a propositional variable. Thus far Russell would have agreed, for in *The Principles of Mathematics*, Ch. VIII, he tells us that 'no apparatus of assertions enables us to dispense with the consideration of varying one or more elements in a proposition while the other elements remain unchanged'. But, now, with the notion of a propositional variable we have the idea of propositions related in a certain way. The question is how are they related. A propositional variable gives us what is common to a group of propositions, but how can we express what it is they have in common? We cannot say that they contain the same symbol since on the account we have been giving of the nature of a symbol in order to understand 'same symbol' we would need to refer to the propositions in question. In order to understand what it is for propositions to have sense we need to understand how propositions can have something in common in such a way that what it is that they have in common is an unaskable question at least if the question is asked expecting an answer which states the common factor. The notion of a part of a proposition that can serve to characterize its sense, the notion of a symbol, an expression or an idea, involves a conception of unsymbolizable, unexpressable or unidealizable relations between propositions. A variable, as Wittgenstein has it, gives us the prototype of a proposition. What is in common to the propositions which are the values of a variable is a certain form or structure; that is to say such propositions exhibit internal relations. The consideration which Russell endorsed leads to the conclusion he wished to reject.

Given that these considerations about symbols leads to a doctrine about internal relations between propositions we might try asking how such relations stand to what might properly be called relations. Consider the relational proposition 'London lies to the south of Newcastle'. In order to get at the contribution to the sense of the proposition made by its parts we shall need to hold one part of it constant while allowing the rest of it to vary. So initially we have 'London lies to the south of . . .' The same operation can be performed again and so we get '. . . lies to the south of . . .' We now have a propositional variable which has for its values all those propositions in which suitable candidates can be substituted in the argument places. The contribution which '. . . lies to the south of . . .' makes to the proposition 'London lies to the south of Newcastle' is an internal or structural relation between certain propositions. It is by virtue of such relations that relational propositions make sense. This gives us the way in which internal relations stand to relations proper and it explains an otherwise baffling remark in the notes dictated to G. E. Moore.

Internal relations are relations between types which cannot be expressed in propositions, but are all shown in the symbols themselves, and can be exhibited systematically in tautologies. Why we come to call them 'relations' is because logical propositions have an analogous relation to them, to that which properly relational propositions have to relations (*Notebooks 1914–16*, 116).

At first sight this is baffling for we would be inclined to say that relational propositions express relations but we know that Wittgenstein would not allow logical propositions to express relations between types; in fact he maintained that such relations could not be expressed in propositions at all. However, given that the sense contributed to a relational proposition by a relational expression is the internal relation between those propositions which contain it we can see that such a contribution is not something which could itself be expressed in a proposition and so could be said to stand to relations proper as logical propositions stand to relations between types.

The idea that a symbol is a variable, or that an idea is a loosened adjective, leads then to a doctrine of internal relations between propositions or judgments. Yet this might seem a far cry from the doctrine of internal relations associated with idealist philosophers and in particular it might seem a far cry from the doctrine of internal relations as it appears in Bradley's *Appearance and Reality*. Recall the passage that almost every philosopher has stumbled over about the red-haired man.

> By being red-haired the two men are related really, and their relation is not merely external. If it were so wholly it would not be true or real at all, and, so far as it seems so to that extent it is but the appearance of something higher. The correlation of the other circumstances of and characters in the two men with the quality of red-hairedness cannot in other words possibly be bare chance. And if you could have a perfect relational knowledge of the world, you could go from the nature of red-hairedness to these other characters which qualify it and you could from the nature of red-hairedness reconstruct all red-haired men. In such perfect knowledge you could start internally from any one character in the Universe, and you could from that pass to the rest (Appendix Note B, p. 520).

In this passage the talk is not about propositions or judgments at all but about men; it is between them that internal relations are said to hold. As it stands the view expressed looks like some version of Leibniz. In fact I think it is because he sees it as some version of Leibniz that Russell reacts to it as he does, seeing it as the consequence of the false doctrine that all propositions are of the subject predicate form. He says, for example, in his account of Leibniz's philosophy, that

> The view that a subject and a predicate are to be found in every proposition is a very ancient and respectable doctrine: it has, moreover, by no means lost its hold on philosophy, since Mr Bradley's logic consists

almost wholly of the contention that every proposition ascribes a predicate to reality as the only ultimate subject (*The Philosophy of Leibniz*, 12).

Now we have already seen that this version of Bradley's contention that judgments have the form 'Reality is such that S is P' is misleading and that the correct way to interpret such remarks is to see them as pointing to the connection of the notion of a judgment to the notions of truth and falsity. Bradley's 'Reality is such that S is P' is not an affirmation that in every judgment there is a subject and a predicate but rather an insistence that as parts of judgments ostensible subjects are in the same position as predicates, that is to say they are ideal. Reality cannot be considered as part of a judgment at all, although all judgments are of reality. What a proposition is about cannot be part of the proposition itself. Considered as parts of propositions subject terms are characters, they are not individual but general, and so considered a doctrine of internal relations like that of Leibniz is as obviously false as critics like Russell who foist it on Bradley suppose it to be. Such a doctrine would be a version of the distinction between analytic and synthetic propositions in which it is urged that when properly understood all propositions will be seen to be analytic. This is precisely the doctrine which Leibniz held to be fundamental, namely that in every true proposition the predicate is contained in the subject, even if in certain propositions this could only be shown to be so by an infinite analysis of the subject which mere mortals are not capable of performing. Over and over again Bradley is prepared to admit that subjects so construed can be either extrinsically or intrinsically related to their predicates but equally persistently he insists that this misses the point that he wishes to make with regard to internal relations.

> For a thing may remain unaltered if you identify it with a certain character, while taken otherwise the thing is suffering change. If, that is, you take a billiard-ball and a man in abstraction from place, they will of course—so far as this is maintained—be indifferent to changes of place. But on the other hand neither of them, if regarded so, is a thing which actually exists; each is a more or less valid abstraction ... The billiard-ball, to repeat, if taken apart from its place and its position in the whole, is not an existence but a character, and that character can remain unchanged, though the existing thing is altered with its changed existence (Appendix, p. 517).

To assert against his views that predicates may be internally or externally related to the subjects of propositions when those subjects are considered as parts of propositions is an *ignoratio elenchi*. The distinction between analytic and synthetic propositions in the fashion of Leibniz misconstrues the point that all judgments are of reality, it mistakes the way in which judgment and truth go together.

One of Bradley's ways of making this point, although not the only one, is to argue that if we construe judgments in this way then the only sense in which they could be said to be true is hypothetically. Now the curious thing here is that most commentators actually have Bradley himself maintaining that all truth *is* hypothetical. I find it difficult to understand how this can have come about, and can only suppose that it goes with the Russell gloss on 'Reality is such that S is P' as all propositions contain a subject and a predicate and the consequent Leibnizian interpretation of the doctrine of internal relations. But the view that all judgments are hypothetical is seen by Bradley as a consequence of the mistaken view that judgments are unions of ideas, a view which Bradley is centrally concerned to reject in the first two chapters of the *Principles of Logic* on the grounds that it miscontrues the adjectival nature of ideas as they enter into judgments. The consequence that all judgments are hypothetical Bradley puts forward as the *reductio ad absurdum* of the thesis that judgments are the union of ideas

A categorical judgment makes a real assertion in which some fact is affirmed or denied. But since no judgment can do this, they all in the end are hypothetical. They are true only of and upon a supposition. In asserting S–P I do not mean that S, or P, or their synthesis is real. I say nothing about any union in fact. The truth of S–P means that, *if I suppose* S, I am bound *in that case* to assert S–P. In this way all judgments are hypothetical.

The conclusion thus urged upon us by Herbart, follows, I think irresistibly from the premises. But the premises are not valid. Judgment . . . can not consist in the synthesis of ideas . . . To see clearly that if judgment is the union of ideas, there then can be no categorical judgment is a very great step in the understanding of Logic (*Principles*, 44).

To bring this point out consider one of Bradley's examples, 'Gold is yellow'. If we maintain that the subject of the judgment is itself part of the judgment which is somehow joined with other parts of it, as part of the judgment it can only be so in its ideal nature, not as some mental fact. But in judging that gold is yellow I surely did not want to say something about goldness but rather to say something about gold itself. In making the subject of the judgment part of the judgment I prevent myself from making the judgment I wanted to make. The subjects of judgments considered as parts of judgments are adjectival. 'But reality is not a collection of adjectives nor can it be so represented' (*Principles*, 46).

The doctrine of internal relations is then not a thesis about the relations between subject and predicate when these are thought of as constituents of judgments. Relations, Bradley says, hold in the symbolized and not between symbols. What constituted for him a problem is that we can only get at them by means of symbolizing. No doubt everything is what it is and not another thing more, but we can only approach things through our idealizations. The reality of which we judge is transformed in judgment into something which is not real but ideal, or to put the matter the other way round our idealizations aim at something they can never attain. It is in the nature of reality not to be ideal and it is the nature of ideas not to be real, yet the real is what ideas are ideas of. This is the grand dilemma Bradley tells us lies behind the doctrines of *Appearance and Reality*.

> There is a difference between on the one side truth or thought, . . . and on the other side reality. But to assert this difference seems impossible without somehow transcending thought or bringing the difference into thought, and these phrases seem meaningless. Thus reality appears to be an Other different from truth and yet not able to be truly taken as different (Appendix, 492).

Our judgments of reality force us into a relational mode which reality itself can never exhibit, since any relational mode is not real but ideal. Bradley's point is that although in our judgments we of necessity fall short of reality we should nevertheless endeavour to make the distance by which we fall short as small as possible. The relations which we attribute to reality should be no more than the business of idealization itself requires namely the internal relations between judgments which, we have seen, is what an idea from the point of view of judgment is. When we judge that Jones is red-haired, while no doubt it is true to say that he could have remained Jones even if he had ceased to be red-haired, and presumably red-haired if he had ceased to be Jones, to insist on this is to remain at a level of ideas or idealizations. Whereas we began by wanting to say something about the man himself we end up by saying something only about ideas; viz. the idea of Jones and the idea of being red-haired. And while it is true that the business of judgment forces us into a relational mode it is not the case that it forces us into that relational mode. Being red-haired, or for that matter being Jones is an *abstractable* feature of reality but it is not a *detachable* feature. The false view that in judgment we have to do with a union of ideas forces us to treat abstractables as detachables and hence to attribute to reality relations which hold only between abstractions. When we pick out a subject as part of a judgment we are dealing not with a bit of reality which can exist apart from the rest but with an idea, so that when we talk about the relations it stands in to other ideas we cannot be talking about relations between bits of reality. The doctrine of internal relations on the other hand has the merit of only ascribing to reality those relations required for the business of idealization as such, for with them we are dealing not with relations between ideas but with relations between judgments, which is what an idea is. The judgments 'Jones is red-haired' and 'Smith is red-haired' are internally related. When both of these propositions are true then such internal relations could be said to hold in reality. But of course there will be internal relations between judgments that are false. Knowledge of the internal relations between judgments by themselves will not give us knowledge of reality but the relations that you have knowledge of when you have knowledge of reality are internal relations. All internal relations are not real but all real relations are internal. In the end, Bradley held, any relational talk is inadequate so far as reality is concerned, only some such talk is more inadequate than others. We operate at a level which is least inadequate if we stick to relations which belong to the very business of idealization or symbolising. In so far as we move away from these and think of reality in terms of relations between subjects and predicates when the subject itself is considered as part of the proposition thus far do we leave reality behind.

I have argued then, that for Bradley the doctrine of internal relations is the view that if we are to attribute relations to reality at all then they should only be those which the nature of thinking about reality itself requires, and these are the internal relations between judgments which constitute ideas. On such a view the distinction between analytic and synthetic judgments into which the doctrine later developed or, as I think we should more properly say, regressed is irrelevant to his views. But what to my mind makes this more interesting than an exposition of a neglected philosopher's views is that the distinction between analytic and synthetic propositions has been presented to us in modern times as the distinction which gives us the nature of philosophical investigations. The idea that the business of philosophy is the analysis of concepts which results in the production of analytic truths has been seen as the methodological precipitate of our concern in the present century with the nature of meaning. But if ideas or symbols are as I have argued both Wittgenstein and Bradley took them to be, this conception of philosophy will turn out to have been a misconception of the notion of meaning from which it is allegedly derived.

Transcendental Arguments and Idealism

ROSS HARRISON

'Metaphysics', said Bradley, 'is the finding of bad reasons for what we believe on instinct, but to find these reasons is no less an instinct.' This idea that reasoning is both instinctive and feeble is reminiscent of Hume; except that reasons in Hume tend to serve as the solvent rather than the support of instinctive beliefs. Instinct leads us to play backgammon with other individuals whom we assume inhabit a world which exists independently of our own perception and which will continue to exist tomorrow in a similar fashion to today. However, when instinct leads us also to reason about these beliefs they are all subject to sceptical attack. Their defence provides a challenge, a challenge which in thumbnail histories of the subject is met by Kant. He does this by use of a powerful new form of argument which he calls transcendental argument and which, in my opinion, provides not only reasons but also good reasons for the defence of some of our most central instinctive beliefs. The strategy involved in this kind of argument is to reflect on the necessary preconditions for comprehensible experience. In this way, some beliefs which are subject to sceptical attack, such as that there is a causal order between objects which exist independently of our experience of them, can be found to be the essential preconditions for having comprehensible experience at all. The reason for accepting them is, therefore, that they are the necessary preconditions of having any beliefs at all; and this provides a good, rather than a bad, reason for accepting these particular instinctive beliefs.

As well as these more traditional areas of philosophical criticism and defence, modern philosophy also operates in areas which were relatively unfamiliar to Kant, such as the philosophy of mind or of language. Here again instinctive beliefs, such as the belief that other people have sensations similar to our own, or that we understand what other people mean by their language, have been subject to sceptical attack. Here again these beliefs have been defended by using the Kantian weapon of transcendental arguments. Strawson and Wittgenstein argue, for example, that the possibility of attributing sensations to others is a precondition for having language of sensation at all; Davidson and Wittgenstein argue that the presumption of general agreement is a precondition for having a language at all. In both these cases we have a sceptical argument based upon an assumed premise, such as that we can talk of our own sensations or that we understand our own language, which is then held to provide inadequate support for our natural, instinctive, beliefs, such as that others have similar sensations or that we can understand the language of others. In both cases the transcendental argument meets this threat by showing that the negation of the sceptical conclusion is a precondition for the truth of the accepted premise; the ability to attribute sensations to others is, for example, shown to be a precondition for attributing them to ourselves. The last words of Strawson's book *Individuals*, in which the argument just given occurs, allude back to the aphorism of Bradley's with which I started. Strawson ends his book by saying that 'if metaphysics is the finding of reasons, good, bad or indifferent, for what we believe on instinct, then this has been metaphysics'. In my opinion, as I said, good reasons.

This is not, however, the universal opinion. The last fifteen years has seen, besides continuing use of transcendental arguments, increasing discussion of whether they do provide good reasons after all. It has been objected that we can never establish necessary conditions of thought. It has been objected that sceptical doubts are doubts about what there really is, and cannot be met by transcendental arguments which only tell us what we must believe. It has been objected that we can only move from what we must believe to what there is by use of the verification principle. In this paper I ignore all these objections and concentrate on the objection that transcendental arguments only work because they presuppose idealism, which is taken to be an unacceptably high price to pay. According to this objection, finding the presuppositions of belief, the beliefs we have to have if we have any at all, only legitimates the truth of these beliefs because it is also assumed that the existence of the objects of the beliefs depends upon our having these beliefs. It is only because it is assumed that existence depends upon belief, that to be is to be believed, that the necessary conditions for belief can also be taken to be the necessary conditions for the existence of those objects which make the beliefs true.

The objection that the recent use of transcendental arguments involves idealism was first made by Bernard Williams in an article in the *Philosophical Review* for 1968. Criticizing the recent arguments of Strawson and Shoemaker in the philosophy of mind, he says that the recent users of transcendental arguments 'perhaps pay insufficient attention to Kant's insistence that his transcendental arguments give knowledge of how things must be only because the things are not things in themselves'. 'The idealism', he adds, 'was what was supposed to make the whole enterprise possible' (p. 218). In a later paper on Wittgenstein which he contributed to the *Understanding Wittgenstein* volume of the Royal Institute of Philosophy lectures, Williams repeats some of his argument of the former paper, and this time quite specifically accuses Wittgenstein of idealism.

As Williams remarks, Kant himself was clearly some kind of idealist. Kant's problem, in answering scepticism, was the problem of how we can know certain very central features of the world *a priori*; that is with a necessity which is independent of the particular experience we happen to have. The mind can only know such necessary truths about the objects of its knowledge, he supposes, if we presume that the objects conform to the mind rather than the mind to the nature of the objects. As he puts it in the famous passage which leads up to the image of the Copernican Revolution in the Preface to the second edition of the *Critique of Pure Reason*:

> Hitherto it has been assumed that all our knowledge must conform to objects. But all attempts to extend our knowledge of objects by establishing something in regard to them *a priori*, by means of concepts, have, on this assumption, ended in failure. We must therefore make trial whether we may not have more success in the tasks of metaphysics, if we suppose that objects must conform to our knowledge (Bxvi).

Kant's idealism, that is, depends upon a picture of the mind and the world in which it is supposed that the mind can have *a priori* knowledge of itself and of its powers in a way that it cannot have of mind-independent entities. If, therefore, we may suppose that the objects depend upon the mind then we may have *a priori* knowledge of them as well, at least with respect to the features which so depend. So with idealism, *a priori* knowledge of the objects, that is, transcendental arguments which establish with necessity some very general features of our world, becomes possible. Without idealism, there can be no such arguments and no such knowledge.

On historical grounds alone, therefore, Williams clearly has a strong *prima facie* case. Kant invented transcendental arguments and Kant was an idealist; the idealism, furthermore, was taken by Kant to be an essential and central component of his arguments. He presents transcendental arguments to posterity as a package; and the onus of proof must therefore be on those who say that the real gift is the form of the argument and that the idealism is only the dispensable wrapping. In *The Bounds of Sense*, Strawson claims that in many places in Kant's *Critique* the doctrine of idealism is 'superfluous to the essential structure of reasoning, . . . an extra wheel, zealously but idly turning' (p. 257). He, and such other contemporary Kantian commentators as Jonathan Bennett, wish to redeploy the form of argument without getting involved in the 'dark side' of Kant's metaphysics. Now I do think myself that this assumption is correct, and the central aim of this paper is to show that it is possible to use transcendental arguments without being involved in idealism. It must be realized, however, that this assumption clearly needs to be defended. Before the argument begins the presumption must be that it is false.

There is an alternative way of meeting Williams' objection to transcendental arguments, and this would be by allowing his central claim that transcendental arguments involve idealism, but then going on to claim that idealism was not really an objection to them. Both Williams and his opponents, that is, have assumed that if the arguments are convicted of idealism, this forms a crucial objection to their use. Any argument accused of anything so dark must be removed from the society of right-thinking argument. This, however, might be resisted by examing the history of the argument more carefully than in the above, crude, sketch. Kant, it might then be argued, was not really an idealist at all in any problematic sense. He had his own special, highly idiosyncratic, kind of idealism. Understood in this quite special way, there is nothing wrong with idealism, and so nothing wrong with transcendental arguments if they are involved in it. Instead of trying to employ Kant's arguments without Kant's dark side, the aim of this reply to Williams would be to show that this side of Kant was not dark after all.

I do not myself wish to use this kind of defence because I think that Kant's form of idealism is sufficently objectionable to make it worth showing that transcendental arguments need not be committed to it. It is, however, important to realize that Kant himself did think that he was an idealist in a very special manner. He called himself a 'transcendental idealist', but held that he was also an 'empirical realist'. He added to the second edition of the *Critique of Pure Reason* a 'Refutation of Idealism' designed to meet the objection that he was an idealist. He held that judgment of 'inner experience', of states of mind, presupposed judgment of 'outer experience', of states of a spatial, causally connected world, existing independently of our individual selves. He was clearly not just a subjective idealist in the way that Berkeley without God would be. However, even if we discount passages which appear only in the first edition, Kant clearly says in both editions such things as the following:

> We have sufficiently proved . . . that everything intuited in space or time, and therefore all objects of any experience possible to us, are nothing but appearances, that is, mere representations, which, in the manner in which they are represented, as extended beings, or as series of alterations, have no independent existence outside our thoughts. This doctrine I entitle *transcendental idealism* (A490–491/B518–519).

This seems to me to be a clear enough statement by Kant that the objects of experience depend for their existence on our thoughts, and that this is still a feature of his special kind of idealism. His special kind of idealism is therefore sufficiently full-blooded for me to think that it is worth showing that transcendental arguments are not committed to it.

Let me now leave Kant and set out in more general terms why transcendental arguments might be thought to involve idealism, and why they do not. It seems that transcendental arguments try to show that certain very central beliefs we happen to have are in fact true by showing that they are necessarily true. Our instinctive beliefs are defended by showing that they are necessary beliefs; transcendental arguments show what there is by showing what there must be. It may seem, therefore, that these arguments depend upon using the following form of argument.

$$\frac{\Box p}{p}$$

So far there are no problems about the validity of the argument, the problem is rather how the premise, $\Box p$, is established. It seems that it is meant to follow from consideration of the necessary conditions of having judgment, or conceptualizable experience, of a world. If 'j' symbolizes 'there is judgment of a world', that is, it seems that the whole argument is meant to have something of the following form:

(1) j
(2) $\Box (j \rightarrow p)$
(3) $\dfrac{\Box p}{}$ (from 1, 2)
(4) p (from 3)

For example, if 'p' is 'there is a causal order', it seems that we defend our belief that there is a causal order by showing that there must be a causal order, and we show that there must be such an order by showing that it is an essential presupposition for judgment (that is, necessarily, if there is judgment, there is a causal order). The trouble with this argument, however, is that it is invalid as it stands, since line 3 does not follow from lines 1 and 2. It would, however, be valid if, instead of line 1 above, we had:

(1a) $\Box j$

The argument would be valid, that is, if we could start from the assumption that it was necessarily the case that what there is was judged, but is not if we start from the assumption that the world in fact happens to be judged (or be judgable). Yet the assumption that it is necessary that what there is is judged, that *esse est concipi*, is precisely the assumption of idealism. Without idealism, that is, there is always a possibility that the world could not be judged by us, and so we make a mistake in applying the above argument to the world. Whereas if we assume that the world depends upon our judgment, and is necessarily judgable by us, then we know that the necessary conditions of judgment must apply to the world. So, it could be argued, without idealism, no valid transcendental arguments.

I have laid out this argument in the above, rather elaborate, fashion because I hope that this makes it apparent how obtuse is the way of understanding it which involves adoption of the idealist premise. If we look at it again, it is quite obvious that we can reach the desired conclusion, p, from the given premises, j and $\Box (j \rightarrow p)$, without any invalid argument. We do not need line 3 in the above argument. We do not need, that is, to establish at any stage that anything is necessary *tout court*; all we need is the necessity of various hypothetical statements which lay out the essential preconditions of judgment (or of conceptualizable experience). Given these hypotheticals, we may move directly and validly from the purely contingent assumption that there is a judgable world to the purely contingent conclusion that, say, this world must exhibit causal connection. The world might be otherwise. It might not exist at all. It might not be judgable, and so it might not exhibit causal connection. However, *if* it is judgable, *if* we can make any judgments at all, then it must be the case that it exhibits causal connection. In this way our belief that the world exhibits causal connection is defended. The transcendental argument gives good reasons for it. For the transcendental argument says: either you can make no judgments at all, or else this judgment about causal connection is correct. Since we can make judgments, we have therefore the best possible reason for thinking that our judgment about causal connection is correct. The transcendental argument works without establishing the necessity of anything apart from hypothetical statements. It therefore does not need the idealist premise that what exists is necessarily judged.

The objection to the argument as first given depended upon the claim that it confused the necessity of the conse*quent* with the necessity of conse*quence*. Being given j and $\Box$ (j→p), it was thought that a necessary consequent, $\Box$p, could be detached instead of just p. The reply is that the necessity of conse*quence* is all that is involved in transcendental arguments, and there is no confusion. This, however, may seem to be an unsatisfactory reply if transcendental arguments are to succeed in making their conclusions impregnable to sceptical attack. For it may be felt that they are impregnable to such attack only if the necessity goes all the way through. If, on the contrary, the argument merely derives purely contingent conclusions from purely contingent premises, it may seem that the sceptical attack can be moved back to the premises. To show that the world is necessarily causally connected is one thing, to claim that we do, as a matter of fact, make judgments about the world may well seem to be quite another thing. If the world is not such as that it is necessarily judged, as in idealism, how are we to know that all this apparent judgment is not mere illusion? Although, that is, it may be allowed that the validity of the argument can be saved without adopting the idealist premise, only the idealist form may be felt to be satisfactory in fulfilling the task that transcendental arguments are required to perform. Unless we have line 3 in the original argument, unless we can show that it is *necessary* that the world is causally connected together, then sceptical doubts about causation cannot finally be laid to rest.

This reply, I think, merely brings out how crucial it is exactly which kinds of judgment or experience have their essential preconditions examined in transcendental arguments. We do not need necessary premises for such arguments, but we do need certain ones. They must be such that, although not necessary truths in themselves, they are unavoidable for us, and we have no alternative to believing them. This certainty or unavoidability will then be transferred to the conclusion by the hypothetically necessary steps of the argument. If, therefore, the transcendental arguments examine the necessary preconditions for some quite specific kind of judgment, such as attributing sensations to ourselves, then it may be possible to avoid their force by moving the sceptical doubt about their conclusion back to their premise. It is not necessary that we attribute sensations to anyone; it is not unavoidable, and so it may not be felt to be certain that we can do so. If, however, we restrict transcendental arguments to examining the preconditions of judgment, or of conceptualizable experience, as such, as in the original Kantian arguments, then this premise is unavoidable. The alternative is silence. Either we must accept that we can can make judgments, or else we can say nothing at all, including not being able to object to transcendental arguments. That we make judgments is unavoidable, and so therefore is also any necessary preconditions for making judgments. The conclusions to transcendental arguments will therefore be sufficently certain, using no other necessity than the necessity of consequence, if we adopt such premises as that we make judgments. For, although such premises are not necessary truths, if we make the claim involved in them, then, if meaningful, it must be true. The judgment that we make judgments is similar to Descartes' 'I think': it is not a necessary truth, but it is the case that, if asserted, its truth is a necessary condition of its meaning what it does. It can only be asserted with that meaning if it is true. That we make judgments is something, therefore, which we are justified in assuming because the only options before us are that it is true or we can say nothing at all; either it or silence.

It is not necessary for transcendental arguments, therefore, to try to establish any other necessities about the world than those of consequence. Only the necessary preconditions of judgment are required, not anything which is necessary in itself. To put it like this may help, I think, to show how Kant was pushed on into idealism even though idealism was not necessary for his transcendental arguments. For Kant not only wished to establish hypothetical necessities about the preconditions of judgment but also categorical necessities that the objects of our judgment had a particular, necessary, character. He wishes to show, for example, that the necessary truths of arithmetic and Euclidean geometry are truths about the objects of our experience. He wishes to show not just that it is necessary that this world we experience has causal connection but that this connection is itself a necessary connection. Consider, for example, the following passage from the 'Second Analogy' section of the *Critique of Pure Reason*:

On the contrary, the appearances must determine for one another their position in time, and make their time-order a necessary order (A200/ B245).

In this sentence two quite separate necessities are claimed by Kant, the necessity that there is an order determining the appearances in time, and that this order is itself a necessary order. The former could be taken as a hypothetical necessity to the effect that, *if* we have judgment of appearances, then it is necessary that the appearances occur in a determinate order. The second is clearly a categorical necessity, a necessity which the appearances possess themselves. If, therefore, we remember that Kant's original problem was not just how there could be conformity of knowledge with objects but, rather, how there could be conformity between knowledge of necessary truths and objects, then we can see how Kant is forced into idealism. The necessities can apply unproblematically to the objects because the objects are just objects of the mind. Because appearances depend upon us there is not a crucial distinction between hypothetical necessities in which something is only true if it is judged and categorical necessities which are true in themselves. For appearances are not things in themselves; their existence depends on judgment. Without the idealism, however, the further necessities that Kant wants would be inexplicable. This does not mean that idealism is needed for transcendental arguments, but it does suggest that it may be needed for the particular conclusions which Kant wished to derive from his own arguments.

Distinguishing between hypothetical and categorical necessities in a way in which Kant, with his idealism, does not need to, also enables us, I think, to solve a problem which Broad has set for Kant. Holding as he does that the understanding is the 'lawgiver of nature' (A126), Kant holds that the mind imposes necessary connections, or laws, upon nature. He also holds, however, that what particular laws there are is a truth independent of us which needs empirical, scientific, investigation. In Kant's metaphor, the particular laws are part of the matter on which the mind imposes the form. This leads Broad to object, in his recently published lectures on Kant, that Kant seems to commit the 'fallacy that one could impose complete law-abidingness without imposing *any* set of determinate laws' (*Kant*, 136). The fallacy here is similar to the fallacy of thinking that one could impose a colour upon something without there being any particular colour which one imposed upon it. How can the mind make necessary connections in nature, even a nature which depends upon it, without there being particular necessary connections which it makes? This is a serious problem for Kant, but it is only a problem for him because of his idealism and his claim that the mind imposes certain things on nature. If we did not have the idealism, but just a transcendental argument which showed that there must be laws in nature if we are to be able to judge it, then there is no problem. For there is no fallacy in claiming that it is necessary that there are *some* laws (if we are to be able to judge), while denying that there are any *particular* laws which it is necessary that there should be. This would merely be like claiming that it is necessary that we eat some food (if we are going to survive), while denying that there is any particular food which it is necessary that we eat. So, if we do not accept Kant's idealism, there is no problem in having a transcendental argument similar to Kant's that it is necessary that the world we judge exhibits law-like connection, and yet holding that the particular laws it exhibits are a matter of empirical, scientific, discovery. Kant, however, who does accept idealism, does have a problem.

In his two papers Bernard Williams does not only make the general charge that transcendental arguments involve idealism. In both papers he backs up the charge by constructing a particular argument-schema which he thinks looks as if it gives the general form of arguments used in the philosophy of mind by such makers of transcendental arguments as Shoemaker, Strawson, and Wittgenstein, and yet which is an 'unappealing sophism' which leads directly to idealism. I give the argument in the shorter form in which it appears in the second paper:

> (i) 'S' has the meaning we give it.
> (ii) A necessary condition of our giving 'S' a meaning
> is Q.
> *ergo* (iii) Unless Q, 'S' would not have a meaning.
> (iv) If 'S' did not have a meaning, 'S' would not be true.
> *ergo* (v) Unless Q, 'S' would not be true.
> (*Understanding Wittgenstein*, 93)

Williams comments that:

> any number of substitutions for Q in (ii) which relate to human existence, language use, etc., make it true for any 'S' one likes (p. 93).

Examples would be that we exist or that we think; unless these were true, we could not give meaning to portions of our language. Yet, given this,

> We can get the truth of any true 'S' dependent on human existence, etc.; that is, prove unrestricted idealism (pp. 93–94).

The argument Williams gives does seem to be of the same general form as transcendental arguments, since it sets out the necessary preconditions of our making a particular kind of judgment. Yet the conclusion seems to show that any truth whatsoever, such as that there are mountains on the back of the moon, would not be true unless we existed or thought; and this is, as Williams says, a very severe form of idealism.

After his presentation of the argument in the second paper, however, Williams himself suggests ways in which his argument could be met which he did not suggest in the first paper. He comments that

> on some traditional views, there is no need to find anything wrong with the argument in order to avoid this [proving unrestricted idealism],

since (i) will be taken to be true just in case 'S' names a sentence, and in that case (v) can be harmlessly true, as meaning 'Unless Q, "S" would not express a truth . . .' (p. 94).

This, I think, is a perfectly acceptable answer. If nobody ever existed or had existed, then the *words* 'there are mountains on the back of the moon' would have no meaning, but it would still have been true that there are mountains on the back of the moon. The language of English would not have existed, but the truths we can now express in this language would still have been true. It is a presupposition, that is, of our being able to use language meaningfully and of our being able to express anything at all that we exist and that we think; this does not mean, however, that the truth of what we express depends upon our thought or existence. Again, it is not the case that idealism is required to make such arguments work. Unless certain conditions are met we are not able to think about and judge a world. Such conditions are that we think and exist, and all the less obvious preconditions of judgment discovered in transcendental arguments. This does not mean, however, that the truth of all these preconditions depends upon us. It is just that, if they are not met, as Williams puts it, ' "S" would not express a truth'. They are preconditions for the meaningfulness rather than the truth of what we say. The options, as I put it above, are: either this or silence. Either we exist or silence; either the world exhibits causal connection or silence. This does not mean that we would not exist unless we thought about it, that is that our existence depends upon our conceiving ourselves; it is just that, *if* we *do* think about it, then we must exist.

I hope that it is now clear why I do not think that transcendental arguments involve idealism. The general point could be put in the following, rather different, way. Sceptical problems arise about our normal beliefs, beliefs which we normally take to be well founded upon experience. Since the scepticism is precisely about whether experience justifies these beliefs, it is no good trying to meet it by further observational evidence. Instead of using experiential evidence, therefore, we may follow Kant in trying to refute it *a priori*. However, it seems, again like Kant, that we cannot tell the nature of the world directly while operating wholly *a priori*; and so may follow him in shifting our attention from the *objects* of our knowledge to the *medium* by which they are apprehended by us. Although we cannot establish anything directly about the object, we can establish some things about the nature of our sensibility or understanding while operating purely *a priori*. So, let us suppose, we may establish that anything perceived by us exists in a single space, or that anything of which we have conceptualizable, understandable, experience exists in a causal order. In this way we use the necessary conditions which we discover about the medium by which we apprehend the world to tell us about the nature of that world. Because we can only understand, only apprehend, a causally connected world, we therefore deduce that our world is causally connected.

If we put it in this rather picturesque way, I think we can see both how it is natural to suppose that we are committed to idealism, and also why we are not in fact so committed. It is natural to suppose that we are, because it is natural to think that we cannot discover anything about the nature of the *object* by discovering truths about the *medium* unless the medium makes the object to be as it is. If, that is, the existence of the world, of the object, depends upon its being perceived or judged, depends upon the medium, then it is clear that truths discovered about the medium will apply to the object. If, however, the object is totally independent of us, is totally independent of the medium, it may seem that any things we discover about the medium merely remain truths about the medium and in no way tell us about the object. If we have a machine which makes lollipops, and we know that the machine cannot make lollipops bigger than four inches across, then this knowledge of the capacities of the machine will enable us to know something about the lollipops it produces; but this is because the lollipops depend upon the machine. If, however, the machine is just set up beside a stall containing completely independent lollipops, it does not seem that any amount of knowledge of the nature or capacities of the machine would tell us anything at all about the nature of the lollipops.

So much for the argument that we cannot find out about the nature of the object by studying the nature of the medium unless we also suppose that the object depends upon the medium. It is important to realize that it applies both to the supposition that objects depend for their existence on the medium and also to the weaker supposition that they only depend for their nature on the medium. For Kant's own, idiosyncratic, form of idealism was that the objects depended for some of their nature on the nature of the mind. This is why he sometimes calls it 'formal idealism'. The idea is that the mind forms matter which exists independently. So the relevant image would not be so much a machine which produced lollipops from scratch but, rather, a machine which was given a sweet mixture and formed it into lollipop-like shapes. Again it is the case that, knowing the machine, we know the shapes; but that we can only do this because they depend for their form (although not their existence or matter) on the machine.

Whichever form of idealism is thought to be involved, however, the claim that we cannot legitimately move from discovery about the nature of the medium to reasonable belief about the nature of the object is mistaken. Even if the object is totally independent, in its existence, matter, and nature, we may still make reasonable, justifiable, judgments about it. This is because these judgments have the hypothetical character that I have stressed throughout this paper. Since we presuppose that the medium *is* applied to the object, we may legitimately suppose that the object possesses the necessary conditions of such application. If, that is, it is a necessary condition for our apprehension of a world that that world is causally connected together, then we may legitimately suppose that any world that we *do* apprehend is causally connected together. Supposing this does not prevent our also supposing that the object is quite independent of the medium, and would have existed in the way that it does even if the medium had never been applied to it. Take the analogous case of visual perception. We know that it is a necessary condition of visual perception that objects reflect light, and hence that, *if* an object is perceived, then it must be the case that it reflects light. We move from knowledge of the medium by which the object is apprehended to a justifiable belief about the nature of the object. To do this, however, it is not necessary for us also to suppose that the object depends, either for its existence or its nature, upon us or upon the medium of apprehension. For it is quite open for us to allow that the object would exist in exactly the same way, including its ability to reflect light, even if it was never perceived by anyone.

It may be felt, however, that there is one further thing that needs to be explained and for which only idealism provides an explanation. This is the fact with which Kant started, the fact that we are able to have knowledge of a world, the fact that there is agreement between the forms of judgment and the world to which they apply. The above argument results in the conclusion that we do not need to suppose that the mind makes the world in order to use transcendental arguments; all we need suppose is that the world is accessible to the mind. Yet it is just this supposition that might seem to need further explanation, an explanation which could only be supplied by idealism. Without idealism, we would seem to be left with the unappealing alternatives that the coincidence between thought and its objects was pure luck or that it was the product of the conscious design of some external cause, or God, who had established a harmony between thought and its objects. Kant, after all, in the famous letter to Herz of 21 Febuary 1772 in which he raises the general problem which the Critical programme is designed to solve, namely

> how is the understanding to construct for itself entirely *a priori* concepts of things with which the things are necessarily in agreement ((ed.) Kerferd and Walford, p. 113).

immediately goes on to dismiss the solution of a pre-established harmony:

> in determining the origin and validity of our knowledge, however, the *deus ex machina* is the most absurd argument one could choose (pp. 113–114).

That is, if we leave a designing God out, does not the above argument make to be purely a matter of luck a harmony for which idealism would form a perfect explanation?

I think that this objection can be answered satisfactorily; and my answer
to it derives from a rhetorical question thrown out by Jonathan Bennett in
his book *Kant's Dialectic*. Bennett says there that if he has to explain at all
how experiences 'happen' to be just of the sort which the mind can receive,
then

> what is wrong with an analogue of the explanation of why the air on this
> planet 'happens' to be of just the sort human lungs insist upon having?
> (p. 54).

Bennett leaves the matter there, but I think that the implication of his
question is clear. Just as the harmony between the nature of an animal's
organs and the environment which it inhabits can be explained by natural
selection, so also can the harmony between a human's general forms of
judgment and the world. In both cases it depends neither upon a designer
nor upon pure luck, but is the result of normal causal processes. Any
individual who thinks (or acts as if) there is no causation in the world, or
that the future does not resemble the past, is an unsuccessful mutation,
ill-adapted to survive or breed. Ralph Walker has objected to the adequacy
of such evolutionary explanation in his recent book on Kant, and claimed
instead that 'the hypothesis of a benevolent designer is . . . what our system
of thought requires to secure its own coherence' (*Kant*, 176). This is because he thinks that such evolutionary accounts cannot meet the problem
posed by Goodman's paradox: just as past experience cannot give inductive
support for something being green rather than it being grue, so natural
selection cannot select between the adequacy of the concept of greenness
and the concept of grueness (pp. 173–174). There are two reasons, however,
why I do not think that this reply of Walker's is appropriate. The first, less
important, one is that even if he is right about quite specific concepts, the
same points may not apply to the very central features of thought and the
world with which transcendental arguments are concerned. The second,
more important, reason is that the harmony we are trying to explain is the
harmony which exists at present between our thought and the world. I
have said nothing in the previous argument which implies that it is
necessary that the harmony between thought and the world will continue
into the future. If causal relations cease to hold in the world, then we will
no longer be able to judge it and will be condemned to silence in the way
that I have outlined above; this does not mean that it could not happen.
The argument is merely that, *if* we can judge it, then it must exhibit causal
connection. This is the present situation: we can judge it, and so it does
exhibit causal connections. This present harmony is all that it is required to
explain and for which idealism was thought to be the only possible explanation. This is not so, because the harmony can be explained by the
survival value in the period up to the present of a belief in causal connec-

tions. An evolutionary account only explains the present situation, but it is only the present situation which needs to be explained.

Bibliography

Bennett, Jonathan, *Kant's Dialectic* (Cambridge University Press, 1974).
Broad, C. D., *Kant, An Introduction*, C. Lewy (ed.) (Cambridge University Press, 1978).
Kant, Immanuel, *Critique of Pure Reason*, translated by Norman Kemp Smith (London: Macmillan, 1933).
Kant, Immanuel, *Selected Pre-Critical Writings*, translated by G. B. Kerferd and D. E. Walford (Manchester University Press, 1968).
Strawson, P. F., *The Bounds of Sense* (London: Methuen, 1966).
Strawson, P. F., *Individuals* (London: Methuen, 1959).
Walker, Ralph C. S., *Kant* (London: Routledge & Kegan Paul, 1978).

Bradley's aphorism is in his *Aphorisms*, and repeated on page x of *Appearance and Reality* (Oxford University Press, 1930).

Anti-realist Semantics: the Role of *Criteria*

CRISPIN WRIGHT

§1. Anti-realism of the sort which Michael Dummett has expounded[1] takes issue with the traditional idea that an understanding of any statement (here, declarative sentence) is philosophically correctly analysed as involving grasp of conditions necessary and sufficient for its truth. Many kinds of statement to which, as we ordinarily think, we attach a clear sense would have to be represented, according to this tradition, as possessing *verification-transcendent* truth-conditions; if true that is to say, they would be so in virtue of circumstances of a type transcending our range of possible awareness. Exactly where to draw the boundaries of our possible awareness might be controversial; but there is clearly no being aware, in the relevant sense, of the kind of state of affairs which would make true a generalization of theoretical physics, an assertion about James II weight on his twenty-eighth birthday, a claim about what would have happened if Edward Heath had not sought a fresh mandate during the miners' strike, or—from your point of view—the statement that my left ear aches. In each of these kinds of case the traditional view, while granting that we (or you) cannot experience the truth-conferring states of affairs as such, would nevertheless credit us with a clear conception of the type of thing they would be. To be sure, there is then no possibility of a straightforward construal of this conception as a recognitional capacity. But the traditional view tends to conceal from itself the problematic status which the alleged grasp of truth-conditions therefore assumes by working with the picture that the 'conception' is *indirectly* recognitional, that it *issues in* a cluster of unproblematic recognitional capacities; in particular, the ability to recognize what is or is not good evidence for the relevant statement and the ability to recognize its logical relations to other statements.[2]

Now, what the anti-realist urges that we enquire is: what good reason is

[1] I do not mean to imply that Dummett's exposition has remained uniform throughout his writings. The principal sources are the articles reprinted as chapters 1, 10, 11, 13, 14, 21 in the collection of his papers, *Truth and other Enigmas* (Duckworth, 1978), and 'What is a Theory of Meaning? (II)' in *Truth and Meaning*, Evans and McDowell (eds) (Oxford University Press, 1976). See also *Frege: Philosophy of Language* (Duckworth, 1973), *passim*.

[2] See, for example, Strawson, 'Scruton and Wright on Anti-realism, etc.', *Proceedings of the Aristotelian Society* (1976).

there to postulate any such ulterior 'conception' from which these abilities are supposed to flow—why, indeed, describe our understanding of these statements as involving knowledge of truth-conditions at all? His challenge to the realist is to make out a respectable notion of explanation in terms of which the truth-conditional account can be seen to be needed in order to explain these recognitional abilities. And his suspicion is that the challenge cannot be met.

If this suspicion is correct, the traditional truth-conditional account actually conveys, at least in the case of verification-transcendent statements, no substantial philosophical insight into what understanding essentially is. However, an account which, it seems, cannot possibly be open to objection in the same way would *identify* understanding with the cluster of abilities of which the truth-conditional view aimed to provide a unified explanation. Understanding a statement, on this view, would simply be a matter of practical mastery of all aspects of its *use*.

If a statement has truth-conditions whose actualization is something which our experience can encompass, then part of this practical mastery will be the ability to recognize such an actualisation, if one is appropriately placed to do so, and to respond accordingly; in such a case, knowledge of the truth-conditions will be a sub-species of knowledge of the conditions which warrant assertion of the statement—its *assertibility-conditions*. But it is now a grasp of assertibility-conditions which, for statements in general, will play the central role in the account of understanding. Such grasp can play this central role because, first, a practical knowledge of the logical relations of a statement is simply a knowledge of the role played in its assertibility-conditions by possible argumentation; and because, second, whether there is what the traditional account would regard merely as good evidence for a particular statement is something which—unlike whether or not it is true—a reasonable man can *always* recognize, which can never be transcendent. The thought is, in short, that understanding a statement is essentially a practical, discriminatory skill of which knowledge of assertibility-conditions is always, while knowledge of truth-conditions is at most sometimes, a satisfactory interpretation.

An endorsement of this assertibility-conditions conception of meaning is taken by Dummett, I believe rightly, to be part of the intent of the later Wittgenstein's identification of (knowledge of) meaning with (knowledge of) use. It is therefore natural to wonder what if any part ought to be played in a theory which elaborates the assertibility-conditions conception by the notion of a *criterion* deployed in Wittgenstein's later work. That is the main question which I want to consider: if we find ourselves in sympathy with the anti-realist's criticisms, and are led thereby to seek a philosophical account of meaning in which conditions of warranted assertion rather than of truth play the central role, ought we to try to substantiate and utilize something at least interestingly akin to Wittgenstein's notion?

§2. In the *Blue Book*, as is familiar, Wittgenstein does not always sharply distinguish the concept of a criterion from that of a sufficient—or even a necessary and sufficient—condition of a statement's truth. (See, notoriously, the passage about Angina on p. 25.) But the use which Wittgenstein makes of the notion both elsewhere in the *Blue Book* and throughout the *Investigations* make it plain that he did not in general intend that satisfaction of the criteria of a statement should be the same thing as realization of truth-conditions. Consider for example *Investigations*, 377:

> What are the criteria for the redness of an image? For me, when it is someone else's image, what he says and does . . .

But Wittgenstein explicitly disavows the behaviourism which would hold that the truth-conditions of 'X is experiencing a red image', said of another, are constituted by his verbal and non-verbal behaviour.[3] Compare 354:

> The fluctuation in grammar between criteria and symptoms makes it look as though there were nothing at all but symptoms. We say, for example: 'Experience teaches that there is rain when the barometer falls but it also teaches that there is rain when we have certain sensations of wet and cold or such-and-such visual impressions'. In defence of this one says that these sense-impressions can deceive us. But here one fails to reflect that the fact that the false appearance is precisely one of rain is founded on a definition.

The criteria of a statement, as Wittgenstein intends the notion, are, first and most importantly, in contrast with its symptoms, conditions which justify its assertion as a matter of 'definition'—as a function purely of its meaning—but which fall short of making it true. We can add that if the statement has a communally well-understood use, as Wittgenstein argued any genuine statement must, the conditions in question must, secondly, be *publicly accessible*. And Wittgenstein stresses, thirdly, that the criteria of a statement are generally *multiple*; see, for example, *Blue Book*,. p. 51, on the multiplicity of criteria for statements about the perceivable world; *Brown Book*, 7, p. 144, on the multiplicity of criteria for someone's sincerity; *Investigations*, 164, for the case of reading, and many other passages.

Both Hacker[4] and Baker[5] take it to be an essential fourth feature of Wittgenstein's notion that the satisfaction of criteria confers *certainty*. Naturally, this cannot be so if we regard as certain only statements about which the possibility of error can be definitively excluded. But if certainty is taken to apply to all and only statements which may not reasonably be doubted, then—since what may reasonably be asserted cannot simul-

---

[3] For any agnostic about this claim, *Investigations* 393 should be explicit enough.

[4] In *Insight and Illusion* (Oxford University Press, 1972), concluding chapter.

[5] In 'Criteria: a New Foundation for Semantics', *Ratio* (1974).

taneously be reasonably doubted—the satisfaction of a statement's criteria will indeed pre-empt any reasonable doubt about it; for it will now be part of the *content* of the statement that it may reasonably be asserted in those circumstances. (Classical scepticism therefore presupposes something other than a criterial account of meaning; it requires an account which makes it coherent to call into question our warrant to assert a particular kind of statement in all the kinds of circumstances which we typically consider to justify its assertion without *eo ipso* calling into question the identity of the statement. The truth-conditional account will generally serve the sceptic's purpose admirably.)

§3. A natural thought is that the assertibility-conditions theorist will need to avail himself of something at least very close to Wittgenstein's distinction of criteria from conditions of warranted assertion in general if he is to give an account of what it is to *misunderstand* a statement. If somebody uses a statement in what seems to the rest of us a quite aberrant manner, factual misapprehension, prejudice and simple ignorance are among the most likely explanations. But another possibility, as we should ordinarily suppose, is that he doesn't understand the statement. The traditional view would mark this difference by drawing a distinction between aberrant uses which respectively do and do not flow from a misconception of a statement's truth-conditions. But it looks to be unclear what account an anti-realist can give of the distinction so long as he is content to talk vaguely of understanding a statement as consisting in a practical knowledge of its assertibility-conditions; for the ignorant, mistaken or prejudiced man, after all, does in one way not know the assertibility-conditions of the statement of which his use is aberrant. If assertibility-conditions are divided into criteria and symptoms, on the other hand, then the anti-realist can propose that aberrant use betrays misunderstanding when and only when it is caused by misconceptions about, or ignorance of, the criteria for the statement in question.

Now, it is clear that, whatever else it may achieve, this proposal does not of itself convey a full account of misunderstanding. Saying that a misunderstanding consists in misconceptions about, or ignorance of, criteria is no more an account of the notion than saying that it consists in misconceptions about, or ignorance of, truth-conditions. In both cases we continue to await an explanation of how such a misconception is supposed to be manifest *as such* in a person's behaviour. Talk in terms of criteria, or truth-conditions, puts us in a position to *label* the notion of misunderstanding; and our desire to have such a label has whatever respectability the belief possesses that no satisfactory philosophy of language will be able to jettison the notion of misunderstanding altogether. But the fact is that to introduce the idea of aberrant usage which is attributable to misconceptions about, or ignorance of, criteria really makes it not one whit clearer how to provide a substantial account of misunderstanding: it merely serves to include provision of one on the (already packed) agenda.

This objection is reinforced if we look a little closer at the question how a substantial account might run. From whatever standpoint it emanated, it is clear that the account would have to respect the *holistically interlocking* character of the key concepts in the system whereby we explain a person's linguistic performance. In order to make his willingness to assent to, or dissent from, a particular statement in particular circumstances intelligible to us, we need to come up with hypotheses about his desires, beliefs, and the manner in which he understands the statement. But his performance will be good evidence for any particular one of these hypotheses only against the background of the other two. (The same point applies, of course, to the simpler system of belief and desire in terms of which we interpret non-linguistic human behaviour. A person's behaviour will support a particular hypothesis about his desires only if we presuppose certain beliefs on his part about how he can achieve those desires and about the prevailing circumstances; conversely, we can support the claim that he has certain beliefs only if we are allowed to presuppose certain desires on his part.) We do not require a more refined account of this sort of holistic structure of explanation to appreciate the corollary that there is no behaviour which is absolutely distinctive, of and by itself, of a misunderstanding of a particular statement. Whatever someone does, he can be acquitted of the charge of misunderstanding if we are ready to plead his possession of suitably idiosyncratic desires or factual beliefs; in fact, there will be *no end* of explanations of his behaviour available to us none of which involves attribution of any misunderstanding. So a full account of the notion of misunderstanding must do no less than tackle the complex question: what makes an explanation in terms of misunderstanding preferable to one of another kind, given the freedom that the holistic character of this system of explanation in principle affords us?

One possibility, certainly, is that the assertibility-conditions theorist will have to invoke the notion of a criterion in order to answer that question; that, for example, responses to situations in which arguable criteria for a statement are realized are particularly important in determining our preferences concerning what sort of explanation to give of an aberrant use of it. But, in advance, there seems no very clear reason for expecting this to be so. It may be that wholly pragmatic considerations govern our preferences here; considerations, that is to say, which have to do solely with how powerful and manageable an overall theory of the individual's behaviour the contrasted explanations admit of integration into—our preference being, for example, to describe someone as misunderstanding only when a large *range* of aberrant usage can be elicited from him in which certain expressions recur of which we can furnish an interpretation sanctioning a large part of the range.

Where that was the situation, we should expect, *ceteris paribus*, that patient re-explanation of the meanings of the relevant expressions, with perhaps a special eye towards ruling out the deviant interpretation in question, would bring our miscreant into line. And it will be, of course, in general a crucial element in our preferences about what kind of account to offer of aberrant use of a statement just what kind of 'further education' we anticipate will serve to eliminate it—explanations of meanings, or adduction of empirical fact, or neither. This reflection, however, provides a reason for supposing that the assertibility-conditions theorist will need to invoke criteria if he is to account for the notion of misunderstanding only if it is already assumed that he will need to invoke criteria in order to make good the distinction between explaining meanings and calling attention to empirical facts. And that assumption is correct only if at least some explanations of meaning are distinguished as such precisely by serving to elucidate criteria for the correct use of certain statements. If *that* were clear, however, we should already have sufficient reason for supposing that an assertibility-conditions orientated philosophy of language ought to utilize Wittgenstein's notion; special consideration of misunderstanding would be a detour.

There is at any rate, as it seems to me, no easy path from the assumption that such a philosophy of language ought to provide an account of the notion of misunderstanding to the conclusion that it will need to distinguish among assertibility-conditions between those which are criterial and those which are merely symptomatic in status. That is not to say that there may not be a harder path.

§4. Let us experiment with the following *Criterial Schema*:

If an agent has verified each of $\{D_1, \ldots, D_n\}$, and possesses no information telling against S and no information which would explain, without the need to suppose S, why $\{D_1, \ldots, D_n\}$ are true, then it is reasonable for him to believe S.

The Schema is satisfied for any particular statement S only by statements $\{D_1, \ldots, D_n\}$, which (collectively) describe conditions knowledge of whose realization is capable of justifying assertion of S. But as it stands, it embraces certain trivial cases: $\{D_1, \ldots, D_n\}$ may, for example, entail S; or they may include the statement that it is reasonable to believe S, or entail that statement independently of the additional conditions that no information telling against S, or equally good alternative explanations of the truth of $\{D_1, \ldots, D_n\}$, should be on hand. Let us therefore stipulate, first that $\{D_1, \ldots, D_n\}$ all be *decidable* statements; we thereby ensure that whenever S is verification-transcendent, knowledge of the truth of $\{D_1, \ldots, D_n\}$ will constitute at best a defeasible ground for asserting S, and will moreover be knowledge of an unproblematic recognitional sort (provided, of course, it is right to suppose that knowledge of the truth-conditions of decidable statements is correctly so regarded[6]). And let us also stipulate, second, that $\{D_1, \ldots, D_n\}$ are to be *S-predicative* statements: that is, statements which involve in particular no occurrences of S and, more generally, an understanding of which presupposes no understanding of S; we thereby ensure both that the second and, I believe also, the third trivial kinds of case are excluded, and, most importantly, that any $\{D_1, \ldots, D_n\}$ which satisfies the Schema for a particular S is suitable material for a non-circular explanations of the assertibility conditions of S—for, from the point of view of the assertibility-conditions theorist, it obviously has to be possible to explain S's assertibility-conditions without presupposing that the recipient already understands S.

To locate a set, $\{D_1, \ldots, D_n\}$, which, for a particular S, satisfies the Schema, understood—as from here on we shall understand it—as so restricted, would not yet be fully to explain the use of S; full explanation would at least require, in addition, an S-predicative account of what it was to have no information telling against S, nor any competitive alternative explanation of the truth of $\{D_1, \ldots, D_n\}$. Nevertheless it appears that we can now formulate our leading question in rather sharper terms: is the assertibility-conditions theorist committed to holding that, if S is a well-understood verification-transcendent statement, a set, $\{D_1, \ldots, D_n\}$, can be located whose introduction with S into the Schema will result in a *non-contingent* truth? If so, then for each such S, he will be constrained to acknowledge a set of conditions which can be explained independently of an understanding of S and of which it is non-contingently true that their satisfaction defeasibly warrants S's assertion. That would surely be a commitment to something 'interestingly akin to' Wittgenstein's notion, even though the proposal does not speak directly to Wittgenstein's conditions concerning the publicity and variety of criterial support.

In order to try to clarify the matter, let us suppose the opposite: that there are verification-transcendent statements of whose assertibility-conditions we can, perhaps, give a general, though impredicative, description but of which no more specific, predicative description can be given generating a non-contingent instance of the Schema. For any such statement, S, we then confront two possibilities: either (i) such S-predicative characterizations as can be given of S's assertibility-conditions yield contingent instances of the Schema; or (ii) no S-predicative characterization can be given at all. The question which it is now fruitful to consider is: how are the kind of circumstances which justify assertion of S to be conceived as initially communicable? On alternative (i), it appears that an explanation could at least begin by reference to an S-predicative description, C, of features, $E_1, \ldots, E_k$, of certain such circumstances. But it would be *contingent* that the circumstances so described ever justified

---

[6] A question to be aired in §7 of this paper.

assertion of S—so before one could reasonably offer this sort of explanation, it would be necessary to have empirical grounds supporting it; empirical grounds for supposing that the appropriate instances of the Schema were (contingently) true. Evidently, in order to be in possession of such grounds, we should have to have had some anterior idea of *other* features, $F_1, \ldots, F_k$, which would distinguish (at least some) circumstances justifying assertion of S. For unless we had some such idea, capable of elucidation in advance, it would be impossible to defend against the suggestion that we did *not* find empirical grounds for regarding C-type circumstances as justifying assertion of S but rather tacitly adopted a *convention* that they did so—contrary to (i). So the question now arises, in what manner is this anterior idea to be thought of as capable of explanation? Perhaps the relevant features, $F_1. \ldots, F_k$, can be S-predicatively characterized; but in that case, given (i), it will be contingent whether circumstances which exemplify them justify assertion of S, so the explanation given will in turn require empirical support. And, again, we shall be able to adduce such support only within the framework of yet other features, $G_1, \ldots, G_k$, regarded as distinguishing assertibility-conditions of S. Clearly, however, *these* features must not be those features, $E_1, \ldots, E_k$, originally specified in C—otherwise our putative empirical grounds for regarding C-circumstances as justifying assertion of S become circular. So we embark on a regress.

The position, in other words, is that if we are allowed recourse *only* to S-predicative descriptions of assertibility-conditions of S, then alternative (i) requires that in order to be entitled to regard our explanation as correct, we shall need to establish empirical support for infinitely many independent such descriptions—*per impossibile*. That is, if it is possible to give an S-predicative characterization of assertibility-conditions of S which we are entitled to regard as correct, the case for saying so will have to advert to something other than an S-predicative characterization.

Notice, however, that for the assertibility-conditions theorist it must not be *unavoidable* for us to invoke an S-impredicative characterization at this point. For knowing S's assertibility-conditions is to involve more than grasping that certain types of circumstance justify its assertion—it is to involve attaining all the understanding of S which we, the trainers, enjoy. So if C-type circumstances merely contingently justify assertion of S, one thing the trainee has to learn is *why*—by what principle—they are rightly judged to do so. But if we really cannot avoid bringing in reference to an S-impredicative characterization of S's assertibility-conditions in order to defend the correctness of C, then there cannot be any explanation of this principle intelligent receipt of which does not presuppose a prior understanding of S—and that is just to say that there is no full explanation of what it is for circumstances to justify the assertion of S save one which presupposes an understanding of S, an absurd situation from the point of view of the assertibility-conditions theorist.

The consequences of alternative (i) for the assertibility-conditions theorist are therefore as follows. In order to be entitled to regard any S-predicative description as characterizing a class of circumstances which justify S's assertion, we shall need to advert to features which we *cannot* capture by S-predicative description but which *can* be explained without recourse to S-impredicative description. Only someone who is apprised of these features and their role understands S; so no S-impredicative description of them is of any explanatory use. S's assertibility-conditions, alternative (i) therefore forces us to conclude, do not admit of a complete descriptive explanation.

If, on the other hand, as supposed on alternative (ii), it is somehow the case that no S-predicative characterization can be given at all of features distinctive of S's assertibility-conditions, the same conclusion swiftly follows. Now the only characterizations of S's assertibility-conditions which we will be entitled to regard as correct will all be S-impredicative; whereas if such a characterization is to be genuinely explanatory, it will have to be possible to presuppose on the part of its recipient a prior understanding of S, conferred in some other way than by a characterization of its assertibility-conditions. The truth-conditional conception has at least *scope* for such a presupposition; the requisite prior understanding of S will have been conferred by exactly an explanation of its *truth-conditions*, so there is no formal obstacle to an explanatory but S-impredicative characterization of its assertibility-conditions. But the assertibility-conditions theorist, obviously, has no such scope except in cases where he regards grasp of truth-conditions as unproblematic—contrary to the hypothesized situation of S. It therefore appears that in the case of any well-understood verification-transcendent statement he must either reject *both* alternatives, (i) and (ii), or else embrace their common consequence (for his point of view) that no description of the statement's assertibility-conditions can be given which is a full and adequate introductory explanation of them. To reject both alternatives, (i) and (ii), however, is just to postulate the existence of non-contingently true instances of the Schema—restricted as described—for the statement in question; that is, *criteria* for it. So we have an affirmative answer to our leading question as one disjunct of the conclusion of the foregoing argument.

§5. The other option is that the theorist discard the idea that a full understanding of S can be imparted by description of its assertibility-conditions. Since, for him, an understanding of S *consists* in grasping its assertibility-conditions, this option immediately necessitates some other model of how a grasp of S's assertibility-conditions can be conferred. The only other form for a model to take is, of course—using the word in its broadest possible sense—*ostensive*: it has to be possible to make manifest what type of conditions justify the assertion of S by demonstration and example.

Granted the soundness of the reasoning of the preceding section, the situation is therefore that an assertibility-conditions theorist is committed to elucidating criteria for any verification-transcendent statement, S, whose sense he considers to be well-determined but whose assertibility-conditions he considers could not be explained ostensively.

It might be thought that, bearing in mind that we learn the overwhelmingly greater part of our language by direct immersion, as it were, the demand on the assertibility-conditions theorist actually to spell out criteria is one which it will hardly ever be possible to make stick. Confidence in the correctness of that thought ought to await an investigation how it could be made apparent, *purely* by ostension, demonstration and example, under what circumstances past-tense, or unrestrictedly general, assertions—to take two potentially problematic-looking cases—were justifiably assertible. But even if the thought is correct, we still need to consider, before concluding that no reason is apparent for supposing that an assertibility-conditions theorist will have much work for criteria, whether even within the class of assertibility-conditions whose explanation does proceed, in the relevant broad sense, in purely ostensive terms, something 'interestingly akin to' the distinction between criteria and symptoms can still be explained.

It is natural to think that the answer must be negative. For the distinction as so far understood turns on whether a state of affairs of a particular type justifies assertion of a particular S contingently or non-contingently. And how can that issue so much as make sense if the type of state of affairs in question is associated with no particular description but is identified by ostensive means? All that can settle the question of contingency or non-contingency, it might be thought, is consideration of the meanings of S and of the description given of the type of state of affairs in question. So where, in the relevant sense, *no* description is given, the question cannot arise. Or if it does arise, some radically *de re* conception of contingency/non-contingency seems to be required to give it content.

Surely, though, of *any* explanation of assertibility-conditions of S, descriptive or ostensive, it has to make sense to enquire whether it admits of an empirical defence. If the community considers that a certain sort of state of affairs, of which they can give no better than an incompletely descriptive, largely ostensive characterization justifies asserting S, it ought to be a reasonable enquiry what, if any, type of ground they have for thinking so. Three possibilities then open. The first is that they consider that they have empirical grounds; as when, for example, a particular behavioural syndrome, visually distinctive but difficult distinctively to describe, has been found to be associated with a particular kind of poisoning. Second, they may find that they are unable to adduce such grounds, and tend to treat that as calling into question the correctness of asserting S in that type of circumstance. Or, third, they may be disinclined to respond to their lack of empirical grounds in that way and, very likely, puzzled to know what to do to meet the demand for justification of this aspect of their practice. Obviously, it is this third possibility which is of interest in the present context. It is a possibility which it is certain would in actual practice be realized repeatedly. But the question is how to elicit a respectable notion of *convention* of such a sort that we can then regard communal responses of the third kind as possible indications that the association between the assertibility of the relevant statement and the obtaining of an instance of the ostensively explained species of circumstances is a conventional matter.

The obvious proposal is simply this: the connection between the occurrence of a particular ostensively explained type of state of affairs and a particular statement, S, is one of *conventional support* if and only if we would consider it acceptable in certain circumstances to assert S on the basis of knowledge of such a state of affairs; and we would not require, in order for someone to be credited with a full understanding both of S and of what type of state of affairs had been ostensively explained, that he know what it would be empirically to investigate whether occurrences of that type of state of affairs really did provide reason for believing S and to find that they did not.

In contrast, the connection is one of *contingent support* if and only if we would, once again, consider it acceptable in certain circumstances to assert S on the basis of knowledge of such a state of affairs; but would regard no one as fully understanding both the statement and what kind of state of affairs had been meant *unless* he grasped how it might be empirically investigated whether occurrences of the latter provided reason for believing the former and what it would be for it to turn out that they did not. If, for example, we give an ostensive demonstration of the syndrome of movements characteristic of mercuric poisoning, no one will be credited with a full understanding both of what kind of state of affairs we intended to demonstrate and of the statement, 'X is suffering from mercuric poisoning', unless he has some idea of what it would be empirically to investigate whether occurrences of that syndrome provided a reason for believing appropriate statements of that kind, and what it would be for it to turn out that they did not.

Let us say that a particular type of state of affairs is a **criterion* for a particular statement if and only if it affords that statement conventional support in the sense just described. Truth-conditions, clearly, where, if anywhere, they are capable of ostensive explanation, are a sub-class of **criteria* so characterized. Our question now is: will an assertibility-conditions theorist who is ready to grant that a particular class of verification-transcendent statements possess no criteria be committed to their possession of **criteria* instead?

Consider what sort of model the theorist is in a position to give of how an understanding of any one member of the class, S, is to be conferred if he tries to proceed without recourse to *criteria. By hypothesis, he has abandoned the hope of elucidating criteria for S. So the materials at his disposal include only S-predicatively characterizable but symptomatic assertibility-conditions of S and ostensively explicable but merely contingently S-supportive states of affairs. The most immediate difficulty, as before, has to do with the defensibility of whatever explanation he chooses to advance. It has to do, that is to say, with how he can support the claim that his explanation enjoins *correct* use of S. For whatever type of explanation, ostensive or descriptive, which his model involves will connect only contingently with the justifiable use of S—will be such that competent members of his speech community will have a concept of how the adequacy of the explanation might be investigated empirically and of how it might turn out to be doubtful. If the explanation is ostensive, the point follows directly from the definition of contingent support; if the explanation is descriptive, it follows from the contingency, ergo possible falsity, of the appropriate instance of the Schema, the possibility interpreted—as an anti-realist must interpret it—constructively. So, either way, in order to provide a defence of the model explanation, the theorist will have to provide a reason for thinking that such an investigation would turn out favourably. In fact, though, it is clear that the most he will be able to provide will be reason for thinking that his explanation enjoins the same pattern of use as another, antecedently accepted as correct. And since this in turn can, by hypothesis, only be an ostension of contingently supportive circumstances or a predicative description of symptoms, the issue of *its* defensibility will immediately arise. Failing recourse to criteria or *criteria, then, the theorist lands himself in the incoherent position of having to grant that there is an empirical question about the adequacy of any particular explanation of the use of S into which no *effective* (i.e. finite, non-circular and persuasive) investigation can be conducted.

To be sure, that is a predicament which the truth-conditions theorist might be prepared to tolerate. He might be prepared to accept that it is an empirical issue whether the grounds which we standardly accept for asserting a particular type of verification-transcendent statement are indeed a good indication that its transcendent conditions of truth are realized—it is just that the appropriate 'empirical investigation' is one which mere human beings cannot perform. But the only coherent stance for the anti-realist assertibility-conditions theorist is to postulate, for any communally well-understood verification-transcendent statement, S, the possibility of an explanation of its assertibility-conditions which, if ostensive, is associated with no communal conception of how its adequacy might be empirically investigated; or, if descriptive, results in a non-contingent instance of the Schema.

The same conclusion emerges another way if we draw on another of our earlier reflections and recall that, while the meaning of S is now viewed as being fully explained by fully explaining its assertibility-conditions, no one will count as fully understanding S whose responses to what we consider to be contingently S-supportive or S-symptomatic circumstances are more or less what we think of as the right ones but who had no conception of how it might be empirically investigated, and confirmed or disconfirmed, whether we are right. So the assertibility-conditions theorist must provide in his model a way of communicating such a conception; and it is clear that so long as his model makes play only with contingently supportive and symptomatic circumstances, the problem will be intractable. For no matter what lengths the model goes to, no matter how specification of assertibility-conditions is piled on specification, if, for each combination of the circumstances explained, the thesis that its realization would provide reason for believing S is in principle empirically defeasible, no one has fully grasped the meaning of S who has not grasped what it would be for that possibility to be realized—and that is something which the model itself cannot have made clear. A full understanding of S, therefore, if it is to be conferrable by an explanation of assertibility-conditions at all, has to be conceived as involving a knowledge of criteria, or *criteria, or both.

It should be stressed that what has been established, assuming the soundness of these considerations, is the theorist's commitment to the existence of assertibility-conditions, for each statement for which he regards the truth-conditional account as problematic, of which there is no communal conception how they might be found *not* to provide reason for believing the statement. A full understanding of the statement, that is to say, will be required to involve grasp of the role of these conditions; but it will not be required to involve grasp that their status is susceptible to empirical investigation. Something *weaker* is therefore being said than that each such statement will be associated with assertibility-conditions for which there is a communal understanding that their status as such is *not* susceptible to empirical investigation. Critics of the Wittgensteinian notion[7] are usually realists holding, more or less consciously, the truth-conditional view; but they also tend to labour under the belief that the proponent of criteria is confronting them with some such strong notion. And the fact is that lots of *prima facie* examples of the weaker kind of thing tend not to be clear-cut examples of the stronger. I suggest, however, though I shall not attempt to argue the point here, that play with a notion of the weaker kind will subserve well enough the *Investigations* strategy with traditional forms of scepticism; and that Wittgenstein's talk of the 'fluctuation between

---

[7] See most notably Putnam, 'Brains and Behaviour' in *Analytical Philosophy*, Butler (ed.), second series (Blackwell, 1965); also Chihara and Fodor, 'Operationalism and Ordinary Language: a Critique of Wittgenstein', *American Philosophical Quarterly* (1965).

criteria and symptoms'[8]—an idea crucial to his diagnosis of the way in which the sceptics's ideas are able to take hold of us—is correctly interpreted as pointing in particular to the phenomenon whereby it can at one time be no part of understanding a certain statement to know what it would be empirically to investigate whether a particular kind of state of affairs, standardly taken to justify its assertion, really does so but at a later time essential to have a conception of just such an investigation. That some such thing has happened to, for example, statements identifying samples of the elements between the era of the alchemists and the present day seems clear enough; and that it reflects a change in concepts like 'gold' is also clear, since the requirements imposed on a full understanding of these concepts have changed. But whether the point is correctly interpreted as somehow compromising the continuity of the objects of scientific enquiry is quite another matter.

§6. A major area of enquiry opens up at this point. If the assertibility-conditions theorist is committed to finding either criteria or *criteria for every communally well-understood statement for which he finds the truth-conditional account unacceptable, then if ever reason can be given for doubting that either criteria or *criteria can be found in a relevant class of cases, that will tend to suggest that there is something amiss with the assertibility-conditions conception of statement meaning; and that in turn will pose the question whether anti-realism can succeed in proposing any defensible alternative to the truth-conditional view. How far, then, can the assertibility-conditions theorist meet this apparent commitment?

The question is too big for this lecture. But let me at least make some rather cursory remarks about one central problematic case: that of statements about the past. An immediate reaction would be that the case looks promising for the anti-realist; for is it not most implausible to suppose that our apparent memories, or the possession of historical documentation, merely contingently provide reason for believing such statements? Is it not out of the question to suppose that a conditional like:

> If we all seem to recollect that S, and possess no countervailing evidence, nor any other explanation, equally as good as the supposition that S, of our possession of such an apparent memory, then it is reasonable for us to believe that S,

although, as we should ordinarily suppose, true, could in principle turn out to be incorrect if certain contingencies were realised? No doubt an appropriate genre of *scepticism* would contest the truth of such a conditional; but it would do so on purely *a priori* grounds. And a philosopher who is not

---

[8] In addition to the *Investigations* passage quoted above, see also *Zettel* 438.

prepared to don the mantle of sceptic about the past, and who can adduce no plausible account of *what* contingent facts would have to change in order for such a conditional to cease to be true, seems to have no alternative to admitting that statements about the past are capable of defeasible but non-contingent support.

Even if the conditional is indeed a non-contingent truth, however, as a prospective indication of a source of criteria, in the sense in which we are interested, for statements about the past, it is, obviously, uselessly S-impredicative. It may well be true that apparent memory enters into some sort of non-contingent connection with the reasonableness of certain kinds of belief about the past; but there will be no milking criteria out of the connection unless an S-predicative characterization can be given of what it is to have an apparent memory that S, and a characterization, moreover, whose correctness in any particular state of affairs is a decidable matter. The prospect of doing so, however, looks very opaque: what distinctive but essential features *are* there of an apparent memory that S which could be captured by descriptions presupposing no understanding of S and whose collective realization would *constitute* an apparent memory that S? Nothing plausible comes into view; and the corresponding question about historical documentation looks, for its part, no less daunting.

Memory and documentation apart, our judgments concerning past events and states of affairs rely entirely upon more or less theoretically inspired beliefs concerning their presently accessible physical traces. That no such traces can enjoy the status of criteria seems to be settled by the simple reflection that their provision of a reason for believing a particular past-tense statement will always be contingent *either* on the outcome of a direct appeal to documentation or memory *or* on the degree of empirical support possessed by the theory which credits them with that status—itself a contingent matter. So the criteria, if there are any, for past-tense statements must, it seems, be sought in the areas of apparent memory and documentation. If, therefore, the suspicion is correct that none save S-impredicative characterizations of apparent memories and documentation will serve to generate non-contingent instances of the Schema for a past-tense statement, S, we must conclude that there are no criteria for statements about the past.

It appears, then, that the assertibility-conditions theorist must make a case for regarding apparent memory and/or documentation as possible sources of *criteria for past-tense statements; and part of the case will have to be to argue that it is possible to explain ostensively, without presupposing an understanding of S, what it is for one to seem to remember that S or to have documentation that S.

In the case of documentation, it seems to be plain that little headway can be made. No doubt we could ostensively train someone to recognize written, or spoken, occurrences of the statement (that is to say, remember, declarative sentence); but only a language-user could tell whether it was meant to be received as having been asserted or not—and, besides, the knowledge that others, dead or alive, assert the statement is next to useless as a clue to its content. Knowledge of the *criteria of a statement ought to confer a *non-parastic* knowledge of its correct assertoric use; so the kind of non-contingent connection which documentation, and hearsay in general, has with reasonable belief is of no help to the theorist here.

The crucial question is therefore: could we make intelligible to someone by, in the relevant broad sense, ostensive means, what it was for him to seem to remember that S without in any way presupposing a prior understanding of S on his part? One's first suspicion is: no. Obviously, it it possible for us to drill someone in a broadly ostensive way in the correct use of a particular statement only if we are in a position to know in what way, from situation to situation, he *ought* to use it. But, it is plausible to suppose, someone's apparent memories are a feature of his mental life of a kind of which, in contrast to many sensations and emotions, there is no distinctive behavioural manifestation *save* his report of them. So if, as is our hypothesis, someone is in no position to report his apparent memory that S, how can it be determined how the envisaged drill should proceed? How are we supposed to know what someone's apparent memories are, if he is not in a position to tell us? And how, therefore, could we drill him in their correct description?

If there are neither criteria nor *criteria for past-tense statements, then, assuming the soundness of the reasoning of the preceding sections, it cannot be correct to view our understanding of such statements as consisting in knowledge of their assertibility-conditions. But we only have a *prima facie* case for that conclusion—and one to which the assertibility-conditions theorist is by no means bereft of a reply. He could point out, to begin with, that it is not as if a man's linguistically mature descriptions of his apparent memories are granted an absolutely unchallengeable authority. We often have a fairly definite idea when to expect someone to seem to remember something; and a fairly definite idea, too, of what it is to have a reasonable suspicion that someone is lying, or even sincerely mistaken, in claiming to seem to remember something. And if there are public standards for the correctness of apparent memory reports, ought it not to be possible to guide the envisaged ostensive training by these standards? After all, correct use of statements concerning one's own past is something in which most of us have been successfully trained simply by immersion within a linguistic community, something which we have learnt purely by example, prompting and correction. This training, somehow or other, gets across to us the distinction between making such statements on the basis of apparent memory and making them on other grounds. It helps to imagine our own practice changed in the following respect: we now never make, as it were, unguarded assertions about our past but always explicitly acknowledge the type of ground which we have for them: 'I am told that I was very angry', 'I seem to remember being very angry', 'I guess I must have been very angry', and so on. This new practice involves making no assertions in circumstances in which it would not have been correct to assert them before; so it could not be any more difficult to learn from scratch. Since its mastery, in contrast with mastery merely of the past tense, involves *explicit* knowledge of what it is to have apparent memories, surely there is no alternative to supposing that such knowledge is capable of ostensive communication.

This reply is more of a strong protest than a strong argument. I shall not try to take the matter any further here. The foregoing is at least a preliminary illustration of the way in which our leading question has a wider bearing than on the issue, interesting enough in itself, how Dummett's anti-realism connects with the ideas of the later Wittgenstein.

§7. We have so far been considering the role of criteria/*criteria* in an assertibility-conditions account of the meanings of verification-transcendent statements. In this final section I want briefly to consider the assumption that an anti-realist need have no quarrel with a truth-conditional view of the meanings of decidable ones.

If, as in Hacker[9] and Baker,[10] the criterial relation is regarded as holding between statements, then an anti-realist who held that the meaning of *every* statement is determined by its association with criteria would commit himself to an impossible model of how an understanding of any statement could be acquired. When the criterial relation is so understood, therefore, a criterial theory of meaning cannot be a global theory of meaning; a base class of statements is required whose meaning is not determined by association with criteria, and the obvious strategy for finding it is to see whether, or how far, the truth-conditional conception can be regarded as unproblematic from an anti-realist point of view.

How should the idea of an (effectively) decidable mathematical statement best be generalized? The obvious proposal is simply to replace the notions of proof and disproof in the mathematical characterization by more general ones of verification and falsification. An (effectively) decidable statement would then be any statement for which (we can recognize in advance that) we have a finite procedure whose implementation will culminate in its verification or falsification.

In terms of this proposal, perhaps the most immediate contingent candidates for the status of effective decidability would be statements which concerned presently observable characteristics of particulars which we can presently effectively find and identify; or, more generally, which

[9,10] See works cited above.

concerned finitely surveyable episodes or states of affairs in presently accessible regions of space and time. Thus 'My car is parked on the Scores', 'Tabitha is in her basket' and 'The sea is choppy today' would, making appropriate allowances for context and, where necessary, vagueness, turn out to be effectively decidable in these terms. The decision procedure appropriate in each case is: position yourself in the appropriate situation and observe.

Now, one might worry about what it is for a characteristic to be 'presently observable' or whether the idea of an 'effectively identifiable' particular has any legitimate place in a purported characterization of effective decidability. But the most major complication with the sort of example illustrated is that the role played by the idea of *position* has no counterpart in the mathematical cases form which we are trying to generalize. Anywhere is as good a place as anywhere else to determine whether or not 283 is a prime; and the same goes for time. But observation of the properties of spatio-temporal particulars, or of the goings-on within particular spatio-temporal regions, essentially requires getting oneself into an appropriate spatio-temporal position. Examples of this type, it might be argued, are therefore properly regarded as effectively decidable only if where and when one is itself an effectively decidable question; and it is proper to regard it as such only if we can rightly regard ourselves as having an effective finite procedure for determining where and when we are. But can it plausibly be claimed that we have any such procedure? Consider the case of spatial position on its own. Each of us finds his way around by relating the sequence of his experiences to a complex theoretic 'map' that he carries in his head of how the world is, by and large, disposed to affect his senses in different places. But the sense-affective dispositions of any particular place are, of course in no way *essential* characteristics of it: how the world is at any particular place is something which we conceive to be capable of radical change. The theoretic map which we employ is thus a revisable empirical theory. Granting, then, that there is no effective procedure for settling the truth or falsity of such a theory, and that it is only within the framework which it supplies, that the sort of statement illustrated can be determined to be true or false, how can such statements be regarded as effectively decidable at all? After all, if any statement counts as effectively decidable of which we can recognize that its truth or falsity can be settled within the framework of what is merely a *well-supported* theory, there is likely to be no clear barrier against the effective decidability of many examples of the sort of statement for which the anti-realist finds the notion of truth unacceptably transcendent.

A more general doubt about the propriety of thinking of the sort of statement illustrated as capable of verification pivots on their essential *defeasibility*. For verification ought or so it is natural to think, to be *conclusive*—otherwise there is no difference between data which verify a statement and data which merely support it. But no matter how sure a statement of the simple observational kind illustrated seems to be, developments are conceivable which may force us to retract it. For in addition to the complications generated by the role of spatio-temporal position, we have to acknowledge also possiblities like illusion and deception, possibilities which in any particular case may always suddenly open up on us.

The obvious thought at this point is that we may merely have picked the wrong type of example. But if there is to be a class of contingent statements about whose status as genuinely (effectively) decidable the above doubts do not apply, then the above sources of defeasibility must not apply either. In the first instance, therefore, their verification must not presuppose that the agent verifies his own spatio-temporal position. So they will have to deal in what is happening *here* and *now*. Secondly, they will have to involve no modes of reference to or description of particulars whose appropriateness turns on presuppositons about their history or future; and this promises to proscribe all proper names, all definite descriptions involving sortal terms—'man', 'tree', etc. (which always presuppose a certain sort of history); and all predicates, indeed, save ones which can be applied purely on the basis of present observation. But, thirdly, statements can meet these conditions, e.g. 'something here and now is red', but still be prone to a further source of defeasibility affecting every categorical assertion, however closely tied to present observation, which we venture about the external world: the possibility of developments which suggest that the conditions of observation are in some way radically *abnormal*. Any characteristic which we might easily take to be purely observational—characteristics, that is, which like colour, or the pitch of a note, or the texture of a surface, can be determined simply by looking, listening, feeling—will be such that a thing can *seem* to have it yet not do so because the conditions of observation somehow disqualify our findings.

It begins to look as though a retreat will be needed to statements concerning how things here and now *seem*. The statement, 'Something here and now seems to be red', for example, will not be compromised by the discovery, say, that it is subtly bathed in red light. But defeasibility is not to be shaken off so easily, provided such statements are construed as dealing in publicly accessible facts—provided, that is, the question of how things appear is sharply distinguished from the question of how they appear to any particular individual. For still the requirement of normality of the *observer* remains a source of defeasibility: something can here and now appear red to me, though not appear red *simpliciter*, because I am drugged, or colour-blind, or whatever. Indefeasible verifiability, it appears, is therefore going to require a retreat to description of how things seem to a single observer from his point of view—in short, to *privacy*; for each of us the statements in question will have to concern how things here and now seem to him, irrespective of his state, the conditions of observation, precisely what particulars of what kinds are within his experiential field, or where and when he is. But the price of taking statements of this kind to be indefeasibly certain will be that the anti-realist, following Wittgenstein's polemic in the *Investigations*, will be constrained to doubt whether we are concerned with a genuinely fact-stating type of statement at all.

It begins to look, at this point, to be only in a 'loose and popular sense', to borrow Butler's phrase,[11] that any contingent statement can be regarded as capable of verification. Strictly they are all verification-transcendent; capable of evidential confirmation but as little capable of verification, properly conceived, as Dummett's original examples: 'A city will never be built on this spot' and 'Jones was brave'.[12] And it would, moreover, be a mistake, though one with a long history of attraction, to suppose that the situation is any different with decidable mathematical statements. For:

> ... one cannot contrast *mathematical* certainty with the relative uncertainty of empirical propositions. For the mathematical proposition has been obtained by a series of actions that are in no way different from the actions of the rest of our lives, and are in the same degree liable to forgetfulness, oversight and illusion (*On Certainty* 651).

If these considerations are correct, then we have to acknowledge that the contrast between any kind of statement which we can verify—whether as the result of implementation of an effective procedure, or by good fortune and/or ingenuity—and verification-transcendent statements is not to be explained, if indeed it can be made out at all, by the susceptibility of the former to indefeasible certainty. Moreover the strategy of trying to construe verifiability merely as a high-grade but defeasible kind of confirmability is certain not to produce a distinction between verifiable and verification-transcendent statements coinciding with what the anti-realist intuitively wants. There are, for example, lots of unrestrictedly general scientific hypotheses, and associated counterfactual conditionals, which have been confirmed to saturation point, so to speak; say, 'All men are mortal'. So is not the class of verifiable contingent statements at best loosely so described and at worst mythical?

The possibility of a negative answer to that question would not compromise a genuine distinction drawn by refinement of the following idea. Some statements, including all decidable mathematical statements, have the feature of being associated with a procedure which it is within human power to implement and which is such that if it is implemented correctly and the agent correctly apprehends what goes on in the course of its implementation, he will thereby have determined whether the statement is true or not.

[11] 'The Analogy of Religion'; see *Personal Identity* Perry (ed.) (University of California Press, 1975), 101.

[12] In 'Truth', *Proceedings of the Aristotelian Society* (1958), reprinted as chapter 1 in *Truth and other Enigmas*, cited above.

Effectively decidable statements in general are those of which we can recognize that this is a correct characterization without yet knowing what their truth-value is. Both effectively decidable mathematical statements and the sort of contingent example which we started out considering come under this general rubric. It is just that in neither case can we conclusively, i.e. indefeasibly certainly, verify that the appropriate procedure has been implemented correctly and that we have correctly apprehended the course things took. Moreover, the rubric appears to put in the right place all the standard contingent examples for which the anti-realist urges that we should see problems in the truth-conditional account. There is, for example, no procedure within human compass such that if it is correctly implemented and its whole process correctly apprehended, the truth-value of an unrestricted generalization would *eo ipso* be among the information at one's disposal. The same, plausibly, applies to statements about the past, contingent counterfactual conditionals and statements about others' mental states: the best investigative procedures that we have for these statements are such that, no matter what good luck we enjoy or ingenuity we summon, if we carry them through correctly and correctly apprehend what we have done, we can *still* form an incorrect opinion. To put the matter in terms which an anti-realist would not accept: after implementation of any investigative procedure in these cases, the truth-value of the relevant statement may possibly be at our disposal in the sense that we have managed to form a correct opinion about it; but our investigations will have failed to *determine* the truth-value in the way they do when we are concerned with statements about which an incorrect opinion is possible after implementing the appropriate procedure only if the procedure was botched somehow or we misapprehended the course which things took.

If, however, it is only along these lines[13] that the contrast between decidable and verification-transcendent statements can be made out, the urgent question is whether it was right for the anti-realist to regard 'grasp of truth-conditions' as a problematic notion only in verification-transcendent cases. His original point was that 'grasp of truth-conditions', knowledge of the distinction between circumstances which make a particular statement true and circumstances which do not, ought to be an ability to *make* a distinction; i.e. to tell the difference. But it is so only when decidable statements are concerned; only then can someone show he has mastered the distinction in the way that fundamentally counts—by applying it directly to the two kinds of circumstances which it divides. For only in the case of decidable statements can truth-conditions be realized within the compass of our experience. But, now, if our best efforts at verification or falsification of decidable statements always remain in principle defeasible,

[13] For misgivings about this way of drawing the contrast, and an attempt to improve upon it, see §3 of my 'Strict Finitism', forthcoming in *Synthese*.

then in just what sense *are* the truth-conditions of such statements realizable 'within the compass' of our experience? With what justification does the anti-realist credit us with a practical, discriminatory knowledge of truth-conditions in decidable cases but not in verification-transcendent ones if in *both* kinds of case only a defeasible purchase is possible on the facts by reference to which our putative knowledge is to be tested?

Provided defeasibility is, as it seems, absolutely pervasive and ineliminable, it does not in this context matter how (effectively) decidable statements are characterized. For it will remain unclear what the *special* problem about the truth-conditional view of verification-transcendent statements is supposed to be. But it would not follow that the anti-realist ought to suspect error in his original doubts.[14] The logical conclusion for him to draw would be rather that truth-conditional semantics is a distortion right across the board; that everywhere it is at best a mere slogan to think of statement-understanding as consisting in knowledge of truth-conditions. Rather, what it fundamentally consists in, the ability in which it is fully manifest, is just the ability intelligibly to participate in the community's use of its language; the ability to join non-parasitically in a community of assent concerning the justifiability of asserting a particular statement. It is this ability which, whether it is verification-transcendent or decidable, provides the ultimate touchstone of understanding a statement. A recognitional grasp of truth-conditions ought to be testable; and it is testable only by assessment of the agent's responses to situations whereby the truth-conditions are, or are not, realized. But now it is unclear whether that is something which we can ever, strictly speaking, do. All we can do is test his responses to situations in which our best *but defeasible* opinion is that the truth-conditions are, or are not, realized. So his performance is assessed in relation not to how things are but to how we take them to be; and it is in the agent's ability to bear up favourably under this comparison that his understanding of the statement in question resides.

Lest there be any misunderstanding, I do not claim that it is clear that the anti-realist must follow this path, but only that it is at least understandable if he does. We are steering close now to a possible point of contact between anti-realism and the Idealist tradition in philosophy which forms the subject matter of this series of lectures. The essential spirit of the realist philosophical outlook is captured by a three-term picture: whenever (a) I form an opinion, there is (b) the question whether others agree with me and (c) the quite independent question whether I and/or they are right about the matter. All Idealists, whatever other differences there may have been between them, have agreed in holding either that there is no intelligible question (c) or, at least, that it cannot intelligibly be construed as 'quite independent', that how things are is some sort of conceptual function of

---

14 Again, however, see 'Strict Finitism', §3.

how human beings take them to be. Now, so long as the anti-realist is content to allow that there is a base class of statements for which the truth-conditional account is appropriate, he has done nothing to cut himself off from realism about any subject matter debatable by the use solely of statements within that class. It will be open to him, that is to say, to endorse the three-term picture as appropriate to any opinion one forms on an issue within such a subject matter. If, in particular, he takes no issue with the truth-conditional view for all effectively decidable statements, then it is open to him—and perhaps required—to endorse the three-term picture for all effectively decidable questions. But if he takes the above considerations to heart and jettisons the idea of a truth-conditionally determined base class of statements, then his contention will have to be that the three-term picture everywhere encourages misdescription of the character of linguistic competence. The realist tries to see competence as a matter of the propensity to suit one's use of statements to correct answers to question (c); but the anti-realist is urging in effect that all that we can *display*, in any case where at most defeasible certainty is possible, is an ability for whose adequate description no acknowledgment of the legitimacy of question (c) is required. So he is within a whisker of Idealism; and he can avoid an idealist stance only if he can somehow argue that question (c), although we do not have to acknowledge it in order to do justice to the character of statement-understanding, has to be acknowledged on other grounds. A leading corollary of the later Wittgenstein's recurrent discussion of rule-following is, I suspect, that the anti-realist cannot coherently develop such an argument. But I will not try to pursue that thought here.[15]

We noted that anti-realism cannot coherently suppose that the meaning of every statement is determined by association with criteria. If it cannot coherently look, either, to a truth-conditionally determined base class of statements, there seem to be two remaining possibilities, one remaining within the walls of the assertibility-conditions conception and the other by way of a sortie. The first course would be to look to a base class of statements whose meaning was determined by their association with *criteria. But of the realization of these *criteria there would be provision for no other description save by the use of the very statements whose assertion they non-contingently support. There would be, that is to say, no purer description of them whose assertion, over and above being non-contingently justified by them, they actually *made true;* for any attempt to formulate such a description would merely result in something defeasible, an understanding of whose truth-conditions would therefore be, for the anti-realist who has taken this path, an unproductive fiction. Certain passages in Wittgenstein's later work suggest that he may sometimes have had some such idea

---

[15] See my *Wittgenstein on the Foundations of Mathematics* (Duckworth, 1980), chapters II, XI, and elsewhere *passim*.

as this in mind; e.g. *Zettle* 114–116. But of course the idea cannot be so much as addressed unless we refuse Hacker's and Baker's proposed regimentation of Wittgenstein's equivocal pronouncements about the terms of the criterial relation, and are prepared to countenance the idea that a state of affairs can non-contingently justify a particular assertion in a way which is not parasitic on its description.

That is the first possibility, then: to look to a base class of statements whose meanings are fixed by ostensive training in the conditions which justify their assertion, of which conditions there is, however, no description save by the use of these or other statements for which they are less than truth-conditions. This would be to conceive of the nexus between language and reality as, so to speak, through and through *crititerial*.

The second alternative is to break with the assertibility-conditions conception of meaning and to look to a base class the correct use of whose members, while something on which any opinion is essentially defeasible, is thought of as founded not on the satisfaction of certain external conditions—even if not truth-conferring ones—but in human consensus alone; certain passages in Wittgenstein suggest this idea too (e.g. *On Certainty* 204).[16] And its radical abnegation of the third term of the realist picture means that an anti-realist who takes it will have little justifiable compaint if he is regarded as a neo-Idealist.

---

[16] I have in mind, also, the 'Limits of Empiricism' remarks in the *Remarks on the Foundations of Mathematics*.

Wittgenstein and Idealism

NORMAN MALCOLM

Recently some philosophers have proposed that the later philosophy of Wittgenstein tends towards idealism, or even solipsism. The solipsism is said to be of a peculiar kind. It is characterized as a 'collective' or 'aggregative' solipsism. The solipsism or idealism is also said to be 'transcendental'. In the first part of this paper I will be examining a recent essay by Professor Bernard Williams,[1] in which he presents what he takes to be the grounds for such an interpretation of Wittgenstein. After that I will try to offer convincing evidence that no tendency towards any form of idealism is to be found in Wittgenstein's later philosophy.

1. Professor Williams starts off by referring to the solipsism of the *Tractatus*. The solipsistic passages in that work have perplexed many readers. Some have even doubted that any genuine solipsism is present there at all. However, from the propositions that 'The world is *my* world' (5.62) and that 'I am my world' (5.63), it follows that 'I am the world'—which surely is an assertion of solipsism. From this, together with 'The world and life are one' (5.621), it follows that 'I am life'. At 6.431 it is said that 'So too at death the world does not alter but ceases'. Now, if *I* am life, then *my* death is the end of life. And since life and the world are one, *my* death is the end of the world. It would be hard to deny that this is a severe solipsism. Furthermore, 5.62 declares that 'What solipsism wants to say (*meint*) is entirely correct; only it cannot be *said*, but shows itself'.

One's understanding of the solipsism of the *Tractatus* is complicated by the fact that the *I* that is talked about in the foregoing propositions is not something *in* the world. Thus, this *I* is not L.W., nor any other human being, nor any mind or soul. It is not anything *in* the world, nor is it anything outside of the world, for there is nothing outside. Then *what* is it and *where* is it? The answer is that it is the boundary of the world. 'The subject does not belong to the world, but is a boundary of the world' (5.632). Here it is said to be *a* boundary (*eine Grenze*)—which might suggest that there could be more than one boundary. But what was surely meant is that the subject ('the metaphysical subject') is *the* boundary (*die Grenze*)—which is how Wittgenstein actually puts it in 5.641.

The assertion that the subject is 'the boundary' of the world is a pretty

---

[1] Bernard Williams, 'Wittgenstein and Idealism', in *Understanding Wittgenstein*, Royal Institue of Philosophy Lectures, Vol. 7, 1972–73, G. Vesey (ed.) (New York: St Martin's Press, 1974).

Norman Malcolm

dark saying. My guess is that it means that if there were no subject there would be no world. I think here of the relationship of the boundary of a circle to a circle. The boundary is neither within the circle nor outside it: but if there were no boundary there would be no circle. A circle *pre-supposes* a boundary. This is actually how Wittgenstein puts the matter in the *Tractatus Notebooks* (p. 79): 'The subject is not a part of the world but a presupposition of its existence'.

It would perhaps be right to call this a form of 'transcendental idealism'. The *I* is a necessary condition (presupposition) of the existence of the world; but not being *in* the world, it is not itself a possible object of experience or knowledge, and in this sense is 'transcendental'.[2]

---

[2] The remarks on solipsism in the *Tractatus* are exceedingly compressed, even for the *Tractatus*. Some thoughtful interpreters of those remarks believe that Wittgenstein was not actually stating a solipsistic position. I disagree; but also I apologize for my peremptory treatment of the matter, my excuse being that it is not my topic in this essay. The bare way in which I have sketched the position may make it appear that Wittgenstein's adoption of solipsism was ridiculous and dogmatic. I believe it was ingenious and profound.

The most fundamental step in the development of solipsism in the *Tractatus* is the observation that 'There is no thinking, representing subject' (5.631). In the *Tractatus Notebooks* (p. 80), this idea is expressed in the remark that 'The I is not an object'. A basic doctrine of the *Tractatus* is that each significant proposition is ultimately analysable into a grouping of 'names', each of which designates an object. To say that 'The I is not an object' means that the word 'I' is not a *name* and so does not appear in the final analysis of any sentence in which it occurs. For example, the pronoun 'I' will not appear in the final analysis of 'I am angry', nor in the final analysis of any first-person psychological sentence. What about third-person psychological sentences, such as 'He is angry'? It is sufficiently obvious that if 'I' is not a name, neither is 'He'. The sentences 'I am angry' and 'He is angry' differ in meaning; but the difference cannot consist in the two pronouns designating numerically different objects, i.e. numerically different 'thinking, representing subjects'.

Where then can the difference in meaning of those two sentences lie? It must lie in the predicates. The predicate 'angry' must differ in meaning in the first-person and third-person sentences. Let us say that in the first-person sentence 'angry' refers to something genuinely 'mental', while in the third-person sentence it refers to *physical behaviour*. Thus, 'I am angry' is equivalent to 'There is anger', whereas 'He is angry' is roughly equivalent to 'The behaviour of *that* body is similar to the behaviour of *this* (my) body when there is anger'. According to this model, first-person psychological sentences do truly assert the existence of thoughts, feelings, sensations, whereas third-person sentences only assert the existence of physical behaviour. This is a form of solipsism, although a no-self solipsism. Let us call this *psychological solipsism*.

How do we get from psychological solipsism to *world solipsism*? There is an easy transition by way of *phenomenalism*, which is the doctrine that propositions about physical things and events are analysable in terms of propositions about

2. Professor Williams acknowledges the criticisms of solipsism that occur in Wittgenstein's later work. He speaks of 'The well-charted moves in the later work from "I" to "we" . . .' and of 'the emphasis in the later work on language's being an embodied, this-worldly, concrete social activity, expressive of human needs . . .' (Williams, op. cit., 79). However, he goes on to say:

> My chief aim will be to suggest that the move from 'I' to 'we' was not unequivocally accompanied by an abandonment of the concerns of transcendental idealism . . . Rather, the move is to something which itself contains an important element of idealism. That element is concealed, qualified, overlaid with other things, but I shall suggest that it is there. I shall suggest also that this element may help to explain a particular feature of the later work, namely a pervasive vagueness and indefiniteness evident in the use Wittgenstein makes of 'we' (ibid.).
>
> Perhaps there is a form of transcendental idealism which is suggested, not indeed by the confused idea that the limits of *each* man's language mean the limits of *each* man's world, but by the idea that the limits of *our* language mean the limits of *our* world (ibid., 82).

First of all, I am surprised by the assertion that Wittgenstein's use of 'we' is vague and indefinite. Williams himself notes how Wittgenstein frequently compares the 'language-games', 'forms of life', and 'world-pictures' of various groups of human beings who differ in their upbringing and interests, and how he uses such comparisons to indicate the possibility of different concepts.

To give an example, not mentioned by Williams, Wittgenstein imagined a society of people who measure tracts of land and determine boundaries solely by pacing off distances, and who have no interest in employing measuring tapes or surveyors' instruments. It appears right to say that those people have a different *concept* of 'exactness' in measurement to the one *we* have. The 'we' here would obviously refer to the great majority of people in Western cultures who would not dream of fixing property lines by merely

---

sensations and sense-impressions. There is evidence from Wittgenstein's *Philosophische Bemerkungen* (pp. 51, 84), and also from Waismann's record of conversations with Wittgenstein (*Wittgenstein und der Wiener Kreis*, 45) that at an early stage Wittgenstein accepted phenomenalism. The conjunction of psychological solipsism and phenomenalism yields world solipsism, i.e. 'I am the world', which of course cannot be said but shows itself.

The foregoing is a very skimpy outline of the case for interpreting the *Tractatus* as presenting a no-self solipsism. I derived this interpretation of the *Tractatus* from reading the doctoral dissertation of my friend and Cornell colleague, Professor Richard Miller. Miller's interpretation has been recently published: Richard W. Miller, 'Solipsism in the *Tractatus*', *Journal of the History of Philosophy* **18**, No. 1. (January, 1980).

pacing off distances. It would be the 'we' of one actual segment of mankind, contrasted with another (imagined) human society.

In an example from *On Certainty*, to which Williams does refer, Wittgenstein imagines a people who are guided in their actions by the pronouncements of oracles in perference to the propositions of physics. Wittgenstein remarks:

> Is it wrong for them to consult an oracle and be guided by it?—If we call this 'wrong' aren't we using our language-game as a base from which to *combat* theirs? (*OC* 608, 609).

The 'we' here includes Wittgenstein and all others who would rather put their trust in physical principles than in oracles. The 'we' refers to one human group in contrast with another.

Wittgenstein does indeed use 'we' with a shifting reference. For example, in the *Investigations* he speaks of the philosophical temptation to hold that the sentence, 'Red exists', is nonsense, 'because if there were no red it could not be spoken of at all'. He goes on to remark that

> What we really *want* is simply to take 'Red exists' as the statement: the word 'red' has meaning. Or perhaps better: 'Red does not exist' as ' "Red" has no meaning'. Only we do not want to say that that expression *says* this, but that *this* is what it would have to be saying *if* it meant anything. But that it contradicts itself in the attempt to say it—just because red exists 'in its own right' (*PI* 58).

This 'we' refers to all of those philosophers, including Wittgenstein himself, who feel the temptation that he is describing. In the following remarks 'we' has a different reference:

> When philosophers use a word—'knowledge', 'being', 'object', 'I', 'proposition', 'name'—and try to grasp the *essence* of the thing, one must always ask oneself: is the word ever actually used in this way in the language-game which is its original home?
>
> What *we* do is to bring words back from their metaphysical to their everyday use (*PI* 116).

In this example, unlike the previous one, 'we' refers to Wittgenstein and to any other philosophers who are trying to follow the method of his later philosophy, in contrast to, say, the method of the *Tractatus*. But in both cases the 'we' refers to actual groups of human beings.

Wittgenstein certainly gives different references to 'we'. But there is nothing vague or indefinite about it. Williams thinks that the supposedly 'curious use that Wittgenstein makes of "we" ' (ibid., 85), may be explained by Williams' hypothesis that there is a tendency toward transcendental idealism in Wittgenstein's later philosophy. Williams says:

> While the 'we' of Wittgenstein's remarks often looks like the 'we' of our group as contrasted with other human groups, that is basically mis-

leading . . . Thus, while much is said by Wittgenstein about the meanings *we* understand being related to *our* practice, and so forth, that *we* turn out only superficially and sometimes to be one *we* as against others *in* the world, and thus the sort of *we* which has one practice as against others which are possible in the world . . . One finds onself with a *we* which is not one group rather than another in the world at all, but rather the plural descendant of that idealist *I* who also was not one item rather than another in the world (ibid., 92).

The new theory of meaning. like the old, points in the direction of a transcendental idealism . . . (ibid., 95).

Although the reference that Wittgenstein gives to 'we' often changes from one remark to another, his use of 'we' is not on that account 'vague', 'indefinite', or 'curious'. A moderate amount of attention and thought suffices to make it clear to a reader what the reference of 'we' is in each case. And in each case the reference is to some actual human group, society, or culture. Consider the following remark from *Zettel*:

A tribe has two concepts, akin to our 'pain'. One is applied where there is visible damage and is linked with tending, pity, etc. The other is applied to stomach-ache, for example, and is tied up with mockery of the complaining one. 'But then do they really not notice the similarity?'—Do we have a single concept everywhere there is a similarity? The question is: Is the similarity *important* to them? And need it be so? And why shouldn't their concept 'pain' split ours up? (*Z* 380).

Wittgenstein is imagining a society of people who have a word, 'W', to which they respond in two different ways when one of their group complains of 'W', depending on whether the complaining person has or hasn't suffered some visible injury. If he has, they respond with concern and help. If he has not, they regard the complaining one with indifference, or even with contempt and ridicule. We may suppose that a complaining person spontaneously exclaims 'W!' in both cases, and that his primitive behaviour in both cases is like the behaviour that surrounds our use of the word 'pain' in the first person present tense. But the marked difference in reaction of those who observe the complaining one, depending solely on whether there is visible injury, justifies Wittgenstein's remark that the tribe 'has two concepts, akin to our "pain" '. This may strike us at first as strange and irrational. 'Don't they notice the similarity?' Of course they do. But they also notice *the difference*! Their difference in response will perhaps seem *less* unintelligible if we remember that we too have some tendency to react with *more* pity, concern, anxiety and help where there is visible bodily damage (after a child has a fall, say) than where there is none. So this difference affects our reactions too. But we don't draw as sharp a line as they do.

Now when Wittgenstein asks, 'Do we have a single concept wherever there is a similarity?', who is the 'we'? Clearly it refers to everyone, including you and me, who do not draw as sharp a line as do the people of the tribe that Wittgenstein imagined. An actual human group is being compared with an imagined one. The point of the comparison is to show how the same behavioral phenomena could give rise to different concepts. How another group could be more struck by a difference in circumstances than we are.

In Wittgenstein's writings the reference of 'we' is precise. The reference is always to some actual human group or society, in contrast with another real or imagined one. I do not find 'a *we* which is not one group rather than another in the world' but is instead 'the plural descendant of that idealist I' of the *Tractatus*. I am unable to gather from Williams' essay what it is that leads him to think either that a transcendental *I* has been replaced by a transcendental *we* or that some form of idealism is obscurely present in Wittgenstein's later thought.

3. Williams' interpretation of Wittgenstein seems to be influenced by a worry about what Williams calls 'the *evaluative* comparability of different world-pictures' (Williams, 87). He remarks that, on Wittgenstein's view, different world-pictures 'are accessible to one another, to some extent, but that does not say anything, or anything much, about whether one could compare them with regard to adequacy' (ibid., 87–88).

According to Wittgenstein, the concepts of reasons, justification, evidence, proof, certainty, doubt, are *relative* to various language-games and forms of life. Illustrations of this point can be more, or less, obvious. To take an obvious example: suppose there is a tribe which has a technique of counting (say, from 1 to 100) that is taught and employed in the life of the tribe. But this tribe has no arithmetic. For certain purposes these people make arrangements of stones. Let us suppose that they arrange three vertical rows with six stones in each row. They want to determine the number of stones in this group and they do this by counting the stones one by one. Now *we*, who have arithmetic, could look at the arrangement, note that there are three rows with six in each row, and say: 'Three times six is eighteen; so there are eighteen stones here'. The people of the tribe cannot speak or think in that way. That three times six is eighteen cannot be, for them, a reason, justification, or proof, that the arrangement contains eighteen stones. Our arithmetic provides us with reasons and proofs that are meaningless to them. Is there a hint of idealism in this? Not at all. The stones could be there, and there could be eighteen of them, even if no human beings or other creatures were, or ever had been, present. This relativity of reasons, justification, proof, to language does not yield idealism.

Now what about Williams' question as to whether different language-games, forms of life, world-pictures, can be compared 'with regard to adequacy'? The question seems to assume that there could be such a thing as 'adequacy' in some absolute sense. But 'adequacy' is obviously relative to interests, problems, purposes. If these are not taken into account it has no meaning to ask whether one method of doing something is more or less adequate than another. If we were to declare to the members of the tribe, who have counting to one hundred but no arithmetic, that our arithmetical calculations are swifter, are better for dealing with large numbers, and are more reliable than counting, they could reply (or rather, someone could reply for them), that they are in no hurry, they don't deal with large numbers, and as for reliability isn't it possible to make mistakes in calculation as well as in counting? For their limited purposes and interests, counting is adequate. It would be silly to insist that calculating is better for them.

It is to be noted that there is no equality between them and us in respect to 'accessibility' of language-games: for they have no arithmetic, and so cannot compare it with their counting; whereas we have both. Since we use both techniques we can make an 'evaluative comparison'; and this comparison enables us to see that for the concerns of the tribe, counting is a satisfactory technique, not to be judged inferior to calculation. The point is the same as with the previously imagined people who determine areas of land lots solely by pacing. Perhaps they are not troubled if different pacers obtained different results. Or perhaps there is an official who does the pacing for all of them. In either case they don't get into squabbles about boundaries. It would be foolish to assert that they ought to adopt the more refined technique of surveying. Their concept of 'same area' is good enough for their life.

4. But probably these examples are too easy for dealing with Williams' worry about the comparative adequacy of different language-games. Wittgenstein's example of the tribe that has two concepts similar to our 'pain' presents a harder case. If there is no visible swelling, bruise or laceration, those people regard a person's groans and writhings as pretence, malingering, or illusion. Apparently those people have no concept of an invisible cause of physical pain. To us this seems strange and even absurd. We would want to bring them over to our point of view, perhaps explaining to them that there are various internal organs, veins, intestines, which when infected, injured, blocked, swollen, can produce physical pain. We give them reasons for changing their view. Suppose those people go along with us in conceding that there are these internal parts and that they can become impaired. But suppose they hold that this doesn't produce physical pain but merely complaining behaviour?

This difference between them and us would be an example of what Wittgenstein calls a difference in 'world-pictures', not merely a difference in language-games, as in our previous easier examples. The attitude of the other community would seem incomprehensible to us, and we would feel that they were not just wrong but crazy. This is like the case of the people who rely on oracles in preference to physics. Of those people Wittgenstein asks: 'If we call this "wrong" aren't we using our language-game as a base from which to *combat* theirs?' (*OC* 609). And he adds:

> I said I would 'combat' the other man—but wouldn't I give him *reasons*? Certainly; but how far do they go? At the end of reasons comes *persuasion* . . . (*OC* 612).

We can imagine how the attempt at persuasion would go. 'Why should pain be produced solely by visible injury? Why shouldn't a diseased or damaged internal organ also produce pain?' And much more. But this other man might resist our reasons and persuasion. He might reply: 'How do you *know* that internal physiological conditions cause pain and not merely pain-like behaviour? How can you prove it? Why shouldn't pain be produced solely by external damage?'

This arguing back and forth might get nowhere. The real difference in world-pictures would not lie in evidence and argument but in different ways of *acting*. The people of the other community do not respond with concern and help unless there is visible bodily damage; whereas we do not draw that sharp line in our behaviour towards persons who complain of pain. The fundamental conflict would consist, not in reasoning, but in action and reaction. We would be convinced that our perception of reality is superior to theirs, and that we know something which they don't know. But our preference for our view of the matter is, in the end, something that cannot be justified. As Wittgenstein puts it:

> Giving grounds, . . . justifying the evidence, comes to an end;—but the end is not certain propositions' striking us immediately as true, i.e. it is not a kind of *seeing* on our part; it is our *acting*, which lies at the bottom of the language-game (*OC* 204).
> At the foundation of well-founded belief lies unfounded belief (*OC* 253).

In our present example, the 'unfounded belief' would be our belief, or we would call it *certainty*, that people can and do suffer physical pain even without visible bodily damage. This belief or certainty is displayed in our actions and reactions. It is not the result of reasoning; it could be called 'instinctive'. Wittgenstein makes some remarks that can be applied to this case.

> Now I would like to regard this certainty, not as something akin to hastiness or superficiality, but as a form of life (*OC* 358).
> But that means I want to conceive it as something that lies beyond being justified or unjustified; as it were, as something animal (*OC* 359).
> I want to regard man here as an animal; as a primitive being to which one grants instinct but not reasoning. As a creature in a primitive state.

Any logic good enough for a primitive means of communication needs no apology from us. Language did not emerge from reasoning (*OC* 475).

It is a help here to remember that it is a primitive reaction to tend, to treat, the part that hurts when someone else is in pain; and not merely when oneself is. . . (*Z* 540).

But what is the word 'primitive' meant to say here? Presumably that this sort of behaviour is *pre-linguistic*: that a language-game is based *on it*, that it is the prototype of a way of thinking and not the result of thought (*Z* 541).

Each of *us* normally has an instinctive reaction of concern when someone behaves as if in pain, usually in disregard of whether there is perceptible bodily damage. The people of the tribe imagined by Wittgenstein do not have this same primitive reaction. They respond with concern only when they perceive bodily injury. This difference in natural response would give rise to different language-games with the word 'pain'. Two different uses of the word 'pain' would be based on two sharply different forms of primitive behaviour—on two different 'forms of life'. One difference in the two 'grammars' of the word 'pain' would be the following: If a young member of that tribe were to declare in all sincerity, 'I really was in pain yesterday even though I had no bodily injury', he might be told by his elders: 'You merely *thought* you were in pain'. In contrast, the grammar that *we* give to the word 'pain' does not permit such a sentence as 'You thought you were in pain but you really were not'. Wittgenstein has invented a fictitious natural history (*PI* 230) in the light of which we are enabled to see the possibility of a different concept of pain.

5. I wish to return to Williams' question about 'the evaluative comparability of different world-pictures'. We surely have a strong inclination to think that our concept of pain, the grammar that the word 'pain' has in our language, is correct, and that the concept of pain employed by the fictitious tribe is mistaken. But what can this mean? In relation to *what* is our concept more correct than theirs? Do we want to say that our concept more accurately portrays the actual nature of pain? Do we think that we derive our concept from the nature of pain? Wouldn't this be like thinking that it follows from 'the nature of negation' that a double negative is an affirmative? About *this* Wittgenstein remarks that

There cannot be a question whether these or other rules are the correct ones for the use of 'not'. (I mean, whether they accord with its meaning.) For without these rules the word has as yet no meaning and if we change the rules, it now has another meaning (or none), and in that case we may just as well change the word too (*PI* 147, fn.).

Similarly, it cannot be a genuine question whether our rules for the use of the word 'pain' are more correct than are those of the fictitious tribe. Their use of the word is both like and unlike our use. In so far as it is unlike we can rightly say that they give a different meaning to the word. On the other hand, their use of the word has much in common with ours: to that extent, they don't give it a different meaning. Neither they nor we can be said to have a more accurate conception of the nature of pain. It is not as if these two societies had both observed the nature of pain and drawn different conclusions, ours right and theirs wrong, or theirs right and ours wrong.

Williams raises a question about the 'accessibility', by which I presume he means the 'intelligibility', of concepts that differ from our own. I think this would be different in different cases. There is nothing perplexing about the people who determine the number of objects in an arrangement solely by counting, nor about the people who measure land boundaries solely by pacing. We see in both cases that their methods are satisfactory for them, and also that if their interests widened they could be trained in arithmetical calculation or in new methods of measuring. Their methods are included in our methods. There is no baffling instinctive difference between them and us.

But the case is different with the fictitious tribe whose members respond with concern and help only when there is visible injury. Wittgenstein remarks that

> Concepts other than though akin to ours might seem *very* queer to us: deviations from the usual *in an unusual direction* (*Z* 373).

That is how it is with the fictitious tribe. How strange that they should use visible injury to mark off pain from the absence of pain! We cannot imagine ourselves responding this way in all cases. I would apply to this example Wittgenstein's remark: 'We are here describing a language-game that *we cannot learn*' (*Z* 339).

Is this strange concept of pain intelligible ('accessible') to us? Two things can be said about this. It *is* intelligible in the sense that we can *describe* their language-game with the word 'pain'—how they react, how they speak, how they differ from us. But there is also a sense in which neither those people nor their use of the word 'pain' is intelligible to us; and this consists in there being a striking difference between them and us at the level of instinctive reaction. It would go against the grain for us to feel pity and concern, in the presence of pain-behaviour, *only* where there was visible injury.

This difference between them and us at a primitive, instinctive level does not indicate that our world-picture, form of life, or language-game is better, more true, than theirs. To suppose that it was would indeed be using our own language-game as a base from which to combat theirs.

Williams remarks that when it comes to comparing different world-pictures 'with regard to adequacy', Wittgenstein 'tends to say things which cast great doubt' on the possibility of

> Whether there is some objective basis from which one 'we' could come to recognize the greater truth of what was believed by another 'we' (Williams, p. 88).

Williams appears to think that there should be an 'objective basis'. But what could that be? Our concept of pain has a certain grammar; the concept of the imagined tribe a different grammar. The difference between the two is rooted in different instinctive reactions, in different forms of life. Wittgenstein rightly says that our language-game 'is not based on grounds. It is not reasonable (or unreasonable). It is there—like our life' (*OC* 559). The same holds for the language-game of the imagined tribe. Each 'we' finds the language-game of the other 'we' strange, absurd. What more can be said? To suppose that there is an 'objective basis' in terms of which one language-game could be judged to be more adequate or more 'true' than the other, is to suppose that the true concept of pain is stowed away somewhere like the standard metre, available for comparison when differences arise between merely human concepts. But we may be certain that there are no principles of justification which lie outside of all human conceptual frameworks and world pictures.

6. What bearing has all this on 'idealism'? We employ a particular concept of pain; the imagined tribe employs a different one. Their concept contains the condition that attributions of pain are justified only if there is visible injury. Thus their use of the word 'pain' will be surrounded by a use of the words 'justification', 'reason', 'evidence', 'proof', that is different from ours. This difference has wide ramifications. For example, costly medical research into causes of bodily pain when there is no visible injury, is supported in our society; whereas the imagined people would consider such an activity as nonsensical; they would look on it with the same attitude of incredulity that many of us take towards astrology. They would not regard the presence of pain in the absence of visible bodily damage, as anything that could be explained by empirical investigation—just as many of us would not take seriously any purported scientific backing for the presence of 'astral influence'.

Previously I said that, on Wittgenstein's view, the concepts of reason, evidence, justification, proof, are 'relative' to language-games. This now seems to me to be an understatement. For the way in which those words are used are *part* of a language-game, not just 'relative' to it. And the concept of pain that a group has, *is* their language-game with the word 'pain', not something 'relative' to that language-game.

Williams says, quite correctly, that

> It looks as though the question, whether something is empirically

explicable or not, is itself relative to a language; for such explanation, and *a fortiori*, particular forms of scientific explanation, are just some language-games among others (ibid., 89).

But Williams draws a conclusion from this which I cannot follow. He says:

> Thus our view of another world-picture, as something accessible, and empirically related, to ours, may just be a function of our world-picture ... Thus we lose hold at this level on the idea that they are *really* accessible. Once that alarm has broken out, we may indeed even begin to lose the hard-earned benefits of 'we' rather than 'I'. For if our supposed scientific understanding of the practices of other groups is to be seen merely as how those practices are *for us*, and if our experience of other forms of life is inescapably and non-trivially conditioned by our own form of life, then one might wonder what after all stops the solipsist doubt, that my experience which is supposedly of other individuals and the form of life which I share with them, cannot fail to be an experience only of how things are *for me* (ibid., 89–90).

Let us assess these remarks in terms of the example of the concept of pain of the imagined tribe. As I said previously, we can *describe* the language-game of those other people. In this sense it is 'accessible' to us. It is trivial to say that this description is formulated in *our* language. How else could we formulate it? But this does not imply that we may be failing to see their practice as it really is. The failure of understanding would be, as I said, not at the level of description, but at the deeper level of instinctive action and reaction. We can describe this difference *too*. What makes those people incomprehensible to us is that we cannot imagine ourselves instinctively rejecting all pain-behaviour as expressive of pain if it is not accompanied by visible injury.

It is a huge *non sequitur* to infer that this opens the way to first-person solipsism. What 'stops the solipsist doubt' is the realization that language cannot be the creation of an individual thinker but must involve activities and reactions that are shared by a group, whose members *agree* in the application of words within those activities, which agreement is the measure of the right or wrong use of language by individual speakers of that group.

But probably Williams does not really mean that the 'relativity' of concepts to language-games threatens us with *first-person* solipsism. For he goes on to put his point in what he says is another way—although actually it is a very different point. He says:

> The point can be put also like this, that there is the gravest difficulty ... in both positing the independent existence of culturally distinct groups with different world-views, and also holding that any access we have to them is inescapably and non-trivially conditioned by our own world-view. For the very question from which we started, of the existence and

relative accessibility of different world-views, becomes itself a function of one world-view. In fact what we have here is an exact analogue, at the social level, of aggregative solipsism (ibid., 90).

Thus the real threat, according to Williams, is not first-person solipsism, but 'aggregative solipsism'. But is 'aggregative solipsism' a meaningful expression? Solipsism in its original, stern sense, is the idea that no person other than myself can understand what I mean by my words, because my words obtained their meaning from my inner, private, ostensive definitions. But if this idea is untenable, as Wittgenstein has sufficiently demonstrated, what room is there for solipsism in any form? Each one of us grows up in a linguistic community and gradually comes to share in the uses of language that are embedded in the activities and reactions of that community. There can be no place for solipsism *within* the common use of language of an 'aggregate'. In this sense, 'aggregative solipsism' is a contradiction in terms.

Presumably Williams wants to say that there is a solipsism *between* different aggregates. To speak of 'solipsism' here should mean that one community cannot *understand* the different world-pictures and language-games of another community. But as I have said, there is an ambiguity here. We can understand the use of the word 'pain' of the imagined tribe, in the sense that we can *describe* it. I cannot see what Williams means in saying that our description is '*non-trivially* conditioned' by our own use of the word 'pain' and our related form of life. It is completely trivial to say that we describe their use of the word in terms of our own, and that we compare it with our own. Yet we do perceive the difference between their use and ours.

What we find puzzling, even incomprehensible, are *those people*. The trouble is *not* that we cannot *explain* why they instinctively react as they do. For that matter, we cannot explain why *we* react as we do in *not* demanding visible injury as a rigid condition for applying the word 'pain'. Such attempts at explanation do not belong to our philosophical job. As Wittgenstein says:

> Our interest certainly includes the correspondence between concepts and very general facts of nature. . . . But our interest does not fall back upon these possible causes of the formation of concepts; we are not doing natural science, nor yet natural history—since we can also invent fictitious natural history for our purposes (*PI* 230).

What was gained by the invention of the fictitious tribe was the realization that there could be a concept of pain that deviated from ours. This helps to free us from the assumption that our concept is 'absolutely the correct one'; but also it helps us to understand our own concept better; for we are now able to perceive how it is rooted in our own form of life—that is, in our instinctive, unlearned, reaction of concern in the presence of the pain-behaviour of other persons, independently (for the most part) of whether there is visible injury.

There is nothing in all of this that hints at either solipsism or idealism. In fact, quite the contrary. For in describing forms of life, world-pictures, language-games, real or imaginary, that differ from our own, we are enabled to reflect on our own concepts and to see them objectively: we distance ourselves from our concepts and view them from outside, as it were. There is no analogue here of the doctrine of *Tractatus* that 'the limits of *my* language means the limits of *my* world'. Williams suggests that this has been replaced, in Wittgenstein's later philosophy, by the doctrine that 'the limits of *our* language means the limits of our world' (Williams, p. 82). I see nothing in this except the tautology that our language is our language. One of the great endeavours of Wittgenstein's later philosophical work is to show how we can detach ourselves from our own concepts by making them objects of study, through comparison with other imagined concepts and corresponding forms of life. In this way we can also contemplate world-pictures other than our own.

Nor, as I said previously, is there any basis whatever for Williams' suggestion that in Wittgenstein's later philosophy a 'transcendental "we"' replaces the 'transcendental "I"' of the *Tractatus*. Contrary to what Williams says 'we' in the later writings always refers to an actual group *in* the world, which is being compared in its practices and language-games, with some other group that is actually, or imagined to be, *in* the world. There is no *we* that is 'the boundary' of the world—no *we* that is 'the plural descendant of that idealist *I*' of the *Tractatus*, as Williams supposes (Williams, p. 92). Nor is there a language which is *the* language that defines *the* limits of thought—but only different language-games, real or imagined.

7. But now I will turn to a difficulty that seems to me to present a temptation to think that Wittgenstein's later philosophy implies a form of idealism—a temptation that is greater than any suggested by the points brought forward by Williams, in so far as I understand his paper. I refer to the fact that the word 'know', like any other word, has its place in a language-game. Indeed, this word is used by us in a number of different language-games. Sometimes 'I know' is offered as a guarantee that confirming evidence can be produced. Sometimes the force of 'I know' is to *exclude* further tests, evidence, confirmation, as being *irrelevant*.

Leaving aside such differences, it seems that 'know' is always governed by this rule: if I know that p then p is true. Philosophers sometimes mistakenly take this to mean that if I know that p then I *cannot* be mistaken. Actually it should mean only this: If I know that p then I *am not* mistaken.

But to proceed to the apparent idealistic consequence: If I am trained in a language-game in which the word 'know' is used, then if I say, 'I know that p', using my sentence in conformity with the conventions of that language-game, including (let us suppose) a backing of evidence that is deemed in that language-game to be adequate or even overwhelming—does it not follow that p is true? Isn't that what the language-game tells us to say? Doesn't this language-game *define* my statement as being true? If so, the nature of reality, what is the case, is determined by human language. This is a conclusion that surely deserves the name of idealism.

I think that a concern with this problem is prominent in *On Certainty*. It is particularly conspicuous in Wittgenstein's study of the expression, 'I cannot be mistaken'. Previously I said that 'I know that p' entails, not 'I cannot be mistaken', but only 'I am not mistaken'. However, 'I cannot be mistaken', 'I can't be in error about that', certainly are sentences of ordinary language. Wittgenstein raises an interesting question about how those sentences are used:

> The sentence 'I can't be making a mistake' is certainly used in practice. But we may question whether it is then to be taken in a perfectly rigorous sense, or is rather a kind of exaggeration which perhaps is used only with a view to persuasion (*OC* 669).

I think the answer is that it is used in both ways. Wittgenstein certainly concludes that it has a rigorous sense. He says:

> There are, however, certain types of case in which I rightly say I cannot be making a mistake, and Moore has given a few examples of such cases (*OC* 674).

Some of Moore's examples would be: 'I have clothes on'; 'I am standing up'. Normally, 'I know', would not be used in such cases. But we can imagine circumstances in which another person would be in doubt whether Moore's statements were true, and there Moore could rightly say, 'I *know* I have clothes on', the sense of Moore's assertion there being the same as, 'I can't be mistaken as to whether I have clothes on'.

Wittgenstein gives his own examples:

> If someone believes that he has flown from America to England in the last few days, then, I believe, he cannot be making a *mistake*. And just the same if someone says that he is at this moment sitting at a table and writing (*OC* 675).
>
> I might ask: '*How* could I be making a mistake about my name being L.W.?' And I can say: I don't see how it would be possible (*OC* 660).

What does it mean to say that 'I can't be making a mistake' is used 'rigorously' in these examples? Wittgenstein understands it to mean that a 'mistake' is *logically* excluded. He distinguishes between 'subjective certainty' and 'objective certainty' in the following remark:

> With the word 'certain' we express complete conviction, the total absence of doubt, and thereby we seek to convince other people. That is

subjective certainty. But when is something objectively certain?—When a mistake is not possible. But what kind of possibility is that? Mustn't a mistake be *logically* excluded? (*OC* 194).

But are we not now confronted with a 'linguistic' idealism? If when I say that my name is N.M., or that I am seated and writing, or that I am living in England, or that I have never been to the moon, and so on—I can't be *mistaken*; and if 'I can't be mistaken' is used here in a rigorous sense to mean that a mistake is logically excluded—then doesn't it follow that the *truth* of my statement is *guaranteed* by this correct use of the expression 'I can't be mistaken'? It is not merely that *I* say that I can't be mistaken: the actual use in ordinary language of the word 'mistake' does not admit of its correct application to those statements of mine. If the language-game with the word 'mistake' forbids its application to those statements, does it not by the same stroke establish them as true? Here again we seem to be presented with the consequence that the conformity of reality with certain statements is secured by a language-game.

There is a tiny hint in Williams' essay that he interprets Wittgenstein in this way. In talking about 'the evaluative comparability of different world-pictures', he speaks of 'those elements in the world-picture which purport to be truth-carrying' (Williams, p. 88). He doesn't say to what 'elements' he is referring: so I can only guess at his meaning. I can, however, see the temptation to regard the use of 'I know that *p*', and of 'I can't be mistaken', in their appropriate language-games, as 'truth-carrying'. These might be some of the 'elements' that Williams has in mind.

I wish to show, however, that this is a misinterpretation of Wittgenstein. First of all, the statement, 'I know that *p*', even when one is perfectly *justified* in making it, is not 'truth-carrying'. Wittgenstein says:

> It would be wrong to say that I can only say 'I know that there is a chair there' when there is a chair there. Of course it isn't *true* unless there is, but I have a right to say this if I am *sure* there is a chair there, even if I am wrong (*OC* 549).

The same holds for the statement, 'I can't be mistaken'. Suppose I have to give my name to an official. For some reason he suspects that I am suffering from some delusion about my identity, and says 'Are you sure that that is your name?' I might reply, 'Come now! I can't be mistaken about my name'. Wittgenstein remarks:

> I have a right to say 'I can't be making a mistake about this' even if I am in error (*OC* 663).

Even if I am completely justified in saying, 'I know that my name is N.M.', or in saying, 'I can't be mistaken about that', it does not follow that my name is N.M. For me a mistake about my name can rightly be said to be 'logically excluded', in the sense that *I* can't conceive of anything that I would regard as evidence that my name is not N.M.—but from this it doesn't follow that that is my name. We have a temptation (I know that I have been influenced by it) to think that 'the impossibility of being mistaken' is a super-strong concept, which when correctly applied is 'truth-carrying'. But in fact it is a down-to-earth expression, containing no magic.

> 'I can't be making a mistake' is an ordinary sentence, which serves to give the certainty-value of a statement. And only in its ordinary use is it justified (*OC* 638).

But how is this ordinary sentence used? One thing it does is to exclude a particular *kind* of *failure* (*OC* 640). I can make a mistake in a calculation, or about what day it is, or mistake that person across the street for someone else, and so on. But could I be 'mistaken' about my name, or whether I am in England, or have been to the moon, or am now sitting down? If I *were* wrong in *these* cases it could not be called a 'mistake'. Wittgenstein says:

> In certain circumstances a man cannot make a *mistake*. ('Can' is here used logically, and the proposition does not mean that a man cannot say anything false in those circumstances.) If Moore were to pronounce the opposite of those propositions which he declares certain, we would not just not be of his opinion, but would regard him as mentally disturbed (*OC* 155).

Being *mentally disturbed* is quite a different thing from *being mistaken*. Wittgenstein remarks that

> It would be completely *misleading* to say: 'I believe my name is L.W.' And this too is right: I cannot be making a *mistake* about it. But that does not mean that in this I am infallible (OC 425).

The important point here is that if I say that '*p*' is true, then even if it is one of those cases in which I can't be *mistaken*, it doesn't follow that '*p*' is true.

> When we say 'Certain propositions must be excluded from doubt', it sounds as if I ought to put these propositions—for example, that I am called L.W.—into a logic-book. For if it belongs to the description of a language-game, it belongs to logic. But that I am called L.W. does not belong to any such description. The language-game that operates with people's names can certainly exist even if I am mistaken about my name—but it does presuppose that it is nonsensical to say that the majority of people are mistaken about their names (*OC* 628; see also 519). On the other hand, however, it is right to say of myself 'I cannot be mistaken about my name', and wrong if I say 'perhaps I am mistaken'. But that doesn't mean that it is senseless for others to doubt what I declare to be

certain (*OC* 629). It is simply the normal case, to be incapable of mistake about the designation of certain things in one's mother tongue (*OC* 630).

In the overwhelming number of cases, adult speakers are not wrong about their names, or about this being called a 'chair', or that a 'tree'. This is a general fact about human ability, without which the practice of giving names could not exist. Being wrong has to be an exception. This has the consequence that one's statements in such matters will have *weight*—will normally be relied on by others.

This general fact cannot, however, prevent the occurrence of events so extraordinary that they would leave me dumbfounded. Suppose that I made a casual remark to my wife about being in England now—whereupon she looked at me with amazement and exclaimed, 'You are not in England, but in Ithaca, New York, USA! Don't you feel well?' Going to the window I saw, or seemed to see, familiar scenes of Ithaca. Some Ithaca friends came into the room and assured me, with apparent sincerity and concern, that although there had been talk of my moving to London, in fact I am still in Ithaca. What would be my reaction? Probably I would feel that I no longer understood anything—that indeed I had gone crazy! Certainly I would *not* say, 'Well, I guess I made a mistake' (see *OC* 420).

Wittgenstein imagines a similar case:

> What if something *really* unheard-of happened?—If I, say, saw houses gradually turning into steam without any obvious cause, if the cattle in the fields stood on their heads and laughed and spoke comprehensible words; if trees gradually changed into men and men into trees. Now, was I right when I said before all these things happened 'I know that that's a house' etc., or simply 'That's a house' etc.? (*OC* 513).

We move about in our language-games with confidence. We name things, report events, give descriptions. In an overwhelming number of cases we are entirely free from any doubt about what to say. Furthermore, our language is blended with action. We *act* with complete certainty. But this ease and confidence in speech and action is possible only because the world and life go on in regular ways—because, as it were, things 'behave kindly' (*OC* 615). Wittgenstein says:

> Certain events would put me into a position in which I could not go on with the old language-game any more. In which I was torn away from the *sureness* of the game. Indeed, isn't it obvious that the possibility of a language-game is conditioned by certain facts? (*OC* 617).

This conception is surely contrary to idealism. If the logical possibility of language, and therefore of thought and judgment, depends on regularities in the world and life, than it cannot be that reality is *created* by language, thought, judgment.

Then there is the other anti-idealistic feature of Wittgenstein's thinking, which I have already mentioned but will repeat. Suppose that the world and life go on evenly, in the sense that the stability of language is not undermined by wild irregularities. Among the language-games we master are those that employ the expressions, 'I know', 'It's certain', 'I can't be mistaken'. When the presuppositions and requirements of those language-games are satisfied, then one is *entitled* to say, with confidence, 'I know that so-and-so', 'I can't be mistaken'. But nevertheless, *one might be wrong.* Being contradicted by other evidence is not one of those unheard-of occurrences that would destroy language. Thus, even if one says with *complete* justification, 'I know it to be so', reality, the facts, may give one a surprise. This is perhaps the meaning of Wittgenstein's remark:

It is always by grace of nature that one knows something (*OC* 505).

Life-form and Idealism

DEREK BOLTON

In this paper[1] I shall suggest that philosophy which bases itself firmly in life is incompatible with idealism. The example of such a philosophy to be discussed is the later work of Wittgenstein, and I shall define in what sense this is 'based in life', with particular reference to his concept of 'Lebensform', or 'life-form'. I shall understand idealism to be, in general terms, the doctrine that *idea* is the primary, or the only, category of being. Various kinds of idealism may then be distinguished according to the precise definition each gives of 'idea', and of the category, if any, which is held to be less fundamental. Thus, in brief, in Platonic idealism, absolute immaterial being is ontologically prior to the changing world given to sense-experience; in the idealistic systems of more modern thought, mind is more fundamental than matter; or again, subject, or spirit, is more fundamental than object. While the various systems of idealism are properly classed together so far as they assign priority to the concept *idea*, it is clear that they differ in their interpretations of the concept. When one has in mind these differences, it is of course misconceived to speak of idealism as a single doctrine; nevertheless, it is plausible to suppose that philosophers have been led to apply the term 'idealism' to various systems despite their differences, because there is indeed a common tendency of thought to be found in them. The present paper takes this supposition as a working hypothesis, with the particular aim of establishing that philosophy based in life is incompatible with philosophy based in idea, whatever be reasonably meant by 'idea'. In brief my argument will be this: that *life is no idea*.

I begin, then, with discussion of the concept *form*. The concept has been a fundamental one in Western philosophy. It appeared in full splendour in Platonic thought. Form appears there as the basis of what *order* there is in nature; it is by virtue of their relation to forms that particular things in nature are unified into classes, as opposed to being unordered. And therefore, form is the object of thought, of knowledge and wisdom, and is also the condition under which meaningful language is possible. The particular account Plato gave of form is familiar: form is absolute and immaterial, outside and prior to the natural world of space, time and change. Plato saw that if form is absolute, it cannot exist in nature; on the assumption that there are absolute forms, for example of equality, beauty, and justice, Plato infers from the imperfection of such qualities in nature

[1] I am grateful to Professor Vesey for his helpful comments on an earlier draft of this paper.

and human society, that they must have existence elsewhere. It is clear that this concept of form pervades the Platonic philosophy, being fundamental to ontology, epistemology, the account of thought and language, and so on. The concept is connected also to an account of the soul: in so far as we have knowledge, or recognition, of form in Plato's sense, then we are not material, not dependent on the bodily senses for knowledge, but we are rather spirit, and immortal.[2]

The concept of form re-appears, though differently interpreted, in more modern philosophy. It is fundamental, for example, to Wittgenstein's *Tractatus*, appearing there as: the form of reality, pictorial form, logical form. Form is the *order* in reality; that is to say, objects are not a random collection, but have a particular structure, the possibility of which is form (2.02's and 2.03's). Form appears also as the essential feature of thought and language. Signs have a particular form, logico-pictorial form, by virtue of which they can represent the order in reality (2.1 to 3.1). We can therefore say that the concept of form in the *Tractatus* is in certain respects analogous to the concept of form in Plato's philosophy: in both cases form constitutes the order in what exists, and is the condition of thought and language. However, the *accounts* of form given in the two cases are very different. In particular, Platonic form underlies the ordering of things into classes, while *Tractatus* form orders objects *spatially* (by relations). Further, *Tractatus* form does not order objects from outside; spatial form is reasonably interpreted as belonging to the natural world, not to another world.

Let us turn now to Wittgenstein's later philosophy. We find there, in the first pages of the *Investigations*, the suggestion that the signs of language have meaning because they are used in human activities; activities such as shopping, building, playing. This account of meaning, like the others already mentioned, may naturally be expressed in terms of the concept *form*. Thus, form becomes *life-form*. Wittgenstein writes at §19:[3]

> To imagine a language means to imagine a form of life.

And at §23:

> Here the term 'language-*game*' is meant to bring into prominence the fact that the *speaking* of language is part of an activity, or of a form of life.

Language originates in life-form. Life-form is the order in which signs must be used if they are to have meaning; just as according to the *Tractatus*, signs, if they are to be meaningful, must mark out a logico-pictorial form.

---

[2] On the notion that form orders things into classes, see, for example, *Parmenides*, 130b–131a. On the account of form as absolute, see, for example, *Phaedo*, and *Cratylus*, 439b–440e.

[3] *Philosophical Investigations*, G. E. M. Anscombe and R. Rhees (eds), trans. G. E. M. Anscombe (Oxford: Blackwell, 1953).

The concept of life-form, or, we can also say, the concept of human activity, informs Wittgenstein's later philosophy of language, but its implications are more widespread. It becomes inevitable that the same concept should be fundamental to epistemology. Thus, for example, in the *Investigations*, p. 226:

What has to be accepted, the given, is—so one could say—*forms of life*.

And in *On Certainty*, for example:[4]

7. My life shows that I know or am certain that there is a chair over there, or a door, and so on. —I tell a friend e.g. 'Take that chair over there', 'Shut the door', etc. etc.

196. Sure evidence is what we *accept* as sure, it is evidence that we go by in *acting* surely, acting without any doubt. . . .

204. Giving grounds, however, justifying the evidence, comes to an end; —but the end is not certain propositions' striking us immediately as true, i.e. it is not a kind of *seeing* on our part; it is our *acting*, which lies at the bottom of the language-game.

Activity appears also as an order in reality. However, in contrast with both Platonic form and *Tractatus* form, form of life is *creation of order*. We act in an ordered way; as it were, according to a rule. However, as is argued in the *Investigations* between about §§143 and 202, the rule is not given or laid down in advance, but is rather *made in practice*. Further, the concept of life-form belongs with a particular account of 'subject', namely, that it is the living human being. To interpret form as life-form is equivalent to according human beings the traditional role of subject, that which thinks, knows, understands language, etc., since the form of thought, knowledge, and language, must then be human. Wittgenstein gives a fundamental place to human beings in his later philosophy; from the beginning he speaks of men and their common activities, this being the point of reference for philosophy of language, for epistemology, and so on.

Philosophy based on the interpretation of form as life-form, that is to say, which asserts that form is *alive*, I shall call 'life-philosophy'. Let us turn now to the relations between life-philosophy, so defined, and idealism, considering first the original idealism of Plato. To describe briefly Platonic idealism is in effect to repeat what has already been said about the Platonic notion of form; for the Platonic forms are ideas. Thus, Platonic idealism rejects the natural, material world given to the human senses, in favour of the absolute, immaterial world of ideas or forms, known by the spirit (thought, or intellect). With this thought, the idealism tends inevitably to a transcendental or divine viewpoint, which sees nature from outside, as

[4] *On Certainty*, G. E. M. Anscombe and G. H. von Wright (eds), trans. D. Paul and G. E. M. Anscombe (Oxford: Blackwell, 1969).

only appearance obscuring true being, which is immaterial, akin to spirit, outside space, time and change. Life-philosophy excludes idealism of this kind, and the reasons are straightforward. Form as life is not absolute, but is always active, changing and developing. And it is this activity, not an immaterial faculty, which is taken to be the means of knowing. Life is essentially (even if only partly) material; the living body is a body among others in nature, it is made from the same stuff as earth, plants and air, in complex organization, and at death returns to its material constituents. Thus no philosophy to which life is fundamental can assign secondary place to matter, or generally to nature, in favour of 'the other world'. So also the transcendental viewpoint of Platonic idealism has no place in life-philosophy. Life is born of and into nature, is part of a greater whole; the living being does not view the world from outside, but from within.

These points of contrast between idealism in the Platonic sense and life-philosophy will recur in more or less related forms when we consider more modern systems of idealism. They appear with particular clarity in the context of Platonic idealism, a fact which can be explained with reference to the development of that theory. For it was Plato's rejection of philosophy based in life and nature, the philosophies of Protagoras, Heracleitus, and others, as being unable to account for intelligible form, in particular his search for what is absolute, perfect, and unchanging, that led Plato to his idealism.[5]

The Platonic interpretation of form belongs with idealist presuppositions, the interpretation of form as life-form contradicts those presuppositions. This thought raises the question: how does idealism stand to the third interpretation of form discussed above, namely, *spatial* form? This is a complex question, and there is time here for only a brief examination of it. Space may be construed either as absolute, or as relative to human perception, and was so construed, in modern philosophy, by Newton and Berkeley respectively.[6] In this respect, then, the Newtonian conception of space was ideal, in Plato's sense, while Berkeley's was not. However, in the context of modern philosophy, the term 'idealism' is used usually to refer to the doctrine that mind is more fundamental than matter, or indeed, is the only existent. As concerns this doctrine, however, it seems that the concept of space does not yet determine whether spatial objects are material or ideal (mental); either interpretation may be given, as for example by Locke and Berkeley respectively,[7] or the issue may be left open,

[5] On Plato's criticism of the pre-Socratic philosophy, see particularly the *Theaetetus*.

[6] Sir Issac Newton, *The Mathematical Principles of Natural Philosophy* (1687), Scholium to the Definitions; G. Berkeley, *The Principles of Human Knowledge* (1710), Part I, §§11, 110–117.

[7] J. Locke, *Essay Concerning Human Understanding* (1690), e.g. bk. II, chs. IV, VIII; G. Berkeley, op. cit., Part I, §§1–39.

as seems to be the case in the *Tractatus*. It can be seen, then, that the implications of defining form as spatial are uncertain; in particular, the definition seems to be neutral between idealist interpretations and their contraries. This is connected with the fact that in a certain general respect, spatial form is intermediate between Platonic form and life-form. Platonic form is outside space and time, and so to interpret form as spatial is already to move one step away from Platonic idealism. However, spatial form is not yet life-form, for life-form is a form of movement, or activity; it is a *spatio-temporal* form.

Let us turn now to consider the more modern forms of idealism, particularly those belonging to nineteenth century thought, the Kantian system and those which followed. In accord with the limited aim of this paper, I shall examine a general characteristic or tendency to be found in these systems in so far as they are called 'idealistic'. This idealistic tendency may, I suggest, be expressed as follows: nature, the material world in space and time given to human experience, is taken to originate in immaterial and transcendental being, called by several names, for example, 'reason', 'spirit' ('Geist'), or 'will'; and further, in so far as the ego can conceive nature transcendentally, by means independent of human experience, the ego is itself taken to be, or to be part of, the transcendental origin of nature.[8]

If we now compare idealistic philosophy of this kind with life-philosophy, we find, I think, fundamental opposition between the two. Firstly, the idealism is based on a concept of spirit, consciousness of some kind, as opposed to matter, but life is not spirit as opposed to matter; the living being is at least a living body, and cannot be identified with spirit alone. Secondly, a connected point, in life-philosophy, the subject is the human being within the world, and is not, as in idealism, a transcendental ego.

The incompatibility here can be expressed, as would be expected, in terms of the concept *form*, in particular by comparing the concept of life-form with the Kantian notion of form, which underlay Kant's own transcendental idealism, and at least some of the idealism that followed. Kant proposed that the forms of sensible intuition, space and time, and certain categories of the understanding, such as causality, were transcendental, in that they were given *a priori*, not founded in human experience, and ideal, in that they derived from the transcendental subject alone, having no

---

[8] Brief statements relevant to idealism in the nineteenth century German tradition include the following: I. Kant, *Kritik der reinen Vernunft* (1781), Introduction, and Preface to 2nd edn (1787); J. G. Fichte, first part of *Grundlage der gesammten Wissenschaftslehre* (1794); F. W. J. Schelling, Introduction to *System des Transzendentalen Idealismus* (1800); G. W. F. Hegel, Preface to *Phänomenologie des Geistes* (1807); and A. Schopenhauer, first section of *Die Welt als Wille und Vorstellung*, Vol. i (1819).

reality as things in themselves.[9] By contrast, however, form construed as life-form is neither transcendental nor ideal. Life-form is activity, and this activity implies awareness of space and time; for the real activity of a living being, unlike particularly the ideal 'activity' of a transcendental ego, is a true *movement*, i.e. through space and time. Further, in ordered action, action according to a rule, there is already ground for application of a concept of cause and effect. This is to say, space, time and causality are the form of human experience precisely in so far as they are the form of *action*. And so we can comprehend these very general features of experience, I do not say 'explain' them, without postulating a source of cognition other than the human. Or instead we can say this: the source of cognition is extra-human, in that it is the human being in relation to the world in which he lives, but still it does not lie outside this world, it is not transcendental. This leads on to the second point, concerning the ideality of form. The action which is life-form is more fully called *interaction*, that is, between the living creature and its environment. Life-form is clearly conditioned by the natural world, not only by the living creature. That action is possible at all, that it continues to be possible, depends on nature, for example, on the ground supporting our feet. Particular forms of activity likewise are determined by what is independent of us, as well as by ourselves; for example, agriculture depends on the good nature of plants, on favourable conditions of soil and climate, as well as on certain capacities in human beings. Life-form, then, is not ideal, in that it is not determined by subject alone; nor is it determined by object alone, but always by a combination of both.

We have considered so far several forms of idealism, and I turn now to the question whether their common element, the priority assigned to the concept *idea*, can be defined more closely. The concept *idea* has been variously defined, but always in such a way that an idea is an *immaterial form*.[10] The concept is to be found in both idealist and dualist philosophies,

[9] I. Kant, op. cit., in the 'Transcendental Aesthetic' and the 'Transcendental Logic'.

[10] It is clear that to define ideas as immaterial is not necessarily to say that they are 'in the mind', or subjective in origin. Plato's ideas, particularly, have absolute existence. Myles Burnyeat, in his paper in the present series, argues that we find in Greek thought no idealism, by which he means, no basing of philosophy in the concept 'mind', or 'subject'. My description of Plato's theory of forms as a kind of idealism does not contradict Burnyeat's point, with which I agree, but rather employs a broader definition of 'idealism'. It is fruitless, I assume, to ask which among the several plausible definitions of 'idealism' is 'the correct one', provided it is made clear which similarities and distinctions the term is intended to mark. Burnyeat wishes to contrast the 'realism' of Greek thought with the mentalist and subjectivist themes in modern thought, and uses the term 'idealism' for the latter. My aim has been to contrast the primary emphasis on human activity, to be found in Wittgenstein's later work, and in other recent philosophy, with immaterialism, usually in the context of transcendental philosophy, which is

but the former are distinguished by their claim that the category *idea* is fundamental. This claim can have two general forms. According to one, nature is itself made of immaterial ideas. This interpretation of nature characterizes Berkeley's idealism uniquely, and it contradicts the assumption common to other systems of idealism, also to dualism and materialism, that the natural world given to human experience is material. Under this assumption, idealism appears in the second and most common form, namely, as the claim that ideas are in some sense *prior to* nature and human experience. That is to say, idealist systems most commonly interpret ideas as being transcendental. And so we may summarize the opposition between life-philosophy and idealism in this way: to interpret form as life-form is to treat life as fundamental, but life is no idea, that is to say, it is not immaterial, and nor is it transcendental.

This opposition can be expressed also in another way, in terms of the definition of 'subject'. To interpret form as life-form is equivalent to according human beings the traditional role of subject. Life-philosophy is therefore incompatible with idealism in this sense: so far as concerns the concept 'subject', it refers only to human beings, not to an immaterial soul, or ego.

It is important to note that the criticisms of idealism made from the standpoint of life-philosophy give no credence to materialism.[11] The traditional doctrines of materialism have been based on the same conceptions of matter as are found in the idealist systems we have considered. Thus the material world has been conceived, after Plato, as possessing no intelligible form, since it is in flux; according to more modern conceptions, matter is inert and mechanical; or again, it is merely dogmatically postulated object, and so far excludes subject. Life is not 'material' in any of these traditional senses. To interpret life as form is to ascribe to the living human being certain of those characteristics denied to matter, and ascribed by the idealists to ideas, namely, intelligible form, thought and consciousness. Form is now taken to be embodied in space and time, in the activity of the living being. The living being is 'material' in the minimal sense that it has solidity and is spatio-temporal, but it is distinguished from other natural bodies precisely by its form, by its intelligent activity. In this way the con-

---

found in both Platonic and more modern thought, and which I have called 'idealism'. This broad conception of idealism, within which important distinctions may doubtless be made, accords with those employed by, for example, H. B. Acton in his entry 'Idealism' in the *Encyclopedia of Philosophy*, Vol. 4, P. Edwards (ed.) (London: Collier–Macmillan, 1967); B. Russell, in his *History of Western Philosophy* (London: Allen and Unwin, 1946), 139 *et passim*; and W. Windelband, *Geschichte der Philosophie* (Freiburg i.B., 1892), §11 *et passim*.

11 I should like to thank Professor H. G. Adler for his suggestion that I include this remark.

cept of life bridges the old dichotomies between idealism and materialism. Life contains some elements of 'idea' and 'matter', as previously conceived, but the extremes of neither, and it comprises new elements, for example, the capacity for change by intelligent activity in reality. I have said that idealism is incompatible with life-philosophy because it accords no fundamental place to matter. But this does not yet define the true nature of the incompatibility. One should equally say that materialism is incompatible with life-philosophy because it includes no proper account of form, of thought and consciousness, in this sense of 'idea'. The conclusion is, therefore, that life-philosophy excludes both idealism and materialism, since neither treat *life* as fundamental, and so also because neither can do justice to man.

Having described the opposition between idealism and life-philosophy, I wish now to remark on certain points of contact between the two, specifically with respect to nineteenth century idealism. We find in the more modern systems of idealism a view uncharacteristic of Platonic idealism, namely, the view that the ideal origin of nature is *active*, or dynamically productive. And this emphasis on activity is shared by life-philosophy. Indeed, the recent idealistic systems tended towards life-philosophy precisely in so far as they construed action as real action in the world, and the subject as human; but they stopped short precisely in so far as they construed action as ideal, and the subject as transcendental, i.e. precisely in so far as they were systems of *idealism*. There was in nineteenth century philosophy a tension between, or a wavering between, these two interpretations of action, the one real and human, the other ideal and transcendental; and so far as the former interpretation dominated, that philosophy may be seen to anticipate certain features of non-idealistic philosophy in the present century, of which the later work of Wittgenstein is an example.[12]

Leading on from these remarks, I shall next consider Wittgenstein's later philosophy in further detail, particularly in the context of the suggestion made by Professor Williams, in his paper 'Wittgenstein and Idealism', that this philosophy contains a form of transcendental idealism.[13] In

[12] Patrick Gardiner's paper in the present series brings out this point clearly with respect to Fichte. He points out that Fichte's active epistemology anticipates the view that our practical concerns shape our apprehension of the world, a view found in various forms in pragmatism, existentialism, also in Wittgenstein's later work. But he stresses that this is only part of Fichte's concern, which is also to define a transcendental basis of experience in the activity of the ego, pp. 119–122.

[13] Bernard Williams, 'Wittgenstein and Idealism', in *Understanding Wittgenstein*, Royal Institute of Philosophy Lectures, Vol. 7, 1972–73, G. Vesey (ed.) (London: Macmillan, 1974). An 'idealist' interpretation of Wittgenstein's later work has been proposed also by Ernest Gellner, 'The New Idealism—Causes and Meaning in the Social Sciences', in *Positivism and Sociology*, A. Giddens (ed.) (Heinemann Educational Books, 1974).

accord with the points so far made, I shall argue that this suggestion is a plausible one in so far as it points to what may be called the 'active epistemology' in Wittgenstein's later work, but it is mistaken in supposing that this implies idealism. Certainly human beings are active in the construction of their knowledge, but this construction is not ideal, nor is it transcendental. Let us consider these points in turn.

Professor Williams suggests that according to Wittgenstein's later philosophy, our language 'shows us everything as it appears to our interests, our concerns, our activities' (op. cit., 85). He continues:

> The fact that in this way everything can be expressed only via human interests and concerns, things which are expressions of mind, and which themselves cannot ultimately be explained in any further terms: that provides grounds, I suggest, for calling such a view a kind of *idealism*.

Now it does indeed follow, if form is interpreted as life-form, that the form of appearance is relative to our activity; the human being knows the results of his activity, and those results depend partly on what he himself is and does. This activity, however, is not 'mental' as opposed to 'material', neither in its means nor in its effects. Alternatively, it might be said that, according to Wittgenstein, appearances are determined by our interests and concerns; and it is customary to describe these as 'mental phenomena'. But it must be added then that 'mental phenomena' are not left undefined by Wittgenstein, but are rather to be understood with reference to our practice and our behaviour. Either way, then, the concept of mind does not have that crucial role in Wittgenstein's later philosophy which Williams suggests; what is taken as fundamental is rather human action, and this being so, there is no reason here for calling this philosophy a kind of idealism.

If Wittgenstein's later philosophy is no idealism, then *a fortiori* it is no transcendental idealism. Let us consider, then, Williams' reasons for giving a 'transcendental' interpretation. His arguments, like their subject-matter, are complex, and I hope I do not misrepresent them in the following summary. He describes a view, which it is plausible to attribute to Wittgenstein, according to which language admits of no empirical explanation; here the term 'language' is used, after Wittgenstein, in a broad sense which embraces world-view (op. cit., 86). The basis of this view is said to be that all empirical explanation is already expressed in terms of our language. Professor Williams writes (op. cit., 84):

> Any empirical discovery we could make about our view of the world, as that it was conditioned by our use of count-words or whatever, would itself be a fact which we were able to understand in terms of, and only in terms of, our view of the world.

Further, a connected point, our language can be construed as conditioning *everything* that is comprehensible to us; it is the expression of the whole, and what lies beyond its scope is meaningless to us. The above quotation continues:

> And anything which radically we could not understand because it lay outside the boundary of our language would not be something we could come to explain our non-understanding of—it could not become clear to us what was wrong with it, or with us.

In this way, Williams makes plausible the claim that there is a 'transcendental' feature in Wittgenstein's later conception of language. His argument is particularly interesting and illuminating, in that it leads him to suggest that the later philosophy implicitly contains an analogue of the transcendental solipsism of the *Tractatus*. In place of 'the limits of my language mean the limits of my world', we find: 'the limits of *our* language mean the limits of *our* world' (op. cit., 82). And just as the 'I' of the *Tractatus* was transcendental and unique, not an item in the world among others, so the 'we' in the later work, Williams suggests, is not one social group among others. He concludes (op. cit., 92):

> One finds oneself with a *we* which is not one group rather than another in the world at all, but rather the plural descendant of that idealist *I* who also was not one item rather than another in the world.

This conclusion, however, is rather an incredible one. Williams is himself aware that it apparently conflicts with what is commonly found in the texts. He notes (op. cit., 87–88) that Wittgenstein speaks of various possible languages or world-pictures different from ours, and quotes, in a discussion of relativism, *On Certainty*, 298, which gives every appearance of defining us as one social group among others:

> 'We are quite sure of it' does not mean just that every single person is certain of it, but that we belong to a community which is bound together by science and education.

Williams goes on to suggest, however, that this impression that 'we' are contrasted with other human groups is 'basically misleading' (op. cit., 92). Speaking of the possibility of groups different from ourselves, he writes (loc. cit.):

> If they are groups with which we are in the universe, and we can understand that fact (namely, that they are groups with a language, etc.), then they also *belong* to 'we'.

This is a powerful argument, though, I shall argue later, mistaken. But for the moment I wish to examine the meaning of the term 'transcendental' which is at issue here.

Even if the term 'we' refers to only one group, still this does not mean that it refers to something *outside* the world. On the contrary, the 'we' of Wittgenstein's later remarks refers to human beings; and human beings are in the world, they are part of it, not outside, and in this sense not transcendental. This much, I think, Williams does not wish to deny. Rather, I think, his paper raises the possibility that the 'we' is transcendental in a less straightforward sense, namely, in that our language has a certain non-empirical status, and reaches right to the limits of what is comprehensible to us. But indeed this possibility does point further: in so far as our language is *not* based in experience, and if it does indeed embrace *the whole* of what is comprehensible, does it not after all follow that we and our language are related to the world from the outside, transcendental, then, even in the traditional sense? And so, notwithstanding the simple demonstration that the 'we', referring as it does to human beings, is not transcendental, Williams' arguments point in the opposite direction, making plausible the claim that, after all, Wittgenstein's later work did not move so far from traditional transcendentalism.[14]

The claim is, nevertheless, mistaken, and the apparent paradox it produces can be resolved. For if we consider more closely the nature of the non-empirical in human language, and the nature of its limitation, we shall find that they arise not because we, the users of language, have a transcendental status, but precisely the reverse; they belong with the fact that we are *within* the world.

Let us begin with the assumption that the meaning of language is grounded in human life. What can be said then concerning our concept of experience, and concerning the 'limits' of our understanding? Man acts in the world, and how he acts determines what he discovers. Or, we can say: *the method of activity determines what is experienced.* And so, what is found by a method is empirical, but *what characterizes the method itself is non-empirical.* Therefore in so far as we describe a method by propositions, these propositions will not be 'based in experience'. This is part of the epistemology that belongs with Wittgenstein's later account of language and meaning (see *On Certainty*, e.g. §§136, 151, 167, 308–309, 318–319). Propositions functioning as rules are not derived from or tested against experience; and therefore in this sense thay cannot be *explained* empirically. A useful explanation of a particular method of enquiry cannot be given in terms of those empirical facts which it alone makes possible and brings to light; for the method is not derived from those facts, it is rather the necessary condition of them. Certainly we might speak in general terms

---

[14] Professor Malcolm, in his paper in the present series, shows convincingly by argument and by textual reference that the 'we' in Wittgenstein's later remarks always refers to some actual human group or society. However, he does not see the reasoning behind Professor Williams' 'transcendental idealist' interpretation, as he himself says (p. 254), and consequently does not bring out its full strength.

of the presuppositions of a given practice, making reference to very general facts of nature, of human interests and education, in the way that, as Williams notes (op. cit., 87), Wittgenstein sometimes does. But to describe the general conditions of a form of life is not yet to give an 'empirical' or 'scientific' explanation of it. For this, it is necessary to adopt the standpoint of *another* method, together with the kind of facts it reveals. Here belongs the fact, then, that we use *various* methods of enquiry; 'our worldview' is not one thing, and therefore one part of it may be used in explanation of another. Although a method cannot be explained by reference to the experience to which it gives rise, still it may be explained, more or less well, by reference to empirical facts of another kind, derived from another method. What serves to guide empirical judgment in one context, may have empirical status in another. It must be added, however, that explanations of a form of life made from an external frame of reference must fail to define its internal nature. If form is interpreted as life-form, it follows that each form of life experiences its own form of reality; here the term 'reality' does not refer to a status, but directly to movement, change, interaction. And the reality given to a life-form can be seen only from within, that is, by *being the form*; it is not visible from the outside.

In conclusion, then, our language does have non-empirical characteristics; but this is not because we and our language are transcendental, related to the world from outside; it is rather because our understanding employs methods, and these methods, and the language which interweaves with them, belong within the world; they are methods of activity. And the non-empirical status of a particular language-game is relative, not absolute; this is another aspect of the reason why 'non-empirical' no longer means the same as the old concept 'transcendental' (or '*a priori*').

Let us turn now to the question of limits. This question is familiar in the context of postulating a transcendental subject, but is equally important for an understanding of what it means for the subject to be inside the world. For the transcendental subject, as postulated in the *Tractatus*, the world appears from outside as a limited whole. In another sense, however, the world appears from outside to be unlimited, in that there is nothing other than it. Consider now the subject that is inside, related to the world as part to whole. So far as concerns this subject, the world is unlimited, for its limits cannot be circumscribed. In another sense, what this subject knows is limited, for there exists more than what is immediately given. Pursuing the metaphor of part and whole, the subject inside reality knows directly that part of the world which he is, or which is next to him; but he also *knows of*, indirectly, the existence of things beyond these boundaries. This distinction between what is known and what is known of makes no sense, however, to the transcendental subject; for this subject is no closer to one part of the world than to any other, and therefore all knowledge stands at the same level. A similar point can be made in connection with the concept of understanding. The transcendental subject understands all descriptions of the world, and all else is nonsensical non-description. But the subject inside understands best what is closest to him; the further away reality from him, the less his understanding of it, gradually less and less, until descriptions of it make no sense to him at all.

Limited, in the sense of partial, knowledge and understanding, belongs to us as human beings; we take our experience to be part of something greater. On this, in *On Certainty*:

> 276. We believe, so to speak, that this great building exists, and then we see, now here, now there, one or another small corner of it.[15]

Human beings, limited as they are to a particular position within the world, cannot experience, nor draw boundaries around, the whole. The limits of human understanding cannot be precisely drawn; rather, the reality that we do understand fades gradually into the reality that we do not. Still it might be said that vague limits are nevertheless limits: suppose we stretch our imagination as far as possible, to include all that we can conceive, would we not find limits to our understanding, beyond which, so far as we are concerned, there is nothing? But here belongs the remark that the concept 'all we can conceive' (and its equivalents) is a misleading one, in that it does not refer to a fixed and unified whole. In terms of language: 'our language' is not a single and uniform instrument of expression, but is many and various things, and is always changing. Or again: there are diverse forms of life, and new ones constantly replace the old. This means that we can sometimes see what lies beyond reach of one conception, by adopting another point of view. For example, I discover that the values and attitudes I grew up with are limited, even though at the time I had no idea this was so, by hearing of alternatives in conversation with a Chinese. This kind of discovery is frequent, so what reason should I now have for saying: 'Now I know of everything there is to know, and all the rest is nonsense'? Or another kind of example: I sometimes dimly recall what it was like to be a very young child, and I realize, or think I realize, that my experiences and beliefs then were very different from now, so much so that I can no longer make sense of them. So if we use the expression 'the limits of our language', which language do we mean? We speak many languages, and know that any one of them expresses but part of what can be expressed. And the apparent totality of 'our language' is vague and always changing; is it to include, for example, the language of the child, which we know of, and once understood, but no longer use? We use many languages, we have used others, we hear and read of still more, always new ones. Diversity and change, and therefore also expectation of something new, characterizes

---

[15] This metaphor seems to me in the spirit of Kafka; compare, for example, his short story, *Beim Bau der Chinesischen Mauer*. Kafka has explored deeply what it means to have only partial, limited, understanding.

life-form, which is constantly developing. So it is that we can reasonably say: there are possibilities even beyond the penumbra of our present understanding, which we cannot now so much as conceive of. And in this case, 'the limits of our language' never reach the limits of what we believe is possible, but always no more than approach them.

At this point we may return to Williams' argument that the 'we' in Wittgenstein's later remarks does not refer to one human group contrasted with others. The argument is that if we can understand that there is another group, that they have a language, then they also belong to 'we'. In the light of the above remarks this can be seen, I think, to be too black and white. 'Our understanding' is many and various things, and admits of degrees. For example, we might understand and be able to communicate with another group so far as they shared with us certain activities, such as drinking water, or building shelters. On the other hand, we might be unable to follow other of their practices, involving, let us say, magic and ritual. Here communication would be problematic; for language, it is proposed, derives its meaning from life-form, and therefore if a form of life of another community is absent from ours, so too is the language involved in it. Thus we would have here an example of a community different from ours; strictly speaking, different from ours in certain respects, but colloquially, just 'different'.

It is assumed here that there are grounds for believing that if a group is intelligent in some of what they do, particularly in the minimum that makes them a human life-form, then they are intelligent in other matters, even in practices unlike our own. These grounds may be partly that we can see in different ways of life something like our own, so that we can find at least *some* sense in them. But further, we can have reason to believe that even a way of life radically different from our own is indeed a genuine *form*, intelligible not to us, but to its participants; for we ourselves are constantly realizing new possibilities, so that we always find more than we understood before, and always expect there to be more than we understand now. Thus it may be said that whatever peoples we understand belong to 'we'; nevertheless, we may understand to a limited degree a people who are unlike ourselves and who cannot be included in 'we'; and further, we may see signs of radical alternatives to what we are familiar with, even if we cannot grasp them.

Let us consider now the basis of the proposition that we can (best) understand only what is like us; i.e. that we can (best) understand only ourselves. This is connected with the fact that we are ourselves the means of understanding. And that the human being is the measure of things follows from the assumption that form is human life-form. Because the human being is the form of understanding, he must use himself to comprehend all things, and his understanding is therefore relative to himself. And since among what is to be understood there are things unlike himself, understanding is at times difficult. It may be difficult, for example, for a child to make sense of what an adult does, or vice versa; or again, it is difficult to grasp the meaning of practices in an alien culture, using concepts drawn from our own. In his discussion of Wittgenstein's 'relativism', Williams suggests that if indeed our experience of other forms of life is inescapably conditioned by our own, it is difficult to see how we could come to know of *another* form of life, difficult to see how we could avoid the conclusion of 'social solipsism', or 'aggregative solipsism' at the social level, as he terms it (op. cit., 90). Now the difficulties that arise when we try to follow practices very unlike our own are certainly signs that our understanding is *limited*. But I suggest that the experience of limitation in these contexts is precisely experience of inadequacy and ignorance, and precisely not an experience of completeness and omniscience. That is to say, the limits of our understanding encountered here are not of the kind drawn by a transcendental, solipsistic subject, but are rather of the kind that we work on from within. And in this case, what we know is that there are indeed people different from ourselves, whose way of life so far exceeds our understanding.

To summarize, then, the present argument: Williams suggests that we can find in Wittgenstein's later work a form of transcendental idealism, because it implies that our language, in so far as it has no empirical explanation, is an expression of mind, and its limits mean the limits of our world. Against this interpretation, I have argued that Wittgenstein's philosophy is based in human action, not in mind. Further, no transcendentalism is implied. Our language, our view of the world, is not determined wholly by empirical facts, nor is it to be fully explained by reference to them; but this is not because our language originates outside the world we experience, rather because it originates in our activity in the world, and serves to guide that activity, and therefore also the construction of our experience. And in so far as we can speak of the 'limits' of our language, they are not commensurate with all that we believe is possible, but only with part of something greater; the limits are not prescribed transcendentally, but are rather encountered from within. Those aspects of reality which we discover in our activities might be called 'our world'; but what conditions our activity, and what always limits it, is *the world* we are born into. And this world shows itself also in our language; for our language derives its meaning from its use in our form of life, and the world has a say in our language, since it has a say in our life.

It can be seen that these considerations are closely connected to those previously brought against Platonic idealism, and also against more modern idealism. To interpret form as life-form, to affirm that human beings are the agents of knowing, understanding, and so forth, is to exclude all kinds of idealism.

The exclusion of idealism is already guaranteed by Wittgenstein's move from the 'I' of the early work to the 'we' of the later. This move cannot take place, as Williams suggests it can, 'within the transcendental ideas themselves' (op. cit., 79). The subject of the *Tractatus* must be unique *because* it is defined transcendentally. Another subject can never be an object of knowledge for a transcendental subject because all objects of its knowledge are part of the world, and whatever is part of the world cannot be another subject. Conversely, if one subject can identify another, if it is ever possible to say 'we', then both must be part of the world, inside it. The move from 'I' to 'we' *is* the move from being transcendental to being in the world, to being human. It is not a move across, staying at the same level, but is rather a move downwards; and with this descent, idealism is finished.

Men are more or less like one another, they are born into, and later join, some groups opposed to others; there is diversity between individuals, sub-cultures, and whole cultures. This diversity is one reason why human knowledge is imperfect and incomplete, in contrast to the knowledge of the 'I' which rises above the human world. Let us consider, finally, whether we can imagine this to be otherwise. Perhaps we can imagine that all human beings shared in common not only the basic elements of life, such as the need for nourishment and shelter, perhaps also for friendship, but also the practices, attitudes and beliefs of higher culture; or at least, if these practices were not universal, that each human being could understand in himself the meaning and purpose of what his fellow men do. If this were so, there might be no use for a fundamental distinction between 'we' and 'others'; we, mankind, would comprise everything human, would be a unity in all respects and not just in the minimal ones. Then we might speak of a degree of transcendence achieved on earth; but this possibility, which we can hardly conceive, is not now reality.

Index of Names

Index of Names

Index of Subjects

abstraction, 13, 14

acting, and language-games, 256, 271

action, and event, 139; Fichte on, 125; Hegel on, 141–154; life-form and, 274–277; Schopenhauer on, 127–140

agency, human, 165; knowledge of, 133–139; primacy of, 120

animism, 176

appearances, and perception, 24; idealism and, 84, 88

apperception, unity of, 97

arguments, transcendental, 130, 211–224

assertibility conditions, 226–248

atomism, 30, 33

beauty, 6

bedeutung (reference), 75

behaviourism, 227

causality, concept of, 163–165, 215, 220–224; seen from within, 131

certainty, 263

cogito (I think), 10, 43, 47, 217

conceptualism, 35

conventionalism, 3

cosmology, 79

craftsmen, divine, 7

criteria, 225–248

critical principle, Kant's, 73, 77, 79, 84, 91

deductions, empirical and transcendental, 16

determinism, 113, 117, 147

distance, perception of, 60

divisibility, infinite, 62–65

dogmatism, 116

dualisms, two, 12–14

ego, 118; absolute, 123; transcendental, 273

Eleaticism, 32, 61

empiricism, pure, 108

Epicureanism, 35, 37

equality, Form of, 13

externality, 40, 51, 53

falsehood, 23

flux, 3, 26

Forms, theory of, 1–9, 15, 18, 33, 274

force, idea of, 164

framework, categorial, 167–178, conceptual, 259

freedom, 111–126, 143, 146–150

geometry, 9, 58

God, 14, 105

good, Form of, 4, 6, 8

grammar, 17

harmony, pre-established, 222

idealism, absolute, 111; as monism, 23; empirical, 16, 52, 81–90, 128, 214; ethical, 125; immaterialist, 19, 21, 51–69; Platonic, 269–273; problematic, 53, 68; refutation of, 53, 66–69, 89; subjective, 142; transcendental, 16, 18, 51–69, 71–92, 111, 113, 128, 214, 249, 252, 276, 279.

ideas, abstract, 13; and idealism, 1; as immaterial forms, 274; clear and distinct, 10; definitions of, 269; ideality of, 198, 200; immediate objects of perception, 85; inert, 27; innate, 13; real, 15; simple, 14; unions of, 203, 207

identity, mind–brain, 134

imagination, 12, 17

immaterialism, 19, 21, 51–69

intentionality, 59

internal relations, 181–195, 197, 203–207

judgment, 188–190, 193–195, 197–202; necessary conditions of, 215

knowledge, 3; as perception, 21

language, 14; and reality, 15; divine, 60

language-games, 165, 255

libertarianism, 117

life-form, 269–284

289

Index of Subjects

mathematics, 9, 15
materialism, 23, 33, 166, 275
matter, 6; and form, 31; for Descartes, 9; for Plotinus, 30; prime, 8
Maya, veil of, 136
meaning, assertibility-conditions concept of, 226–228; truth-conditions concept of, 225–226
measure doctrine, Protagorean, 24
mechanism, 112
memory, 17
metaphysics, 211
mind, embodied, 107
misunderstanding, 228–230
monism, 23, 31; neutral, 28
motion, absolute, 57, 62; relative, 56

Neoplatonism, 30–32
Notion, the, 103, 106, 108
noumena, 73, 115–116, 122

opposites, 2, 6
oracles, 252, 256
outness, 60

pain, 17, 253–262
parasites, cut loose, 197–209
perception, and appearance, 24; and knowledge, 21; Cartesian theory of, 11; causal aspects of, 28; Gricean theory of, 138; immediate, 26; passive, 27; veil of, 85
personalism, 175–179
phenoma, 73, 113
phenomenalism, 83–91, 175, 250
phrenology, 148
practice, primacy of, 155–179
prime mover, 127
Pyrrhonism, 36

qualities, primary and secondary, 64, 82, 163

realism, empirical, 81–90, 214; Greek assumption of, 32, 44; naive, 84; transcendental, 52, 81–90
reason, practical, 120; principle of sufficient, 132
recollection doctrine, 4
red-hairedness, 181, 183, 205, 208
relativism, 24, 90, 283
relatively, 254, 259
rule-following, 247

scepticism, 15, 32, 36–40, 51, 72, 96, 228, 238
self-activity, 118
self-consciousness, 141
semantics, anti-realist, 225–248; non-realist, 73; realist, 76
sensation, 106
Shinto, 176
Sinn (sense), 16, 74
snow, 172
solipsism, 123, 249–251, 260–262, 278
space, 6, 8, 9, 15, 51–59, 66–69
Spirit, Hegel's doctrine of, 98
Stoicism, 33, 35, 37
substance, 7, 8, 15, 55, 66, 160–163
surrealism, 174
sweetness, 20

teleology, 5–8
things-in-themselves, 122, 128, 133–136 140, 156, 173, 212, 274
thinking, 13
third man argument, 33
time, 66–69
touch, primacy of, 161–163
truth, 38, 167, 194

understanding, 226
universals, 1, 5, 35

vacuum, 56
variables, 201–204
verificationism, 76, 212

will, 127–140, 148